Simplified Boatbuilding

The V-Bottom Boat

Simplified Boatbuilding

The V-Bottom Boat

Harry V. Sucher

W · W · NORTON & COMPANY · INC ·
New York

Copyright © 1974, 1973 by W. W. Norton & Company, Inc.
First Edition

Library of Congress Cataloging in Publication Data

Sucher, Harry V
  Simplified boatbuilding.

  Companion volume to the author's Simplified boat-
building: the flat-bottom boat.
  Bibliography: p.
  1. Boat-building. I. Title.
VM351.S772   623.82′02   73–22340
ISBN 0–393–03180–2

Published simultaneously in Canada by
George J. McLeod Limited, Toronto

Printed in the United States of America

1 2 3 4 5 6 7 8 9 0

To Margery—the best small boat sailor of them all.

Contents

PART 3   The V-Bottom Boat

List of Illustrations

PLATES

FIGURES

Foreword
By Howard I. Chapelle

In my time I can recall many sessions held in the homes of yachtsmen, in yacht clubs, and in designers' offices, where we sat around bewailing the loss of boatbuilding skills. We did not realize that most of the fine cabinet work that we thought we were losing was always uneconomical and was entirely an expression of pride on the part of the owner or boatbuilder.

Well, we lost the "fine workmanship and boatbuilding skills" as we foresaw, but wait—did we? The answer is *no*, for amateur boatbuilders began to appear. At first we laughed at the crude "boxes" they built—you could hardly call them boats—but a few of us did take notice of the gradual changes that have been taking place. Some of the "box-builders" began to turn out very fine craft from their backyards, garages, cellars, and shops. Pride in workmanship led amateur boatbuilders to become interested in things that related to their hobby: yacht design, new building materials and methods, adhesives, paints, and such.

While there are many books published on boatbuilding and design, many amateurs feel they are too complicated. *Simplified Boatbuilding* by Harry V. Sucher is presented to answer these complaints. The material is divided into two volumes, this one on V-bottom hulls, the other, already published, dealing with flat-bottom craft.

This work discusses boatbuilding in general, beginning with estimating materials and blueprint reading to trim tabs. Details of construction and of engine installation are outlined in plain, nontechnical language. The types of V-bottom craft are discussed, their designs analyzed, and their construction examined. Their performance is also described.

The author takes much care with a simple but thorough explanation of lofting methods required for each hull example. He also examines fastenings, a much-neglected area. Another valuable feature of the book is the straightforward treatment of erecting the hull frame and the attention given to wood preservation.

11

There is a wealth of information here on high chine V-bottom boats, especially the Northern skipjack and the Chesapeake Bay skipjack, with little-known (in the West) data on the development of the Yamato boats and sampans. Dr. Sucher also deals at length with the low chine models—modified sharpies, double wedge power launches, Chesapeake Bay bateaux, fantail-stern skipjack launches, utility launches, and cruisers.

Whether a small craft enthusiast or a yachtsman dreaming about a scow or sharpie schooner cruiser, here is a profusely illustrated source book of new ideas.

Preface

Many practical boating enthusiasts who are somewhat skilled in the use of carpenters' tools will wish to consider building their own small boats, whether for pleasure or commercial use, in order to secure a substantial boat at moderate cost. The practicality of such a venture is enhanced by the universal availability of mass-produced power woodworking tools at moderate cost. These tools enable a workman of modest skill to produce a boat of professional quality, given the proper time and care. The prospective home boatbuilder, however, is often discouraged by the fact that many small boat designs, based on traditional building methods, appear unduly complicated. Too, he has often been led to believe that even small boats must have certain arbitrary features of complex construction that could tax his ingenuity or be beyond his capabilities. The steam-bent frames of the Viking ships or the carefully shaped planking of the caravels of Columbus still have their modern counterparts and are assembled by the same laborious methods. The innate conservativism of seafaring men has often resisted any change toward less-complicated methods.

Due to the stereotyped designs of many of our small pleasure boats, which slavishly follow "yachting standards," many enthusiasts have turned to the wholesome functionality of the traditional "working" boat, and have found to their delight that they could obtain a simple craft that was eminently seaworthy, economical, and had an air of distinction and character. Conversely, the working commercial boatman has added some of the "frills" of the pleasure boat to his craft and thereby produced an aesthetically pleasing boat with no sacrifice of utility. Some of the designs given in the following pages show how ideally this marriage of two apparently opposed views can be worked out.

In the following chapters the aspiring boat owner will learn the basic fundamentals of small boatbuilding, some instructions leaning toward simplified traditional methods and some taking a radical departure therefrom. Wherever possible the use of modern materials is advocated. The instructions are presented in logical sequence, each chapter building on the previous one. Included are a number of drawings for practical, proven, small pleasure and commercial boats, and the reader may readily discover a boat of his choice well within the capabilities of the average amateur boatbuilder.

Acknowledgments

It is impossible for me to recall the name of everyone who has contributed to the pleasure and enjoyment of nearly five decades of boating. Yachtsmen, commercial boat operators and working fishermen, professional designers and others within this sphere of interest, appear to be ever helpful with ready advice and counsel when approached with intelligent questions put by a sincere inquirer. The fascination of the sea, with its infinite pleasures and continuing perils, creates strong fraternal feelings among those who follow it. This at once becomes manifest when a bond of common interest is evidenced. To this now somewhat faceless but well remembered crew of gallant gentlemen from the distant past I offer my most grateful thanks.

Among those whose contributions ultimately led to the production of these books, I must mention Howard I. Chapelle, distinguished naval architect and marine historian, Curator Emeritus for the United States National Museum, for his very helpful advice and encouragement during the many years of my studies of traditional small boat types; David R. Getchell, Editor of the *National Fisherman* magazine, for a very pleasant association during the years when a series of my designs for simple, low-cost boats appeared in that publication; John Gardner, Technical Editor of the *National Fisherman,* for his helpful suggestions and constructive criticism; the late Rogers Winter, N.A., for his friendship of many years standing and for his valued advice on technical matters; Charles W. Bond, N.A., for his contribution of material concerning historical small craft of the Florida and Caribbean area; Ito Fugama and S. Takahara for their interesting data on oriental sampans; Martin Seligmann, late octogenarian master boatbuilder for his information on boat carpentry and joinery; the staff of the United States National Museum for their kindness in making available for my reference a large number of plans and drawings of historical small boat types preserved in the extensive Watercraft Collection; Charles Stokes for his information concerning modern marine engines and automotive conversions of the same; the Manhattan Marine and Wilcox Crittenden concerns for their data on fastenings and marine hardware; Acadia Gas Engines, Ltd.,

15

the Lunenburg Foundry Company, and the Easthope Marine Engine Company for their information on heavy duty gasoline marine engines; William T. Hutchins of the McInnes Boat Company and William Tighe of the Willard Boat Works for their courage in building to some of my more controversial small boat designs.

I should also like to acknowledge the contributions of my many correspondents throughout the world, who, in a common search for practicalities and economies in boating, have offered material of inestimable value which is incorporated in this effort.

And lastly, my wife, Margery, who has typed and edited most of my many manuscripts through the years, and who has provided the domestic tranquillity so necessary for creative effort.

Garden Grove, California 1972

Part
1

Small Boat Design and Classification

1

The Origins of Small Craft Design

Boating enthusiasts inquiring into the origins of common small boat forms will learn that modern sailing and power craft are derived from small working boats of the past. In the consideration of basic hull forms, it should be kept in mind that they are the result of empirical reasoning and trial-and-error experimentation over the span of countless centuries, long before any concepts of mathematical principles or formal engineering were discovered to apply to them. Small boat form has gradually come about through a process of evolution, such as primitive man's observation that a hollowed-out log could be more easily paddled if its ends were pointed and turned upwards. As maritime activities expanded, and trade, commerce, and commercial fishing became commonplace, boats were developed to meet the economic demands for useful craft that were seaworthy, able, and adapted to the work intended.

The small sailing craft of today, including racing classes, have their origins in the dozens of variations of small sailing workboats that were employed in vast numbers in the United States and abroad during the days of working sail. Before the coming of power, in the opening days of the twentieth century, many boat types were built to suit local conditions of offshore and inshore fishing and commerce. Most of them were very able and useful craft of marked distinction and good form. Built mostly by highly skilled craftsmen, who were often practical sailormen as well, their satisfactory performance and good form inspired later variations of many of the attractive pleasure yachts we see today.

While modern architecture of small boats is largely based on mathematical calculations for displacement, stability, and hull resistance, hull form cannot be projected entirely by mathematical formulae. The small size of the hulls in relation to their speeds, together with inevitable variations of material weights and loading factors, make definitive mathematical projections impossible in the strict practical sense. The designing of small boats can be best defined as a combination of mathematics, art, experience, observation, and a dash of intuition. The designing of an attractive and functional set of hull lines is often said to be an art that has to be inspired, and many engineers who are able to comprehend the calculations involved cannot draw hull lines.

The incorporation of changes in a boat's original plan is a serious undertaking which some amateurs often attempt, often at the suggestion of some waterside "expert." When a change in length, beam, height of cabins, or shifting of any principal weights occurs, the design becomes completely new, and its performance then depends upon another set of conditions that can ruin the boat completely for normal use. If the plan under consideration does not suit the intentions of the owner a new design should be selected.

While small sailing-cruising auxiliaries and sailing-racing classes have become standardized as to their most efficient form, many of the so-called ultramodern high-powered planing pleasure cruisers have taken on extreme forms in recent years. Many of these show excessive beam-length ratios and shallow, flat bottoms in the interest of high speeds. Wide beam enables house trailer type accommodation with this spaciousness enhanced by very high cabin structures. While these types are satisfactory in protected waters, their ability as sea boats is open to question. It would appear that attempts to equate the boat with the automobile for the benefit of sales promotion has not always been in the best interests of sound boating.

Small boats of accepted proportion of beam to length, freeboard, and sheerline generally show what is called good balance upon visual inspection. Many small craft built to traditional lines established over one hundred years ago make very attractive, satisfactory craft, as a developed and proven near-perfection is ageless. Amateur boat enthusiasts with the desire to develop their knowledge and judgment of good hull form would do well to examine as many boats as possible, both at anchor and under way. The opinions of experienced sailors is most valuable, and should be sought wherever possible. Boatmen of experience and ability are generally good judges of boats, as, in the old axiom, "what looks right is right."

2

Fundamentals of
Small Boat Design

1. Power Boats of Displacement Type

The principal governing factor influencing the hull form of a powerboat is its projected speed, and is under the direct control of the designer as he undertakes to lay out its lines. Once the speed is decided upon, the overall proportions, such as displacement, beam, draft, and freeboard, as well as interior space, are more or less predetermined. The basic differences between a high-speed power launch designed to carry only passengers and fuel, and a large, heavy, displacement commercial fishing boat that must load and carry a cargo of fish, have their origins in their respective speeds.

At the outset it must be noted that the science of naval architecture as applied to the design of large ships has little or no relation to that of small powerboats. The reason for this is that small craft travel at proportionately much greater speed in relation to their size than do ocean-going freighters and passenger liners, and their resistance factors which govern the resistance of the water against their forward motion through the dynamic force of their power are many times greater.

The speed of a boat is generally calculated in knots rather than statute or land miles. A knot is a unit of speed equal to one nautical mile per hour. A nautical mile is 6,080 feet or one minute of latitude on the earth's surface.

Speed factors in design are based upon what is defined as the speed-length ratio, expressed mathematically by dividing the projected speed in nautical miles by the square root of the waterline length of the hull in question.

$$\frac{\text{Speed in Knots}}{\sqrt{\text{Waterline Length in Feet}}} \quad \text{equals speed-length ratio}$$

An example is

$$\frac{10 \text{ Knots}}{\sqrt{16 \text{ feet Waterline Length}}} \quad \text{equals 2.5 speed-length ratio}$$

The reason small powerboats must inevitably show high speed-length ratios in proportion to their size is that practical considerations of their employment make certain speed capabilities mandatory. If the lines of a small boat were drawn to approximate a speed comparable to an ocean liner, with a speed-length ratio of 1.1, the cruising speed for a launch with 25 feet of waterline length would then be 5 knots which is not acceptable for most purposes. Ratios of small boats, therefore, must be projected for speeds of at least 7 knots, and, in most cases, much more is demanded. The point of beginning, then, must be for speed-length ratios at least 1.5 when a small powerboat is designed for average uses.

The resistance factor set up by the water surrounding the hull as a small displacement-type power launch approaches a speed-length ratio of 1.5 is approximately 150 pounds for each ton of its overall weight or displacement. In comparison with the resistance factors present in considering large ship design, a low-powered coastal freight ship will show an economical 5 pounds of resistance for each ton of its displacement, an ocean-going freighter 10 pounds, and a high-speed passenger-carrying liner 20 pounds. It is, therefore, easy to visualize why data used in calculations for ship design have no application in the architecture of small power craft.

The high-resistance factor of small boats is due to the transverse wave system that is set up as cruising speed is reached. At a speed-length ratio of 1.5, this wave system is longer than the hull itself, the bow riding its forward crest, the after part of the wave crest being some distance behind the transom, with the stern then settling down into its trough. It is obvious that spreading the weight of a boat over as long a waterline length as is practical lowers resistance factors by lengthening the crests of the transverse wave. It also explains why heavy-displacement launches with wide beam and very full hull lines are capable of only mediocre performance and show an inefficient utilization of power.

The speed capabilities of small, displacement-type powerboats are generally predicated at their so-called cruising speeds, often described as their terminal hull speed. If the boat is overpowered, or an attempt is made to drive it faster than this terminal hull speed, the stern is drawn further down into the deepening transverse wave, causing the boat to squat and wallow, thus inhibiting forward travel.

Many small commercial craft and heavy-displacement pleasure cruisers intended for offshore use have fantail or canoe-type sterns in the interest of greater seaworthiness, and they show speed-length ratios of 1.2 or 1.3. They can be economically driven with proportionately moderate-size engines showing good fuel economy. If speed length ratios of 1.3 and 1.5 are demanded, a hull must then show reduced displacement for the same overall length, less draft, and a broad and flat transom stern. At speeds above 1.6, very high power and a wider transom is necessary, and the underwater lines from amidships aft must assume a nearly flat surface.

The critical area for speed in displacement-type power launches is between speed-length ratios of 1.1 to 1.6, or the difference between the hull form and power criteria for 4–5 knot speeds, and the more practical 8–10 knot speeds demanded for increased performance.

The matter of actual hull form is, of course, quite critical. While it is obvious that a square-ended box or scow-type hull can be pushed through the water under power, conditions of seaworthiness, practical demands for effective speeds, coupled with economical running, demand a refinement of underwater shape for hydrodynamic efficiency. In considering a displacement boat, it is visualized that the bow cuts into the water, forces it aside, and turns a part of it under the bottom of the hull where it flows back and returns to the surface by passing back out behind the transom. As water resists being disturbed by flowing around solid objects, the hull lines must be gentle to avoid forming eddies which set up further resistance to forward motion. To counteract this resistance it is desirable to have a moderately fine waterline entrance angle, some flare in the sides of the hull to hold the waterflow to the load waterline, moderate beam for minimum resistance factors, and a flattened underbody rising aft to the surface. This suggests that most displacement-type launches perform best with a flat transom stern to hold the hull in a nearly horizontal position in relation to the waterline against the thrust of the propeller, allowing the water to return to the surface without creating an unduly steep stern wave.

An excessively broad transom stern, however beneficial to speed, can lead to less satisfactory conditions of seaworthiness. In a following or stern sea, a wave may strike the flat surface with such force as to swing the boat broadside into the wave trough, causing it to capsize. This condition is called *broaching*. In practical small boat design, sterns are made as broad as possible in relation to the overall length of the hull, together with a full length keel and a moderately deep skeg or deadwood to act as a brake against the hull pivoting about from the bow.

Another poor feature in an excessively broad-sterned launch, designed for optimum speed, is that the wide quarters offer excess buoyancy in rough water causing accelerated pitching or up-and-down motion when traveling at necessarily reduced speeds. In very wide-beamed boats this causes much violent motion in a confused sea. Some small power launches intended for offshore use often have fantail or canoe-type sterns in order to minimize this buoyancy. While such hulls show greater seaworthiness and comfort for the occupants, the more abrupt upward sweep of the after waterlines seriously impairs speed by offering less support to the stern sections against the thrust of the propeller. Most small canoe-stern or fantail type hulls cannot be economically driven at speeds of over 7 to 9 knots in waterline lengths up to 50 feet, and the application of excessive power causes much squatting of the hull aft with much wave making and no increase in speed.

To express the most desirable proportions of hull form for satisfactory attainment of the somewhat opposed considerations of speed and seaworthiness, the efficiency is defined as the prismatic coefficient, and two other interrelated factors known as the block and midship coefficients. The midship coefficient is defined as the ratio of the immersed area of the hull below the waterline amidships to the area of the surrounding rectangular area that encloses the load waterline. In average power boats this varies from about 0.57 to 0.72. The block coefficient is the ratio of the immersed displacement of the entire hull below the waterline to that of the circumscribing waterline rectangle, and its amount is largely determined by the fullness of the midsection. The prismatic coefficient is the ratio of the displaced volume of the hull to a prism with the immersed midship section area, and equal to the length of the load waterline. This ratio indicates the fullness of the ends of the hull in relation to that of the midship section and serves as a guide to the fore-and-aft distribution of the displacement. A further interpretation of these principles is:

$$\frac{\text{Block Coefficient}}{\text{Midship Coefficient}} \text{ equals Prismatic Coefficient}$$

This is shown graphically in Figure 1.

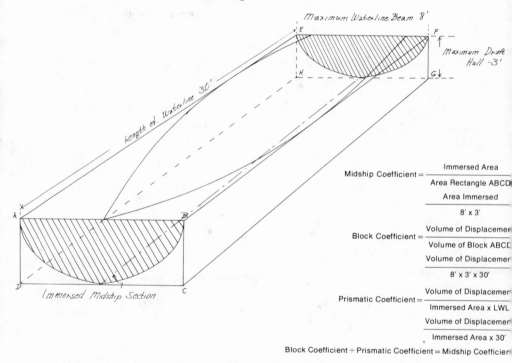

$$\text{Midship Coefficient} = \frac{\text{Immersed Area}}{\text{Area Rectangle ABCD}}$$
$$= \frac{\text{Area Immersed}}{8' \times 3'}$$

$$\text{Block Coefficient} = \frac{\text{Volume of Displacement}}{\text{Volume of Block ABCD}}$$
$$= \frac{\text{Volume of Displacement}}{8' \times 3' \times 30'}$$

$$\text{Prismatic Coefficient} = \frac{\text{Volume of Displacement}}{\text{Immersed Area} \times \text{LWL}}$$
$$= \frac{\text{Volume of Displacement}}{\text{Immersed Area} \times 30'}$$

Block Coefficient ÷ Prismatic Coefficient = Midship Coefficient

Figure 1   Determination of midship, block, and prismatic coefficients

An ideal prismatic coefficient will vary with the speed-length ratio, and increase with it. This means a rather full-ended hull for best efficiency in power utilization, as obviously a boat with very fine ends and a very full midship section will pitch in rough water and will squat badly under power when an attempt is made to drive it at high speed.

To effect the most practical compromise for speed and seaworthiness in small, displacement-type launches under 50 feet in length, the terminal hull speed for boats of normal hull form is about 12 knots. Cruising speeds of 9 to 10 knots are the most practical for the best operating economy. It is possible, however, to attain much higher speeds in the displacement-type hull if provision is made for a very narrow beam in relation to waterline length, coupled with very light displacement. In the early days of powerboating, many small launches were designed and built to this form. In copying the beam-length ratio of the then newly developed naval torpedo boat destroyers, resistance factors comparable to ship-type vessels and resultant higher speeds were achieved utilizing the contemporary, low-powered engines. A racing-type, V-bottom launch built in 1902 with an overall length of 37 feet and a 4 feet, 2 inches beam made over 26 statute miles per hour with a slow-turning, two-cylinder marine engine of 15 horsepower. The noted Hooper Island launches, much in evidence on the Chesapeake Bay until recently, were more practical adaptations of this extreme form with beam-length ratios of about 1.6 on overall lengths of from 25 to 50 feet. They proved to be very seaworthy and able boats, given substantial deadrise in the midship sections, and were capable of speeds of 12 to 14 knots with very moderate power. The noted Thorneycroft concern in England experimented with a series of similar hulls in the 1930s and finally produced a model 50 feet long with 8 feet beam making 18 knots with a 100 horsepower engine.

While these hulls are eminently seaworthy and economical to drive, they are useful only where somewhat reduced carrying capacity and interior accommodations are acceptable. After observing some of the undesirable characteristics of many modern pleasure cruisers with very wide beam and high power, such as impaired steering in high winds and rough water, coupled with excessive pitching, small boat designers are again considering the older form of narrow-beamed hull.

2. Power Boats of Planing and Semiplaning Type

Any power launch will plane to some degree if its underwater lines are such that high power will lift the hull above its static load waterline at speeds near terminal hull velocity. The planing attitude is described as that point where the dynamic thrust applied through the propeller will raise the hull to the point where the factors of buoyancy for actual hull support decrease.

Planing is necessary for high speeds in small launches. Pure displacement types, excessively overpowered and driven at high speeds, will, as we have seen, create a wave disturbance around the hull to draw it deeper into the water. The resultant suction may even sink the boat by swamping as the stern settles down and the water comes up over the sides of the boat. If the underwater lines of a boat are flattened sufficiently, and if these strike the surface of the water at the correct angle, a pressure area is created that supplies the lift, given sufficient dynamic thrust.

It will be observed that weight becomes more of a consideration than displacement in the planing attitude. The overall efficiency in relation to speed is highly dependent upon the lightness of the hull and its contents. In fact, some authorities on small boat design consider weight more of a critical factor than the intricacies of actual underwater form.

Resistance factors to be considered in a planing hull, as in the displacement type, are dependent upon wave disturbance and friction of the water against the forward motion of the hull. In a desirable condition of high power-to-weight ratio, the hull is progressively lifted as the resistance is lowered, allowing high speeds.

The choice of hull in a planing boat, whether of round-, V-, or flat-bottom type, depends upon the speed desired and the degree of seaworthiness demanded. Round-bottom hulls, with the after underwater sections suitably flattened, are fully capable of planing speeds. They are the most comfortable for the occupants in rough water when speed must be reduced, and the boat then functions as a pure displacement type. Many small pleasure cruisers intended for limited offshore use are of this type, as are many small commercial craft such as lobstering launches and certain small combination boats. In these cases, comfort and economy are compromised with moderate speed.

The V-bottom hull is obviously capable of being designed for higher planing speeds, as its underwater sections can be made comparatively wider on similar beam-length ratios than the round-bottom type. The angle at the chine can also exert more pressure to keep the water from being forced up the sides of the hull.

The flat-bottom hull can be made to plane at very high speeds due to the lack of resistance from a more normally shaped keel or forefoot, but present problems of directional stability and hard steering in rough water, not to mention excessive pounding and the structural strains set up against the hull. The flat-bottom is used in fast runabouts and water-ski boats in protected waters, and in combination with lifting sponsons in racing hydroplanes that produce high speeds due to lowering of resistance factors from a reduction of wetted surface.

It is generally considered that at speed-length ratios up to about 3.5, the round-bottom can be more easily propelled with the added advantage of greater seaworthiness. If higher speeds are demanded, the V-bottom must be used, even at a sacrifice in comfort and seakeeping abilities. In these cases, beam-length ratio and the angle of deadrise become critical factors in design. Decrease in the latter and widening the beam are helpful in creating better lift as planing power is applied, but may induce higher resistance factors. Then, too, excessive beam in relation to overall waterline length may produce a boat very hard to steer and one with excessive pitching in rough water. As an acceptable degree of comfort and safety must be attained to make a boat practical under most conditions encountered, the lines of a high-speed planing boat must be drawn with these opposed considerations in mind.

A variation of the conventional V-bottom boat, when high planing speeds are required, is the monohedron bottom. The usual V-bottom hull shows a warped plane in its bottom which is described as a flattening of its angle of deadrise from 12 to 15 degrees at the bow to 3 to 4 degrees or even less at the transom. In a monohedron hull, the deadrise from just abaft the stem to the transom is at a constant angle of 12 to 15 degrees. With very high power, the thrust generates lift all along the bottom of the hull, and the hull lifts at a more horizontal angle to the static waterline. Such hulls provide more comfort in rough water because the deep V is in constant contact with the water and they have the further advantage of nullifying the wide bow angle that many conventional V-bottom types show at their highest speed. While these hulls are often considered as a late invention, their action was well understood in the pioneer days of power boating. It was only the lack of sufficiently high-powered engines that precluded earlier development as these hulls require enormous power to perform properly.

Another variation of the V-bottom hull for higher planing speeds in the same waterline length is the stepped hydroplane. The forward section of the underbody is shaped in a deep V, the chine line is widened as it sweeps aft as in the conventional type, but a step or break is interposed amidships and the after portion of the hull is made flat to the transom. The step is made several inches higher than the lowest portion of the terminated V forward. The hull rises on its forward section as the power is applied, and the water flow passes under the step forming a partial vacuum. This phenomenon greatly lowers the resistance and friction forces due to a marked reduction in wetted surface along the bottom of the hull, as the boat is supported at speed only on a small section of the V-bottom just forward of the step and is balanced aft only on a small portion just forward of the transom.

There is some loss of efficiency in the hydroplane hull under low speeds or when it is forced to proceed as a displacement boat under rough water conditions. This is due to the eddying produced from the consequent drag of the step, but many of the larger hydroplanes, other than pure racing boats, are surprisingly seaworthy. Although the hydroplane is considered a purely racing craft, these hulls have, in fact, been widely used as offshore launches. In the years just prior to World War I, the British and Italian navies experimented with hydroplanes as torpedo-carrying launches. The English developed a 40-foot hydroplane capable of carrying a 4-ton military load and crew at speeds of 40 knots with a 250 horsepower engine. A 55-foot type was later developed that could carry a 6-ton load, and both models proved acceptably seaworthy in offshore use. Later experiments to gain more efficiency from the hydroplane principle included the use of multistep hulls with two or more steps along the bottom, but the added resistance and increased wetted surface appeared to decrease rather than add efficiency.

While the hydroplane can show a 25 percent increase in speed in comparable size and power to a conventional V-bottom, it is less efficient as a weight carrier and is quite sensitive to balance factors, as the main weights must be concentrated over the area just forward of the step for proper performance. With special attention to its limitations, and strict attention to its overall demands of power-to-weight ratios, it can be designed as a practical and useful high-speed boat.

The latest efforts to effect high speeds from small planing launches include turbo-jet engines to drive the propellers, as well as aircraft jet engines providing air propulsion. However, apart from highly developed racing craft, it appears that, for the time being at least, natural physical forces somewhat limit higher speeds to conventional planing hulls. The latest efforts are directed toward the use of hydrofoil supported hulls which lift the hull to high speeds after the usual planing hull supporting them reaches terminal speeds. While the future here looks promising, efforts are at present beyond the technical capabilities of the amateur boatman.

3. Sailing Boat Design

Factors in sailing boat design include both the form of the hull and the shape and area of the sails that drive it. These two entities are intimately connected as a sailing craft is said to be a combination of an aerofoil and a hydrofoil, each being dependent upon the other and their reciprocal action.

Sailing craft, in the majority of cases, are displacement-type hulls, and as these are driven at speeds only moderately higher than the square root of their waterline length, resistance factors play an important role in hull efficiency. It will be seen that both racing and cruising sailboats show spindle-shaped hulls intended to travel through the water with a minimum of wave disturbance. The latter will usually show a more burdensome hull due to the need for cruising accommodations. Apart from the considerations of the required form of the hull and its displacement, the designer must consider problems of skin friction, sailing efficiency at varying angles of heel, and the form above the waterline which will best enhance seakeeping ability.

The amateur or professional boatbuilder can gain a working knowledge of modern sailing boat hull forms by a study of the standard treatises on naval architecture. As the intricacies of the subject cannot be entirely covered by mathematical formulae, an examination of various hauled-out examples of known performance will aid in obtaining a practical knowledge of the subject. Experience with various individual boats is also invaluable, as the most noted of sailing yacht designers were also practical sailormen.

4. Seaworthiness

In the initial examination of a small boat design, one of the first considerations is that of its seaworthiness. This, however, is a purely relative factor. No vessel of any size can be deemed seaworthy in the ultimate sense, as witnessed by the numerous marine disasters involving so-called unsinkable ships during the last hundred years.

While designers naturally endeavor to produce safe boats, any craft of small size has very definite limitations in withstanding unusual conditions of wind and sea. All the designer can do is to incorporate design elements that will enable the boat to weather what might be termed normal emergencies.

The desires of the prospective owner are frequently at variance with the dictates of safety. The commercial fishing boat operator will demand a small boat of good carrying capacity, acceptable speeds and seakeeping ability for working offshore, yet may want very low freeboard amidships for ease in handling nets and boating fish. The pleasure boat owner will specify a craft of good all-around performance and ability, yet may suggest vast interior accommodation and large, glass-enclosed deckhouses that could render the boat vulnerable to disaster in an unexpected storm.

Small boats by virtue of their size and limiting design factors must arbitrarily fall into a rather circumscribed area of use. A fast, open launch used for short day excursions and water-ski towing in smooth water is definitely an unsafe boat to go to sea in, though it may be an admirable performer in its intended use. Fast, planing pleasure cruisers offering luxurious accommodation with their wide beam and shallow draft might be in serious difficulty if they lost engine power in rough water or high wind.

Seaworthiness, in the final instance, is in the hands of the individual operator who knows the limitations of the boat in question and does not venture to overtax its capabilities.

Stability in a boat is a prime requisite for safety. This simply means that to have normal seagoing ability a small boat should be capable of righting itself if thrown over on its beam ends. Small, displacement-type power cruisers and commercial fishing boats are usually capable of righting themselves at angles up to 80 or 90 degrees. Wide-beamed and shallow draft high-speed planing types have a much narrower range of stability and may capsize at angles of 50 degrees or less. Sailing cruisers with ballast keels are ordinarily considered to be very stable, but more shallow centerboard types may easily swamp when thrown on their sides.

Factors other than the stability of the boat itself may alter the picture. For example, while a boat may be capable of righting itself up to 90 degrees, the occupants may be thrown out or washed overboard before the critical angle is reached. A small light boat of indifferent righting qualities may have seakeeping abilities enhanced by natural buoyancy that allows it to ride high in the water, and by the presence of tight decks that keep solid water out of the hull. A keel-ballasted boat with an ordinarily high degree of stability may swamp through water filling large cockpits or pouring into the cabin, or the decks may be torn away if dismasted from rolling the rig into the water. Some light draft centerboard sailing cruisers may right themselves if their decks are watertight and the masts and rigging are cut away shortly after rolling under.

The true stability factors inherent in a small boat may not be readily apparent as the amount of roll enters the picture. A long, narrow hull of moderate displacement may have a long, slow roll that creates a feeling of uneasiness, yet be thoroughly capable of a 90-degree righting. A wide, shallow hull may show greater initial resistance to rolling, but display a quick, jerky motion in rough water and ultimately demonstrate but half the righting moment of the narrow boat. Many of our more modern types of wide-beamed hulls have less comfortable motion than some of the older types.

Stability itself depends upon the interaction of buoyancy and gravity when the two enter into opposition as a boat heels over (Figure 2). When

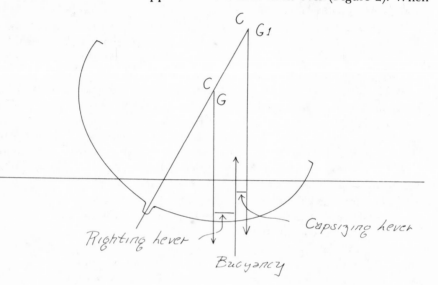

Figure 2 Diagram illustrating the variable factors of metacentric height

the hull is upright, these factors balance themselves, buoyancy acting vertically upwards and gravity downwards. As the hull rolls down, the newly immersed hull form has its buoyancy shifted to the low side, the flotation forces on the other side being reduced as the bilges leave the water.

Stability factors in new designs are very tiresome and lengthy to calculate. Most designers, if they do them at all, figure stability at one large angle of heel. Other practical considerations are beam-length ratio, displacement, and weight distribution throughout the hull and its contents. Every hull possesses what is known as metacentric height. This is an overall indication of loading factors, taking into consideration stability as related to heights of cabins and deckhouses, windage, and other factors having a bearing on stability.

While stability is a basic function of the underwater shape of a hull, other factors must be considered. Flare in the topsides adds righting levers to the hull as it rolls down and picks up the consequent buoyancy. Freeboard is critical as it keeps water off the deck that might add extra weight at a crucial angle of heel. Watertight decks are important in seagoing craft as are watertight doors and hatches. High bulwarks in some commercial and pleasure craft aid in keeping water off the decks, but may also put the boat in danger if adequate scuppers or freeing ports at the deckline are not provided. Small fishing boats carrying large deckloads are especially vulnerable in this regard.

While the foregoing are practical considerations gained from experience and observation, safety factors are often negated by authenticated accounts of long ocean voyages in ordinarily unsuitable vessels. Their owners, however, are generally highly skilled, experienced sailors. It is an old saying that the seaworthiness of a boat is in proportion to the skill of its master. Caution and good judgment are the best insurance for safety at sea.

3

The Classification of
Small Boat Types

The prospective builder generally selects the overall size of a boat by an estimate of its projected cost, and possibly to suit the building space available,
but it is also essential to select the type or model best suited to the work intended. It is also important to select a design that is well within the mechanical capabilities of the builder to insure its successful completion
within a reasonable length of time. A familiarity with the various small
boat types should increase the prospective builder's general knowledge of
the subject, and make him a better judge of boats, and of small boats in
particular.

There are three basic types of models of small boat hulls, whether intended for sail or power, and these are classified as to the transverse section
of their hull, i.e., flat-bottom, V-bottom or round-bottom. In this book we
will concern ourselves with hulls of the V-bottom type, with plans of various
examples together with details of their construction.

The V-Bottom Boat

The V-bottom boat is a refinement of the flat-bottom types. With the V-
bottom hull it is possible to employ greater beam and increased displacement for enhanced carrying capacity and interior room than with the flat-
bottom hull. Both as a sailing and power craft, it shows better seaworthiness
and overall performance than the flat-bottom, but is more complicated in
building and material requirements. It has numerous variations as to hull
form, generally induced by the chine profile, which also determines cost and
building complication.

1. The *flattie* is the most primitive type of V-bottom boat, and was originally developed from the early sailing sharpie. Wide-bottom hulls are
   slow to come about when tacking, and it was discovered that by reducing the displacement aft, maneuverability was somewhat in-

creased. In these boats the bottom is flat from the bow to a point just aft of amidships, where it is formed in a shallow V to the transom. The chine line shows a pronounced rocker from the heel of the stem to the transom. This type has been virtually abandoned since the days of working sail and is often thought to be a transitional type.

2. The *Roslyn* or *"non-pareil" sharpie* was developed by Thomas Clapham shortly after the American Civil War, its common name being derived from the area of its building on Long Island Sound. This is another variation of the old sailing sharpie, the bottom being dead flat amidships but with shallow deadrise at both forward and after thirds of the bow and stern sections. Clapham attempted to publicize it as an improved variation of the flat-bottom type, as well as the flattie.

3. The *modified sharpie* or *"diamond bottom"* shows a slight amount of deadrise all along the bottom but deepest amidships, the chine line meeting the heel of the stem forward. These boats are usually planked herringbone fashion on the bottom, the planking being of short pieces extending outward at an angle of 10 or 12 degrees from the keel to the chine. These are easy hulls to build, and are seen in small class racing-sailing boats. In some cases, the hulls are planked lengthwise, and have ballasted fin keels. A few types of moderate-speed power launches have been built to this model.

4. The *garvey* has been often built as a V-bottom as an improvement over the flat-bottom type in both sailing and power craft. It was much used in the days of working sail. These boats are smart sailers, and are very fast as powerboats if large engines are fitted; in these cases, the bottom is made dead flat from amidships aft. The V-bottom is generally quite pronounced forward, and cuts down on pounding. Very small V-bottom garvey types are widely seen in small sailing classes, where they are often referred to as *prams*. They are also used as dinghies, as they can carry large loads for their lengths and can be easily stowed on the deck or cabin top of small yachts.

5. The *Northern skipjack* is considered by many marine historians as the original V-bottom type. It was developed shortly after the American Civil War in the Long Island Sound area, and was built along the lines of the small, shallow-draft, wide-beamed center-board sloops that were used in the commercial fisheries. The chine showed a pronounced rocker, particularly forward, landing high on the stem. This form allowed the longitudinal bottom plank to be laid on in natural sweeps without the hard twist found in hulls with lower chine lines forward. The bottom had a complete framing system with closely spaced sawn futtocks. As in the parent type, the boats were about 20 to 30 feet long, and were very fast sailers with their lofty rig, wide beam, and large centerboards. After the coming of power, motor launches of various sizes were built to this form, but with lower chine lines aft to retain the advantage of easy planking.

6. The *Chesapeake Bay skipjack,* or *"deadrise boat"* or *"bateau,"* originated in the Chesapeake Bay area, and is a modified Northern skipjack with low chine line forward and much more simplified construction. It is thought that it was developed by professional shipwrights
   as a cheaper and more quickly built version of the boats used earlier
   on Long Island Sound.

   The old sailing skipjacks built in lengths of 35 to 60 feet to the
   original model are still used in limited numbers on Chesapeake Bay
   for oyster dredging, as this activity is legally limited, as a conservation
   measure, to sailing craft. Since the coming of power, the Bay boats
   have been built in various forms as power work boats, adhering to the
   old style and often in lengths up to 60 or 70 feet. While this style of
   building is only satisfactory for small angles of deadrise and creates a
   boat of rather shallow draft, the boats are surprisingly able and seaworthy in the rough and steep seas often seen on the Bay.

7. The *Cape Hatteras boats* are power launches developed for offshore
   use from the Carolina Sounds, and were derived from the Chesapeake
   Bay power boats developed from the sailing skipjack. They show
   more deadrise and less beam for enhanced seaworthiness, and usually
   have rounded or elliptical sterns to cut down the risk of being
   broached in a steep, following sea. Their forward lines are quite
   sharp, the chine line fading into the bow sections just aft of the stem,
   and they often have a straight line in the forward frames from rabbet
   to sheer. Some of the boats have a complete framing system and are
   longitudinally planked on the bottom. These boats are very seaworthy
   and are capable of being operated offshore under very severe weather
   conditions.

8. The *Oriental sampan* is a powered version of the old sailing Yamato
   boats of Japan, and curiously enough, their hull forms bear a close re-
   semblance to both the Northern skipjack and the Cape Hatteras boat.
   The parent Yamato boats were built as the successors to the fourteenth century log canoes, after large logs became unavailable. These
   were narrow-beam boats built up of five very thick and wide planks,
   with very fine lines dictated by the difficulty of springing the planks
   into a boatlike form. One plank formed the keel, being tapered to a
   point forward, two more formed the angles of the bilge, and the sheer
   strakes formed flat sides. The sides and bilges were laboriously sprung
   into place in a building frame, by the use of jacks, chains, and levers,
   the planks being hewn to fitting shape, and held in place by cleats and
   edge nailing. A complete framing system was not needed, due to the
   thickness of the planks used, which were often some 24 inches wide
   and 2 or 2½ inches thick, with solid lengths up to 24 or 26 feet. The
   boats were fitted with two or three lug sails, and were rowed or
   sculled with a long oar in light airs or when maneuvering in the harbor. With the coming of power, larger boats were built with a com-

plete framing system in larger sizes, but retaining the characteristically heavy plank. As the early Yamato boatbuilders knew that a
sharp rake to the stem and a high chine line were necessary to form
the shape, the powerboats naturally assumed the same form, the high
chine line fading out some distance aft of the stem. These boats, with
their moderate beam, sharp forward sections, strongly raking stem,
and the great weight of their hulls, are very seaworthy and able craft,
and work far offshore in the commercial fisheries.

9. The *high-chined V-bottom* is usually seen in auxiliary-powered, sailing-cruising types, with a strongly raking stem, cut away forefoot, and
a moderate rocker in the chine line from bow to stern. The bow form
here is intended to cut down the tendency of the V-bottom hull to
pound in head seas. The sailing speed is somewhat reduced by the resistance set up by the curved chine. This type of hull generally shows
more interior room than a round-bottom hull of comparable size, and
is usually thought of as a cheaper and more easily built compromise
for a small cruising boat offering better accommodation. Many are indifferent sailers, because excessive free-board and high cabin sides
produce much windage. They are built either as centerboard boats
with shallow draft, or as keel boats with ballasted fins. As their sailing ability is limited, and their ability to sail to windward is less than
that of comparable round-bottom types, they are usually seen in sizes
under 30 feet of overall length. The most familiar example of this
type is the well-known *Seabird* yawl, upon which the design of most
small, V-bottom sailing auxiliaries is based.

10. The *flat-chined V-bottom* is used in power craft for high speeds, and is
seen in specialized racing boats, high-speed runabouts, water-ski towing launches, sports-type fishing cruisers, and other fast launches. The
stem is cut away somewhat, the chine, moderately high on the stem,
curves downward running just below or at the waterline in a flat
plane to the transom. The type of bottom varies as to the speed intended, or to the dictates of more seaworthiness. The monohedron, or
constant angle V-bottom, shows this chine profile.

11. The *Multi-chine V-bottom hull* is sometimes built as a simplified version of the round-bottom type, and is usually seen in small sailing hulls
intended for amateur construction. These are usually built with ballasted fin keels. The frames are most often of sawn construction, each
angle in the sides representing a chine. While steam-bent ribs are seldom specified, the construction complication is often enhanced by the
careful fitting and shaping of the side plank necessary to conform to
the lines. These boats often perform well to windward, due to the
more rounded shape possible in the forward hull sections.

Because of its many variations in form, seaworthiness, building complication, and cost, the V-bottom type is less easy to classify than the flat-bottom

boat. And while it is often thought of as a more or less universal type for amateur building, the V-bottom hull can, in some cases, be more difficult to build than the round-bottom type. Various V-bottom models will be thoroughly discussed in Part 3.

Part
2

Fundamentals of Boatbuilding

4

Boating Nomenclature: A glossary of terms describing the structure of a boat

The first step in boatbuilding is to become familiar with the descriptive terms of the various parts of a boat and its internal structure. While the terminology, by tradition, applies to boats built of wood, by popular usage it applies to all boats whether constructed of metal, light metallic alloys, or plastics.

In viewing a boat's outline in profile, the forward and after ends are known as the *bow* and *stern* respectively. The upper edge of a boat's main body is known as the *sheer*. It is the highest portion of the sides of an open boat, or where the deckline is formed in larger sailing or power craft. This line exists without reference to any other upward projections, such as *railings* or *bulwarks* around the deck, and cabins, deckhouses, or steering shelters.

The distances between the outer edges of the bow and stern indicate the *overall length*. The widest part of the cross section of the hull at the sheer is the *beam*.

The point of intersection of the hull and the water when the boat is at rest is called the *waterline, or load waterline*. Some commercial or cargo-carrying boats have two or more load waterlines indicated, according to the condition of loading.

The depth of water needed to provide free flotation of the hull is the *draft,* and is the distance between the static waterline and the lowest portion of the boat's structure, generally the bottom of the keel aft.

The outward projection of the sides of the hull from the waterline upward is the *flare*. While most normal craft show flare in their sides, it is usually more pronounced from the bow aft to the middle of the hull. In cases where the sides extend outward in a curve, in addition to the flare, this is called *flam*. If the edges of the deckline are narrower than the waterline aft, such as in some high-speed runabouts, the condition is known as *tumble-home*.

The area around the hull between the load waterline and the sheerline above is the *freeboard*.

The total weight of a boat is its *displacement*. By physical laws, any floating body displaces the same weight as the medium surrounding it. If it were actually possible to weigh accurately the volume of water displaced by a boat, it would equal the total weight of the boat and its contents.

The foundation of a boat is known as the *keel*, which forms the main backbone member. The *stem* is attached to the forward end of the keel, and is an upward extension of it. The joint between the keel and the stem is the *scarph*, its angle being braced by a triangular member called the *knee*. The stern structure enclosing the after end of the hull is the *transom*, being attached to the after end of the keel and braced by the *stern knee*. In the case of double-ended hulls, such as lifeboats, or hulls with canoe-type sterns, the structure is called the *sternpost*, and is similar to the stem forward.

In deep-hulled sailing craft or heavy displacement cargo-carrying power craft, the timbers attached above the keel at the stern are the *deadwood*. If the transom extends aft behind the keel and rudder post, it is supported by the *horn timber*.

As a means of attaching the planking which forms the shape and mass of the hull, a longitudinal member somewhat wider than the keel is laid along its top. This is the *keel batten* or *keel apron*, and is referred to by the English as the *hog*, or *hog timber*. In some light boats this member is dispensed with, the edges of the first bottom plank being directly attached to the keel by means of a triangular groove cut longitudinally into it along its upper edge. In some cases, such as in the Chesapeake Bay method of building, longitudinal backing for the attachment of this plank is formed by strips of timber bolted along the upper edges of the keel, these being somewhat less deep than the keel itself, and are known as *keel cheeks*.

The first strakes of planking fitted along the keel on either side are the *garboards*, or *garboard strakes*. The line of intersection formed where the inside edge of the garboard meets the keel and the stem forward is the *rabbet line*.

Upon the assembled backbone members, transverse *timbers* or *frames* are erected. The term timber generally refers to the steam-bent pieces used in a round-bottom boat, and frames in a flat- and V-bottom craft having an angle in the outer and lower edge of the hull. The *chine* or *chine line* refers to this angle, where the topsides and bottom areas intersect. In a hard-chined boat, or in round-bottom boats where the timbers or frames are formed from individual pieces, the parts are called the *futtocks*. To further strengthen the hull, or to impart additional bracing to the steam-bent timbers in a round-bottom boat, pieces known as *floors* or *floor timbers* are extended across the bottom of the hull and are fastened both to the keel and the frames. In a flat- or V-bottom boat, these members form the bottom of the frame assembly, and may be called *floor futtocks*.

In round-bottom boats, to keep the hull from sagging or hogging, additional strength is provided by means of longitudinal members known as *bilge stringers* or *hog timbers* placed along the bottom parallel to the keel and near the area where the bottom turns upward. This area, together with the inside of the bottom, is the *bilge.*

In the case of open boats, further longitudinal stiffening is provided by *gunwales* or *gunnels,* which are timbers fastened along the inner and outer edges of the sheer. In decked boats, the inner of these timbers are called *shelves,* and are set a short distance below the sheer line to form the foundation and point of attachment for the *deckbeams* that form the transverse support for the deck above that covers the top of the hull. If railings or bulwarks are fitted, parts of the framing, or members attached to the tops of the frames to support them, are called *stanchions.*

The hull is further braced by a knee, called a *breasthook,* placed forward in the angle formed at the bow. In open boats this is usually fitted at the sheerline, and in decked craft is sometimes placed lower to include the ends of the shelves. Additional bracing is similarly provided at angles between the sides of the hull and the transom at the sheerline aft by *quarter-knees.*

In a power boat, or auxiliary-powered sailing boat, the engine base is fastened through its *lugs* to longitudinal *engine beds,* which are themselves attached to the tops of the transverse frames and floors. In larger boats, the engine beds may have additional support below from *engine bearers* set across the frames and floors and bolted to them.

The propeller shaft from the engine extends outward and usually downward through the hull through a hole in a timber called the *shaft log,* with a *stuffing box* forming a seal around the propeller shaft on the inside, and bolted to the inner end of the shaft log. The outer support of the shaft fastened to the after end of the shaft log is the *stern bearing.*

When openings in the deck are provided for hatches, cockpits, or cabins, the longitudinal pieces that bear against the cut-off ends of the deckbeams are known as the *carlins* or *headers.* The transverse or athwartship members supporting the floor of the cockpit or cabin roof are the *cockpit* or *cabin beams,* and are supported at their ends by *cockpit* or *cabin carlins.*

Some pleasure and most commercial craft have a covering on the inside of the hull known as the *ceiling.* It is fastened to the framing and gives longitudinal support to the hull in addition to the bilge stringers if these are fitted. The lower part of this lining, when it forms the floor of the cockpit or cabin is the *sole.*

The forward portion of the hull below the waterline where the bottom of the keel and the stem intersect is called the *forefoot.* The forward portion of the hull is the *forebody.* The middle portion of the hull is the *midship* section. The after part of the hull is the *afterbody.* The sides of the hull as they extend aft toward the transom are the *quarters.* The underwater portion of the after end of the hull extending toward the rudder is called the *run.*

The angle formed by the bottom of a boat as it projects outward and upward from the keel at the rabbet line toward the outer edges of the bilges or chine line is called the *deadrise.* In some cases, V-bottom boats with hard chines are called *deadrise boats.*

Rigging

Sailing craft are generally classified as to their type of rig. A secondary classification is as to hull type, such as a deep-draft boat fitted with an iron or lead ballast keel, or a shallow-draft type with a movable centerboard. A few shallow-draft sharpie types have been fitted with two centerboards, one abaft the other along the centerline of the hull. Some light draft hulls are fitted with *leeboards,* which are rectangular wood or metal plates fastened along the upper side of the hull along the sheer line and function as does a centerboard.

The *catboat* carries a fore-and-aft rig with one mast and one sail, the mast being set well forward in the eyes of the bow.

The *sloop* is also a fore and after with a single mast, but has one or more headsails. The mast is usually stepped well forward, about at a point one third the distance of the waterline aft of the bow.

The *cutter* is similar to the sloop, except that the mast is stepped somewhat farther aft and two or more headsails are fitted. The differentiation between a cutter and sloop is not often clear cut due to variations in mast position.

The *yawl* is like a sloop or cutter except that a small mast is carried aft for a small fore-and-aft sail. The mast is usually stepped behind the rudder post and is termed a mizzen or jigger.

The *ketch* is like the yawl, except that the mizzen or jigger is a larger sail with a longer mast that is stepped ahead of the rudder post.

The *schooner* also carries two masts. The foremast is shorter and stepped well forward. The mainmast may be stepped at approximately the middle portion of the waterline.

The *pirogue* is much like the schooner except that the foremast is stepped well forward and carries no headsail, as in the catboat. This rig is sometimes called a *catketch.* It is used mostly on very small craft.

The *lug* rig shows a short mast well forward with an irregularly shaped four-cornered sail that is laced to a gaff on its upper edge. No headsails are fitted, the effect being as in a catboat. Some boats carry two lug sails in tandem. This rig is also mainly seen in very small craft.

A further classification of sailing rigs is whether the sails are four-sided and are fitted with a gaff at their upper edge. The gaff rig differs from the lug rig in that the gaff has its forward end attached to the mast by means of a pair of *jaws* that permit it to pivot about to accommodate varying settings. Most gaff sails have a *boom* at their lower edge, also attached to the mast by jaws.

The more modern *jib-headed* rig is triangular and carries no gaff, the peak of the sail being attached to the mast head. To obtain the required sail area, the sail must be taller requiring a taller mast. The English call this a Bermudian rig. It has also been known as a Marconi rig in earlier days.

The rigging of sailing craft is divided into two types. The *standing rig-*

ging is more or less permanently attached to the mast and secures it in position. The *running rigging* consists of the lines and halyards that run through pulleys or blocks to alter the set of the sails.

The standing rigging consists of one or more pairs of *shrouds* which support the mast on either side. Modern jib-headed rigs usually have two sets of shrouds, one set extending to the top of the mast, the other running about half way up. The upper shrouds are kept away from the mast by horizontal struts or spreaders made of either wood or sometimes light alloy metal. Very high masts may have two sets of these. The lower ends of the shrouds are attached to the outer sides of the hull at the sheer by means of long metal bands called *chain plates* which may be bolted to either the inside or the outside of the planking. The shrouds are attached to the chain plates with either dead eyes and lanyards or turnbuckles. *Lanyards* are usually made of hemp and have more elasticity, but must be taken up from time to time and must be renewed periodically. The top mast stay extends from the top of the stem or the outer end of the bowsprit if one is fitted, to the top of the mast. The *forestay* extends from the stem head or bowsprit to a distance somewhat more than half way up the mast.

If a bowsprit is fitted, there will be a stay running from its outboard end to the stem, just above the waterline. This is called the *bobstay.*

There are two lines that extend from either side of the mast at or slightly above the attachment point of the forestay to deck fittings at the sides of the cockpit. These are the *runners* which may be either set up tight or slackened. When sailing, the windward runner is kept taut to give additional support to the mast, and the leeward runner is slacked off to clear the sail.

Some jib-headed craft with tall narrow rigs, such as those fitted to offshore racing boats with short main booms, are usually fitted with a permanent backstay that extends from the masthead aft to the transom.

The running rigging which is used to handle the sails is called *halyards.* On a gaff-rigged sloop there are three of these, two on the mainsail and one on the jib. The jib halyard hoists the jib from its head. The two mainsail halyards are known as the throat halyard and the peak halyard. The throat halyard is attached to a ringbolt near the jaws of the gaff. The peak halyard is attached to the outboard end of the gaff at about one-third the distance from its outer end. These two halyards are handled together to obtain the proper set of the sail. When the halyards are in position they are held taut by twisting or belaying them around a cleat.

There are two lines attached to the clew or lower after end of the jibsail. These are called *jibsheets,* and run through fairleads on either side of the deck to give sufficient leverage for setting the sail. Their ends are belayed to cleats alongside the cockpit.

The *main sheet* is attached toward the end of the main boom and consists of a block and tackle arrangement that runs on a horse or traveler and gives leverage to trim the mainsail.

Running from the extreme outboard end of the main boom to a sheave or block at the mast head and thence down the mast to the deck is the *topping lift*. It is used to keep the boom from falling on the deck when the mainsail is furled.

5

Plans and Lofting

Blueprint Reading and Plan Interpretation

Most boat designers and naval architects assume that prospective builders are familiar with plan reading, and lay out their drawing accordingly. However some amateur builders may have difficulty in the interpretation of boat plans, and, after cursory inspection, conclude that many essential details of the various structural parts have been left out. It is impossible, however, to include every detail of a boat's structure in a set of drawings, as the immense amount of time involved would make the designing cost prohibitive.

Sometimes designs of even very small craft published in hobby or boating magazines as a "how-to-build" feature are presented in elaborate detail for enough clarity to benefit the amateur builder. In such presentations, however, the original effort has been heavily subsidized by the publishers, and they are not representative of the usual stock plan that must be sold at competitive fees.

The two most distinctive features peculiar to boat structures that differ from the more familiar land-based structures are the varying depths of the sectional parts of the hull, and the fact that the exterior parts and general disposition of its form are a series of curved lines. It is this lack of "squareness," or right-angle relationship of the overall outline of a boat, that confuses many prospective builders, even though they may have had extensive prior experience as house carpenters or cabinet makers.

While the profile drawings indicate the size, height, and general disposition of the various parts, the sectional drawings of each area and station line must be used to determine the structures involved at any given point. Using the plan view and profile as a guide, it is possible with a little study to visualize quickly the internal structures by correlating the sectional drawings. On small or very simple boats, one or two sectional drawings generally are sufficient to show all principle structures, material sizes, and details that are typical throughout the entire hull. Large craft of more complex construction and extensive interior fittings may require drawings of several cross sections, and these are usually of half sections only to enable more detail to be worked in. If there is any question about the dimensions of any part not labeled or specified in the drawings, it must be remembered that all parts are drawn to a specified scale. The shape of any part, particularly interior fittings, cupboards, berths, etc., can be determined by applying the scale indicated on the blueprints.

In the correct interpretation of boat drawings, it is essential to consider the profile or plan view together with the sectional drawings as one unit, combining depth perception to visualize the third dimension. The amateur builder should study as many boat plans as possible in order to become thoroughly familiar with the procedure.

Estimating Materials

Few naval architects provide material lists for wooden boats planked conventionally, as varieties and sizes of timber vary greatly in various parts of the country and substitutions are usually necessary. This is less true in the case of boats to be planked with plywood panels or in metal craft, as the larger modules are subject to more uniformity and standardization. The sizes of the various fastenings are generally enumerated in the construction sections, and estimates as to quantity are derived from taking an average number in various typical construction sections. The builder will have to exercise some ingenuity in making substitutions in order that the final dimensions of the various parts approximate those of the designer's specifications. This is particularly true in the case of large wooden craft with large deadwoods, keel members, or horn timbers, where various pieces of timber must be built up to proper sizes.

All hardware fittings are specified by the designer, and are often indicated by the catalog number from some manufacturer's catalog. The builder usually purchases these items as specified, but products of another maker may be substituted if of similar size.

Planning the Actual Construction

When the decision is made to build a boat and the plans are in hand, the next obvious procedure is to select the building site. In many cases the type and size of the projected boat governs the amount of building space necessary. It must be emphasized that building in a clear area greatly facilitates the handling of the material, and, most important, the ability to view the construction from various angles as the work proceeds. Small boats have been built by dedicated amateurs, under very difficult conditions, such as in lofts or attics, cramped areas between existing buildings, in low basements, or even inside of dwellings. Frequently residential backyards are a favored site, but the size of the boat is restricted by the space between adjacent houses, or the presence of masonry fences or shrubbery which cannot be readily removed. Sometimes the presence of a cooperative neighbor will allow adjacent obstructions to be temporarily dismantled for final removal of the finished hull. If a larger-than-average boat is being contemplated, it is often advisable to rent space on an open lot or vacant building, making sure that the area is securely fenced or otherwise closed in and thus is reasonably secure against pilfering or vandalism. If the hull is to be built upside down it is well to plan for its eventual righting, either by block-and-tackle arrangements using sheer poles, or with a portable crane or large truck-wrecking type of vehicle. If building is to be undertaken in a cold climate, some type of covered or closed-in structure that can be heated is almost mandatory.

Lofting

Lofting is described as the laying down of a full-sized drawing of a boat's hull from the designer's plan. These are originally drawn to some arbitrary scale, such as ½, ¾ or 1 inch to the foot, and must be drawn to full size on a lofting floor. When they are completed and templates or layouts are made for the building of the various structural members of the hull, the process is known as *taking off*. The actual representation of the boat is known as the "lines," and consists of three parts: the profile, plan, and sectional or body plan. If a large boat or one with much involved structural detail is proposed, additional drawings may be included to show these to an indicated scale. In any case, (and even in very simple boats), a typical cross-sectional drawing is included which shows the dimensions of the material specified in its building. Sailing craft will have a sail plan, with the disposition and dimensions of all sails and details of the rigging. In every case, the drawings are presented in a flat plane without perspective, that property of optics which reduces the size of the parts farthest away from the eye.

The *profile* shows a side view of the hull with all lengths and heights indicated without reference to any widths. The *plan* shows all lengths and widths without reference to heights, and indicates the form of the hull as viewed from above. In flat- and V-bottom boats which have flat sides standing at an angle with the bottom, the *chine* line is also indicated. Some plan views are drawn to show both sides of the hull. Others may only show one-half of the hull to the centerline, but all dimensions are indicated due to the bilateral symmetry of the hull. The *body* or *cross-sectional* plan shows the hull as viewed from both bow and stern with all widths and heights without reference to length. A representation of typical examples of these line drawings is given in Figure 3.

The outline or profile of the hull is enclosed within a grid of horizontal and vertical lines for purposes of measurement. The vertical lines at the extreme bow and stern are called *perpendiculars* and indicate the overall length of the hull. In the profile drawing, the principal horizontal lines in-

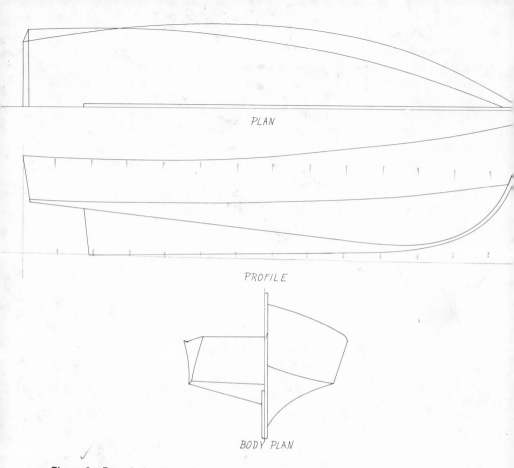

PLAN

PROFILE

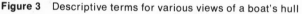

BODY PLAN

Figure 3 Descriptive terms for various views of a boat's hull

clude the load waterline which bisects the lower edge of the hull and indicates its static position of flotation. The base line is positioned at some arbitrary point below the lowest point of the hull, such as near the keel or deadwood, and is used as a datum line for indicating and measuring the heights of the sheer line, chine line (if present), the rabbet line where the forward and lower edges of the planking meet the stem and keel members, as well as the bottom of the keel and deadwood.

The load waterline, from the point of intersection with the bow and stern, is divided into a number of equidistant segments by a series of vertical lines set at right angles to the base line and load waterline. These lines are known as *stations*, and not only function as points of measurement for laying out the hull for building, but are also used by the designer in calculating the hull's displacement and stability factors. The number of station lines will vary with the length of the hull, and are usually numbered consecutively from bow to stern. The distances between the ends of the load waterline and the perpendiculars forward and aft are not equidistant with each other or the station lines in most normal hulls as these dimensions are not critical to flotation or displacement factors and merely indicate the shape of the hull. If either the bow or stern or both are exactly perpendicular or plumb, the perpendiculars may then be considered as also indicating the ends of the load waterline. In any case, these vertical lines at the extreme ends of the hull are called *half stations* and are usually enumerated by alphabetical letters to distinguish them from the consecutively numbered station lines. An exception to this layout of a hull may sometimes be seen in drawings that were made from actual hulls or hulks of existing boats for purposes of measurement and reproduction where original plans are not available or ever existed, such as in empirically evolved or traditional-type hulls built by eye or from carved halfmodels. An example of a profile view of a V-bottom hull with all horizontal and vertical lines indicated is shown in Figure 3.

The *plan* or halfbreadth view indicates the shape of the hull from above or below and includes the shape of the chine line in flat- or V-bottom hulls. The datum line here for plotting the distances for purposes of measurement is the centerline, and as has been stated, may include only one-half of the hull. The station lines bisect the plan view, and coincide with the distances between those shown on the profile. The same half sections forward and aft indicate the overhang of the bow and stern beyond the load waterline, the total length of the hull being indicated by the perpendiculars (Figure 4).

Figure 4   Plan, profile, and cross-sectional views of a V-bottom lobster boat hull showing position of base line, load waterline, and all station lines

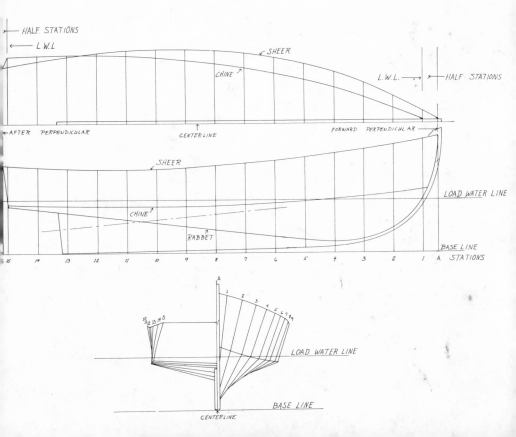

The *body plan* or cross-sectional view of various segments of the hull provides drawings of the transverse or athwartship form without reference to length. It is generally shown as two half sections, one from the bow to a point amidships, and another from the transom to the same point, or one section behind it. This drawing is bisected by the centerline. The lines outlining each section correspond to the vertical station lines of the profile and plan views, and complete the three sets of outlines that indicate the final form of the hull (Figure 4).

While the drawings and outlines described are seen in the plans of small craft generally, the procedure may be greatly simplified in the case of small skiffs or dinghies of flat-bottom form whose general performance and characteristics are well known, and where the designer feels it unnecessary to perform displacement or weight and balance or stability calculations. In such cases, profile, plan, and sectional views are provided to furnish the measurements for setting up the hull, but load waterlines and half stations at the bow and stern are not included. The angles of rake at the bow and transom are shown in their relation to the forward and after perpendiculars and to the base line. In some cases, the base line may be drawn at the upper edge of the sheer, indicating the measurements to be used in building in the inverted position, as is commonly done in such small craft (Figure 5).

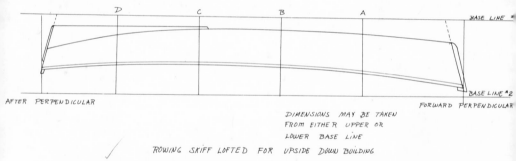

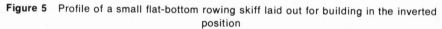

Figure 5 Profile of a small flat-bottom rowing skiff laid out for building in the inverted position

The numerical dimensions provided for laying down a boat's lines are contained in the *offset table*. These dimensions are set down in a grid arrangement that indicates the distances between various points of measurement. In simple flat- or V-bottom hulls this table consists of two parts: the heights above the base line and the distances from the centerline, referring to the profile and plan views respectively. The corresponding stations at which these points are measured from an indicated datum line are shown at the top of each column. The part of the hull to be measured in each case is indicated at the left side of the offset table, and the measurements of any point may be instantly determined by correlating them to the proper station.

The exception to the enumeration of hull and station measurements in such a table is again the case of very simple flat-bottom skiff types where the measurements are indicated on the profile and plan views as well as on as few as three or four body plan drawings (Figure 6).

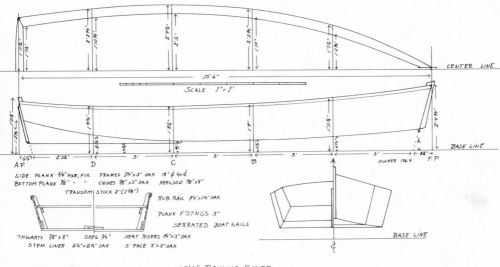

Figure 6 Simplified building plans for a flat-bottom skiff with all principal dimensions shown

    The actual figures set forth on the offset tables are tabulated in feet, inches, and eighths for clarity, and are indicated by using a whole number for each, rather than being written as a set of mixed numbers and fractions. Thus, a dimension of 6 feet 2¼ inches would be written as 6-2-2 in the space provided. A dimension of 10 feet 7⅜ inches would be set down as 10-7-3, etc. This practice eliminates possible confusion in the reading of small fractional figures, compensates for blurring of the numbers in printing, and makes for a more consistent system of measurement.

    The dimensions given in the offset table usually refer to distances that extend to the outside of the exterior planking. This is because the designer's calculations for displacement, weight, and balance factors must include the total hull volume. It is for this reason that the thickness of the planking or hull covering must be deducted from the total measurement shown for each station when lofting the hull. This operation is particularly critical in keel ballasted sailing boats, high speed semiplaning or planing power launches, racing hydroplanes, or specialized racing sail boats, as weight and balance factors become critical for anticipated performance. This condition is less critical in shallow-draft centerboard sailing hulls, heavy displacement cruising launches or load-carrying work boats where flotation factors and total displacement may be varied considerably without upsetting projected performance. The matter must be approached with some judgment, as the addition or depletion of the thickness of one layer of a boat's hull covering could add a ton of displacement to even moderately sized hulls.

The actual layout of a small, flat-bottom, inboard-powered launch is shown in Figure 7, with the offset measurements indicated for each station in the

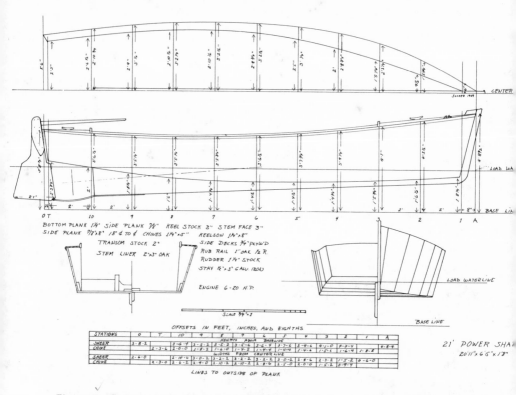

Figure 7 Building plans for a 21′ inboard-powered sharpie launch with principal dimensions correlated to the table of offsets

profile, plan, and sectional views. This is a very straightforward piece of work except for the necessity to visualize the disposition of the transom (Figure 8). Most normal hulls show a slight rake or backward slope here which, of course, cannot be indicated in the sectional view. The actual height of this must be measured from the profile, measuring from the bottom of the transom to the top along the surface of the slope rather than the perpendicular height.

Straight-sectioned V-bottom sailing and power craft are no more difficult to loft than the flat-bottom type except for the extra time involved in plotting the chine line (Figure 8).

While the profile, plan, and sectional views are sufficient for laying out the loft plan for straight-sectioned hulls, some flat- and V-bottom types having flare or flam which produces a curve in the topsides requiring additional points of measurement other than those mentioned to reproduce their lines. These are provided in the form of waterlines in addition to the

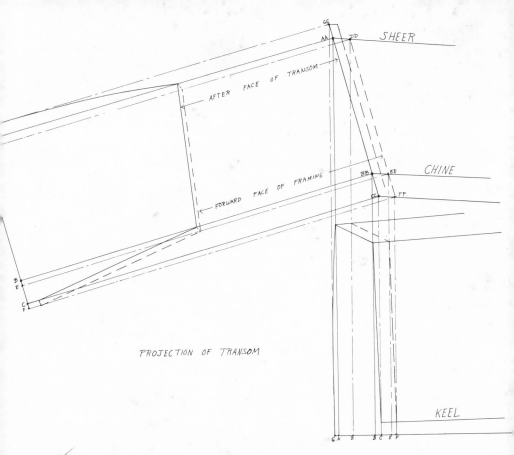

Figure 8 A method for projecting the expanded shape of the transom of a V-bottom boat

indicated load waterline, and are set at equidistant points above it and numbered consecutively from the bottom up for enumeration in the offset table (Figure 9).

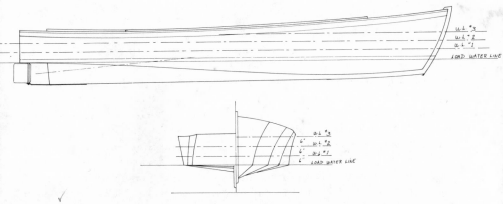

Figure 9 Profile and body plan of a modern Hooper Island launch showing the use of waterlines to indicate the degree of flare and tumblehome of the sides

A further method of measuring hull shapes is provided by the use of buttock lines (Figure 10). These are drawn vertically at equidistant points through the longitudinal aspect of the hull and parallel to the centerline. The intersection of the waterlines and buttock lines may be used as a further aid in fairing the lines.

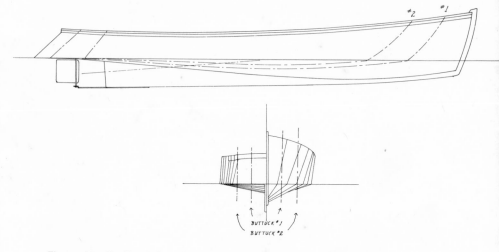

Figure 10   Profile and body plan of an old-style Hooper Island launch showing the use of buttock lines

Lofting Space

The actual lofting process requires a clear floor area somewhat larger than the boat itself to give adequate room in which to work. Commercial boatbuilding yards commonly employ large lofts or sheds with smooth wooden floor areas that are freshly painted before each new job with either white or black paint for either pencil or colored chalk or crayon reproduction of the lines. Such facilities are seldom available to the amateur or casual builder for the building of a single boat, and other means are generally resorted to. If the project is somewhat of an ambitious one for a fairly good-sized boat, it is often worthwhile to build a lofting floor of tongue-and-groove commercial grade flooring or plywood sheets. The foundation should be strong enough to bear the weight of two or three men without sagging. Some builders prefer to use heavy building or wrapping paper that is available in large rolls for laying down lines. If for a large hull, two widths of this paper are joined together with adhesive tape to provide enough space for the drawings. This practice has its limitations, however, as climactic conditions can cause the paper to shrink and stretch and result in inaccuracies in the full-sized reproduction. The recommended procedure is the use of large sheets of light plywood which can be stacked away when not in use. Short blocks can be screwed into the edges, forming a dovetail to hold them together to maintain accurate continuity of the lines over the surfaces of several panels. One side can be used for the profile and plan views and the other for cross sections.

Equipment

The equipment needed for lofting includes well-sharpened, hard-leaded carpenter's pencils together with hard, colored crayons for marking certain of the lines for identification. A large steel carpenter's square is necessary for setting up perpendiculars, and a larger square, accurately made of long hardwood battens is needed for large hulls. For measurement, a long, folding, steel tape is used, together with several stiff hardwood yardsticks. A chalk line of hard twine is used for running long lines, with some long finishing nails for securing the ends. A number of long, flexible wooden battens are used to make curves, along with several small celluloid or plastic draftsmen's battens to make curves of small radii and addenda. Several accurate straight edges should be made up of stiff, hardwood battens, and as long as the material can be and still provide an accurate edge. The wooden battens should be made up out of some clear, straight-grained lumber such as white pine or spruce, although any flexible wood can be used. Several battens 6 to 8 feet long, and of from ¼ to ½ inch in square section, will be needed for the average small boat. In addition, at least one batten will be needed that is somewhat longer than the boat to fair the sheerline. This can be of ¾ to 1 inch square, but will probably have to be spliced from two or more short pieces to obtain the required length. This should be effected by using long, diagonal scarphs, using glue and small nails for fastening. The battens may be held in place when working on lofting floors or plywood sheets by nailing them with thin wire brads. If paper is used over a floor that will be spoiled by nailing, weights must be used. These can be in the form of bricks, or small pieces of iron or lead. In addition to the battens, a few light, hardwood strips called marking staffs should be made up. These are useful in lining up the various heights and halfbreadths at the station lines, and may be marked for individual areas of measurement.

Base Line

The first line to be struck is the base line. This is run either along one edge of the lofting floor, or along the lower edge of the drawing paper or plywood panels, as the case may be. If the hull is longer than any available straight edge, a line must be used. Two nails are driven part way into the floor a short distance beyond the drawing area at each end and the line pulled taut between them. An accurate line can be drawn by adjusting the line to stand about an inch clear of the floor, drawing pencil marks at intervals directly beneath it. This is done using a small square to position the marks perpendicularly beneath it. Another method of running the line is to impregnate the cord with chalk and lay it directly across the drawing. The line is pulled taut and then raised slightly at its center, allowing it to snap back into place. The resulting chalk line is true, and may be penciled in and trued with a straight edge. Before proceeding with other lines, the base line should have a batten tacked along its lower edge so that the heights of the perpendiculars can be made without the measuring sticks or tape overrunning the line.

Stations

The positions of the station lines are next marked along the base line at the proper intervals, the corresponding number of each being indicated just below it. The perpendicular lines are then drawn by the use of a square, and their intersection with the sheer indicated, taking their heights from the offset table. The load waterline is next drawn in, using the same method as described for the base line. In outlining the sheer, a long, flexible batten is used, first making sure that it can be sprung into a long curve with no visible distortions. Lay this along the sheer line, with its lower edge at the top of the points that indicate the top of each station perpendicular. If any slight bumps or hollows are noted, adjust the batten to a fair curve, irrespective of the original offset mark. After the curve has been doubly checked, the sheer line is drawn in, using the lower side of the batten as the edge. It is essential that the batten is not moved from a fair curve in making individual station changes, as this may lead to other bumps and hollows along the sheer.

Keel and Rabbet Lines

The keel and rabbet lines are now drawn, using the heights from the offset table as before. The stem and transom lines are next drawn in to the proper angles. In laying out the stem, a wooden batten may be used for lines of moderate curves. If the forefoot has a sharp curve, a smaller draftsman's batten must be used to form the proper radii. It is essential when large and small battens are used in conjunction with one another that the lines and points of connection be also in fair curves.

Half-Breadth Plan

The half-breadth plan is next drawn, using the dimensions from the offset table, and the same station line configuration as on the profile. It is common practice to superimpose the half-breadth plan over that of the profile, using the base line as the centerline. This method is commonly followed by most professional builders, but is recommended for amateurs only in the case of simple boats where comparatively few lines must be drawn. In more complicated boats, a separate lofting area should be used to insure complete clarity of both drawings. In either case, colored crayons should be used for the superimposed drawing. Whatever method is followed, the lofting procedure is the same as for the profile, fairing the lines and altering the offset dimensions where necessary. If for a flat- or V-bottom boat, the chine line is drawn and faired also.

The cross-sectional or body plan view of the stations is now drawn. It is usual to draw the stations from bow to amidships in one area, and the sections from amidships aft to the transom on another. Each station must be shown in a complete cross section, rather than in half sections only, as in the boat plan itself which commonly shows one-half of bow and stern views. Each station will correspond to its equivalent on the profile and plan views, and all dimensions are taken from the offset table. The perpendicular indicating the centerline is erected with a square. Great care must be taken to draw both sides accurately, and each station should be completed in one operation and not as half sections taken separately. If for a flat- or V-bottom boat, the chine and sheer points when connected with the rabbet line near the centerline will show the outline of the cross section of the hull at any given station line. If for a hull with flare, flam, or tumble-home in any of the sections, waterlines and buttock lines must be drawn, taking the dimensions from the offset table. In drawing cross sections, it is good practice to use small draftsman's battens, so that there will be no flattening of the curves which could lead to flat sections in the finished frames.

It is obvious that the lofting of a small boat of flat- or V-bottom form with straight-sided sections is a relatively simple procedure once the basic system is understood. Only three principal lines form the outline of a V-bottom boat—the sheer, chine, and rabbet. In a flat-bottom boat, only two show the sheer and bottom. The sectional plan being formed of straight lines, these are quickly drawn once the offset points are established.

The beginning or first-time builder is advised to undertake some small, simple hull as an initial attempt at lofting, and it is a good plan to loft two or three very simple hulls until the procedure is well understood. The main consideration is to take plenty of time in the work, and to double check each step as the work proceeds. As one mistake in lofting usually leads to another, care in laying out the lines will save more time in the end. After the fairing procedure is undertaken, it is essential to carefully view the work from several angles at some distance away from the drawing when any discrepancies in line can be more easily noted.

It may be truthfully stated that the lofting of a boat's lines is a lengthy and tiresome process. It is absolutely essential, however, if the finished hull is to be reproduced as the designer intended.

The full-sized drawing of the lines also functions to clarify to the builder details of the hull form which otherwise cannot always be visualized by an initial examination of the plans. If some part of the form and shape cannot be determined beforehand, this becomes clear after lofting. This is also important in projecting the material requirements, as the full-sized layout can be more easily measured. In many cases where lofting is hastily or incompletely done, much time and material may be wasted in rebuilding after a fault becomes apparent.

Perhaps the most significant function of the lofting process is the checking of the accuracy of the designer's lines. Boats are originally designed to scale of one inch or less, and the offset tables and other dimensions are taken from these drawings by use of a pair of dividers and a scale ruler. Even slight inaccuracies in taking off these lines will be much magnified in a full-sized reproduction, and these can be rectified in the fairing process as described.

Certain short cuts in lofting are made by experienced professional builders, especially in cases where frequent reproduction of similar types and sizes of hulls are being built. Such practice, however, is only justified by long experience and good previous results, and becomes an individual attainment. Very simple hulls, such as small punts or skiffs, may be erected from cross-sectional lines only, but again, only by an experienced builder. Straight-sectioned hulls, such as scows or barges need not be fully laid out, as there is no twist to the plank or compound curves to contend with.

A frequent shortcut suggested is the scaling of dimensions from the plans. This usually produces doubtful results, as the shrinking and swelling of the paper causes serious distortions of the dimensions.

The lofting and building of hulls with compound curves in the lines, or traditionally built, round-bottom boats, are generally beyond the capabilities of the average amateur builder. Possible exceptions to this rule are very small hulls such as rowboats or dinghies with U-section forms. Some amateur builders possessed of engineering knowledge and better-than-average woodworking skill often produce good-sized round-bottom boats that would be a credit to a professional yard, but these attainments are few and far between.

A helpful adjunct to the lofting of a boat's lines, as well as a practical illustration of certain details of its construction, is the building of small scale models. A small representation of the hull will more readily allow the prospective builder to visualize its lines. If some aspect of the construction is not fully understood after a thorough study of the plans, a scale model of the part under consideration will usually clarify the details so that the actual full-sized building will not be impeded. Balsa wood in various sizes and lengths is available from hobby or model shops. After the parts are cut to shape they may be put together with ordinary household or modeling glue and pins. Model making was much a part of early-day boat and shipbuilding. Carved models of various types of hulls were used to lay out the full-sized parts in the mold lofts. In the case of very large craft, the models were often built up of individual pieces of wood which were laid on top of each other to form the hull. These individual "lifts" were then used to lay out the full-sized representation of the lines. Model making for this purpose is almost a lost art today, but it is a worthwhile undertaking for the study of the lines of any design where building is contemplated.

6

Tools

Contrary to some popular opinion, a vast array of special tools is not required for building simple boats. Many handy amateurs have actually built various types of good-sized craft with but the ordinary carpenter's tools found in the average home workshop. However, much time and effort can be saved by using adequate equipment, while trying to make do with too few tools will make the work much more difficult. As a guide to the basic tools required, the following list is offered as a composite of those commonly seen in the average small professional boatbuilding shop specializing in wooden construction.

Hand Tools

SAWS

1 24' crosscut saw with 11 points to the inch
1 26' crosscut saw with 9 points to the inch
1 26' rip saw 5½ or 6 points to the inch
1 12" compass saw
1 10" keyhole saw
1 hacksaw with extra blades

PLANES

1 9" general purpose plane
1 6" block plane
1 18" foreplane, wooden soled if possible
1 21" jointer plane, wooden soled if possible

CHISELS, socket-type handles

Full set, ¼" up to 2"—6 to 8 in number
1 "Slick" type heavy chisel, 2" width
1 gouge, ½"
1 gouge, 1"

HAMMERS

1 # 2-sized carpenter's hammer, 13 ounce head
1 # 1½ size carpenter's hammer, 16 ounce head
1 8 ounce ball peen hammer
1 light maul
1 wooden mallet for use with chisels

BORING TOOLS

1 carpenter's brace, ratchet type with ball bearing chuck and head
1 set of auger bits, ¼" to 1¼" by sixteenths
1 expansion bit, adjustable ⅝" to 3" diameter
1 rose bit for countersinking
1 barefoot ship's auger 1" diameter
1 small hand drill with ¼" chuck
1 set hand drill bits, 1/16" to ¼" by sixteenths
1 breast drill with ½" chuck
1 set of breast drill bits—⅛" to ½"
1 medium brad awl

SCREWDRIVERS

1 set hand screwdrivers to fit all common screw heads—¼" to ½"
1 large ratchet of automatic type
1 set of screwdriver bits to fit carpenter's ratchet-type brace

NAILSETS OR PUNCHES

1 set punches, ⅛" to ⅜" tips
1 medium bucking dolly

FILES

8" flat file
6" smooth half-round file
10" bastard round file
12" coarse rasp

CLAMPS

1 door clamp
1 set 6" C clamps
1 set 8" C clamps

MEASURING AND SCRIBING TOOLS

1 try square
1 sliding bevel
1 8" wing dividers
1 steel 6' rule
1 24" x 16" steel square
1 12" combination square
1 drum-type steel tape measure—25' to 50'
1 spirit level
1 sliding T bevel gauge 10" long

MISCELLANEOUS

Ball of heavy twine, plumb bob, pliers, cutters, set machinist's wrenches, caulking irons, spoke shave, 18" Stillson wrench, putty knives, scrapers, adz, oil stones, emery wheel, etc.

Power Tools

These are universally used today in all types of woodworking. They save much time and labor, and aid the amateur in his precision, making up in many ways for lack of mechanical skill. They must be used with care, as all are potentially dangerous instruments.

BANDSAW

A 12-inch bandsaw taking work up to 4-inch thickness is adequate for working material used in most small boats. Most professional shops require one for taking 6-inch timbers.

BENCH SAW

This should be of the tilting arbor type with a blade of at least 8-inch diameter. Set of blades, including rip, crosscut, combination, plywood cutting, and dado type are required for all around work.

SABRE SAW

This useful tool serves as a portable band saw, and can be used in very restricted quarters. It should have a minimum cutting stroke of 1 inch. A number of blades are available for various purposes, including a circle cutting attachment.

JOINTER-PLANER

This tool is required for precision cabinet work and joinery. It is useful for dressing accurate edges on planking.

ELECTRIC CIRCULAR HANDSAW

This tool should have at least a 6-inch blade, and a 7-or-8-inch one is better. The blade housing makes for safety, but the tool should be carefully used.

POWERED HAND PLANE

This tool has been recently introduced and consists of a large metal plane with a circular cutting blade set into the sole. It is, in effect, a portable jointer, and is very useful in dressing large timbers. It must be carefully used, however, as it is a potentially dangerous instrument and due to its high-speed cutting capabilities it is easy to remove an excess of material unless the work is carefully planned ahead of time.

ELECTRIC SANDERS

1. Disk Sander. This is used to fair up rough surfaces and uneven planks or other surfaces. One form is sold as a flexible pad to be fitted to an electric drill.
2. Belt Sander. This is a heavy tool for finishing large smooth surfaces that are flat, such as deck or floor surfaces.
3. Orbital Sander. This is a lightweight tool for finish sanding.

It must be emphasized that all hand tools should be of professional quality, and not of the hobby shop or supermarket type. The power tools should be of commercial, continuous service, heavy-duty variety; any other type will not stand up to the work required.

Anyone contemplating any serious boatbuilding projects should possess a suitable workbench. This should be substantially built with stock 2-inch lumber for the top and back apron supported by 4-by-4-inch legs suitably braced against wracking (Figure 11). The height is optional to suit the operator, and its usefulness is enhanced if it is 12 feet or more in length. It should carry a carpenter's vise at one end, with removable pins at the opposite end to support long planks while being dressed. A wedge-type plank holder is also very useful. Two bench hooks and a peg stop which fits various holes in the top of the workbench are a necessity for working small pieces.

In addition to the usual proprietary hand and power tools, most small boat shops possess a large number of special tools made up by the workmen to perform specific functions in boatbuilding. These include chain clamps,

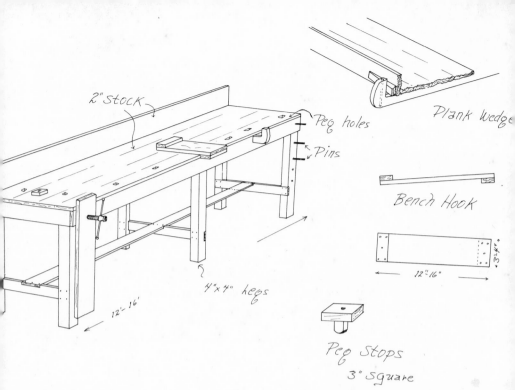

2" stock

Peg holes

Pins

Plank Wedge

4"x4" legs

12'-16'

Bench Hook

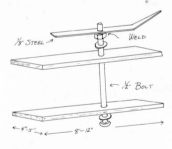

12"-16"

3"x4"

Peg Stops
3" Square

Figure 11 Diagram of a boatbuilder's useful workbench

Figure 12 Clamps used in building wooden boats

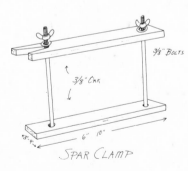

3/8" Bolts

3/8" Oak

6"-10"

SPAR CLAMP

1/8" Steel   WELD

1/2" Bolt

4"-5"   8"-12"

WING CLAMP

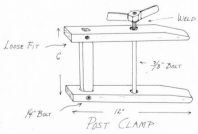

WELD

Loose Fit

6"

3/8" Bolt

1/4" Bolt   12"

POST CLAMP

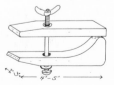

2"-3"   4"-5"

DUCKTAIL CLAMP

1/4" Bar

1/4" Bar   WELD   3/8" Bo...

CHAIN CLAMP

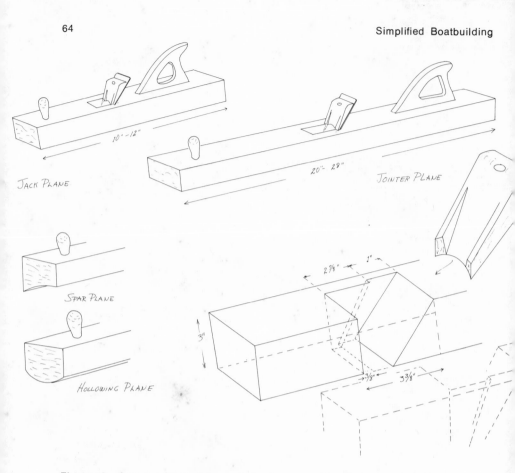

Figure 13 Common types of carpenter's planes used in wooden boatbuilding

plank levers, various types of plank and spar clamps, wedges, and wooden soled planes (Figures 12 and 13). The latter are particularly desirable in boat work as the wooden soles prevent bruising the plank, and are today unobtainable from proprietary tool makers. Because of the relatively high cost of metal clamps, most boat shops make up large numbers to their own design with hardwood frames and ordinary bolts of various sizes.

7

Boatbuilding Materials

Wood

Wood is the classic material for the structure of small boats, and is favored by the amateur builder for its moderate cost and almost universal availability. Contrary to some popular opinion, timber native to the builder's own area is quite suitable for boatbuilding, providing it is sound and of good quality. The primary reason for the use of native woods, other than availability, is that they appear to last longer and are more resistant to dry rot in their own area than is timber imported from other sections of the country.

White oak is the timber of choice for keels, stem pieces, chines, framing, and other structures subject to hard wear, such as rail caps, ladders, steps, cockpit coamings, etc. Its density and great strength, combined with its ability to hold fastenings, make for durable and long-lived structures. It is not generally used for planking because of its weight and its tendency to shrink and swell excessively, but is sometimes used on large commercial boats subject to hard service. While it is commonly stocked in many retail timber outlets, it is somewhat expensive due to its being grown mostly in certain areas of the eastern United States. An acceptable substitute in many cases is native hard pine, longleaf yellow pine, or Douglas fir. If steam-bent timbers are specified, it is almost mandatory to use oak, but it must be cut green and contain a certain amount of moisture, as hard, dry oak is too brittle to bend satisfactorily. If oak is unavailable, rock elm may be substituted.

If light weight, consistent with adequate strength, is necessary for framing material as in high speed launches or specialized racing craft, spruce is often used in place of oak or other heavy woods.

Native woods suitable for planking include eastern or western pine, eastern or western cedar, white pine, longleaf yellow pine, Virginia or loblolly pine, and cypress. Spruce is sometimes used for planking light boats, but it deteriorates rapidly in fresh water. Redwood is a long-lasting wood, but lacks tensile strength and splits easily. Timbers commonly imported for planking include African, Philippine and Honduras mahogany, and teak.

Some planking material, such as cedar, may be ordered in some parts of the country as "flitch sawn," where the boards are cut to the shape of the tree, and have the bark on the edges. This is an advantage as many of the pieces have a natural curve which aids in planking some areas of the hull.

Interior structures and finish are usually made of white pine as its moderate weight and straight grain make it easy to work, but marine plywood, optionally faced with various decorative woods, is becoming almost universal as the large panels are easy to apply and require less man hours for fitting and finishing.

Light cruising and racing sailing craft usually have their masts and spars of spruce, because of its light weight, flexibility, and great strength, but various types of pine can be used where ultralight weight is not mandatory.

In examining a proposed boat plan, it is advantageous to carefully examine the construction sections as to timber requirements, as in some cases the specification of special dimensions of mill cuts can greatly increase the cost. In moderate speed boats, or in commercial craft, most practical small boat designers specify common run timber cuts as they come from the mill. Lumber is sold by the board foot, which is a unit of measurement one inch thick, twelve inches long and twelve inches wide. Lumber is described in even dimensions, such as $2'' \times 4''$, $2'' \times 6''$, $4'' \times 6''$, etc., or $1'' \times 4''$, $1'' \times 6''$, $1'' \times 12''$, etc., but as common mill cuts it is actually somewhat less in overall dimensions, and sometimes as to actual length. A $2'' \times 4''$ is actually about $1\frac{5}{8}'' \times 3\frac{3}{4}''$ or $3\frac{5}{8}''$. A large piece, such as for a deadwood or keel timber specified as $6'' \times 10''$, might be actually about $5\frac{1}{2}'' \times 9\frac{1}{2}''$. The most critical application of this situation is in the specifications for planking material where special milling may be required. If $\frac{3}{4}$-inch thick planking is specified, ordinary 1-inch stock will probably be suitable. If $\frac{7}{8}''$, $1''$, $1\frac{1}{4}''$ or $1\frac{1}{2}''$ thickness is required, the stock will have to be cut from $2''$ or actually $1\frac{5}{8}''$ boards. In some large or heavy boats, such as displacement-type pleasure or commercial power boats, or very large sailing craft, ordinary 2-inch lumber may be specified, with the actual $1\frac{5}{8}''$ thickness being acceptable, and usually of $5\frac{5}{8}''$ width. This practice might not be suitable in the case of light, semiplaning or planing power craft, or in light, racing sail boats, as a small variation from specified plank thickness can add a ton or so of weight to the hull and can seriously upset speed expectations or stability calculations in the design.

Slash sawn milling is commonly provided for land-based structures or cabinet lumber. For boat work, rift sawn milling is more desirable, if available, as the position of the grain is less liable to split when holes for fastenings are bored (see sketch top, right).

The quality of timber materials as to their grade is important for use in boatbuilding, but the standards vary in different parts of the country. The best grades of lumber are either "first quality" or "select," and generally refer to pieces that are free of all knots on one side, and checks or "shakes" and rot on the other. Framing, planking, and decking material should be of this grade. A realistic approach to timber selection is essential, however, as

Slash Sawn

Rift Sawn
for marine use

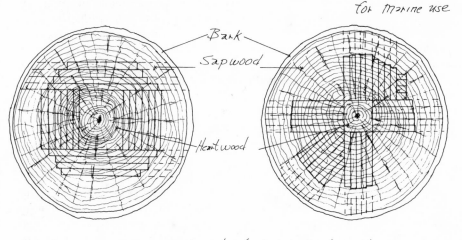

Bark

Sapwood

Heartwood

Two methods of Milling Lumber

some designers' specifications of grade are next to impossible to attain, and could run material costs to fantastic proportions. In actual practice, a few small, tight knots are acceptable in both framing and planking material, as are a few small shakes and checks. The main consideration is to select timber that shows no dry rot or serious structural defects.

The outstanding problem in the suitability of timber for strength and longevity is dry rot. This is caused by various mold fungi that grow within the wood fiber and cause decay. These fungi are found in most native timbers to some degree, and all lumber must be carefully examined before purchase. While fungus spores are universally present, their growth is accelerated by the presence of fresh water, and boats designed for fresh water use should have special attention paid to rot prevention, both as to interior preservation and ventilation.

Under some climatic conditions even young growth can be seriously infected by dry rot and often trees are badly infected while still standing. The proper curing of freshly cut lumber is essential to prevent further spreading or growth of spores usually present, and this was formerly done by air drying through storing the timber in sheds with thin strips of lath between each adjacent piece. This allows evaporation of the fresh water content, with consequent inhibition of fungus spore propagation when the moisture content drops below 10 or 12%. Air-dried timber is practically unobtainable today, however, due to the high cost of handling and stacking, and most lumber is now treated in kilns or drying rooms with artificial heat which materially reduces drying time. Most timber for boatbuilding works more easily if some moisture is present, but to inhibit spore propagation this should not be over 15%. Some commercial boatyards specializing in the finest construction formerly cured their own timber by stacking it in sheds built on wharves over salt water where the salt gradually replaced the fresh water that encouraged fungus formation. Often large timbers or uncut logs were floated in salt ponds, the salt effectively pickling the timbers.

The quality of all domestic timber today is substantially poorer than that cut formerly, as the old first-growth timber has been cut away long ago, and the contemporary second and third growths are less dense. Also, less attention is paid today to the rejection of rot-infested lumber.

To combat rot in timber sold for special purposes, some types are heated in kilns, with the introduction of various preservatives to permeate the wood fiber. As this lumber is generally sold at necessarily high cost and is not universally obtainable, the boatbuilder must take special precautions in the selection of rot-free pieces and in applying preservatives to the structures during construction.

White oak and longleaf yellow pine are satisfactorily rot resistant if purchased in sound condition, the latter having a sap or resin content that appears to inhibit spore formation. Southern cypress, much used for planking along the Gulf Coast, is also quite resistant but becomes quite heavy because of its porosity which encourages soakage. Eastern and western or Alaska cedar are rot resistant, as are the various imported mahoganys. Teak is the most resistant of all, due to its high natural resin content.

As Douglas fir and hard pines are frequently used for framing and planking, it is well to give special attention to their preservation as they rot rather quickly if unprotected, though it is good practice to so treat any boatbuilding timber. The introduction of preservatives under pressure is the most effective, but as this type of treatment is not possible for the amateur builder, the obvious compromise is to paint compounds on the surfaces with a brush. As the faying surfaces, or points where timbers are joined together, are most susceptible to dry rot, it is best carefully to coat all surfaces before final assembly. Creosote is commonly used in large commercial craft, but it has an objectionable odor and forms a poor surface for interior painting. Copper naphthalene compounds are more widely used in pleasure craft. They are very effective, have very little odor, and form a good foundation for conventional paints.

Salting is another method of timber preservation much used in earlier times but rather neglected today. As already noted, dry rot fungi are killed by salt water. Common rock salt can be packed around interior structures; the salt slowly goes into solution from dampness and condensation, effectively pickling the timbers against deterioration. Holes of small diameter can be bored along the insides of the keel, deadwood, and large frame members, and rock salt poured in by means of a small funnel. The insides of planking can be treated by fitting narrow shelves along the sheer strakes, with their outer edges sloping upward at a slight angle. Salt can be added at intervals as the residue seeps down into the bilges. The effectiveness of salting can be seen in many old fishing vessels where the cargoes of salted fish, combined with direct application of salt, have enabled some of these boats to last one hundred years or more.

As the presence of fresh water encourages the growth of the fungus spores, special care should be taken to make decks, waterways, and any structures around the edges of deckhouses and cabin roofs watertight, with provision for ample drainage of rainwater. Dry rot also thrives in damp and unventilated spaces. Such areas are found most particularly in the ends and edges of the hull in decked boats and provision should be made for ventilators and hatches that can be opened frequently to admit a draft of fresh air.

The painting of wooden craft must also be considered from the standpoint of ventilating the various wooden members themselves. While all exterior parts must be painted to avoid weathering and the abrasive action of salt water and air, painting the interior sides of structural members such as planking and framing can actually encourage the growth of the rot-producing spores. Interiors are best covered with either chemical preservatives or raw or boiled linseed oil. This forms a protective covering, but leaves the pores of the wood fiber open to breathe and to evacuate moisture that would otherwise be sealed in by an impervious coat of paint.

The more commonly used native and imported woods for boatbuilding are described in the following alphabetically arranged list.

DOMESTIC WOODS

Ash

White ash rates with oak in strength, hardness, and molecular resistance to shock. It is fairly easy to work with sharp tools and is fairly resistant to rot, although it is not suitable for planking. It is mainly used in light, round-bottom boats for steam-bent framing. Oars, boat hook handles and flag poles are usually made from ash. The weight per cubic foot is 42 pounds.

Cedar

This includes Alaskan, Port Orford, and Western Red cedar. These woods are more or less similar in characteristics. They are light in weight, rather soft, and easily worked, but are somewhat subject to fracturing. Most are available in long lengths with a straight grain free from knots. Holes for fastening should be carefully bored to avoid splitting, especially at the plank ends.

Alaskan cedar is the strongest and hardest of the cedars, and has been available in long lengths. It is also known as yellow cedar, due to its characteristic color. The weight per cubic foot is 32 pounds.

Port Orford cedar is light brown in color and of a rather coarse texture. It is easy to work, and comes in very long lengths, and is of light weight. These woods are mostly favored as planking material, but are also used for interior finishing. The weight per cubic foot is 29 pounds.

Western Red cedar is the softest of the cedars, and has the least tensile strength. It is the least popular of the cedars for this reason. The average weight per cubic foot is about 30 pounds.

White Cedar

There are two varieties of white cedar. The Northern type is native to the Great Lakes region and southern Canada. The Southern type grows in the coastal regions of the southeastern seaboard. Both varieties are very similar in that they are fine, close-grained woods with an aromatic odor, are easily worked and are fairly resistant to dry rot. It is the favored planking for small boats and skiffs.

Unlike the Western cedars, it is rarely obtainable free of knots. These are usually small, and if tight do not adversely affect tensile strength. Cedar swells easily and quickly when wet, which is one of its advantages as planking. It is also popular for fine interior joinery work. Average weight per cubic foot is about 23 pounds.

Cherry

This timber is sometimes called black cherry due to its color, and was much favored in the earlier days of boatbuilding. It is less commonly available today and is expensive. It takes finish well, has a close grain and a dark red color. If well seasoned, it rarely warps or checks. It was formerly much used as naturally grown crooks for breasthooks and hanging knees. It is too stiff and hard for steam-bending. Weight per cubic foot is about 34 pounds.

Cypress

This timber is common in the southern United States and along the Gulf coast. It is highly favored for planking as it has a natural resin which resists dry rot. It is fairly light and moderately strong, and available in wide and long timbers. Its one disadvantage is that it soaks up an inordinately large amount of water when immersed and becomes heavy. It is therefore used mostly in heavy or commercial craft where land transport is not contemplated. Weight per cubic foot is 32 pounds.

Elm

This is rock elm and not American or slippery elm which is not suitable for marine use as it is a very soft wood low in tensile strength. Rock elm is a very strong, hard wood with great shock resistance and is readily bent into hard curvatures when steamed. It is popular for framing round-bottom skiffs and canvas-covered canoes. It is most popular in England for planking. Its native habitat is the Northern Central regions of the United States, and it is unfortunately becoming quite scarce. Weight per cubic foot is about 36 pounds.

Fir

Commonly known as Douglas fir, this is a strong, hard, and somewhat heavy wood with rather coarse grain. It absorbs water readily, as in the case of cypress, and takes up much weight in the process. Its main disadvantage is its low resistance to dry rot, and it was formerly used mostly as interior framing, sheer shelves, bilge stringers, and derrick masts. In recent years it has come into widespread use as planking, particularly in commercial vessels when specially treated with wood preservatives. It is nowadays produced in tree farms by forest products concerns, and is readily available. Vast quantities of fir are made into various grades of plywood. Weight per cubic foot is about 28 pounds.

Hackmatack

Also known as larch or tamarack, it is a very heavy and densely grained wood and is usually found as natural crooks and grown knees for framing purposes. It is becoming scarce and is usually found, if obtainable, from marine timber specialists. Average weight per cubic foot is 36 pounds.

Honey Locust

This is a very heavy, hard wood with a close dense grain that resists splitting and abrading and is very impervious to dry rot. It is the classic material for mooring bitts, cleats, wedges, strongbacks, trunnels, tillers, and steering wheels, hatch coamings and any other area where a hard-wearing wood is required. It is difficult to work and requires very sharp tools to finish. Weight per cubic foot is 43 pounds.

Oak, White and Red

White oak is the timber of choice since time immemorial for ship and boatbuilding. It is principally used in framing and main longitudinal timbering for its density, hardness, great strength, ability to hold fastenings, and lack of shrinking and swelling when wet. When green, it is highly suitable for steam bending in smaller diameters, but this must be selected as such as it is not suitable for this use when dry or seasoned. In any case, it is very resistant to dry rot.

Red oak has similar qualities, but is somewhat softer and is more susceptible to water soakage, making it a second choice for marine use.

Both varieties must be paint finished if used for exposed areas above decks for hard wearing areas, as it turns black when exposed to air and will not take a varnish finish. Weight for both types is about 48 pounds per cubic foot.

Pine, White

There are several varieties of white pine used in boatbuilding. One is the Northern white pine which is native to the eastern United States. The other is the Western or Sugar pine of the west coast. There is another western variety called Ponderosa pine which is less favored.

These woods share the common qualities of uniform texture, ease of working, light weight, good retention of paint, and fair resistance to dry rot. It is a favorite material for interior joinery and trim. It is sometimes used for planking, but absorbs much water to gain weight as does cypress. The weight is about 26 pounds per cubic foot.

Pine, Southern or Yellow

Longleaf yellow pine is a favorite wood for planking as it is dense, hard, and strong and is readily obtainable at moderate cost in long, clear lengths. It is best when specially cut for marine work as quarter or edge sawn.

Its one disadvantage is that it contains a heavy resin which will bleed through paint finish in hot weather, although this quality aids in making it resistant to dry rot. It is mostly used in commercial vessels. In yachts where a fine finish is desired, it has its place in interior framing, as it is very strong and holds fastenings well. It weighs about 38 pounds per cubic foot.

Pine, Oregon

This term is sometimes applied to Douglas fir, which is not a pine, but it is mentioned to clarify its name.

Redwood

This wood is noted for its resistance to dry rot, and is often used for interior joinery for its beautiful color when oiled or varnished. While sometimes used to plank small skiffs, its value is limited as its tensile strength is poor and it is easily shattered by impact. Its weight is about 28 pounds per cubic foot.

Spruce, Sitka

This wood is light in weight and is moderately hard and tough with smooth fibers. It is very strong for its weight, and has long been used for masts and spars. In the earlier days of aeroplane manufacture, it was the material chosen for fuselage and wing spars. It is usually available in very long lengths. It is not highly rot resistant and must be kept sealed with paint, varnishes, or wood preservatives. It is now quite expensive. It weighs about 27 pounds per cubic foot.

Spruce, Eastern

This wood is native to the maritime provinces of Canada and the New England area of the United States. Its weight and general properties are similar to the Sitka variety, except that it shows many knots and clear stock is unobtainable. It is often used for planking and decking, although it must be carefully maintained to avoid dry rot.

Walnut

This is a heavy dense hardwood and is mentioned because it was once favored for interior finishing of fine yachts. It does not markedly shrink or swell with moisture. Its weight is 39 pounds per cubic foot.

IMPORTED WOODS

Imported timber is expensive but has several advantages over domestic woods for certain uses. Included are the various mahoganies and teak.

African Mahogany

This timber is obtained from the Gold Coast and Nigerian areas of Africa. The mature trees are almost uniformly of immense size and may be up to seven or eight feet in diameter. It is a rather soft, light wood with large pores but has a spectacular graining with many variations as to burling and pattern. It is largely used as facing on fir plywood panels. Its average weight is about 33 pounds per cubic foot.

Honduras Mahogany

This term is used to describe most of the mahogany-like timber in southern Mexico and Central America. It is heavier and stronger than the African variety and has a more dense structure. It is usually straight grained, holds fastenings well, and takes a very handsome finish. It weighs about 36 pounds per cubic foot.

Peruvian Mahogany

This timber is native to the region of the upper Amazon, in parts of Ecuador, Peru, Bolivia, and Brazil. Its great expense is due to transporting it from its secluded location. It is somewhat heavier and darker than the Honduras type, is straight-grained and resists splitting. It is perhaps the finest of all the boatbuilding woods, and has been utilized mostly in the better-finished yachts, as it is very durable and takes a very fine finish. It weighs about 39 pounds per cubic foot.

Philippine Mahogany

This is not a true mahogany, but is listed here due to its popular name. It is in reality a mahogany-like native timber of the Philippine Islands, and includes several related species. It is lighter in weight than genuine mahogany, holds fastenings well, and resists splitting. It swells but little on immersion and is easily worked. Due to its porous grain it does not take varnish well, and is usually paint finished. Large quantities of this timber have been exported to the United States and other countries for use in stockboats built in series production. It weighs about 38 pounds per cubic foot.

Teak

A native tree of the East Indies and Burma, teak is the most noble of all boatbuilding woods. Due to a natural resin within its fibers, it resists dry rot and water soakage, and even when left unfinished it appears to last indefinitely. Boats built of this wood have been known to last for centuries. It is characteristically a very heavy and hard wood with dense fibers. It is naturally a light gray or tan which bleaches out to almost a white color on exposure to the sun and salt water. It has long been a favorite for finely finished yacht decking, if used in no other place. Due to its very high cost, it is generally used today as trim material for rail caps, hatches, coamings, pin rails, and other areas subject to hard wear. On the debit side, it is very difficult to work as the resin content quickly takes the edge off the sharpest tools. Due to its high cost, it is seldom employed unless the builder has a high degree of skill in boat carpentry and joinery. It weighs about 48 pounds per cubic foot.

Metals Used in Boatbuilding

IRON AND STEEL

Iron or steel for small boat construction is attractive to many prospective builders who possess skills in its fabrication. Advantages of the use of this durable material are freedom from hull leaks (if properly constructed), elimination of structural deterioration through shrinking and swelling, absence of water soakage, and resistance to damage. It is most frequently used in craft subject to hard usage, such as small tugboats, tankers, utility launches, and fishing boats. Iron or steel is by volume much heavier than wood, but its tensile strength is much greater and its application in thin sheets makes a very strong structure. Its use in large sheets to enclose the hull is comparable to that of plywood, and compound curves, especially in the angle of the forefoot, must be accommodated by using narrow strakes and welding the seams together. Due to its weight, its use in boats under 30 feet long results in a much heavier structure than a comparable one of wood. In hulls over this length, the total weight is lighter due to the increased displacement.

Small steel hulls are usually built in the inverted position and heavy wooden molds are erected on the station lines with suitable notches for the fitting of keel and chine members. The steel panels may be temporarily fastened to the molds with lag screws, the holes being welded shut after the hull is ready for permanent framing.

The keel and backbone structures are usually made up from bar stock set on edge, with the shaft log made of iron pipe welded in at the proper location. Rudder ports are also made of the same material. In some cases, the keel may be made up as a hollow girder. This is usually tapered to a point aft to form the run where it meets the rudder post. In sailing boats made of steel, the hollow keel may be loaded with concrete and scrap iron to form the ballast keel.

The frames of steel boats are often made up of angle iron, though bars may be used, the corners being braced with short tabs to form gussets. The deck and cockpit beams may be made of the same material. The chine and sheer stringers are frequently made of angle iron, although in some cases iron pipe is used, but it must be heated to allow the forming of the proper curve.

The engine bearers should be made extra long to prevent vibration and drumming. Where large engines are fitted, some builders employ heavy wooden bearers bolted to an angle-iron foundation which helps to dampen vibration.

The weight or gauge of the material used will, of course, vary as to the size of the boat or the displacement of the particular design. In motor launches from 25 to 30 feet long and of semiplaning type, hull plate of $\frac{1}{16}''$ to $\frac{3}{16}''$ thickness (10 to 12 gauge) may be used. The framing may be angle iron $1'' \times 1''$ by $\frac{3}{32}''$ up to $2\frac{1}{4}'' \times 2\frac{1}{2}'' \times \frac{3}{16}''$ which will give ample strength. These must be spaced at intervals of not over 18 inches, however, as the light sheets may be prone to buckling and present a "hungry-dog effect" if not well supported. It is this requirement of closely spaced frames in lightly constructed steel boats that somewhat nullifies the otherwise moderate cost of this type of construction. Hulls up to 50 feet in length generally require $\frac{1}{4}$-inch plate which is much stiffer and will be adequately supported by framing set on 20-inch centers.

If any wooden structures, such as deck beams, engine bearers, decking, or deckhouse sills for wooden deckhouses, are attached to metal, they must be well impregnated with a suitable preservative and set in a bituminous bedding compound. This is very necessary as moisture from condensation will cause the wood to deteriorate rapidly.

While iron and steel are subject to rusting and corrosion in both fresh and salt water, proper preservation can result in a long-lived hull. One procedure is to spray all exposed structures with zinc to produce galvanization. Another is the use of metal preservative such as oxide paints or special epoxy compounds. Fiber glass coverings are also popular, as are liquid rubber or latex solutions especially made for this use. No preservative should be attempted, however, unless all surfaces are free of mill scale or bloom. This can be removed by the use of abrasives or sandblasting. All residues from construction may be removed from the interior with a vacuum cleaner. To avoid any moisture being on the surfaces before treating, these operations should be carried on in well-heated quarters or on a warm day with low humidity. Interior condensation or sweating may be controlled by the application of bituminous compounds similar to motor car underseal or tarred felting.

Paint-finished hulls not completely covered with epoxy, fiber glass, or rubber compounds must be carefully protected against electrolytic action from naval bronze propeller shafts, propellers, stuffing boxes, rudders, and shaft hangers. The use of stainless steel fittings in place of bronze is advised, though the cost is higher. The only positive protection is the fitting of sacrificial anodes of zinc alloy to the rudder and anodes of the collar type around the propeller shaft. Anodes must be placed adjacent to shaft hangers and stuffing boxes, and positively connected by means of heavy copper wire to their bases to conduct the galvanic current. In highly saline water, these anodes may have to be renewed every four to six months.

LIGHT METALS AND ALUMINUM ALLOYS

The introduction of various aluminum and light metal alloys that are impervious to the corrosive action of sea water has created much interest in the boating world. A number of small power and sailing craft have been designed for the use of these materials. Another attraction is that aluminum has but one-third the weight of steel for the same strength, and is twice as strong as fiber glass for the same weight. These materials are widely used in aircraft manufacture. The sheets are fastened to either round- or square-sectioned aluminum alloy tubing by means of rivets or heliarc welding. As many boating enthusiasts are skilled in such work, the building of an aluminum boat can be an intriguing challenge.

Aside from light weight and high tensile strength, aluminum alloys possess all the advantages cited for iron and steel together with ductibility that allows them to be worked around compound curvatures and flares. A further advantage is that topside painting can be entirely dispensed with, unless it is desired for aesthetic effect. The underwater sections must be protected from fouling, however, and a number of special compounds are available for this purpose.

Some aluminum alloys used in aircraft manufacture or other industrial applications, while possessing the same ductable qualities, are not suitable for marine work if they contain copper. The alloys used in boatbuilding must be of manganese and magnesium composition to properly resist corrosion, and are metallurgically described as in the 5,000-to-6,000 series.

Aluminum alloy sheets are sometimes used as the hull covering of small skiffs and dinghies, and are either riveted or heliarc welded to angled or sectioned aluminum framing. The latter method makes the stronger structure, but because of its higher cost of fabrication, riveting is more commonly used. These rivets are set by hand with hammer and bucking dolly, and appear to stand up well under ordinary use. However, they will ultimately loosen under severe vibration and this method of fastening is generally limited to small skiffs that will be fitted with small outboard engines.

Sailing and power craft over 25 feet long are built of aluminum alloy plate of ³⁄₁₆ inch thickness, heliarc welded to angle bars or tubes of the same material. The plate may be easily rolled into curves which materially adds to the strength of the hull.

Hull fittings used with aluminum construction must be either castings made from the same material or stainless steel—the use of naval bronze will result in electrolysis. But if naval bronze is used, sacrificial anodes must be fitted as previously described. When an outboard engine is fitted, any bronze underwater fittings on it do not appear to set up electrolytic reactions as these have no direct contact with the hull itself.

While aluminum alloys of the correct metallurgical compositions are not corroded by salt water, an oxide is created which forms a film over the surface after prolonged exposure to salt air. This film appears to protect the metal against further corrosion. Small pits are noted on the aluminum surface after about ten years of exposure.

Aluminum boats require antifouling bottom paint. In preparing the bottom of a new hull, the surface must first be thoroughly cleansed and degreased with detergent soap, and a zinc chromate primer applied as the initial coating. Special antifouling compounds intended for aluminum hulls must be used, as ordinary copper or mercury base paint is antagonistic to magnesium and manganese alloys.

A few boats have been built in England which used aluminum alloy strips as planking and fastened to conventional wooden frames with self-locking screws. A special plastic bedding compound has been developed which is laid over the frames and between the plank strakes to form a flexible, watertight seal.

Amateur building efforts in aluminum have been largely limited to the building of small skiffs and dinghies. Aluminum alloy material is rather expensive.

Fiber Glass

The recent development of polyester resins has resulted in a new plastic material offering variations in methods of manufacture for an infinite variety of products. The chemical bases for these new substances are the hydrocarbons which are derived from benzene, propylene and ethylene.

There are two basic groups of plastics. The *thermoplastic* group includes premolded articles such as automobile ornaments, toilet articles, toys, household utensils, etc. These are made by subjecting granulated plastics to high temperatures in pressure molds. The *thermosetting* group are made by applying a liquid made from polyester resin to cloth made of woven glass fiber. In order to prepare the resin properly for application, catalytic agents are mixed with the resin, causing it to set or harden within a very short time. The thermosetting plastics are the group used in boat construction.

Molded plastic boat hulls are manufactured in series production by placing layers of glass cloth between male and female molds that form the outline of the hull. Resin material is then forced into the molds under pressure, where it forms a bond with the glass cloth. The insides of the molds are treated with parting agents before applying the cloth, allowing the molds to come apart after the plastics have cured or hardened into shape. Another method of molding plastic hulls is to lay up the glass cloth and resin in a female mold, fitting a rubber bladder inside to form the male part of the mold and compressing the material into the proper shape for curing.

The boatbuilding process most suitable for amateur production of fiber glass hulls involves the use of hand lamination, where glass cloth and resin are applied to a wooden structure to form the outline of the boat, remaining inside as an integral part of its structure. In this case the hull is lofted and built up in the conventional manner, with the fiber glass material forming a continuous envelope around it. The advantage of this continuous coating of fiber glass material to the hull is that the reinforced plastics provide a structure which is impervious to water soakage with harmful shrinking and swelling, marine borers, dry rot, superficial damage, or action of the elements. Fiber glass is four times as strong as conventional planking, equal to the strength of steel in similar thicknesses and has the weight of aluminum alloy. Perhaps its greatest advantage is that it eliminates the expensive and time-consuming necessity for caulking, painting, and preservation, as in the case of wooden hulls, or rusting and corrosion in steel hulls, and appears to have an indefinite life. While its use is much at variance with traditional methods of boatbuilding, its proven advantages and adaptability to economical series production of small boat hulls is causing revolutionary changes in manufacture. Its use as a hand laminate is now enabling the amateur builder to produce a boat in every way equal to a professionally manufactured product.

Another synthetic resin product is epoxy, which forms the basis for glues and adhesives, and is produced in solutions that can be applied to the hulls of iron or steel boats, forming a bond that effectively seals the metal against rust and corrosion. Epoxies are chemically described as condensation polymers of bisphenol and epichlorol hydrins. These products cure into surfaces that are harder and more wear resistant than those provided by the polyester group.

Urethane is another derivative of polyester resin, and is produced by treating polyester compounds with di-isocyanates. It can be made as either rigid or flexible structures, according to the type of plasticizers added. It may be produced as foam, often used as flotation material for boats, or as life preservers, or as hardened material for structural interiors. The material is also suitable for incorporation into varnishes as hardeners and makes extremely durable coverings.

Plastic rubber compounds have lately been developed that facilitate the covering of hulls and decks, both for new construction or in the repair of existing hulls. Neoprene is produced in vulcanized sheets that can be laid with synthetic rubber plastic. A product sold under the trade name of Seaprene can be painted on wood and metal surfaces, forming a very durable yet slightly elastic coating.

While steel hulls may be covered with fiber glass materials especially manufactured for this use, new hulls may be coated with tar-epoxy emulsions that form an effective barrier against corrosion and hard service conditions, as it also resists abrasion. It is applied with a paint roller, and various color compounds may be incorporated as a finish coat.

Synthetic rubber polysulfides are useful as flexible seam compounds for caulking planked hulls, and may be applied as a substitute or replacement for conventional cotton or oakum material usually set in oil-based seam compounds. It is also useful in laying decks or cabin roofs where leaks often occur, and sets into an elastic base that compensates for shrinking and swelling of the wood. It is recommended for application between the two layers of double-planked wooden hulls, and it also forms a leakproof bedding material in lap-strake planking joints. In rejuvenating old wooden hulls, interior structures may often be heavily permeated with moisture from old leaks and next to impossible to dry out thoroughly for fiber glass covering. In these cases, it is best to sand the hull vigorously, stop the seams with polysulfide compound, then coat the entire surface with two or three coats of polysulfide which will form a flexible coating that will not leak with the wooden interior's consequent shrinking or swelling.

A significant advance in the production of boat fittings, such as fair-leads, cleats, and pulleys is provided by a hardened plastic known by the trade name of Delrin. This is a derivative of formaldehyde, and can be injection molded into a variety of products that are as durable and corrosion resistant as naval bronze or light metal alloys.

Another useful area of fiber glass application is in the fabrication of new rudders for both sailing and power craft. As the metal fittings of these are normally expensive, sometimes causing electrolysis problems, the use of fiber glass can do much to reduce costs in boating. Masts, spars, and trolling poles made of fiber glass are much stronger than wood and the constant up-keep which the latter requires is eliminated.

Practical construction of fiber glass boats by amateur builders suggests the use of a conventional wooden hull that is built for fiber glass covering of the outer hull and deck or cabin structures, using the hand lamination method. Small sailing, outboard-powered skiffs or dinghies, and fast run-abouts and racing hulls, where lightness and portability are paramount, are best planked up with sheet plywood. This applies also to small sailing and power cruisers designed to be transported and stored on trailers, or fast planing or semiplaning pleasure cruisers of larger size whose speed capabilities are enhanced by light weight. Displacement-type power and sailing craft with conventional planking can also be covered with fiber glass to advantage, as the slight weight increase is not critical, or can be compensated for.

It is absolutely essential that the surfaces to be covered are bare virgin wood, free of all traces of grease, oil, or any other foreign matter, as the resin will not adhere properly to any oily substance. Ignoring this precaution will almost certainly lead to the formation of pockets or bubbles. The wood should be sanded with coarse paper, slightly roughening the surface to promote adhesion. Old wooden and steel or iron hulls may be rejuvenated with fiber glass covering, but special care must be taken to sand off all traces of old paint or other material that would otherwise cause dead areas and lack of proper bonding. Reports of failures and adverse criticism of the fiber glass process can, in most cases, be directly traced to carelessness or poor workmanship in preparing the surfaces. When covering old hulls, it is necessary to remove engines, tanks, heavy interior structures, hull fittings, stern bearings and fastenings, and any other fittings that would interfere with completely sanding down or removing the old finishes. The hull is best turned upside down to facilitate this work. While such an undertaking can be a laborious and lengthy process, it could be well worth the effort in providing a new and long life for a sound and usable craft.

Fiber glass coverings are not difficult to fabricate, but it is essential to follow the proper procedures to insure satisfactory results. This depends upon the correct choice of glass cloth and the resin material for the lamination method to be used. The whole field of fiber glass reinforced plastics is undergoing many modifications, as development and research is constantly going on. While the basic principles have been quite well established, the introduction of new chemical compounds often indicates changes in procedure. Before undertaking any boat construction involving fiber glass, the builder is advised to consult the manufacturing concern of the material to be used for advice and recommendations on the methods of handling its product. Most retailers offer complete lines of material for various methods of fiber glassing boats and it is strongly recommended that the instructions and procedure outlines be carefully studied before starting to build, and followed explicitly during construction.

The possibilities of new approaches to small boat construction with fiber glass components are infinite, and are limited only by the imagination of enthusiasts in developing new techniques for facilitating simplified construction and greater economies in maintenance.

Concrete and Ferro-Cement Boats

The use of cement and concrete building materials in boatbuilding has received attention from both naval architects and empirical builders at times during the past one hundred years as it offers one method of obtaining a monolithic hull structure—the long-standing dream of boatbuilders since time immemorial. Experiments with this material are a matter of record since about 1880, when various builders in France and Germany constructed small skiffs and launch hulls of concrete aggregate, reinforced with iron or steel rods and wire mesh.

Interest in concrete boats apparently languished until after World War II when Professor P. N. Nervi, an Italian architect and yachtsman, built a 47-foot sailing boat of concrete plaster reinforced with an iron and steel framework in 1947.

Nervi's method of building, which he previously developed for land-based structures, did not involve the use of temporary outside forms. Instead, he fabricated a framework of ordinary iron water pipe to the outline of the proposed structure, and reinforced it with closely spaced lengths of welding rod wired on either one or both sides of the main framing. To contain the aggregate, several layers of fine wire mesh, such as is used in poultry fencing, were laid over both sides of this form.

This method of building was, of course, much lighter than with conventional reinforced concrete construction, as the walls could be made very thin, the overall weight comparing favorably with both wood and steel construction. The thickness could be controlled by the size of the pipe and welding rod used for the framing, as determined by the size of the structure to be built, and in small boat hulls could be anything from ¾-to-1¼ inches in section. The only criterion here was that the aggregate should just cover the underlying framing to insure watertightness and to prevent voids in the plaster or the entrance of water into the framing.

Nervi's invention received wide publicity in the contemporary boating press, particularly after the attractive lines of his boat and its good performance capabilities were analyzed. Many prospective amateur boatbuilders, and most particularly those not conversant with conventional small boat construction, but with some professional knowledge of concrete fabrications, immediately became interested in its possibilities. Ferro-concrete boatbuilding in its initial phases remains mostly within the sphere of backyard building, although one small firm in England developed an aggregate market under the trade name of "Secrete" and offered to license its use to prospective commercial builders. Some boats using this have been built in Australia, New Zealand, and Canada.

While the system of building boats of ferro-concrete is basically attractive, a number of problems inherent in the system have prevented a wholesale reversion to this method. The layout and lofting of the round-bottom form which most of the designs so far follow required some prior knowledge and experience. The complete framing requires careful lining up for accuracy of line, and must be either arranged in an inverted position or suspended from another set of temporary framing so that the bottom of the keel or the tops of the gunwales may be thoroughly covered and sealed with the aggregate. As the hull is best plastered in one operation to eliminate seams or voids in the material, a large labor force possessed of the requisite skill must be recruited for a possible round-the-clock operation. Men of experience in this field of endeavor have not yet agreed on the most suitable composition of aggregate necessary for the desired strength, curing qualities, or exact methods of application.

As the building of ferro-concrete boats is a relatively new endeavor, the prospective builder should carefully evaluate all available information before attempting such a project. At this writing several books and pamphlets by builders with some experience in this field are becoming available, and the research of several points of view is seriously advised.

8

Fastenings and Glues

Fastenings

Treenails or "trunnels," to use the shipwright's pronunciation, are wooden dowels of locust, oak, or other hardwoods that are driven into prebored holes fractionally smaller in diameter to make a close fit. The pegs are made more secure with the use of small hardwood wedges driven into small saw cuts in the ends (Figure 14). Where this type of fastening is used to secure planking, a wedge is fitted at either end to effectively jam them into the holes. Where the trunnels are driven "blind" into framing timbers such as horn timbers, keels, or deadwoods, the top wedge is usually omitted. These fastenings are driven with a large wooden maul, and considerable manual skill is required to drive the pegs squarely, as a side blow or deflected stroke can break the shaft.

In the modern construction of wooden boats, metal bolts and drifts are used to secure the framing, with nails or screws for attaching the planking. In every case, with the possible exception of fitting minor trim, all holes for fastenings must be prebored to prevent splitting the wood.

Drifts are lengths of rod made from galvanized steel or naval bronze and are available in diameters of ³⁄₁₆ inches through ⅞ inches. The bronze-type drift is seldom used today, except in very fine work, due to the high cost. Drifts are used to secure framing timbers where the depth of the pieces is greater than 20 inches which is the longest length of commercially produced bolts available. The rule among boatbuilders appears to be "use bolts where you can and drifts where you must." Drifts are also used as edge fastenings in the centerboards and centerboard cases of large, heavily built sailing craft, and also to edge fasten planking, such as in the Chesapeake Bay skipjacks. They are also employed in securing hatch coamings, deckhouses, and other structures in large heavily built, commercial-type power boats.

While in most cases drift rods are driven "blind," it is possible to enhance their holding power where a through fastening is possible by making them up as bolts. The ends are threaded after driving by means of a plumber's

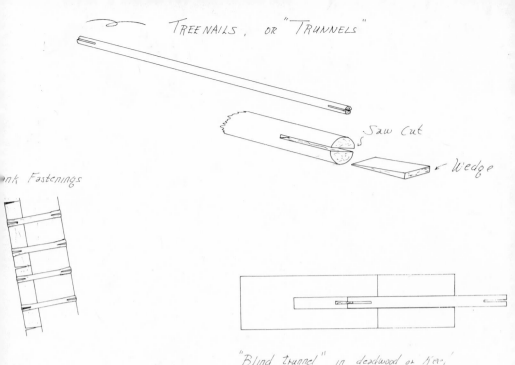

Figure 14   Treenails, or "trunnels," used as fastenings in some older or primitive types of small wooden boats

die and appropriately sized nuts with washers are then fitted. In practice, drifts are generally staggered when set adjacent to one another in the same group of timbers which enhances their holding power and helps to avoid splitting the wood. They are often fitted at varying angles which also increases their holding power through triangulation.

In preparing a drift, the end is roughly pointed with the use of a ball peen hammer to aid in its insertion (Figure 15). With galvanized rod, only the tip should be so treated to disturb as little of the galvanized surface as possible. The lead hole should be somewhat smaller than the diameter of the drift to make a secure driving fit. This varies from $1/32$ inch for oak timbers or other hardwood to $1/16$ inch for hard pine or fir. The depth of the hole should be nearly as long as the shaft, less the length of the pointed end which holds best if driven into unbored timber. To increase the holding power, a clench ring in the form of a shouldered washer is set over the top of the drift before driving. The upper end is then shaped with a ball peen hammer to make a head which is then driven with a small sledge hammer. Manual skill and some experience is required for the driving, as side or deflected blows may bend the drift and render further penetration difficult. If a through fastening with threaded ends for bolting is contemplated, the drift rod is, of course, cut long enough to pass well through the timber and to allow cutting off the driving head for attachment of the washer and nut. The driving should be carried through in one operation, as the drift may otherwise freeze in the hole.

The direction of the lead hole can usually be determined by eye where

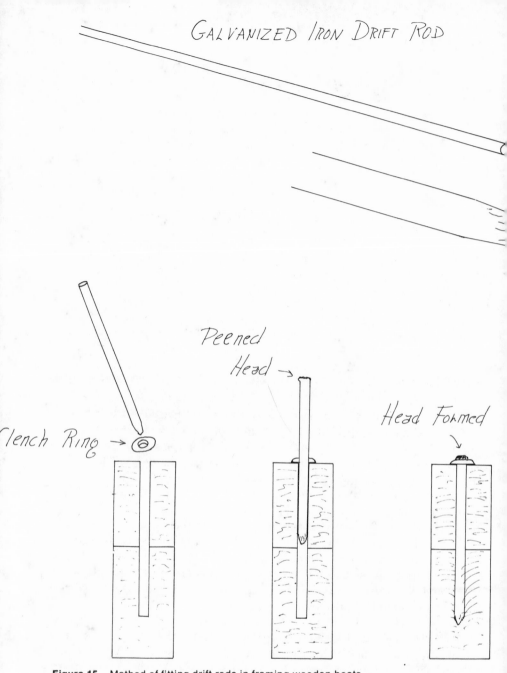

GALVANIZED IRON DRIFT ROD

Peened
Head →

Head Formed
↘

Clench Ring → ◎

Figure 15 Method of fitting drift rods in framing wooden boats

large timbers are to be fastened, or can be readily checked for squareness with a steel try square. In thinner material, such as centerboards, centerboard cases, or for edge fastening of plank, a jig is a necessity to guide the bit in the boring operation (Figure 16). The jaws of the jig should be a close fit over the outside of the material. Most small boatyards possess a number of these jigs to accommodate various common mill-run thicknesses of commercially sawn timbers. The single hole jig is most commonly used, but multiple-holed jigs laid out for staggering the drifts are sometimes made up.

Boat spikes (Figure 17) are used for fastening heavy timbers and planking and decking in large wooden vessels. These are made of galvanized steel and are available in 5-to 8-inch lengths. They are of either round- or square-shaped type, but both have chisel points. In driving, the lead hole is made slightly smaller than the shank, and of a depth just short of the total length of the spike so that the point is driven into the timber. The point should be set with the grain of the wood to avoid splitting. As the head of the spike is usually set below the surface of the wood when used as plank fastenings, the wood is often gouged out with a chisel to countersink this when the hole is bored. A large nail set is used in driving the spike home to avoid leaving tool marks or bruising the plank. Clench rings are sometimes used with spikes fitted in the framing to augment their holding power.

Bolts (Figure 17) are favored fastenings where the depth of the timbers is such that they can be used, and the fitting of washers and nuts enables them to be taken up to make a crush fit between the timbers. Many builders bore the lead holes to the same diameter of the shank, but a closer fit can be obtained by making the hole about $\frac{1}{64}$ inch less diameter for hard wood fastenings, and about $\frac{1}{32}$ inch less in the case of pine or fir. The bolts may then be driven into the holes without damaging the threads.

The carriage bolt with a shoulder under the head is favored over the straight-shanked machine type, as they resist turning and can be more readily taken up.

Figure 16   Two types of boring jigs used in fitting drift rods

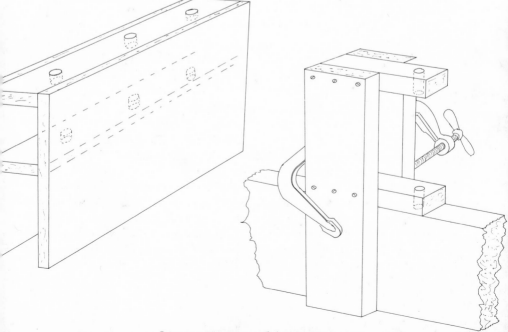

DRIFT BORING JIGS

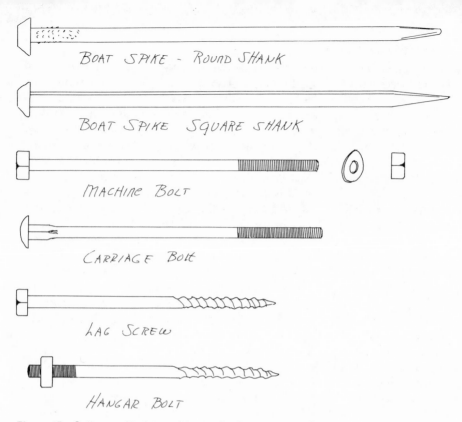

Figure 17 Spikes and bolts used in wooden boat construction

Bolts are widely used for fastening the frame angles or gusseted connections of the framing of V-bottom boats, and are the fastening of choice for fabricating stem pieces when the outer ends are counterbored and plugged to make a watertight joint. In these cases, the head of the bolt is set in the outer edge, with the nuts and washers on the inside.

The sizes of bolts to be used are generally indicated by the designer for the particular hull under consideration. These, of course, will often vary in boats of similar length but dissimilar weight. The keels and backbone structures of boats up to 20 feet may require bolts of $\frac{1}{2}$- or $\frac{5}{8}$-inch diameter. Heavily built boats up to 30 feet may require bolts of $\frac{3}{4}$- to $\frac{7}{8}$-inch size.

Lag screws (Figure 17) as their name implies are large screws with a square or octagonal head that may be taken up with a wrench. The fitting of a washer is usually specified to increase the holding power. The lead hole should be somewhat smaller than the shank to insure a proper grip by the screw threads. Some builders drill a two-stage hole if there is danger of splitting the wood, and the smaller hole fixes the thread while the large one accommodates the shank.

Hanger bolts (Figure 17) are used for securing an engine or other type of machinery that must be securely fastened to the main framing structure but which is subject to removal for replacement or servicing. A two-stage hole is advised for fitting in hardwoods. The nut may be tightened down to the top of the shank for driving with a wrench, then slacked off and removed for the placement of the fitting.

Nails of various types are used in boatbuilding (Figure 18), and should always be of galvanized iron or alloy to resist corrosion. Common wire nails are useless for marine use as they will deteriorate within a matter of days when exposed to moisture. The old-style square cut nail has long been popular for its superior holding power, but the serrated-type boat nail has lately supplanted it almost entirely. These nails, marketed under the trade name of Anchorfast in the United States and Gripfast in England, offer remarkable holding powers as the serrations become embedded in the wood fibers and cannot be pulled loose unless the work is destroyed. They are of copper-silicon alloy which effectively resists corrosion. They are used primarily for planking where their length should be from 2½ to 3 times the thickness of the planking to be fitted. Due to their holding power they are often used in small boats and skiffs to secure frame angles and other structures in place of screws. The shape of their heads makes them well suited for fastening plywood. These nails must be prebored, and to enhance their holding power the hole should not be greater than two-thirds the diameter of the shaft and three-fourths the length to enable it to grip the wood properly.

The nails are driven with a hammer, but a nail set should be used to drive them home to avoid bruises or hammer marks. These fastenings are sometimes counterbored for wooden plugs as will be described for screws, or may be set about ⅟₁₆ inch below the surface and covered with putty or trowel cement. Chart A shows the various sizes of Anchorfast nails.

Figure 18   Nails and screws used to fasten planking and interior finish of small wooden boats

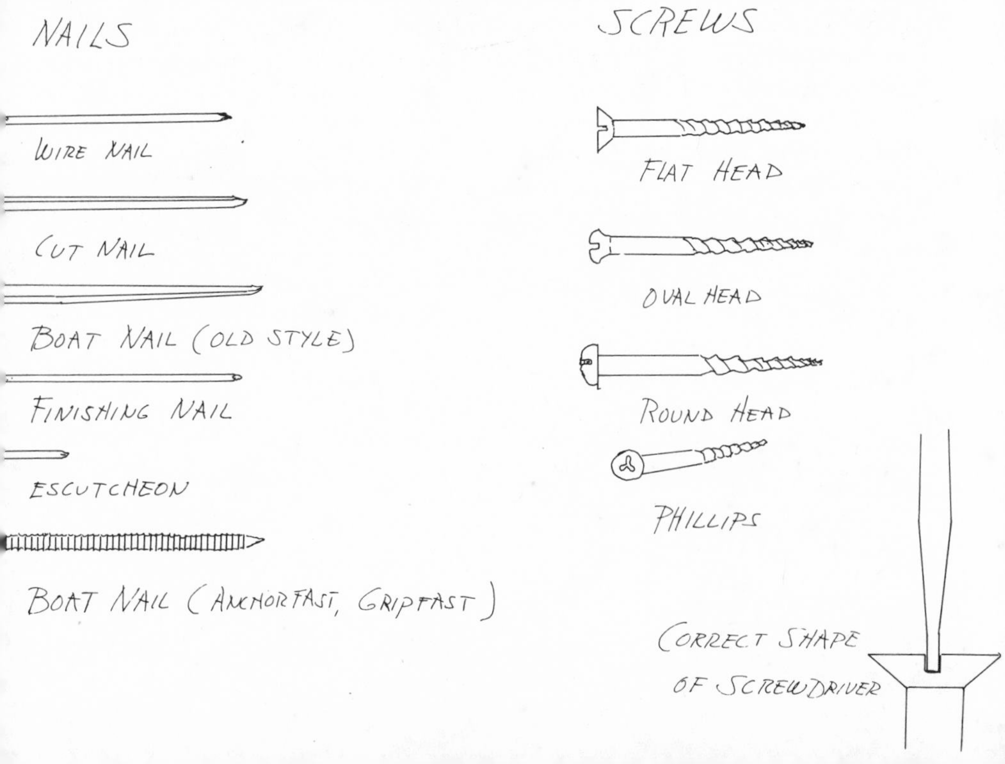

NAILS

WIRE NAIL

CUT NAIL

BOAT NAIL (OLD STYLE)

FINISHING NAIL

ESCUTCHEON

BOAT NAIL (ANCHORFAST, GRIPFAST)

SCREWS

FLAT HEAD

OVAL HEAD

ROUND HEAD

PHILLIPS

CORRECT SHAPE
OF SCREWDRIVER

A. SIZES AND GAUGES OF MONEL ANCHORFAST BOAT NAILS

Gauge	Wire Diameter	Penny Size	Length	Approximate Number per lb.
#14	.083"	4d	1½"	400
#12	.109"	2d	1"	350
		3d	1¼"	280
		4d	1½"	230
#10	.134	4d	1½"	135
		5d	1¾"	120
		6d	2"	105
		7d	2¼"	94
		8d	2½"	84
#8	.165	4d	1½"	90
		5d	1¾"	83
		6d	2"	75
		7d	2¼"	64
		8d	2½"	58
		9d	2¾"	53
		10d	3"	48

While these nails are superior to screws in holding power, plank butts should be secured with screws as it is easier to pull the ends together where the plank may be sprung to a curvature.

Screws have long been popular boat fastenings. They exert satisfactory holding power and may be removed for replacement of a damaged part (Figure 18). As in the case of boat nails, the screws should be of some corrosion-resistant material such as Monel metal or Everdur alloy, or of the hot-dipped galvanized type. Ordinary steel screws are useless in boat work, as are common brass screws which deteriorate within a very short time in contact with water.

There are many sizes of screws available, both as to length and gauge, as shown on Chart B.

B. SIZES OF WOOD SCREWS USED IN BOATBUILDING

Screw Lengths	½"	¾"	1"	1¼"	1½"	1¾"	2"	2¼"	2½"	2¾"	3"	3½"	4"	5"
Gauges	4													
	5													
	6	6												
		8	8	8	8									
			10	10	10	10	10	10	10					
				12	12	12	12	12	12	12	12			
							14		14	14	14	14	14	
										16	16	16	16	16
														18
														20

In selecting the proper size screw for various types of boatbuilding, it is a general rule that the length should be roughly three times the thickness of the material to be fastened. At the same time some judgment should be exercised, as the gauge or diameter should increase with the length for the proper strength. A very long, thin screw has very little holding power. As the size of the head increases with the increase in size, the gauge is of importance in such applications as fastening plywood planking; a thick short screw is best here for the holding power of the head.

The types of screws available are classified as to the shape of their heads, whether round, oval, Phillips, or flat.

Round-headed screws have limited use as they are required only where a structure may be subjected to occasional removal, such as an access panel or inspection door. Care must be used in their removal as it is easy to damage the slot by careless use of the screw driver.

Oval-headed screws are used similarly, but have a stronger head and are less susceptible to wringing. Countersunk washers are available for use with them which makes a more durable fastening.

Phillips screws with the patented driving slot requiring a special screwdriver are a good fastening as there is little likelihood of damaging the slot.

Flat-headed screws are most commonly used in boatbuilding, and most particularly in planking as their heads lie flush with the surface. The heads are usually countersunk with either trowel cement or putty covering the heads to a depth of about $\frac{1}{16}$ inch. In fine work the heads are countersunk to a greater degree and the heads covered with plugs or bungs set in some adhesive or glue to hold them in place and to exclude the water from penetrating to the screw head.

Figure 19   Diagram of the method of preboring for fastenings in wooden boats

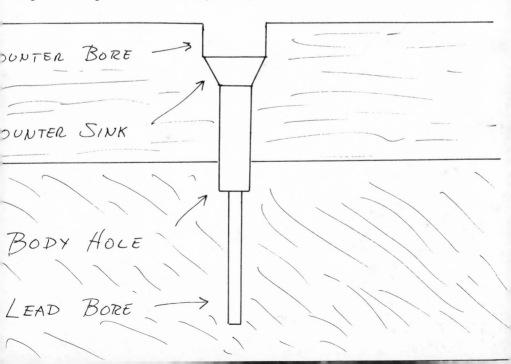

To effect this arrangement, the four boring operations required are for a lead hole, body hole, countersink and counterbore (Figure 19). To facilitate this process, a boring bit known as a patented counterbore is available. It consists of two bits, each with a set screw to predetermine the depth of each hole. These are arranged concentrically to operate simultaneously (Figure 20). As this bit performs but two operations—the boring of the lead hole and counterbore for the plug only—another patented bit has become available which will perform all four operations and is known as the Screwmate. A drawing of this bit and the sizes available for making holes for various screws and plug sizes is shown on Figure 20 and Charts C and D. This tool, while speeding boring operations greatly, must be carefully used, as it has no stop to prevent boring too deeply, and cannot be sharpened as its gauges are then reduced to a smaller diameter.

C. DRILL-SIZE GUIDE FOR BORING FOR WOOD SCREWS

Screw Size	Hard Wood Diameter of bit		Soft Wood Diameter of bit		Shank diameter in inches
	Hole #1	Hole #2	Hole #1	Hole #2	
4	$7/64$	awl used	awl used	awl used	.108
5	$1/8$	"	"	"	.122
6	$9/64$	"	"	"	.136
7	$5/32$	$3/32$	"	"	.150
8	$11/64$	$3/32$	"	"	.164
10	$13/64$	$1/8$	$3/32$	"	.192
12	$15/64$	$1/8$	$7/32$	$1/8$	.220
14	$1/4$	$5/32$	$15/64$	$5/32$	.248
16	$9/32$	$3/16$	$9/32$	$3/16$	.276
18	$5/16$	$3/16$	$5/16$	$3/16$	.304
20	$11/32$	$7/32$	$11/32$	$7/32$	.332

D. SCREW AND PLUG SIZES AVAILABLE WITH "SCREWMATE" THREE-STAGE DRILL BIT

Screw Size	Plug Size
# 8 1"	$3/8$" x $3/8$"
#10 1"	" "
# 8 1¼"	" "
#10 1¼"	" "
#10 1½"	" "
#12 1½"	½" x ½"

In counterboring care must be taken not to bore too deeply as the fastening will then be seriously weakened by leaving too little wood under the shoulder of the screw. The general rule is that the depth of the bung or plug should be no greater than two-thirds of its diameter.

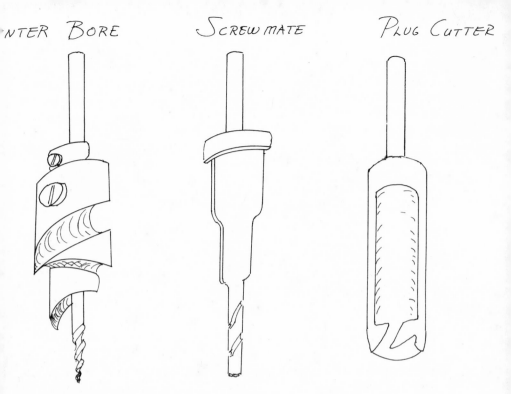

Figure 20   Augers used in wooden boat construction

The bungs or plugs themselves are available in various sizes and cut from various common boatbuilding woods used in planking, such as mahogany, pine, oak, or other woods. It is possible to cut them on the job with the use of a plug cutter which is a type of drill bit that can produce a plug (Figure 20). This can be an economy feature as the plugs can be cut from the scraps left from making up the planking. In no case can dowel material be used, as the grain of the plugs must be straight across and not vertical so the tops of the plugs may be cut off for finishing. Care must be used in setting the plugs to the correct depth (Figure 21) so that the tops may be easily cut off with a chisel for final finishing of the surface.

In driving screws, a certain amount of care must be used so the screwdriver slot will not be damaged. The blade of the screwdriver should be cut square across so it will seat properly in the slot and the shank should be straight through its lower edge to give a firm grip (Figure 18). A screwdriver bit and carpenter's brace should be used for large screws. A rachet-type screwdriver is very useful for ordinary work but it must be held firmly while driving so it does not leave the slot and bruise the adjacent wood. Screw threads may be rubbed with soap or wax to make them drive more easily, especially in the case of the hot-dipped galvanized type which usually has rough spots in the threads.

Copper rivets and *burrs* are used to fasten the adjoining surfaces of lapstrake or clinker planking, and have limited use in the interior framing of small dinghies and canoes. As the rivets are quite soft and will bend readily,

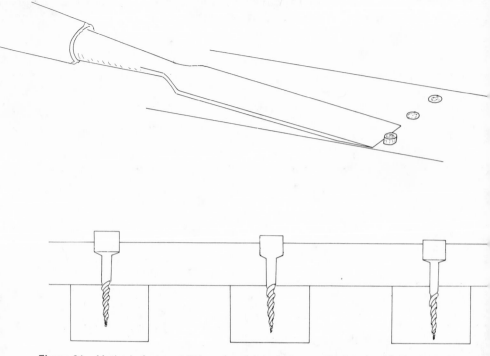

Figure 21   Method of correct fitting of wooden plugs over the heads of fastenings

the prebored holes must be only fractionally smaller than the shank. The method of setting these fastenings is shown in Figure 22.

Clench nails are sometimes used to secure plank laps in place of rivets and burrs. They were often used in building the traditional banks dories, and were set at about 3-inch intervals along the plank laps. The holes for their insertion are prebored and a bucking dolly is required to seat them properly as shown in Figure 22.

Glues and Adhesives

Many changes and new procedures in wooden boatbuilding have been brought about in recent years with the introduction of glues and adhesives. The use of these somewhat simplifies boatbuilding, as well as enhancing structural strength and longevity. In addition to adhesives, the chemical industry has also introduced seam fillers, caulking compounds and surface sealants, and other agents of a flexible nature composed of synthetic rubber, polysulfide, and polyurethane.

Of the older type of resin glue, a compound marketed under the trade name of Weldwood is probably one of the best-known adhesives which is used in various types of woodwork and cabinet making as well as in small wooden boats. This is made from urea formaldehyde and resin compounds and is very easy to use where the structures involved are not continually immersed in water.

This adhesive is prepared by mixing a quantity of the material with water to the consistency of heavy cream. The ideal temperature condition for using it is around 72 degrees. If the working temperature is lower, the glue will take longer to harden, or, conversely, if hotter, the setting time will be much more rapid. Excessive humidity can also influence its action, as it may prolong curing time. It is best to proceed with any work under mild conditions of weather. The moisture content of the wood is also a factor in the curing time, and if the material in question to be worked is excessively wet, it must be dried out before any bonding is attempted.

Another popular type of adhesive that has been widely used is a resorcinol glue derived from a phenolic plastic sold under the trade name of Elmer's Waterproof Glue. This is a much stronger bonding agent than the urea-formaldehyde type, and can be used on underwater or immersed structures.

This glue comes in two portions, a dark red liquid resin and a powdered catalytic agent, and is activated by mixing the two together. This must be done accurately by adding three parts of the powder to four parts of resin in a glass container. If a very small quantity of the glue is required, the mixing

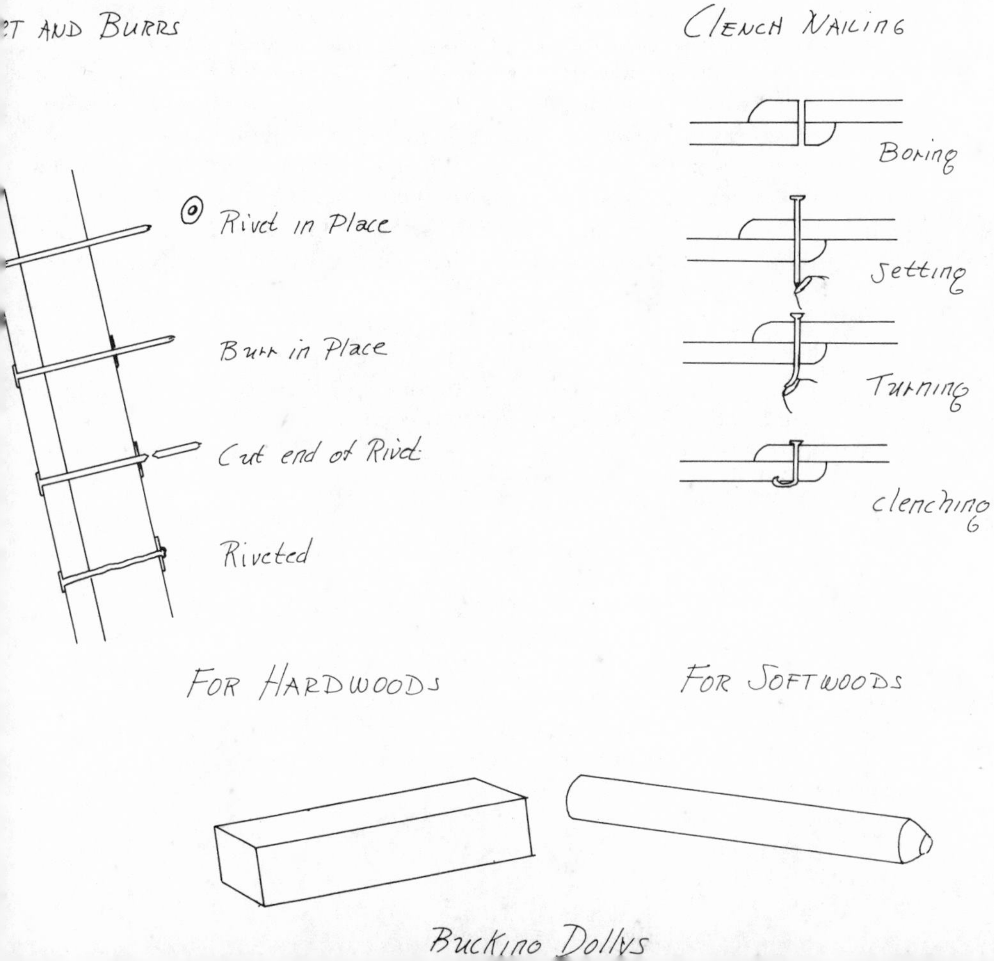

Figure 22   Use of rivets, burrs, and clench nails for plank fastenings

should be done with two large glass kitchen spoons, as the mixture is antagonistic to metals. The optimum temperature for setting this glue is also around 70 to 72 degrees.

These types of glues are only really effective as adhesives if set up under pressure, so the parts involved must be carefully clamped together and allowed to harden for at least 24 hours.

The epoxy glues are superior to the resin types in that they do not require setting under pressure, are waterproof, and are less critical to temperature at the time of application. If used in conditions of extreme heat, their setting time is very rapid—often less than 15 minutes.

There are numerous types of epoxy adhesives on the market, with new ones appearing from time to time. For that reason no specific directions are given for its use. In general, all of them require mixing with catalytic agents, and the maker's directions should be carefully followed in each case.

In spite of good holding power and general satisfactory results obtained from the use of glues and adhesives, the work must be carefully thought out and the proper preparations made to the material to be bonded if best results are to be realized.

The areas to be bonded must be accurately mated, and it is best to employ sawn rather than planed surfaces. With resin type glues which require pressure for bonding, care must be used that the pressure is uniformly applied, as this insures maximum penetration of glue into the pores of the wood, and forces out all air bubbles that might otherwise form voids or pockets and weaken the joint. Soft woods, because of their greater porosity, require less pressure than hard woods. Methods of applying pressure include use of clamps, weights, or wrapping with rope secured with a Spanish windlass. Small work can be temporarily nailed or bolted. If clamps are used, place soft wooden pads under the feet to avoid bruising the wood. When the work is put together, mark both edges with pencil lines to insure proper alignment.

Before setting up a job, it is best to make a test run on scraps of the material to be bonded to check adhesion and setting time.

While epoxy adhesives ordinarily do not require pressure for bonding, it is sometimes advisable to apply some pressure to insure a uniform seam. Any bolt or fastening holes that require boring should be attended to before the adhesive hardens.

9

Framing, Planking, and Decking

Framing

The frame structures of a wooden boat of conventional construction consist of the keel and backbone timbers, deadwoods, horn timbers, if present, stem, and the transverse framing which extends across the hull. The framing supports the shape of the hull and acts as a girder to brace the exterior planking and decking which makes up the form and mass of the boat.

In small skiffs and dinghies, the longitudinal framing is generally not as significant from a structural point of view, as the side and bottom planking in these cases is usually stiff enough to act as the main support of the hull. The transverse framing here also acts as a girder and, in most instances, is utilized as a building frame for the original construction.

The type of framing utilized will vary as to the basic design of the boat. Examples are shown in Figures 23 and 24, and include both light and heavy-weight displacement hulls, keel-ballasted sailing boats, shallow-draft center-board types, light dinghies and power launches with plank or batten-type keels, semiplaning launches with skegs, heavy displacement power boats with full keels and deadwoods, and Chesapeake Bay-type hulls with cross-planked bottoms.

Various methods of attaching the bottom plank to the keel members are shown in Figure 25. Included are the batten type with both horizontal and vertical members whose intersection forms the backing for the garboard, together with rabbeted and nonrabbeted types. Also shown is the heavy log keelson used in the cross-planked Chesapeake Bay method of building.

Examples of various types of transverse framing are shown in Figure 26. Small, round-bottom boats built in the traditional manner have light, steam-bent frames secured to the keel batten with light floor timbers. Similar hulls of larger size and greater displacement employ the same system but with larger scantlings. Some round-bottom hulls are built with sawn frames which eliminates steam bending. With this method the futtocks are cut from straight pieces, and are joined with either a cleat or from doubled

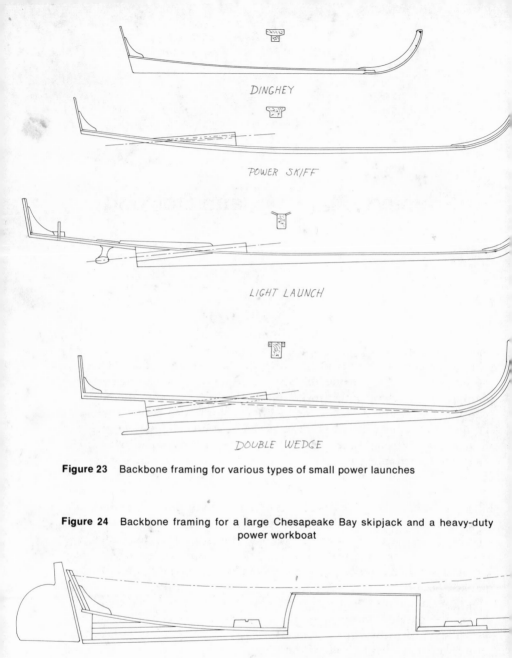

DINGHEY

POWER SKIFF

LIGHT LAUNCH

DOUBLE WEDGE

Figure 23 Backbone framing for various types of small power launches

Figure 24 Backbone framing for a large Chesapeake Bay skipjack and a heavy-duty power workboat

SKIPJACK

WORK BOAT

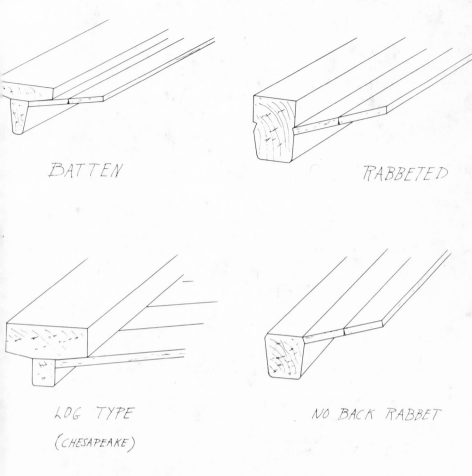

BATTEN

RABBETED

LOG TYPE

(CHESAPEAKE)

NO BACK RABBET

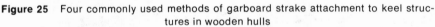

Figure 25 Four commonly used methods of garboard strake attachment to keel structures in wooden hulls

pieces as shown in Figure 27. This type of framing is often used in conjunction with strip planking.

Transverse V-bottom framing varies as to the size and weight of the hull. The weight of the timber is determined by whether it is of planing, semi-planing, or displacement type. The angles at the chine may be either lapped or secured by gussets. Also shown is a drawing of the so-called "frameless" Chesapeake Bay method of building where cross-planked or herringbone type of bottom is fitted, each plank strake then acting as a frame futtock and eliminating the fitting of conventional bottom framing.

To increase the rigidity of the attachment of the transverse framing to the keel structure, the inner or garboard ends of the frames are sometimes let into the longitudinal members by means of shallow notches (Figure 28). This is called "boxing," and may be used in either round- or V-bottom hulls. In the latter type a heavy floor timber joining each of the side frames makes a triangulated girder that imparts substantial resistance to wringing or working of the hull.

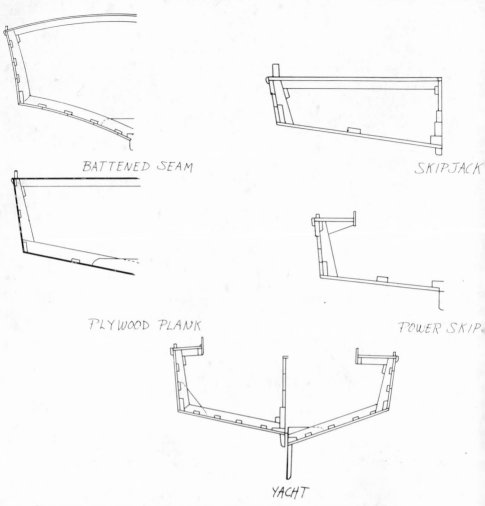

Figure 26   Diagram of various types of construction used in V-bottom boats

In some large and heavily built V-bottom hulls, galvanized iron rods with threaded ends set up in turnbuckles are used to provide additional bracing. These are seen in many Chesapeake Bay skipjacks in the way of the masts where there is much strain put on the shallow hulls, and in power work boats near the derrick mast which prevents wringing the hull when heavy loads are hoisted. Tie rods are also fitted in these hulls to secure the framing of the side decks and to brace the blocking set to brace the deck beams at the mast partners (Figure 29).

In some light-displacement sailing craft covered with plywood planking, the mast may be stepped on deck or on the cabin roof. In these cases two or more arched beams support the mast step which is triangularly braced below by two pairs of heavy knees let into both the roof or deck beams and the side frames. A tenon is worked into the mast step to position the heel of the mast. The main support of the mast is provided by the shrouds which afford triangular bracing when combined with the forestay, and are usually augmented by a movable back stay or a fixed stay secured to a boomkin aft.

Transverse framing must accommodate the lower structure of the hull according to whether keel or centerboard type. In V-bottom boats, a heavy horizontal batten is usually combined with a substantial vertical fin to carry a lead or iron ballast keel. The floor timbers are generally bolted to the keel batten through the centerline of the hull. The through bolts securing the ballast keel through the fin are usually staggered somewhat to provide triangular support against wringing (Figure 30). In some shallow draft centerboard hulls of V-bottom type, ballast is carried in the form of a heavy iron bar or lead casting that is set horizontally rather than vertically as in the case of a fin-type keel.

In most centerboard hulls the board is arranged so as to drop through an

Figure 27 Various types of frame construction used in round- and V-bottom boats

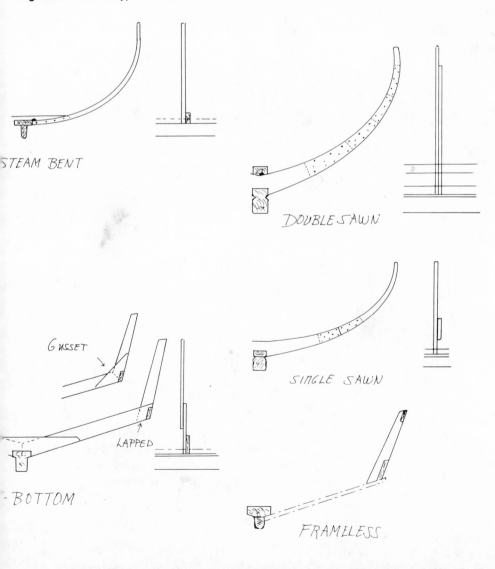

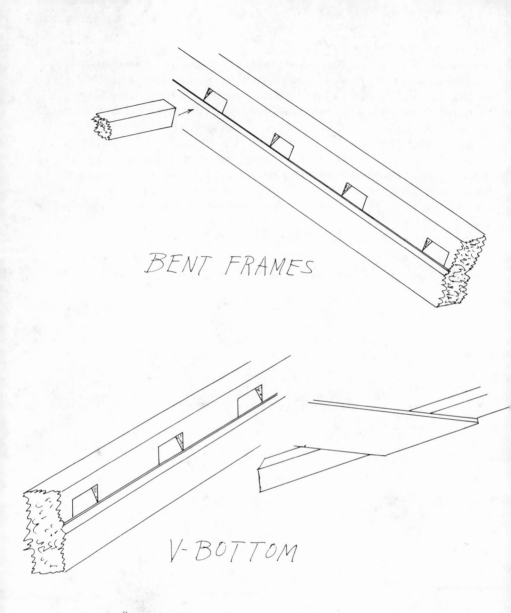

BENT FRAMES

V-BOTTOM

"BOXED" FRAMES

Figure 28   Details of joinery work required to "box" inboard ends of framing in round- and V-bottom boats

aperture cut out of the main keel timbers along the centerline. The foundation for the case itself is made up from heavy sills or logs fastened to the top of these timbers with through bolts or drifts. The upper sides of the case are made of somewhat lighter material, and are either bolted or drifted together from top to bottom.

In some cases, the centerboard may be set slightly off center, the inner edge of the board passing the outside of the keel. This has the advantage of being somewhat simpler to build. The strength of the keel timbers is also not impaired by eliminating the slot for the board, although in heavy craft this factor is probably more theoretical than real. Offset centerboards are also used in sailing boats where the main mast step comes in the way of the after end of the case. For the proper balance of the rig, it is more practical to offset the case rather than place the mast off the centerline of the hull.

In lightly built V-bottom centerboard hulls, the centerboard case can be a source of structural weakness unless some thought is given to proper construction of the attachment of the inner ends of the lower frame futtocks and floors in the way of the case. In most hulls, the floor timbers are made deep enough to be notched over the lower logs supporting the case and are fastened to it with through bolts or drifts. It is good practice to fit angle brackets of either naval bronze or galvanized iron as shown in Figure 30, which give additional bracing to the whole structure.

Figure 29   Details of mast step construction for heavy and lightweight sailing boats

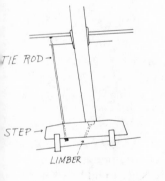

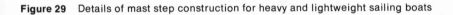

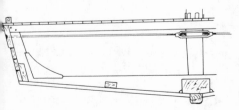

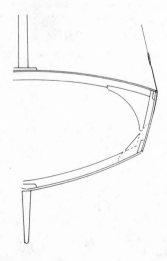

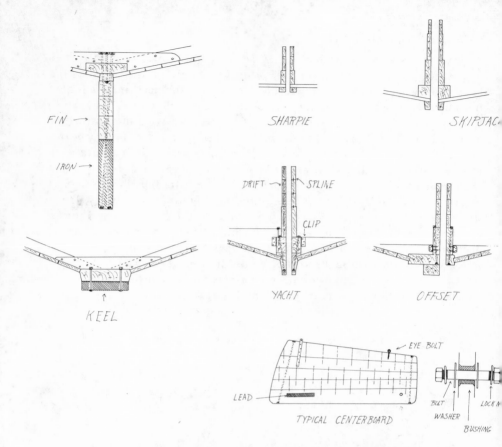

Figure 30 Details of a fin keel with ballast, a flat keel with ballast, and various types of centerboard cases used in wooden sailboats

The centerboard shown in Figure 30 is typical of those fitted to large sailing craft. It is made up of heavy timber, usually oak, the individual pieces being held together with drifts in the sequence shown. Through bolts made from drifts threaded for nuts and washers are often fitted through the ends to keep the structure from separating on a hard grounding, and add substantial weight to the board. If the weight of the various fastenings is not sufficient to sink the board on releasing the tackle, the lower after edge may be ballasted with 10 to 20 pounds of lead. The eyebolt in the forward edge is useful when the board is hoisted from the case for repair or painting.

Planking

There are several methods used in planking a round-bottom boat. These include flush or carvel, lapstrake or clinker, strip, Ashcroft, double diagonal and diagonal, and fore and aft (Figure 31).

Carvel and clinker methods have been used since ancient times in boatbuilding. The latter is sometimes favored as the laps may be fastened to-

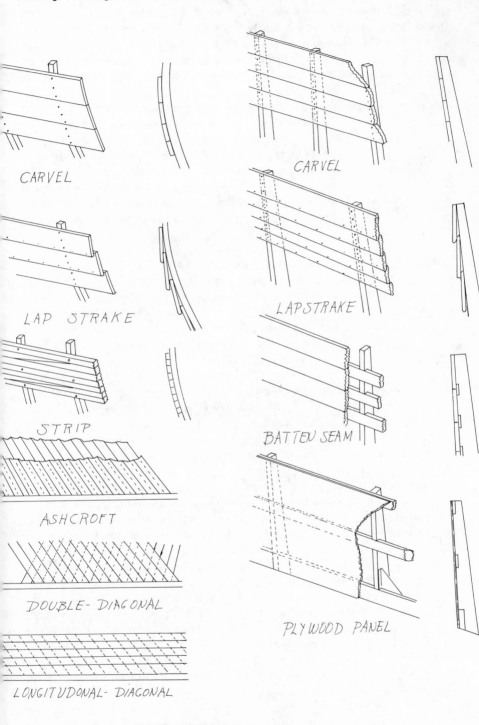

CARVEL

CARVEL

LAP STRAKE

LAPSTRAKE

STRIP

BATTEN SEAM

ASHCROFT

DOUBLE- DIAGONAL

PLYWOOD PANEL

LONGITUDONAL- DIAGONAL

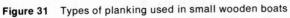

Figure 31   Types of planking used in small wooden boats

gether for a very strong structure. This type is less easy to repair than the former, where an individual plank may be replaced without disturbing adjacent strakes. Strip planking has come into widespread use in recent years, especially among amateur builders, as it is easier to line off than conventional plank as the strips can be run out to a feather edge. The strips are prepared by ripping out conventional plank into square-sectioned battens. These are laid out along the frames and edge fastened at 4-to-6-inch intervals, boat nails of the Anchorfast type being the fastening of choice. Only every fourth or fifth strip is nailed to the frame to minimize the danger of splitting, the requisite strength being obtained by the edge fastenings.

The Ashcroft system of planking was once popular in small dinghies. The double diagonal layers of planking ran at angles to the keel, and usually were separated by a layer of paint-soaked canvas or muslin to insure watertightness and to prevent the plank from drying out when the boat is out of the water.

Fore-and-aft planking combined with the diagonal type is used in generally the same applications as the Ashcroft.

V-bottom hulls may be either carvel or clinker planked over conventional framing, but in the latter case the dory lap is generally used. To insure proper strength of the hull, carvel plank must be backed by frames spaced at fairly close intervals. To minimize the number of frames required, the seams are often backed by battens. This type of construction has long been the hallmark of the classically built V-bottom boat, particularly in lightly built runabouts and planing or semiplaning cruising launches. This method requires much building time, as each plank and batten must be individually fitted due to the lack of predictable width of conventional planking. A faster and more economical method that has come into recent use is the fitting of ripped out plywood panels which can be cut to predictable widths and installed as conventional planking. For proper strength and longevity, this should be covered with fiber glass or polypropylene. Full-sized plywood panels may be applied to straight-sectioned hulls, but suitable sheer and intermediate battens must be fitted to support the material against flexing.

Cross-sectional drawings of several types of V-bottom construction are shown in Figure 26, including examples of the cross-planked Chesapeake Bay method. Attention is called to the drawing of the rabbeted chine. The single-piece type carried two rabbets, an upper one to receive the side plank, the lower accommodating the bottom plank. It will be noted that the outer edge of the chine stringer is exposed and forms the outer portion of the angle. This type of building should be avoided if possible, as it is very difficult to accurately cut the rabbets to make a close fit with both of the plank strakes. A two-piece batten type is shown which is somewhat easier to make if this type of chine construction is favored (Figure 32).

The outer edges of the frames of all conventionally shaped boats, with the exception of straight-sided scows or garveys, must be beveled to accommodate the curve of the planking that encloses the hull. As the bow sections are approached, the depth of this bevel will increase somewhat over the ac-

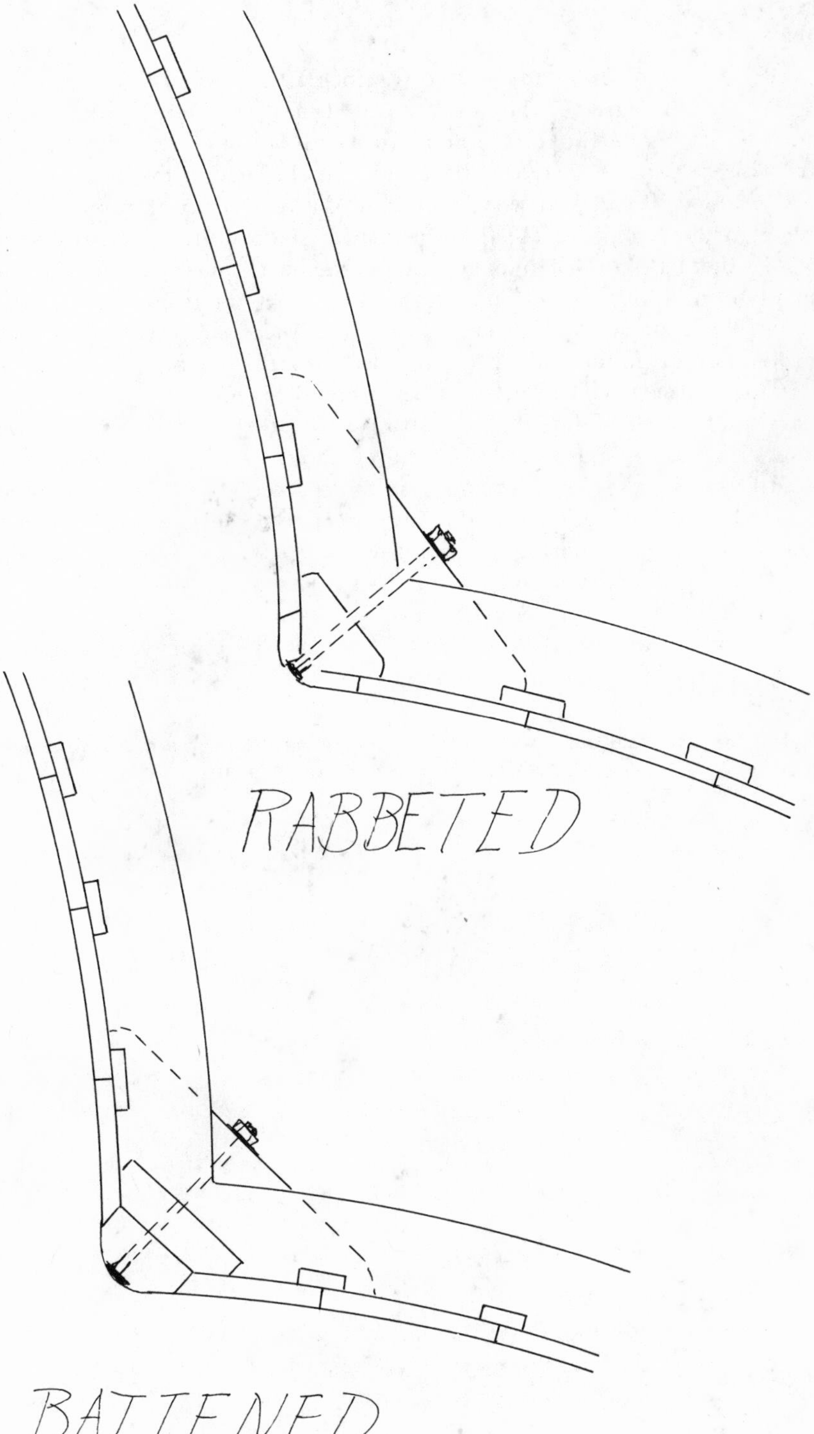

RABBETED

BATTENED

Figure 32 Cross-sectional views of rabbeted and batten-type chine stringers used in V-bottom boat construction

105

tual thickness of the plank due to the increasing curve (Figure 33).

The actual degree of the bevel required may be obtained when the hull lines are faired on the lofting floor. In round-bottom hulls with steam-bent frames, the various degrees of bevel may be obtained in most cases by twisting them while hot and wiring them in the correct position to the temporary ribbands that enclose the outer sides of the hull. In V-bottom hulls with either straight or flammed sections, the bevels must be made by sawing or planking frame edges. The degree of bevel can be taken from the faired lines in plan view, but if a large number of pieces are involved or if series production of similar hulls is to be considered, the fairing process can be facilitated by means of a universal bevel board (Figure 33). To establish the bevels, a number of diagonals are struck across the body plan on the lofting floor. These are transferred to a bevel gauge with the use of the bevel board, which may be drawn on a suitable sheet of plywood. One edge is marked off in half inches, and a perpendicular line is erected at the zero end, its height terminating at a point which will be equal to the interval between the station lines. A series of lines drawn from the top of this point will then indicate every possible bevel.

To take off an actual bevel, the space marked "A" between stations # 1

Figure 33   Universal bevel board used to determine the degree of bevel in the side and bottom frames of V-bottom boats

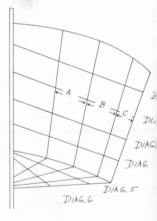

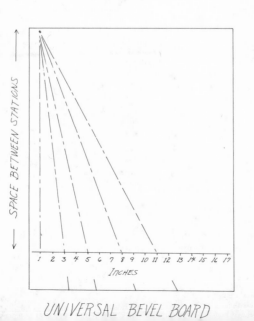

and #2 indicates the bevel for Station #1, space "B" the bevel for Station #2, etc. If the interval between two given stations is, for example, six inches, the angle on the bevel board at the six-inch mark is the one required. This is picked up with an adjustable bevel gauge, and transferred to the work for beveling.

Carvel planking with its flush seams requires caulking between the plank joints if the boat is to be finished conventionally with paint. These caulking seams must be prepared before the planks are fastened in place by planing off a small portion of the upper and lower edges of the outer faces. The V-shaped space formed between each plank by this operation will amount to about two-thirds the thickness of the plank itself, with the inner portions of the planks joining each other in a close hand fit. The approximate dimensions of typical caulking seams for planks of various thicknesses are shown in Figure 34.

After the edges of the planks are dressed, well-mixed oil paint is applied before fitting. In the days of classical boatbuilding, a mixture of thick paint and white lead made up into paste was run into the bottom of the seam be-

Figure 34 Correct dimensions for the depth of caulking seams to be used in various plank thicknesses

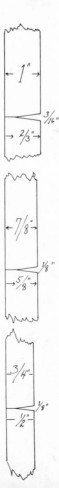

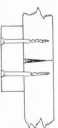

STOPPING FOR

BATTENED SEAMS

fore applying the caulking. In recent years, manufactured seam compounds, which are more adhesive and provide a flexible sealer that is much superior in holding qualities, have become available.

In small boats the caulking material is a special twine which is put up in balls, much as common fastening twine. This is rolled into the prepared seam and pressed into place with a caulking wheel. The outside of the seam is payed or "stopped" with flexible seam compound which is carefully applied over the caulking. This may be quickly done by placing the compound in an ordinary manually operated grease gun with a coarse nozzle and passing it over the opening.

Larger craft are caulked with oakum, a special material derived from hemp fibres that is driven into the seam spaces with caulking irons and a mallet (Figure 35). The latter has a long head to take the "bounce" out of

Figure 35   Caulking irons

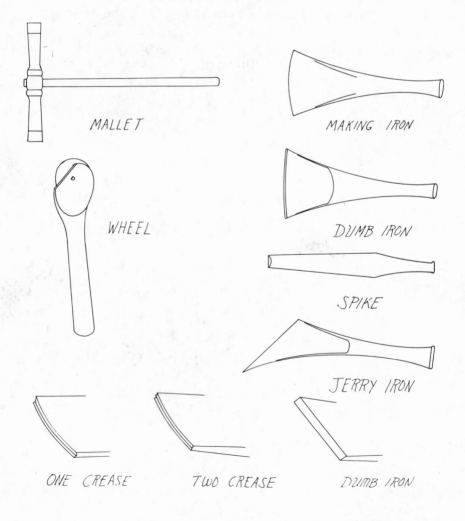

the impact while driving. This is an operation generally considered to be best done by professionals, as it is easy to spoil the work by overdriving and consequently pushing the oakum through the back of the seam. In the actual operation, the oakum or twine is held in the fingers and pushed into the seam as shown in Figure 36. Also shown are examples of some of the caulking irons favored by professionals and in use since the earliest days of boatbuilding. Amateurs aspiring to do their own caulking are advised to make a mock-up of several short pieces of plank, suitably prepared as to the correct seam dimensions and well fastened to framing materials to test their skills before attempting actual work.

Lapped, clinker, or dory-lap type planking should also have the joining or faying surfaces covered with a good quality oil paint before fitting. Some builders use light seam compound under the laps which maintains a tight joint through its flexible qualities, as many such hulls of light construction will have their planks work somewhat under hard going.

V-bottom hulls with battened seam planking benefit from the use of seam compound smeared lightly between the joints. In any case, the joints should be painted at least before fitting. Some builders make a small seam on the inside of the planks behind the battens and fit a small strand of cotton. In no case should these joints be glued as subsequent shrinking and swelling will split the planks in the absence of flexible seam joints.

In considering the shape of the side plank for even simple flat-bottom

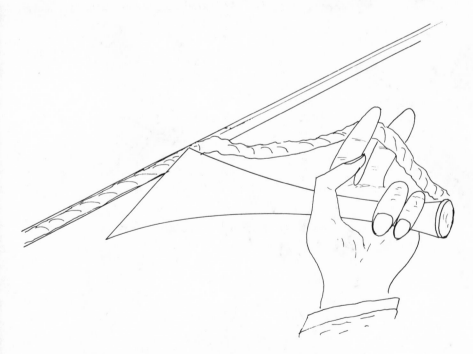

Figure 36   A method of holding caulking material for driving

skiffs or dinghies, it must be noted that the actual or developed shape of the side plank is quite at variance with the apparent shape of the sides of the finished hull in profile. This is due to the curve of the plank and the profiles of the sheer and chine. An example of this optical illusion is shown in Figure 37. In very small or shallow hulls, the sides may be cut from a single wide plank. In most small cheap skiffs the top edge is left as originally milled for simplicity, the curves for the bottom being cut from the bottom edge. The diagram shown in Figure 37 is typical of this practice, and the dimensions shown may be altered somewhat to suit a revision of the chine profile if desired. If two planks are used the upper strake may be fitted as milled, with the chine profile shaped to the bottom strake only.

The same condition exists in flat- or V-bottom hulls with flare and flam, in round-bottom boats, and craft with reverse curves or deepened sections aft in the deadwoods (Figure 38). In some cases short insertions of single planks or "stealers" are used to provide the proper sequence for covering the area involved. In round-bottom boats the planks are individually shaped with the widest portions in their midships sections to allow for the widened girth of the hull amidships.

In getting out the planking after the hull is framed, the actual planking sequence with the number of planks required and their approximate shape must be determined ahead of time. This operation may be plotted ahead of

Figure 37   Diagram of the actual or expanded shape of the side plank for a small skiff

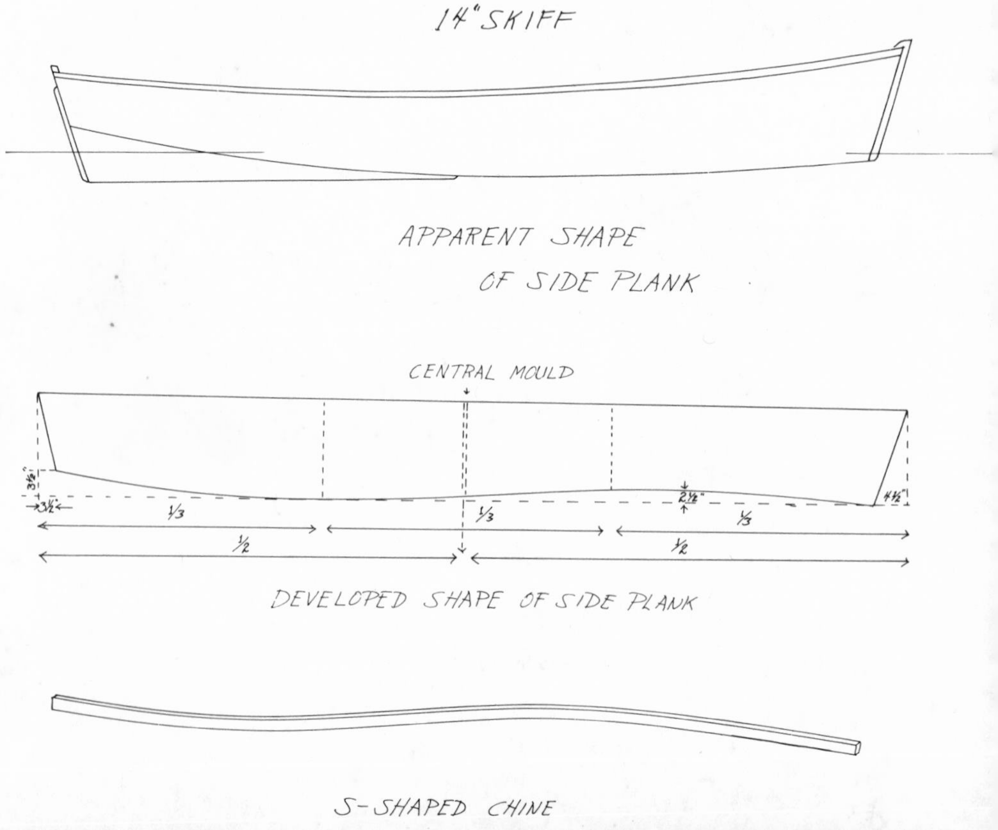

14" SKIFF

APPARENT SHAPE
OF SIDE PLANK

CENTRAL MOULD

DEVELOPED SHAPE OF SIDE PLANK

S-SHAPED CHINE

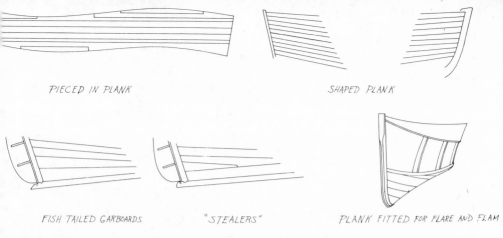

PIECED IN PLANK   SHAPED PLANK

FISH TAILED GARBOARDS   "STEALERS"   PLANK FITTED FOR FLARE AND FLAM

Figure 38   Methods of shaping side and bottom planking and the use of stealers

time by means of a graph (Figure 39). Another method of "girthing" a hull for planking layout is the use of a grid (Figure 40), which can be drawn with a curve at the top to show the shape of the sheer, the lines below indicating the number of plank strakes required between sheer and keel rabbet. When the distances between the rabbet line and sheer are measured on each station line, the dimensions and width of each plank strake can then be determined. If fitted side planks are to be added to a V-bottom boat, the grid can be drawn to indicate the area between the chine and sheer only.

The fitting of plank to enclose the irregularly elliptical form of a boat's hull will involve various plank shapes which in their flat or expanded form appear at first examination to have no relation to the boat's apparent form (Figure 41). However, when bent to their proper curve, they combine with the adjacent planks to form the correct sequence.

Figure 39   Use of a semicircular graph for plotting plank widths

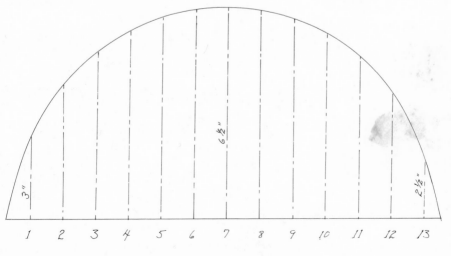

PLANK WIDTH AMIDSHIPS

TH AT STERN   WIDTH AT STEM

PLOTTING PLANK CURVATURES

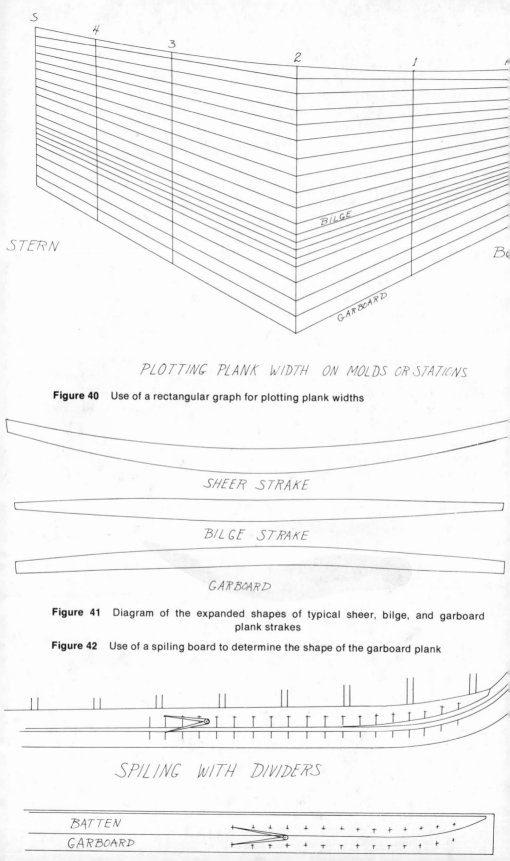

S   4   3   2   1   A

STERN   BILGE   Bo

GARBOARD

PLOTTING PLANK WIDTH ON MOLDS OR STATIONS

Figure 40   Use of a rectangular graph for plotting plank widths

SHEER STRAKE

BILGE STRAKE

GARBOARD

Figure 41   Diagram of the expanded shapes of typical sheer, bilge, and garboard plank strakes

Figure 42   Use of a spiling board to determine the shape of the garboard plank

SPILING WITH DIVIDERS

BATTEN

GARBOARD

In hulls planked with longitudinal strakes in the conventional manner, the garboard must have its inner edge shaped to the profile of the keel rabbet or outer edge of the keel batten and fairing into the stem rabbet. This operation is known as spiling, and requires the use of a temporary batten or spiling board (Figure 42). A series of equidistant marks are made along the bottom of the stem and keel rabbets, the spiling batten being treated similarly. The batten is then temporarily tacked into place and the distance between the keel rabbet and a convenient arbitrary spacing for a congruent set of marks on the batten is made with a pair of dividers, the spacing in each case being marked with a horizontal line. After the required distance has been marked, the batten is removed and the marks are transferred to the garboard plank. To mark the line for sawing, a flexible batten is used as a drawing line which is bent to the required curve.

Another method of spiling is by means of a block as shown in Figure 43.

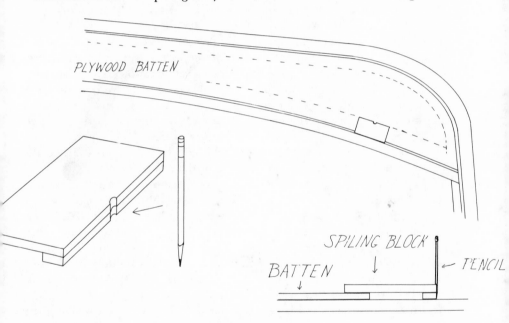

Figure 43   Use of a spiling block to determine the shape of garboard and shutter planks in a V-bottom hull

A notch is cut in one edge so that a pencil held against it will have its point coinciding with it as the block is moved along the area to be marked. This method is often used in marking conventional plank, and is particularly effective when used in laying out plywood sheets. The block will act as a divider as it is moved along the rabbet line.

It might well be mentioned that a common cause of inaccurate spiling by beginning builders is a failure to hold the instrument level (Figure 44). A tilt in the legs will indicate a false or distorted line when the tips are not made to coincide in a flat plane.

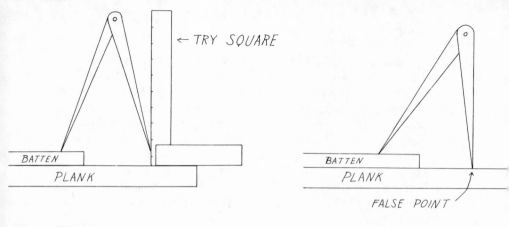

Figure 44   Correct method of holding the dividers on a spiling board

In getting out conventional planking for building, it will be found that few varieties of timber much over 20 feet in length are generally available. Possible exceptions are some varieties of hard pine, Douglas fir, and African mahogany which are commonly cut from very large trees, and which are sometimes available in lengths up to 26 or 28 feet without premium cost. It then follows that in many cases planking timbers must be spliced or butted to make up the required length for hulls over 20 feet in length. There is no objection to this from a structural point of view, as correctly made butts are fully as strong if not stronger than a full-length plank. The cut ends of the planks to be joined are backed with a block which is at least twice the width of the plank involved and may be of the same or somewhat greater thickness (Figure 45). The fastening sequence is shown, and galvanized or bronze screws should be used, according to the metallic content of the rest of the fastenings, as these can better take up the joint than can nails of either conventional or Anchorfast variety, which cannot be drawn tight after initial driving. Sometimes a full-length block is used which takes up all the space between the framing. It is best from a structural point of view to fit only one butt between any given frame space, if possible. If this is not possible, at least three full strakes should intervene between butts.

In hulls to be covered with plywood panels, all frame surfaces should be carefully beveled to present a flat surface. In flat-bottom hulls, a straight edge can be used to check all surfaces from chine to chine. In V-bottom boats, the frame surfaces on either side from keel batten to chine must be similarly checked for truth. This is most easily done by cutting a series of notches at equidistant points at both the inner and outer bearing surfaces (Figure 46), which are made to coincide by means of a straight edge. The spaces between are then leveled by planing. Care must be taken not to cut away an excess of material in the process, and progress can be checked with a straight edge.

Plywood hulls usually require the bottom to be applied before closing in the sides, the reverse of general small boatbuilding practice. This is due to the fact that it would be difficult to trim off the edges of the bottom panels

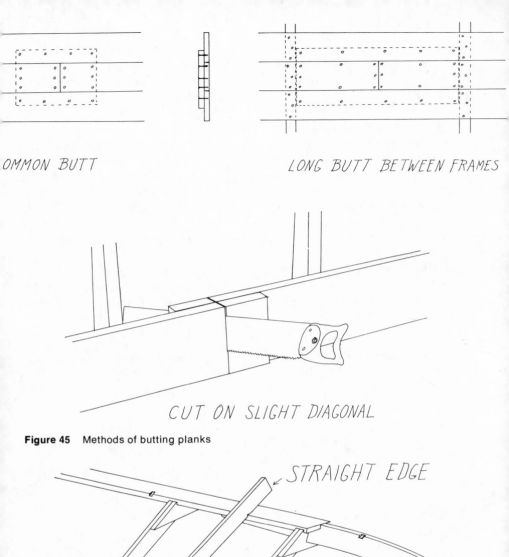

OMMON BUTT

LONG BUTT BETWEEN FRAMES

CUT ON SLIGHT DIAGONAL

Figure 45 Methods of butting planks

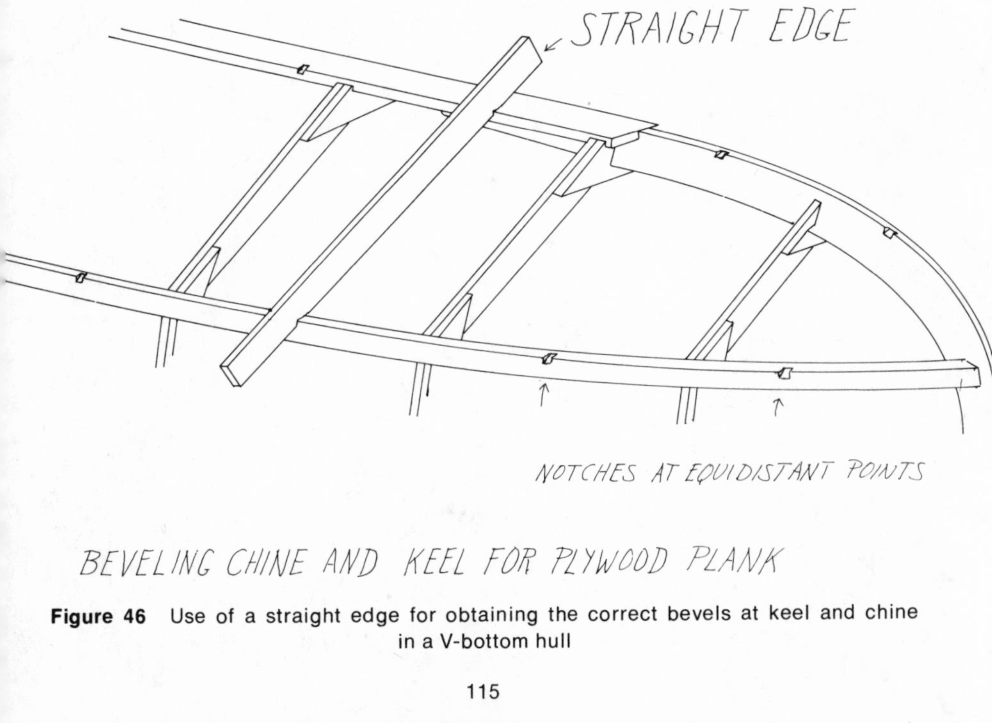

STRAIGHT EDGE

NOTCHES AT EQUIDISTANT POINTS

BEVELING CHINE AND KEEL FOR PLYWOOD PLANK

Figure 46 Use of a straight edge for obtaining the correct bevels at keel and chine in a V-bottom hull

without damaging the topsides. After the bottom is applied, the side panels are bent into place and temporarily fastened into position. At the point where their lower edges will converge with the bottom on the chine stringer, a series of small holes are drilled at intervals of 12 inches to 16 inches through this which allow small finishing nails to be inserted. When the side panels are removed, these point marks may be used to mark the curvature for sawing (Figure 47).

The joining of the side and bottom panels of a small flat- or V-bottom plywood-covered skiff may be made as a lapped joint where the two meet at the chine line. A somewhat neater joint that effectively hoods the core ends of the plywood may be made by beveling each edge (Figure 46). The notch for making a directional change of the bevel toward the bow section is shown.

Most small plywood hulls of the skiff type are designed for a linered stem in place of the more complicated one piece rabbeted type. The sequence for cutting the side panels and the beveled liner finished off with a metal stem band is also shown.

Figure 47 Details of stem construction and fitting of plank panels in plywood-covered hulls

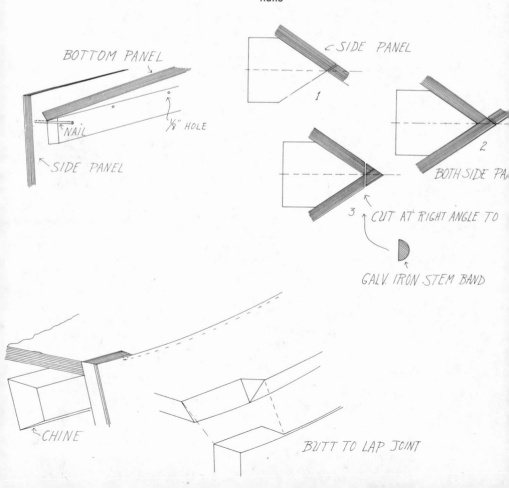

BOTTOM PANEL

SIDE PANEL

NAIL

⅛" HOLE

SIDE PANEL

SIDE PANEL

1

2

BOTH SIDE PA

3 CUT AT RIGHT ANGLE TO

GALV. IRON STEM BAND

CHINE

BUTT TO LAP JOINT

Decking

The decking of a boat's hull functions as the topside and bottom plank to form the mass of the structure and to aid in maintaining its watertight integrity. Full decks in even small craft are considered a necessity for any serious seagoing work. The side decks and foredecks of small boats used in more protected waters do much to keep water from entering an open cockpit if the latter is protected by substantial coamings.

Aside from the structural strength afforded by the decking, the method of construction and the type of material used as well as its manner of finishing was often significant for decorative effect in the days of classical boatbuilding. Conventional planking has been used for deck coverings almost exclusively since prehistoric times until the advent of marine plywood. The continuing problem with the time-honored former material was the difficulty of maintaining watertightness where the inevitable shrinking and swelling occurred. The use of first pitch and then oakum to caulk the seams never entirely solved the problem in olden times, but the later development of flexible seam compounds somewhat minimized leakage if correctly applied.

Another partial answer to the problem of constructing watertight decks was the fitting of two and sometimes three layers of planking with staggered seams. While this expedient made for a very strong structure and did much to cut down leakage, it added considerably to material and labor costs.

Cross-sectional views of various types of deck plank are shown in Figure 47, along with examples of various fastening systems. The use of plywood panels for deck coverings of wooden boats is almost universal today, as its continuous structure appears to have answered the problem of leakage. In some cases, where decorative decks are required, or where a replica of some classic yacht type is to be built, conventional plank is laid over plywood panels and set in some type of bedding compound to discourage dry rot from the effects of rain water.

The fitting of decorative plank decks requires better than average skills in joinery and boat carpentry. One example of such work is the nibbed deck shown in Figure 48. Here each plank is bent to the outside curve of the sheer, with a scarphed covering-board outboard and the end of each plank nibbed into the king plank along the centerline. Teak has long been the favored material for such decks, and is left unpainted to weather to its characteristic light gray color with black seam compound used for contrast.

Another type of plank sequence is the use of straight strakes that parallel the centerline. In either case, shelf beams must be fitted over the outboard ends of the deck beams to support the edges of the deck plank.

Many amateur builders fit common mill run tongue-and-groove flooring to the decks of original or converted small boats, no doubt due to its moderate cost and universal availability. For best results, a subdeck of plywood panels should first be laid (Figure 49).

Most decks in the past have been laid with a crown or curve in sectional view, and, of course, required curved deck beams to support them. This en-

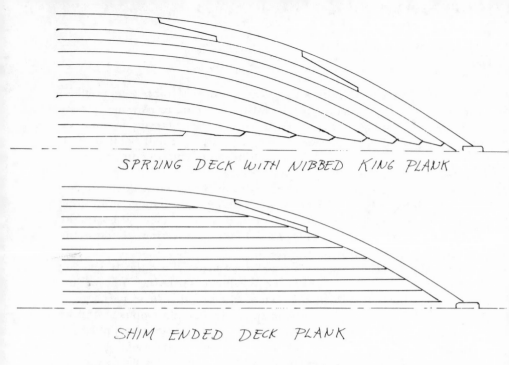

SPRUNG DECK WITH NIBBED KING PLANK

SHIM ENDED DECK PLANK

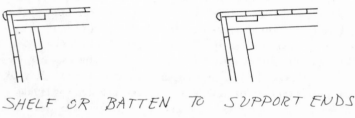

SHELF OR BATTEN TO SUPPORT ENDS

OF DECK PLANK

Figure 48   Two types of deck planking with supporting frame structures

tails the use of wide boards from which the beams must be cut, and involves some wastage of material. In later years many small boats have been designed with flat decks which makes for simpler building when used with plywood decking as the beams may be laid as milled. In spite of some popular opinion, flat decks shed water as readily as the crowned variety because the motion of the boat, in most cases, makes it impossible for solid water to remain on the deck.

In cases where crowned decks are to be fitted, the deck beams must be cut to form this camber on their upper edges. In order to reduce weight, the underside of the beams must be formed to the same curve, as well as to provide as much space below decks as possible. The amount or degree of crown is usually indicated on the plans by the designer, and is generally indicated through the midship section at the point of greatest beam. The degree of camber in the beams forward and aft is subject to a certain amount of inter-

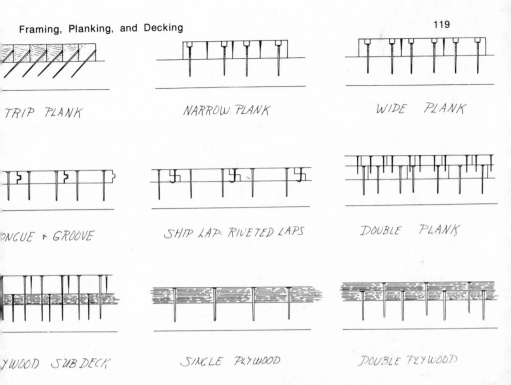

Figure 49   Various types of planking and fastenings used in wooden boats

polation by the builder, however, as the camber must decrease in height as the beam narrows forward aft. At the same time the top of the crown must follow a sweeping curve from bow to stern for proper appearance.

For the initial laying out of the work, a pair of battens are laid out on the lofting floor as shown in Figure 50. A straight line is drawn to indicate the breadth across the widest point of the sheer. The height from this line to the point of intersection of the battens must correspond to the indicated crown of the deck. As the crown or camber is generally given to the outside of the planking, the thickness of the decking must be deducted from this dimension. A fair curve is plotted between the outer sheer points, and a template is made from this outline for making up the deck beam. In practice it will generally be found that the indicated crown will encompass about three or four stations amidships on the average small boat. The height of the crown toward the bow and the stern will be somewhat less.

To lay out the balance of the deck beams, the king plank along the centerline of the hull, or a stiff batten as a facsimile, is laid over the top of the midship deck beams already in place and extending from the top of the transom to the intersection of the deckline with the sheer at the stem. After a fair curve is established by eye, the rest of the deck beams may be gotten out. Their curve may be plotted as shown, or derived by trial measurement of templates made from scrap lumber laid across the hull at the various station lines.

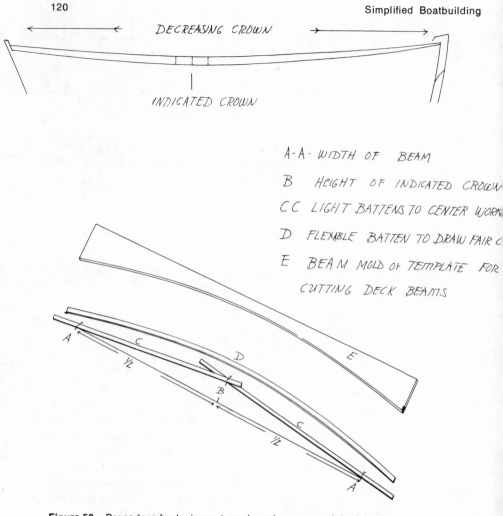

DECREASING CROWN

INDICATED CROWN

A-A· WIDTH OF BEAM

B HEIGHT OF INDICATED CROWN

CC LIGHT BATTENS TO CENTER WORK

D FLEXIBLE BATTEN TO DRAW FAIR C

E BEAM MOLD Ot TEMPLATE FOR
CUTTING DECK BEAMS

A
½
C
D
E
B
C
½
A

Figure 50   Procedure for laying out cambered or crowned deck beams

In cases where trunk cabins, steering shelters, cargo hatches, or other deck erections intervene on the centerline, the deck beams are best first made full length across the hull. The carlins or headers may then be fastened in place so their edges fair into the sweep of the crown, cutting into each beam as the work progresses. This will eliminate discrepancies in the camber line which would present an unshipshape appearance.

10

Boat Carpentry and Joinery

A knowledge of boat carpentry and joinery and mechanical skills in its execution is essential for the proper construction of a wooden boat. While
metal fastenings of appropriate type are the prime agent in holding the various parts of the structure together, accurate fitting of the faying surfaces
and the making of specialized joints is necessary for the required strength
and rigidity.

A type of joint much used in boatbuilding is the scarph. Two forms used
in joining keel and backbone timbers are shown in Figure 51. The common
scarph is a lapped joint with square-cut ends. The hooked scarph provides a
more rigid joint due to the presence of a locking surface. This must be cut
with a chisel after the angle is sawn. Both of these joints are fastened by
bolts. These should be staggered to make for a stronger union of the parts
by triangulation, which lessens the danger of splitting the wood.

The use of joinery to make up keel and backbone structures using various
types of wood is shown in Figure 52. The fitting of curved pieces in the
stem and deadwood is shown, together with the method of adapting straight
pieces for the same purpose. The mortising of the timbers in the stem knee
adds greatly to the strength of the structure. To make the tabled deadwood
requires a high degree of mechanical skill, but the resulting structure is very
strong. The use of tenon blocks exerts a similar effect, and is somewhat easier to fabricate.

The arrangement of the timbers in the stem assembly will vary as to the
profile of the bow. Except in the unlikely event that a very large grown timber of the proper curve is available, the stem must be built up from a number of individual pieces as shown in Figure 53. A close fit between the
pieces is necessary for proper strength, and the use of mortises in the knee
timbers insures rigidity and resistance against wringing.

The stem rabbet must be carefully made so that there is a close fit between the ends of the planking and the horizontal and vertical surfaces of
the rabbet. This accuracy enhances the holding power of the fastenings and
aids in maintaining a watertight structure. The angle and bevel of the rab-

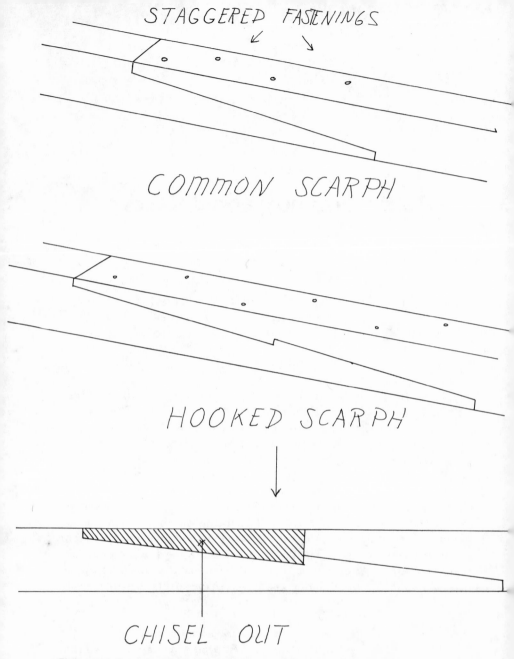

STAGGERED FASTENINGS

COMMON SCARPH

HOOKED SCARPH

CHISEL OUT

Figure 51 Procedure for making common and hooked scarphs

bet are obtained from the loft plan. The depth of the rabbet will be determined by the thickness of the planking. A small piece of material of the same dimensions of the plank, called a fid, is used to check the depth of the rabbet during its cutting to insure accuracy.

Where joints between individual pieces of framing extend outside the plankline, stopwaters should be fitted to make these watertight. These are made by boring a hole through the joint at the rabbet line and inserting a length of softwood dowel. The diameter of the hole in relation to the dowel should be such to make a close driving fit and the dowel will then swell upon immersion of the hull and effectively seal the joint. The positioning of the stopwater is critical, as, if it is placed anywhere outside of the actual surface not covered by planking, water will inevitably seep into the joint. In general, stopwaters should be fitted close to the midline of the rabbet as shown in Figure 54.

Where single planks must be spliced together for either lapstrake planking in round-bottom boats or for a dory lap in flat or V-bottom boats, scarphing must be used in place of butting as the butt block would make a rather awkward if not weak joint if used in conjunction with this method of planking. The procedure is shown in Figure 55. The ends of the plank will have their edges beveled to an equal degree in order to make a continuously flat surface when joined. The length of the bevel will vary as to the thickness of the plank, and a 5-or-6-degree angle will provide adequate bearing surface in most cases.

The proper fitting and fastening of the deckbeams at their outer ends to the shelf or clamp is important for structural strength of the hull. This is especially true of lightly built boats which otherwise have little resistance against wringing and changing shape. Some examples of good joinery in deck beam clamp joints are shown in Figure 56. Also shown are examples of single shelf and clamp and shelf combinations.

Figure 52   Construction of backbone timbers for heavy displacement hulls

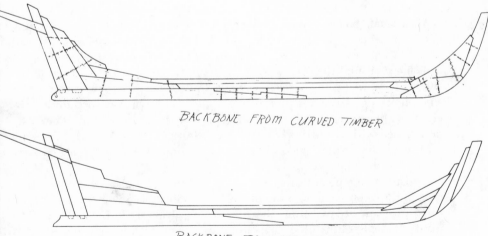

BACKBONE FROM CURVED TIMBER

BACKBONE FROM STRAIGHT TIMBER

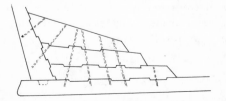

TABLED DEADWOODS

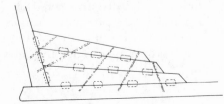

TENON DEADWOODS

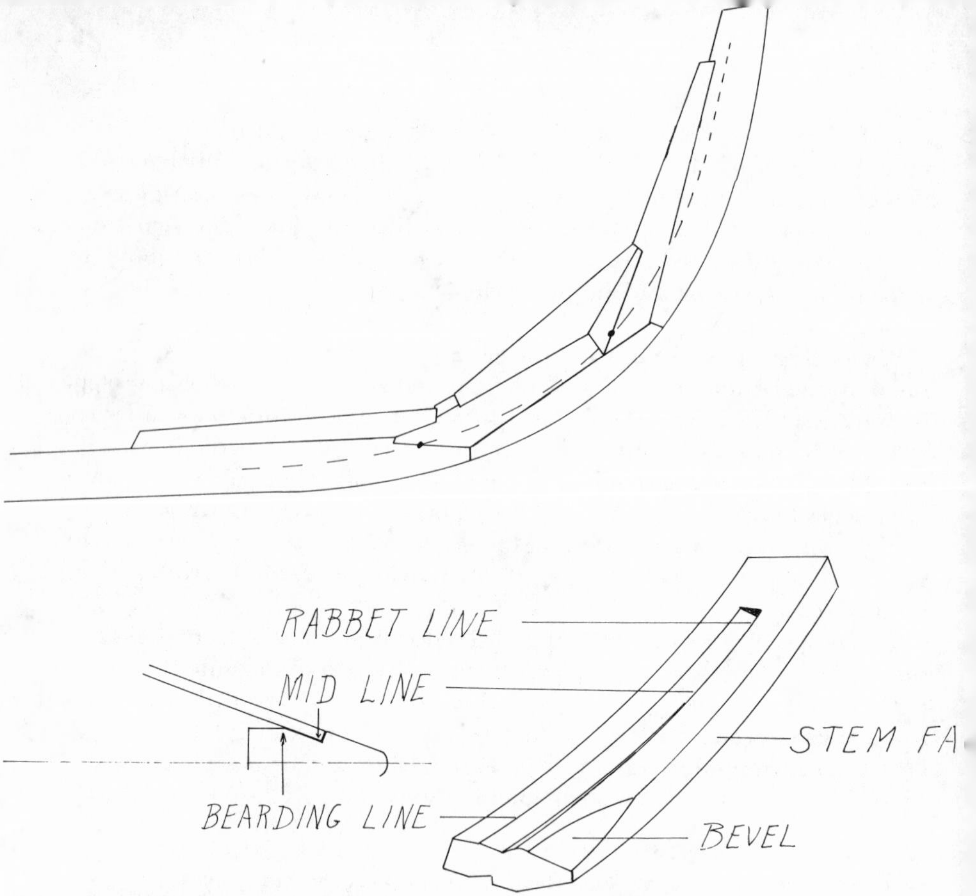

RABBET LINE

MID LINE

BEARDING LINE

STEM FA[CE]

BEVEL

Figure 53 Diagram of stem layout and construction

Most small boats require some type of railing to protect against falling overboard and to otherwise finish off the edge of the sheer. Speed boats, various types of power launches, and small sailing craft generally have low toe rails fitted around the sheer which are actually light battens fastened to the sheer plank with long screws. Heavily built sailing or powerboats sometimes have log rails made from heavy timber. These are fastened to the covering board and into the shelves or clamps with long drift rod. They may be finished with a hardwood rail cap as shown in Figure 57. Log rails are built up from scarphed pieces as it is usually impractical to attempt to force them into the required curve (Figure 57).

A distinctive type of railing is sometimes fitted to both sailing and power craft. This combines a log rail with vertical stanchions made up from galvanized pipe and secured from above with long drifts set in the rail cap. The inside diameter of the pipe varies as to the size of the hull and the height of the stanchions, the most common sizes being ⅜-to-¾ inches. The upper ends of the drifts are secured by clench rings in the manner described in Figure 57. To secure the stanchions against working, the drifts are taken up to make a crush fit of the ends of the pipe into the wood.

For proper appearance, the outer faces of the railing should stand perpen-

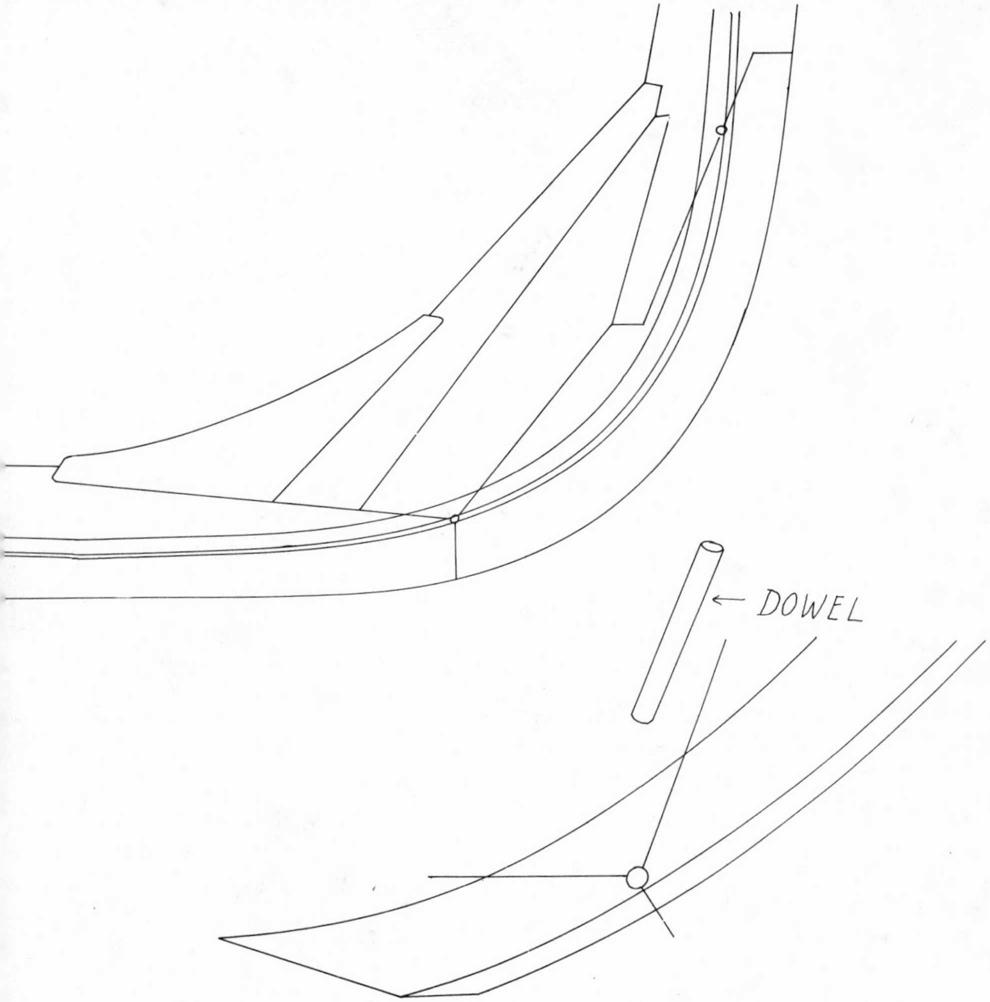

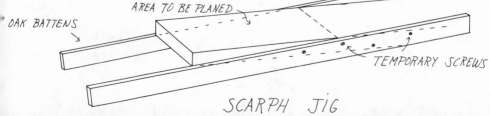

← DOWEL

Figure 54 The fitting of stopwaters in stem scarphs

Figure 55 A method of scarphing plank and a jig for cutting the joints

PENCIL MARKS

PLANK SCARPH

5606° ANGLE

AREA TO BE PLANED

OAK BATTENS

TEMPORARY SCREWS

SCARPH JIG

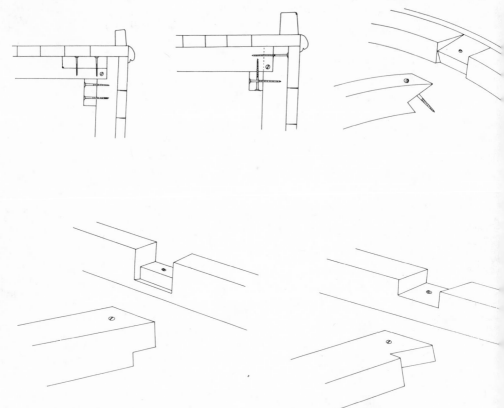

Figure 56   Joinery used in deck beam construction in light wooden hulls

dicular with the waterline, or with a slight tumble-home. The top of the rail cap should be level with the waterline.

Scuppers must be cut into the bottom edge of toe rails and railings to drain water off the deck. These are located along the lowest portion of the sheer line and extended some distance fore and aft. To avoid staining the topsides, a shallow groove or cove should be cut into the lower edge of the guard rail or sheer molding to catch the water from the deck and to allow it to fall clear of the planking.

Where cabin trunks are built from conventional timber, several methods of construction are optional (Figure 58). The main supporting members here are the corner posts, which should be through bolted to both the deck beams and carlins. The sides and end plank may be either lapped, mortised, or rabbeted as shown. In very heavily built craft intended for hard service, cabin trunks and particularly engine cases may be made up from stock 2 by 4 inches or heavier timbers with their edges dovetailed and through fastened with drifts.

Considerable savings in hardware costs can be effected by making up cleats and other fittings from hardwood, preferably locust (Figure 59). Such fittings must always be through fastened by bolting them to backing pieces under the decking. In cases where these fittings are placed on the centerline, they may be secured by bolting into the king plank. If placed outboard of the centerline, doubling pieces are secured between the deck beams.

Examples of joinery for cabin and interior fittings such as cabinets and drawers are shown on Figure 60. These are as used in shore-based cabinet building, and other optional types may be found in any standard textbook on the subject. Whether much fine joinery is incorporated into the boat's interior is optional with the builder, but good construction for doors and windows is essential for proper weather protection and acceptable appearance. Examples of commonly used sash construction are shown in Figure 61. The vertical frames are known as styles, the upper and lower members are

Figure 57 Construction details for railings in light and heavy wooden hulls

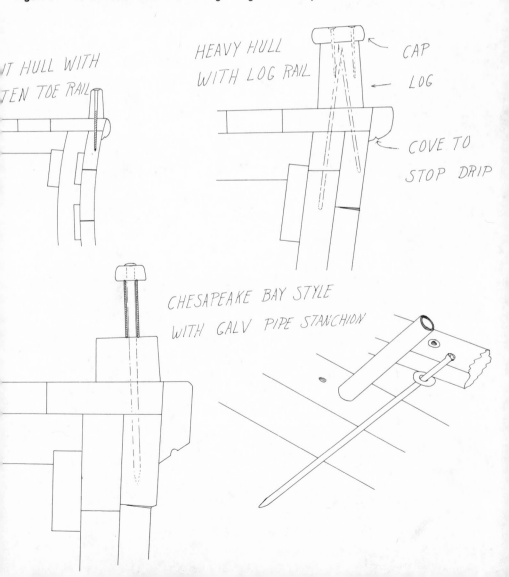

known as rails. The corners may be fastened as shown with either tenons or pegs, or lapped. The inner sides of the styles and rails may be routed and stopped for making a glass window, or grooved for fitting plywood panels for doors. Grooving is seldom used for windows, as replacement of the glass would involve dismantling the window framing. In some cases windows and doors made up for marine use are irregular in shape, such as in the forward end of a pilot house or steering shelter where the roof line follows the curve of the sheer line. Methods of framing various types of cabins, deckhouses, and steering shelters are shown in the volume on building the V-bottom boat.

Plywood panels may be lengthened or enlarged by butting (Figure 62). In cases where a smooth joint is required, such as in ripped out plywood planking or where the presence of a plain butt would spoil the appearance,

Figure 58   Details of trunk cabin and deckhouse construction used in heavy hulls

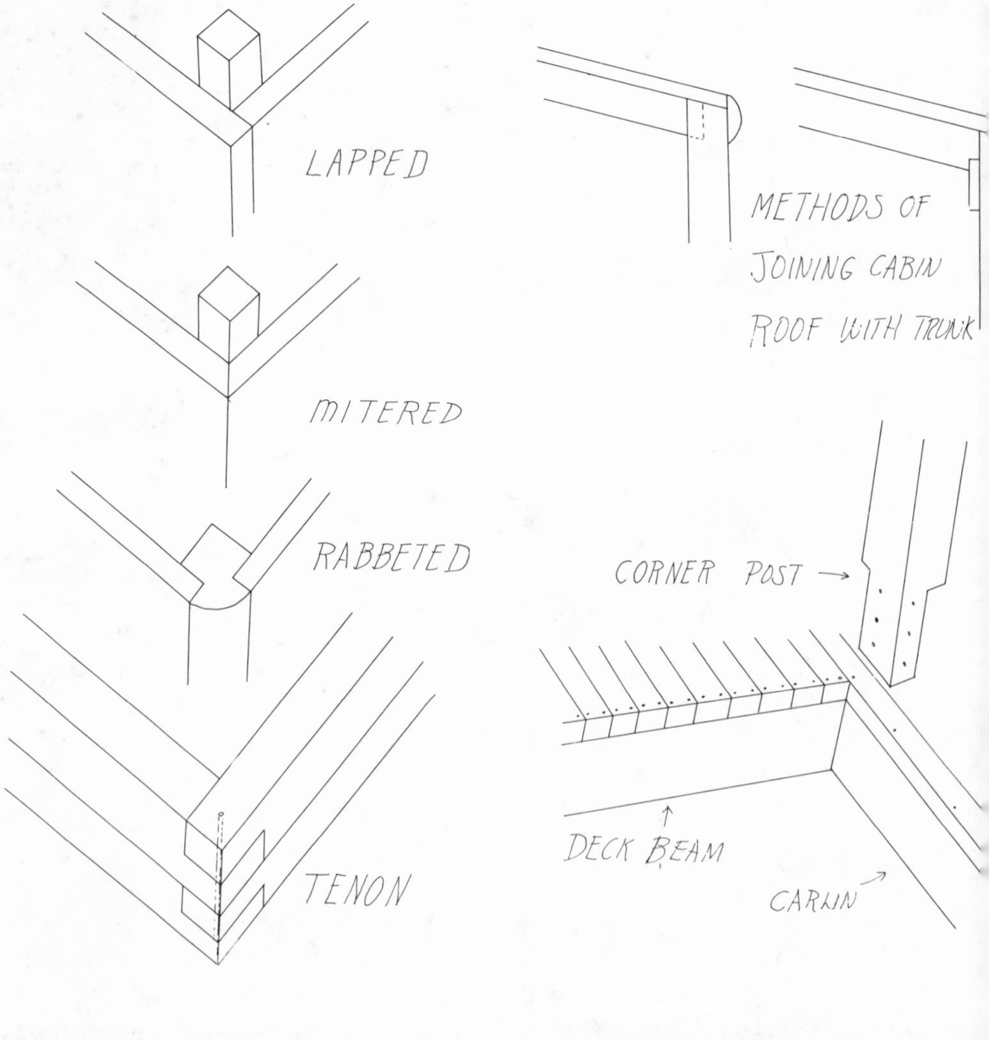

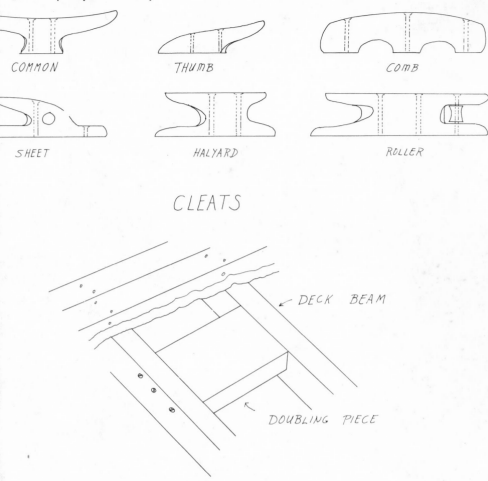

COMMON   THUMB   COMB

SHEET   HALYARD   ROLLER

CLEATS

DECK BEAM

DOUBLING PIECE

Figure 59 Various types of wooden cleats and their method of attachment

splicing is possible if the proper technique is employed. The ends of the material are first beveled, using a plank template that is planed to the proper angle. The degree of the bevel is determined by the thickness of the plywood, this dimension being from 2-to-6 inches for commonly used thicknesses of from ¼-to-1 inch stock. The end of the plywood is temporarily fastened to the template by a screw that is countersunk to clear the plane blade. Each portion of the splice is made identical to the other to insure a straight or level joint between the completed panel.

The splice is secured with epoxy adhesive using a press as shown (Figure 62). The beveled edges of the material are laid together in proper position and a series of pencil marks are made along the outer edges to insure an accurate fit. The adhesive is then applied to each surface, and the ends are clamped together. A duck tail clamp is preferred, as the wooden feet will not bruise the work. Household waxed paper or foil should be wrapped around the splice to contain the adhesive.

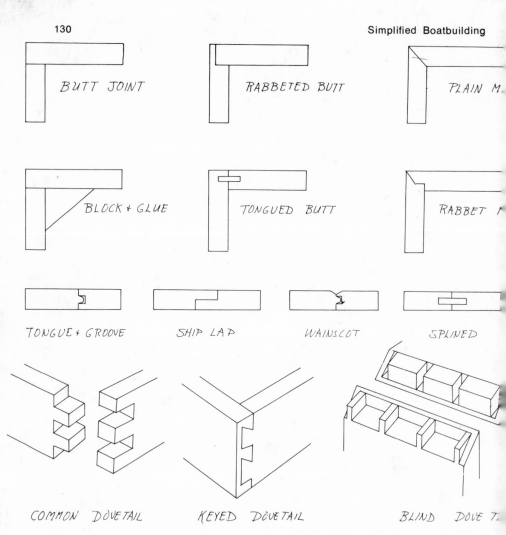

Figure 60 Typical procedures used in small boat joinery

Small sailing craft and power launches with cruising accommodations require special attention to sleeping arrangements to conserve space and to secure the occupants against the motion of the boat (Figure 63).

The box berth is most commonly seen, and its structure is as its name implies. The sides and bottom are made up of light pine or fir planking or hardwood in yachts of fine finish. Where weight saving is an advantage, ⅜-inch plywood is favored, and here the edges must be framed with squared battens as fastening pieces. Several hardwood slats should be placed under the bottom extending across the berth to avoid sagging. The height may vary as to the opinion of the builder, many favoring rather deep sides if the boat is to be used for offshore cruising. The length of an average berth should be at least 6 feet 6 inches long for general use, and not less than 22 inches wide. In some cases the foot end is made more narrow, as where this extends into a restricted area such as near the bow.

Pipe berths are fitted where space below is limited and where it is an advantage to fold up the berths when not in use. The frame is made up of common galvanized pipe, and should be of at least ¾-inch diameter for proper rigidity. A "T" fitting will allow a short nipple to be threaded on for fitting into a vertical part of the cabin framing. The most secure outboard fitting is a pair of chains which will not stretch to allow sagging. A more compact pipe berth may be made up from two lengths of pipe and a section of canvas with sleeves sewn into the outer edges. The berth is stowed by simply rolling up the outside pipe.

Cupboards and dressers with shelves and drawers or both in combination are made up similarly to land-based cabinets, except that special provision

Figure 61   Three types of joinery used in making up window sash

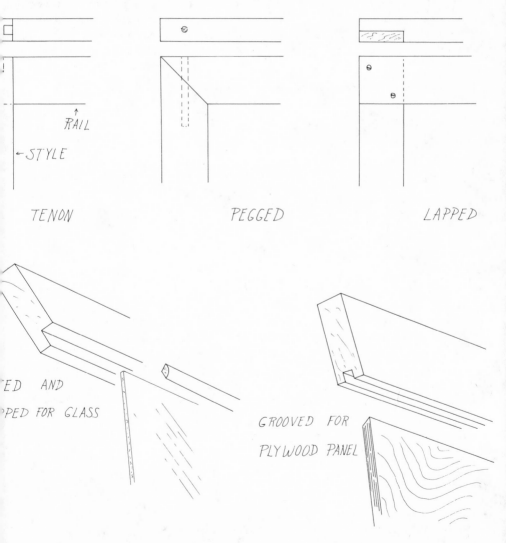

must be made to keep objects from falling out or being shifted due to the motion of the boat. Cups may be hung on hooks, and stops with vertical grooves will secure plates. Removable stops across the outer edges of the shelves will secure miscellaneous objects.

Ice boxes present a problem of leakage of fresh water from melting ice causing dry rot in wooden hulls. Dry rot may also occur behind the case because of the lack of air circulation, so the structure should be made so as to be readily demounted for periodic inspection. The one shown in the drawing is an example of a small-sized structure for a small cruising boat (Fig. 63). The exterior is made from marine plywood well painted inside and out. A layer of cork is fitted inside as a lining and faced with light gauge galvanized sheet metal. A drain is provided under the ice compartment, and should be connected to a through-hull fitting provided with a seacock.

The convertible dinette has, in recent years, become an almost universal arrangement in even very small pleasure and commercial craft. The structure is laid out so that the table top may be demounted and placed between the edges of the seats, the cushions then are rearranged to form a

Figure 62   A method of butting plywood panels

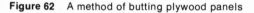

PLYWOOD BUTT JOINT

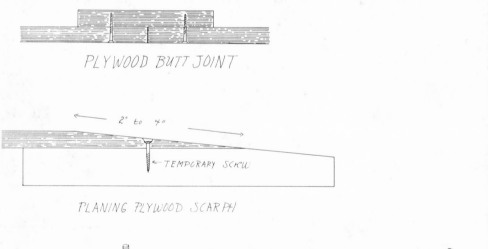

PLANING PLYWOOD SCARPH

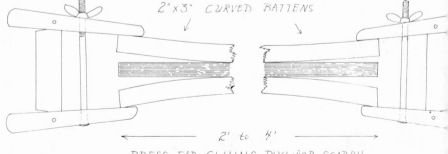

PRESS FOR GLUING PLYWOOD SCARPH

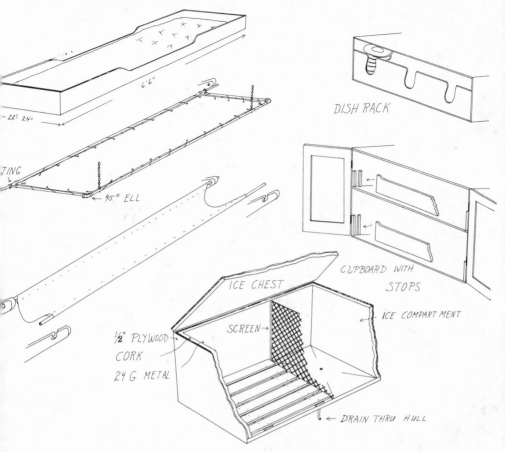

Figure 63 Details of berth, dishrack, and cupboard construction for cabins

mattress. The general dimensions of a dinette are shown in Figure 64, the width being optional to suit the space available or the needs of the builder. If a slightly oversize berth is required, the width of the seats may be increased somewhat. The table top is attached to the wall by means of a pair of hooks, and is supported at its outboard edge by a hinged leg. Two pair of bolt latches under the outer edge of this engage their opposite halves under the fronts of the seats.

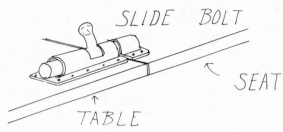

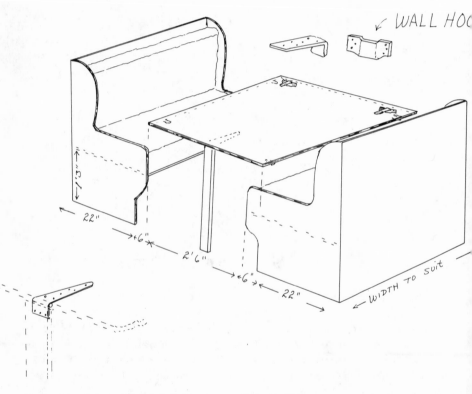

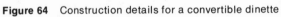

Figure 64   Construction details for a convertible dinette

11

Power for the Small Boat

The selection of the proper power plant for the small motor launch, motor sailer, or auxiliary sailboat is of prime importance for adequate performance, safe handling, and acceptable economy of first cost and running operation. As there is a bewildering array of power plants in an infinite variety of types and sizes on the market today, it is necessary to analyze carefully the requirements of the boat under consideration.

The Internal Combustion Engine

The internal combustion engine burning gasoline or diesel fuel is the power plant of choice for most small boats. Most people are generally familiar with their principles of operation through general acquaintance with automobile and truck units. The application of this power to motorboats, however, presents a number of considerations that are vastly different from their use in land-based vehicles. It is obvious that driving a boat's hull through a surrounding medium of water involves resistance factors not present with a land vehicle that carries its weight upon free-turning wheels in contact with only a few square inches of road surface.

In considering the ability of an internal combustion engine to do useful work, the familiar term "horsepower" immediately comes to mind. While this designation gives some indication of potential engine power in a general sense, it is in reality subordinated to a more important but less-known consideration known as torque. This term describes the amount of force or twisting motion that an engine delivers at the crankshaft to produce actual working power. The amount of this energy is measured in pounds, or "foot pounds," to use an engineering term, and is the true index of actual driving power that the engine produces.

As internal combustion engines are employed in a wide variety of uses, individual torque characteristics vary widely, even in engines of similar size and indicated horsepower development. Torque output is, therefore, prede-

termined when the engine is originally designed and varies as to whether
the engine is to be operated at high or low crankshaft speeds. Factors governing torque output are piston displacement, valve timing or port arrangement in the case of two-cycle types, carburetor breathing, and combustion
chamber shape. Engines designed for continuous heavy service have a
torque output at moderate crankshaft speeds. Those designed for intermittent high-speed operation run at much higher rates, and develop their maximum torque output or driving power at higher points on their power curve.

The advertised horsepower ratings of internal combustion engines tend to
be misleading, as few of them are ever called upon to deliver this power for
any appreciable length of time. These ratings are generally taken from read-
ings at full power and derived from laboratory testing at the factory under
ideal conditions. The engines are run on dynamometers without the power-
absorbing impediments of cooling fans, generators, clutches, or transmis-
sions. Conditions of temperature, humidity, and barometric pressure are
subject to control and optimum conditions for carburetor breathing or fuel
injection are provided. Such tests indicate power impossible to obtain under
normal conditions, and represent only a theoretical performance that can
never be reproduced again. If the usual engine is actually subjected to prolonged full power operation in service use it would soon disintegrate from
the internal stresses produced. While horsepower ratings are given much
sales publicity, reports of actual working torque characteristics are often difficult to obtain.

Some of the common misunderstandings concerning engine power in
boats may be attributed to the fact that most of the smaller marine engines
today, whether gasoline or diesel, are actually conversions of automotive,
truck, tractor, or stationary industrial units. As the public has long been
conditioned to advertised horsepower ratings, it is often erroneously assumed that these indicate the working capabilities of an engine. A rough
guide to the actual output of the commonly used car gasoline engine can be
measured by the fuel consumption. A modern engine in a good state of tune
will consume approximately one gallon per hour for each 11 horsepower de-
livered at the shaft. An example of this could be taken in the case of a 6-cyl-
inder engine of 234 cubic inches piston displacement rated at 110 horsepower at 4,000 revolutions per minute. This engine driving a semiplaning
launch of moderate weight and turning a three-bladed 13-by-10-inch propeller consumes three gallons of fuel per hour at half throttle. It can then be
concluded that the engine is turning out 33 working horsepower at somewhere near its most efficient torque output to drive the boat at cruising
speed.

In the final analysis, the diameter and pitch of the propeller must be selected to suit the requirements of the boat in question as the first consideration. The proper engine must then be selected with the proper torque characteristics to drive it. In this consideration, the matter of the rather narrow
rotative limits of any given propeller for best efficiency will be recalled, as
discussed in the section on propellers. Many small motor boats are ineffi-

ciently powered with fast-turning engines that can swing only small propellers with dimensions that will allow the engine to turn up to the speeds conducive to its best power development. In these cases, it is best to fit reduction gears to enable the engine to turn high enough to develop adequate power. While the problem of mating a small engine to an adequately sized propeller is primarily found in the case of heavy displacement hulls, faster planing or semiplaning types may also require larger propellers for enhanced efficiency. Many of the faster types show better speed and reduced fuel consumption with 1½-1 or 2-1 reduction gearing which enables employing the most efficient portion of the torque band of the engine.

The Gasoline Engine

The gasoline engine is the power of choice for vast numbers of small pleasure and commercial boats for its low first cost, availability, and high power development in its modern form. Most powerboat engines in use today are conversions of popular makes of car engines and provide reliable and trouble-free service if properly converted and installed. The small single or twin-cylinder models used in small auxiliary sailing craft and skiffs are usually conversions of water-cooled industrial engines. For heavy-duty service, car, stationary industrial, or truck and tractor engines are converted to marine use as their design for continuous running and high torque output at moderate speeds is of economic advantage.

The auto engine replaced the true marine power plant only when advanced design and modern lubrication capabilities and metallurgy enabled it to meet the demands of marine service. This was not true in the earlier days of boating, as the usual marine engine was rather heavily built and developed only moderate power from its rather mild compression ratios and valve timing in the interests of reliability and longevity. The price of these engines was rather high as production runs were low and many manufacturers were catering to a limited market. The first auto conversions were homemade adaptations of commercial fishermen who were naturally interested in the lowest possible cost. A discarded car or truck engine purchased from some wrecking yard was cheap and universally available. The results were often satisfactory, but only if the engine was properly converted to marine use and thoroughly rebuilt or overhauled. As the modern car engine can operate for six figure mileages with but routine maintenance in even low-priced cars, it can equal the true marine engine if intelligently employed in a powerboat.

Many converted engines are manufactured and sold ready for installation, with various options as to transmission and reduction gearing. It is also possible to obtain professionally engineered conversion equipment adaptable to an engine the owner buys himself at a considerable saving in cost. In these cases it is essential to select the proper engine for the boat in question, and to be sure that the engine itself is in good condition, or overhauled if required.

In an actual conversion, watercooling is substituted for the usual radiator, and proper mounting lugs, transmission, and backfire arrestor for the carburetor must be fitted. It is also good practice to fit an alternator-type ignition, as this provides battery charging capabilities even though the engine is run at long periods of idling. While conversion equipment marketed today is pretty well standardized, there is a wide option as to the type of transmission offered. As this last item is the most expensive part of the conversion, alterations to the usual car manual shifting gear box are sometimes resorted to. The land-based declutching technique cannot be used. The propeller working in water rotates freely and does not exert braking action on the shaft as do wheels on the ground, allowing the gears to clash excessively. In these cases, first and second gears are blanked out, retaining only top gear and reverse ratios. Reversing is effected by slowing the engine to an idle and then gentle moving the gear lever to the reverse position without declutching. A thrust bearing is necessary, as the motion in the shaft puts undue pressure in the transmission gears themselves. While this adaptation will work after a fashion, it must be carefully used and will not stand up to hard service. Another transmission conversion sometimes used in small commercial fishing launches is to lock the gear train in second where this ratio functions as a primitive reduction gear. While this somewhat enhances the possibilities of propeller efficiency, control of the boat is restricted through lack of any reversing mechanism and is only suited for use where maneuvering around docks or other craft is at a minimum. Another disadvantage is that the locked transmission and solidly fixed propeller and shaft constitute excessive drag in starting and puts an extra load on the starter and battery output. At best such devices are but makeshift transmission arrangements.

If an engine is to be converted by the owner, it is necessary to select one with manual transmission, as automatic shifting types cannot be used due to lack of braking power from the propeller. In some cases it is possible to obtain clutch-type flywheel replacements for these models. The concerns marketing conversion equipment can advise the owner on various makes of engines, and the availability of the necessary parts.

Power requirements in boats are discussed under another heading, as is the necessity for obtaining the proper type of propeller. It is necessary to ascertain if the engine has the proper torque capabilities to turn the correct size of propeller. Most manufacturers of marine equipment can supply the necessary data. Many car conversions function more efficiently with reduction gearing, especially if of high-speed type where their best torque development is high on their revolution spectrum. If first cost is a consideration, and the expense of reduction gears is a limiting factor, it is often best to select a truck or tractor engine for conversion, especially in displacement pleasure cruisers or light commercial craft, as these engines operate at moderate revolutions and have enhanced torque output at more usable propeller speeds.

The gasoline engine is not an economical machine in larger sizes and when run for prolonged periods at high speed its high fuel consumption requires large tank capacity for wide cruising range. This transportation of large quantities of highly volatile fuel obviously contains an element of hazard. Its low cost, availability, and high power to weight ratio for high speed in small launches, however, makes it an attractive proposition.

The Outboard Engine

The modern outboard engine is approaching the capabilities of the inboard engine in durability and longevity. It has a number of advantages that make it the power of choice for a variety of small boat types, as it is marketed in many sizes of model and horsepower rating. The fitting of electric starting to the larger types has made it an engine anyone can operate. Its chief distinguishing characteristic is its portability as a self-contained power unit. While the larger and heavier models are too heavy to be portable in the usual sense, they can be readily removed from the boat for storage or servicing by means of a small crane. While the original intent of the outboard engine was the powering of small rowing skiffs, the modern power plants require hulls of special design for the most efficient performance. Its high power-to-weight ratio makes it efficient power for fast-planing hulls, and its position at the stern is of advantage when a boat rests mostly on its after hull sections in the planing attitude. Heavy duty outboards are now marketed for commercial service. Their engines are derated for continuous running, and some models are fitted with bronze propellers and gear cases that are more resistant to corrosion than the die cast aluminum alloys used in the usual light high-speed types intended only for intermittent running. Outboard engines have lately been introduced into the more undeveloped countries of the world to power various canoes, dugouts, or raft-type boats to aid native fishermen in producing larger catches. Long shaft models are available for various transom heights, and these models also find favor as auxiliary power in small sailing craft. As these heavy-duty models have 2-to-1 or 3-to-1 reduction gearing, they can turn substantially sized propellers at very efficient speeds.

Most outboard engines are of the two-stroke type, and suffer in comparison with the four-stroke in the matter of fuel consumption. While this is not of great importance in small motors, fuel expense in the large types is quite an item if the engine is operated more or less continuously. The commonly seen light-duty types have corrosion problems with their light alloy gear cases and propellers, but this can be minimized somewhat by tilting the engine when not in use. One of the chief drawbacks to outboard efficiency until recently has been the lack of suitable propeller options available for various types of boats. As most outboard propellers were of the "square" type, of equal diameter and pitch, engine revolutions in heavy boats were held down so that they were unable to develop full power when larger diameters and shallower pitch would have been more suitable. With the more recent marketing of mass-produced boat and engine combinations, manufacturers are paying more attention to propeller efficiency and a wide selection of wheels is available for various types of service.

While it is a simple matter to fit an outboard engine on the transom of a small boat, there are certain considerations that must be observed for best efficiency. The cavitation plate above the propeller should be immersed at least an inch below the load-waterline when the boat is at rest and should also be in line with the bottom of the transom to avoid drag. The top of the transom can be cut away, or, in some cases, padded up, to obtain the correct immersion. The shaft should stand in a vertical position which fixes the propeller in an exact horizontal position in relation to the load-waterline. If the engine cants forward the propeller tends to drive the bow of the boat down. If it tilts aft, the engine wastes its power exerting a lever effect against the transom, and the bow may be pulled too far up, immersing the transom with excessive drag. These adjustments can be made by repositioning the stop in the hangar bracket. In each instance the tilting hinge or pivot should be checked for free motion so the unit will automatically swing upward if an underwater obstruction is struck while underway. The clamp screws should be checked periodically for tightness to avoid vibration and possible loss of the motor.

In outboard installations it is essential that the transom structures of the boat are solidly built to counteract engine vibration and propeller thrust, and any weakness here will cause the side plank fastenings to the transom and knees to loosen and invite leaks. This is especially critical in cases where a boat is repowered with a larger engine. As many small boats have a rather deep notch cut into the transom to correctly position propeller immersion, it is often advisable to fit a false transom a little forward of the motor to keep water out of the hull when running ahead of a following sea. Many large runabouts or small cruising launches fitted with large, heavy engines show this weakness. Many small outboard boats benefit from fitting an engine a few inches longer than standard, rather than cutting the transom notch excessively low.

Due to the weight of some of the more powerful engines, a fast runabout or cruiser must be specially designed for proper performance. The hull should be wide enough aft to keep the stern from squatting at speed. The hull should have adequate bearing surface and displacement to cope with the rather high top weight of the power head. Some small runabout types are often excessively overpowered with large engines, and can be dangerous if run at high speed or in choppy water by inexperienced persons. It is always best to consult the manufacturer in regard to the size of boat to be used with various engines.

Small outboard launches of either pleasure or commercial type used for limited offshore work benefit from having the motor mounted somewhat inboard of the stern on a false transom extending the driving unit down through a well. This should open right out aft through an opening in the main transom so that water cannot drag as it is thrown back from the thrust of the propeller. The extra flotation from the sides of the hull makes for a more level ride, and holds the bow down against pounding in a head wind or chop. The power head is also more protected against solid water or spray from following seas.

In small displacement hulls or in double-ended craft, such as banks dories, a low-powered outboard engine is sometimes fitted in a well that opens through the bottom of the hull. This arrangement works well in small boats used offshore where the engine weight is concentrated to a greater degree toward the center of the hull. The boat may be steered either by turning the engine, or with a conventional rudder hung on the transom. The power head is further protected from moisture. Such wells should be carefully designed, however, as a mere boxlike aperture will allow the power unit to pump water right up its sides and into the boat. The well should have a broad sloping bottom aft of the motor to smooth out the waterflow. The engine may also choke up from monoxide fumes trapped in the well that interfere with carburetor breathing. In some cases a large diameter pipe let into the sides of the well and through the outer sides of the hull is necessary for monoxide expulsion.

While it is possible to attach an outboard to almost any type of hull, or to carry long-shaft type engines with large geared down propellers for emergency use in main propulsion failure, it is generally not advisable to convert boats of substantial size from inboard to outboard power. The loss of weight admidships from the removal of the inboard upsets the designer's stability calculations, complicated by the high weight of the power head aft. It is sometimes possible to counteract these changes by ballasting, but most such conversions are of doubtful efficiency.

With the development and engineering refinements that have been incorporated in the modern outboard, small boat designers have developed some very practical and efficient boat-engine combinations.

The Inboard-Outboard Drive

The modern inboard-outboard drive has been developed to incorporate the best points of both inboard and outboard engines. The usual inboard car-type power plant, in both gasoline and light, high-speed diesel form, is coupled to an outdrive unit that allows the drive shaft to extend through the transom. This is attached to an outboard engine underwater unit driven through chains or metalized belts transferring the power to the propeller shaft. The boat is steered by pivoting the drive through a gear control led to the control station on the boat. The drive unit is also fitted to be swiveled upward, as in the case of the outboard engine's transom bracket. It will lift automatically if an obstruction is encountered, and may be rotated manually to aid in beaching, trailer loading, servicing, or changing propellers.

The use of a four-cycle engine or light diesel offers better economy than the more thirsty two-cycle outboard, and the former is generally more quiet and less prone to vibrate. The aft position of the power plant gives more unobstructed cockpit or cabin space and gives the designer wider latitude in planning interior accommodation. The concentration of engine weight aft helps the speed in semiplaning or planing hulls, as in the case of the outboard. Due to the somewhat greater weight of the large engines used, the hulls must be specially designed for correct weight and balance factors, and the units are generally not applicable in boats designed for conventional inboard power. The only disadvantage appears to be handling problems in small boats used in rough water due to weight concentration aft and the overly wide sterns seen in some smaller types. The cost of the unit must also be weighed against the advantages when planning the design.

Light Steam Power

The attraction of light steam power is its simplicity, silence, reliability, longevity, and in the unobtrusive manner in which it operates. Its disadvantages are the weight and bulk of its boiler and rather high fuel consumption, although low cost coal or hardwood can be used. Steam launches are also rather slow, 6-to-8 knots being the general rule unless impractical, expensive, and complicated condensing turbine engines are employed.

There are not a few boatmen interested in steam power as it has a certain unique appeal to those with a feeling for things nostalgic or for small craft with a dash of character. A few firms both in the United States and abroad market small steam engine units of reasonable cost that are ideally suited to this purpose. As the steam engine is a high-torque type producing a driving power far above its modest horsepower ratings, it requires a large-diameter propeller of high pitch. As an efficient power boat, the steam engine is best installed in the old-style, narrow-beamed, easy-driving fantail launch, with plenty of room under the counter to swing the large wheel. With the contemporary development of small atomic reactors for firing steam boilers, light steam power may again become significant in practical small boat propulsion.

The Crude Oil Engine

The heavy-duty, two-cycle marine engine burning crude oil is widely used in various parts of the world to power both large and small boats, although to date it has not been employed extensively in the United States. It is commonly known as the semi-diesel, but this term is a misnomer as it does not operate on the diesel principle.

The crude oil engine was developed during the same period as the diesel, similarly as a low-cost substitute for stationary industrial steam power, with an early adaptation for ship propulsion. Its European developers utilized both two- and four-cycle types, but later concentrated on the former as being more efficient and cheaper to manufacture. The engine operates on the two-stroke cycle as invented by Sir Dugald Clerk, but is further simplified by the elimination of the conventional carburetor and electric ignition. The fuel is forced into the combustion chamber by an injector pump activated by an eccentric on the crankshaft which times its injection to the proper sequence. Ignition is effected by a glow plug of low-heating-point alloy fixed in the cylinder head. This is preheated by a blow torch before starting. Compressed air is used to crank the engine, the air bottles being charged between starts by a pump run off the crankshaft. The fuel valve is then turned on and the heat of the glow plug induces initial fuel combustion. The running cycle is continued from the high temperatures in the combustion chamber created by the moderately high compression ratio.

The crude oil engine is less economical of fuel than the diesel as its compression pressures are somewhat lower. This disadvantage is offset somewhat by its ability to run on very crude grades of fuel oil, other low grades of oil distillates, or even seal oil.

As a consequence of their large cylinder capacities, crude oil engines operate at crankshaft speeds of from 200 to 500 revolutions per minute, but have good torque output because of the inherent characteristics of the two-cycle principle. The primitive simplicity of these engines is enhanced by the fact that most of them are built in single cylinder sizes, with capacities up to 100 horsepower. The smaller sizes are seldom fitted to boats of less than 30 feet long because of their great weight. The massive construction and the low crankshaft speeds and moderate operating pressures make them very long-lived and many are reported to run for thirty or forty years with but routine maintenance. When minor attention is necessary, it can usually be accomplished by semiskilled mechanics.

As a working engine, the type is commonly used in heavy fishing trawlers or small coastal freighters, although some installations have been made in cruising yachts. A late refinement has been the fitting of variable pitch propellers which increases running economy and maneuverability.

The Diesel Engine

The internal combustion engine burning stove oil was invented in Germany by Dr. Rudolph Diesel in the closing years of the last century. It is similar in principle to the gasoline engine, and may be designed to operate on either the two- or four-stroke cycle. The power stroke is activated by subjecting the fuel to very high compression ratios, the high temperature thus produced causing ignition of the fuel. Fuel intake is by injection of the fuel into the combustion chamber by means of high pressure atomizing nozzles, the proper injection sequence being timed by small pumps geared to the crank or camshaft.

The diesel was originally intended as a more economical and compact replacement for the steam engine used as stationary industrial power, but it was soon adapted to large ship propulsion. The early diesels were very large and heavily built machines in relation to their power development to cope with the high pressures and temperatures involved in their operation. Modern diesels operate at increased pressures, but engineering refinements and the advance of metallurgical science have enabled their adaptation to power and weight ratios that compare favorably with gasoline engines of similar horsepower. This has enabled wide employment in automotive, light marine, agricultural, and light industrial applications. Further refinements include supercharging devices that greatly increase power, and the development of air cooling which reduces overall weight.

The diesel is much more efficient than the gasoline engine. Its high compression ratios and high temperatures extract much more energy from a given volume of fuel, with the advantage that a diesel will run more than twice as long on a gallon of fuel that costs one half as much. The safety factor in utilizing a nonvolatile and nonexplosive fuel is of particular interest to boatmen. As a highly efficient engine, the diesel produces a comparatively higher torque output at more moderate crankshaft speeds. This means that a diesel will swing a larger propeller at more efficient crankshaft speeds than its gasoline counterpart.

The elimination of electric ignition and the usual carburetor further simplifies maintenance and enhances dependability, as these two items constitute 90% of gasoline engine breakdowns. The diesel will operate under conditions of moisture that would readily short-circuit electric ignition. As a precision machine subjected to careful manufacture, the diesel will operate more than twice as long as a gasoline engine before even minor overhauls are necessary.

Three admitted disadvantages of the diesel are its somewhat greater weight, rough running and vibration due to high operating pressures, and somewhat noisy exhaust. In recent years, however, these factors have been all but eliminated due to advanced design. The weight factor is somewhat reduced in boating use in that with its lower fuel requirement, an ordinary diesel installation may actually be lighter in the overall sense due to the need for smaller fuel tank capacity.

With the wide ranges of marine diesels marketed today, there is a power plant for every boat. They range from small, single-cylinder air- or water-cooled models for small sailing auxiliaries or skiffs, up to large but lightweight, high-speed, multicylinder engines for fast runabouts and sports cruisers. The ultimate selection of a diesel engine for boat power depends upon initial costs. Due to its design requirements, it cannot, in the foreseeable future, be as cheaply produced as a comparable gasoline engine, even in high production runs. The average diesel will show a purchase price of from two to three times that of gasoline power. The replacement or initial installation of a diesel is largely determined by the running time of the boat during a working year or pleasure boat season. Fuel costs, of course, make a diesel engine mandatory in commercial craft subjected to long seasonal or continuous operation. A few fishing launches used in short working seasons, and many pleasure boats operating for limited distances benefit from gasoline installations where fuel costs would take several years to offset the higher price of a diesel engine. Even at that, the safety and longevity factors still make the diesel the best choice in most instances.

Some boatmen still look upon the diesel as a heavy-duty engine offering complexities beyond their ability to service and maintain. This is not true with today's modern engines. Each manufacturer supplies the new owner with a comprehensive manual fully describing operating and servicing procedures which can be carried out by even the nonmechanical owner. The growing popularity of the modern diesel engine is a sound indication of its obvious advantages.

The Two-Cycle Inboard Engine

The two-stroke-cycle type represents the simplest form of the internal combustion engine. It utilizes the movement of the piston within the cylinder to uncover ports cast in the cylinder wall for the intake of the fuel mixture into the combustion chamber, and for the expulsion of exhaust gases. This cycle is activated by compressing the fuel mixture within the crankcase, the carburetor intake feeding directly into it. Aside from its simplicity, a further advantage of the two-cycle engine is its power stroke at each revolution of the crankshaft that produces even power impulses and smooth running. This feature also gives a torque output that exceeds that of four-stroke engines of comparable piston displacement.

The two-cycle is familiar to boatmen in most outboard motors. It is also widely used in light industrial and domestic applications for powering light machinery, pumps, lawn mowers, and in lightweight, high performance motorcycles. As an inboard marine engine, it is usually recalled only by the older generation of boatmen. In the earlier days of power boating, the comparatively lighter weight of the two-cycle was an attraction in an age of massive and overly heavy engines, and it was the most common form of power in pioneer motor launches. With but three internal moving parts—piston, connecting rod, crankshaft—and ignition produced by dry cell batteries through a simple coil and timing device, it served as a logical introduction to the then-mysterious internal combustion engine. As the heavy-duty, two-cycle with generous piston displacement cannot be made to turn at high revolutions, the growing mania for speed focused attention on the development of the four-stroke type. During the decade following the First World War, the two-cycle gradually fell out of favor. Perhaps one reason for its decline at that time was the rapid wear experienced by its main bearings due to the uncertain metallurgy of the time. This lead to a falling off of power due to loss of crankcase compression, coupled with a reluctance to start readily. Domestic manufacture waned as one maker after another fell by the wayside, and finally ceased altogether during World War II. A few boatmen and commercial fishermen, however, still remain loyal to the type, and two-cycle engines in refined and highly developed form are still being manufactured by two firms in Nova Scotia (Figure 65). Aside from its ability to

Figure 65   The two-cycle single cylinder 6 hp. Acadia gasoline engine

drive heavy displacement boats at moderate speed, its signal advantage is its moderate initial cost due to its inherent simplicity. It is particularly favored in remote parts of the world where the usual service facilities are lacking. Even a novice can adjust and tune the engine without difficulty, and overhauls may be undertaken with a screwdriver and a few wrenches.

The modern two-cycle inboard engine has a definite place in economical boating where heavy, displacement hulls are to be driven at moderate speeds. As a high-torque engine, it can turn large propellers at very efficient rotative speeds which are disproportionate to its modest horsepower ratings. As it is manufactured in a wide variety of one- and two-cylinder models of from 3-to-20 horsepower, in the larger sizes it will power very large boats. While it is ordinarily not fitted with reverse gears, the engine may be made to run backward by manipulating the ignition switch. This further serves to reduce initial costs and maintenance complications.

Two types of ignition systems are available to the purchaser. The jump spark type uses a high tension coil to step up the current from dry cell batteries, and is connected to an ordinary spark plug. The make-and-break system uses low tension current, ignition being effected by a spring-loaded trigger device within the cylinder head. While the former type offers more speed due to its ability to turn the engine faster, the latter is preferred for offshore work, as it is impervious to dampness and the engine will keep running even if doused with water.

A two-cycle inboard is very efficient and low-cost power for moderate-speed launches of easy lines, and is particularly recommended for small sailing auxiliaries for its ability to swing a large propeller. Fuel economy, while not ordinarily an outstanding trait of the two-cycle, is acceptable in the heavy-duty, slow-speed type. A little over one-half pint per horsepower hour is required, and a small quantity of lubricating oil is mixed with the gasoline. As a further concession to economy, one maker offers a kerosene-burning engine that is started on gasoline and run on kerosene after the intake manifold is warmed up.

While the inboard two-cycle requires manual starting, and a little experimentation with carburetor and ignition controls to attain proper running adjustment, it has a certain appeal to the mechanically minded owner who might find an individualistic type of power plant an attraction. In the proper type of boat, the heavy-duty, inboard, two-cycle is an economical and efficient type of engine that will outlast its owner.

V-Drive Units

The V-drive unit is similar to the inboard-outboard drive system in that the engine transfer case and shaft are also an integral unit. In this arrangement the engine is also placed at the stern, but the drive shaft faces forward. The gear case is either attached to the transmission housing, or is a short distance ahead of it and the propeller shaft then extends aft as in the case of the more usual engine-amidships configuration.

These units function similarly to the inboard-outboard drive in that the engine is at the stern. This is advantageous in high-speed launches in concentrating the main weight aft, and also gives more space through the center of the boat for an unobstructed cockpit or cabin arrangement. As in the case of the inboard-outboard type, the hull must be specially designed to compensate balance factors. The advantage of a rotating or swing-up underwater driving unit is not present, as the propeller shaft is fixed and requires the usual rudder arrangement. Various reduction gear options are available with this sytem, which, in some cases, is through the use of skew gears. The size of the engine gear wheel in relation to the transfer gear makes up the reduction ratio.

Powering Auxiliary Sailboats

The application of auxiliary power in sailing craft presents a number of problems due to the fact that sailing hulls are primarily designed for driving efficiency with the principal force centered at some distance above the waterline. This results in an elliptically shaped hull with gentle parabolic curves to minimize resistance factors. Most small sailing-cruising boats can be driven under sail at speed-length ratios of from 1.1 to 1.3, which represent their terminal or absolute hull velocity. Such hulls necessarily have very fine lines in the afterbody, and show an entirely different set of characteristics when an attempt is made to drive them under power. The very moderate resistance factors incorporated in their design allow them to attain speeds up to 1.1 quite easily, this being their speed in knots equal to the square root of their waterline length. If an attempt is made to drive them much faster, however, they merely squat and wallow without any appreciable increase in speed due to lack of bearing aft.

As a displacement boat, the sailing hull performs best with a rather large propeller turning at from 500 to 700 revolutions per minute, and with an engine of moderate horsepower but with high torque characteristics. This suggests the use of a small, heavy-duty, slow-speed engine. The small one- or two-cylinder diesels make ideal auxiliary power for moderate-sized sailing boats, as they are real working engines. The one- or two-cylinder, two-cycle type of heavy-duty gasoline engine is also favored, as they can turn very large propellers in relation to their horsepower ratings.

Small high-speed car-type engines whose torque capabilities allow them to turn only very small propellers at a high rotative speed are most inefficient, as the small propeller lacks sufficient driving power. If this type of engine is installed, reduction gearing must be fitted to enable the use of an adequately sized propeller.

Most auxiliary sailboats are fitted with two-bladed propellers as this enables stopping the propeller so that the blades are masked behind the deadwood for decreased resistance under sail. An ordinary, three-bladed propeller can create enough drag to spoil the sailing qualities of any small auxiliary.

Powering considerations for motor sailing craft are less easy to determine as there are many variations in this class of boat. Some of these are rather heavy displacement power boats with sail added for steadying purposes and have little sailing ability other than before the wind. Other types are best classified as powered sailing craft, as they lean toward sailing efficiency in hull design. In any case, it is best to select power capable of turning large propellers at moderate speeds for good driving efficiency.

The reliability and ruggedness of the modern outboard engine makes it useful in some of the smaller models as auxiliary power for small day-sailing boats and midget cruisers. The engine may be hung on the transom of open boats, fixed to special brackets, or set in an inboard well close to the stern. These make handy compact power plants that require no special equipment to install other than a mounting, and may be readily taken ashore when not in use. Power application is the same as in the case of the larger sailing craft; reduction gearing to enable the small high speed power head to turn as large a propeller as possible. In larger sailing boats, a heavy-duty commercial type outboard engine is the best choice, as it is best suited for prolonged periods of continuous running.

Marine Electrical Systems

Almost every small power launch or auxiliary sailing boat built today is fitted with an electrical system, particularly where the engines are arranged for electric starting. This is also true of the larger outboard engine installations which utilize storage batteries. In small craft constructed by amateurs or where previously built hulls are converted it is possible to install a satisfactory electrical system at moderate cost.

In general, such an installation may be regarded as having three main sections:

1. One or more generators to produce electrical energy.
2. A means of storing this energy in one or more secondary batteries.
3. A system of distribution to carry the electrical charge to lights and other services.

Electric generators may be classified into three main groups:

1. Generators supplied as an integral part of the engine by the manufacturers for electric starting.
2. Auxiliary generators belt-driven from the engine. Small hand-started diesel engines or heavy-duty gasoline engines fitted only with magneto ignition, and two-cycle engines fitted with jump spark or make-and-break ignition may have a power take-off pulley mounted on the propeller shaft.
3. Independent units in the form of either gasoline or diesel-powered generating sets that are self-contained and may be wholly automatic in operation.

Independent generating units are usually fitted to sail and power craft in lengths of over 45 feet, as the number of electrical services required renders propulsive engine generators impractical.

Main engine-driven and auxiliary belt-driven generators should be fitted with an automatic voltage regulator and cut-out. The purpose of the former is to compensate for variations in engine revolutions which would otherwise produce corresponding fluctuations in generator voltage with disastrous results. The cut-out will disconnect the battery or batteries from the generator when the engine is not running, or when it is running at such a reduced rate of revolution that the generator is generating less than battery voltage. Such regulation of the production of electrical current in marine installations is based on current automotive practice and has been subject to such refinement through many years of development as to be virtually trouble-free.

Two types of storage batteries in general use in marine installations are the conventional lead-acid, and the nickel-cadmium-alkaline type. The former, as developed for automotive use, is more generally supplied due to its satisfactory performance and moderate cost. The alkaline batteries have a higher initial cost but offer longer life and do not deteriorate if left standing uncharged for long periods. It is important to remember that if a lead-acid battery is replaced with an alkaline type the automatic voltage regulators must be readjusted to give the correct charging voltage.

Most modern marine engines are equipped with 12-volt systems which are much more dependable than the 6-volt type based on earlier automotive practice, particularly for engine starting purposes. Very large engines often have 24-volt systems for this reason. The independent charging units may be fitted with 24, 50, or 100-volt capacities, according to the size of the boat or its service requirements.

While most boats under 40 feet of overall length are fitted with generators activated by the propulsive engine, some small fishing boats or other commercial craft requiring winches, hoisting gear, large searchlights, or other heavy-duty appliances, are fitted with generator units enhanced for dependability, particularly for offshore employment.

The installation of independent charging sets and their attendant wiring and fittings in large craft is a job for specially trained electricians. Most professional builders of large craft retain the services of personnel trained by the manufacturer of these units to make such installations.

The installation of electrical systems activated by generators driven from the main engine for smaller boats is more simple, but is best undertaken by men with experience in this work. The labor cost is moderate and the material cost is the same in each case. However, if the builder has had some experience in electrical or electronic work, it is possible for a nonprofessional to install a satisfactory system if some special attention is given to the requirements of marine work.

Figure 66 shows a drawing of a simple 12-volt system that is suitable for a small power launch or auxiliary sailing boat. It will be noted that two batteries are fitted and that a large knife switch is placed between them so that either one will activate the system. This is included as a safety feature as

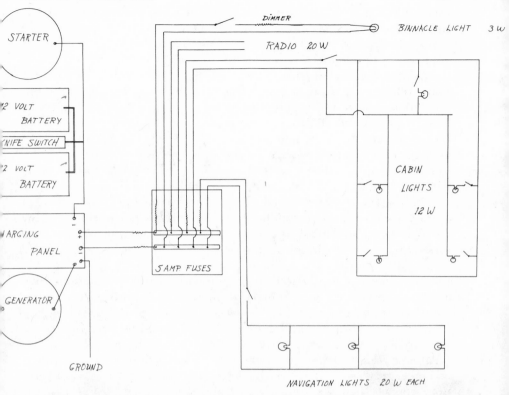

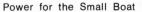

Figure 66   Diagram for a 12-volt electrical system for a small powerboat

both can be kept at full charge at all times. It is important in a low voltage system to keep the cables between the generator, the two batteries, and the charging panel as short as possible to minimize resistance. It is also important to keep the balance of the wiring as short as possible to minimize the dropping off of voltage at the fixtures at the outer ends. Cartridge-type fuses should also be used for the same reason. The wiring should be of 14- or 16-gauge and of the heavily insulated type. Specially armored wire for marine use is available, but any well-insulated commercial type will do. Soft metal clips should be used to fasten the wire to the boat's structure to avoid piercing the covering. Some builders install the wiring in metal or lead conduits, but there is danger here of galvanic corrosion throughout the boat in case of leaks. Galvanic action throughout the system is less likely to occur if the wires are carried high enough through the hull to be kept well away from the bilges. This situation is especially critical in metal hulls. In some cases, however, a ground wire may have to be run to a keel bolt if radio interference occurs while the engine is running. A stranded length of bare copper wire is then fitted from the negative or ground connection of the charging panel.

Twin-type double cables may be used for the wiring circuits, but where switches are to be placed at some distance from the lights it is just as well to use single cables throughout the system. Single cables generally have red in-sulation for the live side of the current connecting the fuses to the switches. Black cable is used from the bar in the fuse box to the lights.

In wiring up the cabin lights, a separate twin cable may be run to each fixture and is preferred where only a few lights are fitted at various loca-tions. Where four or six or even more lights are situated within a rather small area, a loop type circuit is better, as in the sketch (Figure 66), with twin wires running all around the cabin. Short wires are then cut in for each light, and all connections are carefully soldered. The advantage of this arrangement is that the voltage drop of each light is then equalized rather than becoming diminished toward the end of the circuit. Breakage of the wire will also not cause a failure in all of the lights in the system.

With low voltage lighting and current demand, the light wattages are re-stricted to either 12- or 15-watt lights. Due to this low power, shades or cov-ers over the lights should not be used, as condensation may occur inside these fixtures. Several lights of this power in an average small boat cabin will supply adequate illumination.

Special precautions should be taken to firmly secure the batteries against movement. A case made of substantial planking or ¾-inch plywood, lined with rubber sheeting, effectively protects the batteries from damage and should be well fastened to the framing. Covers should be fitted to keep the batteries in place in case the boat is thrown over on its beam ends.

All electrical fittings, such as light sockets, switches, through-deck fittings, and other small parts should be of the marine type to insure against corro-sion. Automotive or household-type fittings should be avoided as these will deteriorate in salt air within a very short time.

12

Propellers and Propulsive Systems

The selection of a proper propeller is essential for the most efficient and economical propulsion of a power boat. The designer usually specifies the type and size of engine to be used, along with recommendations for the correct propeller. If an option is offered for the fitting of various engines, or if the owner or builder selects a different engine, then it is necessary to obtain further information on the subject. Anyone buying a propeller is advised to consult either a manufacturer of engines, propellers, or a firm marketing marine conversion equipment, giving full particulars of the boat and its design. These firms have a vast amount of data on file from thousands of engine and propeller combinations in various types of boats, and can usually supply very accurate information of what propeller to use.

The design of marine propellers is a highly developed science, the complexities of which are beyond the scope of this book. A brief discussion is included only to give the reader some idea on how a propeller works, and some highlights which will enable him to understand the basic principles of propeller propulsion.

The descriptive term "screw propeller" implies that its action is like driving a screw into a piece of wood but this is not wholly correct, as a propeller works within a fluid medium and not solid matter. A propeller does not "screw" its way through unstationary water, but as it thrusts the hull forward, it imparts a sternward motion to the water through which it passes. Its action is, therefore, less of a screw and more of a pump.

The diameter of a propeller, as measured across the outer ends of the blades, is generally indicated by the torque characteristics of the engine to be used. The remaining problem is to determine a suitable pitch. This term is applied to the angle of the blades in relation to the arbitrary straight-line position of the hub. The examination of a typical propeller, however, indicates that the blades show a distinct curve throughout their length. This is necessary for adequate application of thrust, and the true pitch is taken at two-thirds the diameter across the blades.

The selection of proper pitch is most intimately concerned with the problem of "slip." In calculating this, it is convenient to again revert to the "screw" theory of propeller action. Regarding a propeller as "screwing" its way through the water, one revolution will theoretically move the boat ahead a distance equal to the pitch of the blade or "thread." Water, however, being resistant, has a portion of its mass swept backward as the propeller starts to turn, so actual forward progress is always somewhat less than the pitch measurement indicates. The precise amount of slip is very difficult to determine. Various mathematical formulae have been worked out to measure it, but the presence of variable factors in the power developed by the engine, the shape of the hull, and turbulence in the water render most of these purely speculative. Most propeller recommendations are, therefore, based upon much empirical observation in the final analysis.

The shape of the hull greatly influences slip. A heavy displacement hull with full body lines aft will drag much water behind it. This offsets apparent slip to give the impression that there is no slip at all. In some cases a full flow of water passing aft may even suggest a "negative slip" when the surrounding water seems to be flowing faster than the hull itself. The most extreme conditions of slip seem to occur to light, semiplaning launches subjected to various conditions of load. In these cases the propeller pitch must be compromised to give adequate power under a wide range of conditions of use. In these cases, slip may be around 40%, or even a little higher. The heavy displacement types mentioned above will actually show about 15% slip, as large, wide-bladed propellers are installed to give maximum thrust. Light, fast-planing runabouts or racing craft can show very little slip as they are fitted with powerful engines, and hull resistance factors decrease as the hull rises out of the water at speed. The most efficient propellers are found in light, easy-driving displacement launches subjected to carrying fixed loads, where the actual slip may be as little as 5%.

The average power launch is best fitted with a three-bladed propeller for good driving efficiency. Two-bladed propellers are generally fitted to fast-planing launches or racing craft where rotative speeds are over 3,000 revolutions per minute. A small blade area is necessary here to reduce vibration. Two-bladed propellers are also fitted to most small auxiliary-powered sailing craft, as the blades can be stopped behind the deadwood for reduced drag while under sail. Two-bladed propellers are not generally suited to moderate-speed launches, as the blades may be masked behind the deadwood at one point of their revolution and set up much vibration. Another problem in propeller installation is a phenomenon known as "cavitation," but this has more to do with the construction of the boat than the action of the propeller itself. It is obvious that to function efficiently the propeller blades must work within a solid and undisturbed area of water. If the propeller is placed too close to a heavy deadwood timber, or a strut acting as a shaft hangar, the water flow in the run as the boat moves forward may be disturbed to the point where quantities of air become mixed with the water. The design of any powerboat should be carefully inspected with this problem in mind. The propeller should have an aperture large enough to give a full flow of water in heavy displacement hulls, and the after end of the deadwood timbers should be rounded off and smoothed to a streamlined shape. The shaft hangars in high-speed craft should be selected for a narrow, streamlined cross section and should be set well ahead of the propeller itself.

The rotative speeds of propellers vary widely with the type of hull under consideration. Very heavy displacement-type cruising boats or working craft designed for large loads benefit from working speeds of around 350 to 500 revolutions per minute, with large diameter propellers of wide blade area. Small, light-displacement launches show most efficiency with propeller speeds of around 1,000 revolutions per minute. Light- or semiplaning cruising or commercial-type launches require rotative speeds of from 1,500 to 2,300 revolutions per minute to attain acceptable speeds. Higher speed sports cruisers have propeller speeds of from 2,000 to 2,800 revolutions per minute. High-speed runabouts, ski-towing launches, and racing craft have propeller speeds that run considerably higher.

It must be emphasized that a screw propeller must operate within a rather narrow limit of rotative speed for best efficiency. As mated to a hull with an arbitrary condition of diameter and pitch, its driving power falls off badly when run at speeds below the calculated optimum. Conversely, the size of the propeller, and especially the pitch, holds down the rotative speed of the engine itself, as its action is a function of the torque output of the engine.

In projecting the power requirements for a hull whose previous power is unknown, or for a design for which engine specifications are not given, the overall guide to the most efficient power is to obtain an engine that can turn a reasonably large propeller with a pitch measurement that produces the least slip. It is obvious that the best results are to be attained where the propeller will be most suited to the type of boat in question, rather than attempting to arbitrarily suit a propeller to an engine selected at random in the hope that a compromise can be worked out.

It will be readily observed that the propeller requirements and rotative speeds are somewhat arbitrary in various types of hulls, and that in many cases reduction gearing of the engine gives the best results. A high-speed V-8 engine turning a small propeller at high degrees of rotation will be the engine of choice for a fast runabout. The same engine, in direct drive, turning a similarly-sized propeller in a heavy displacement boat would produce inefficient power, as the small, fast-turning wheel would have to show excessive slip to allow the engine to turn at its optimum torque output. The same engine in a heavy hull, but with a 3-to-1 reduction gear, would enable the engine to operate a much larger propeller for good efficiency. While reduction gearing adds to the cost of the craft, it will soon pay for itself in reduced fuel bills. Many small launches are greatly overpowered adding unnecessarily to initial and operating cost. Numerous boat owners purchase oversized engines in the mistaken hope that increasing the power will inevitably produce more speed, ignoring the torque factor in engine and propeller combinations. In some cases a prospective buyer is urged to choose a larger engine than necessary on the theory that "reserve power" might be helpful in some emergency. In all cases it is advisable to seek professional help in boat powering problems unless the owner has had a fair amount of practical experience in the matter.

Jet Drives

Propulsion systems employing the hydrojet principle have limited application in small power launches used in very shallow or weed-choked waters. These consist of a vane-type pump set in a case within the hull, usually near the position of the conventional propeller. The drive shaft of the engine activates this impeller which pumps in water through a forward orifice and discharges it sternward to propel the boat forward. Steering is accomplished by rotating the jet stream, the controls being carried to the steering position. The draft of the hull is materially reduced through the elimination of the propeller and rudder, the jet itself projecting only a few inches below the hull.

Air Screws

Light, scow-type planing hulls are sometimes fitted with aeroplane engines carried on struts above the after portion of the hull, driving an airscrew in pusher configuration to drive the boat. Steering is effected by an aeroplane rudder set in the slip stream of the propeller. These craft are used mainly in swamps or very shallow, weed-choked waters and are able to travel over mud banks and adjacent moist grasslands.

Paddle Wheels

A few small power boats are built with either stern or side paddle wheels for use on shallow lakes or rivers and are especially useful on the latter where large amounts of driftwood can otherwise cause constant propeller fouling. Most of these are replicas of the old-time river steamers and are built by those who like a useful craft with marked individuality. In these installations, the engine is generally set athwartships with the crankshaft parallel to the paddlewheel axle. As the latter can function properly only at very low revolutions, reduction gearing must be employed. This is accomplished with the use of V belts, the engine pulley driving a countershaft which in turn has a pulley geared to the paddlewheel. As the revolutions of the latter are usually between 20 to 40 turns per minute, direct gearing from the engine itself is not satisfactory.

13

Small Boat Conversion

The rebuilding or conversion of an old yacht, lifeboat, commercial craft, or condemned government hull is sometimes an attraction to boatmen. This is often contemplated by prospective boat owners who do not feel that they have the necessary manual skill to construct a boat from the ground up if the hull in question can be purchased at very low cost. In general such undertakings should be viewed with much caution. While it is true that craft ready for junking can be had for the proverbial song, they may well be junk and nothing else. Many of the old time yachts built in the Golden Age of boating were constructed with painstaking care from the best materials, but if built of wood may be heavily infected with dry rot. Such craft were often well maintained and painted frequently, but unless periodically stripped of paint and their wood bared for refinishing, excessive paint coats may well have served to seal in the rot spores which then spread throughout the timbers. Most condemned commercial craft are ill-suited to rebuilding as their owners have usually wrung out a final season of use before putting them up for sale. Power launches condemned from government service are generally in better condition due to well-scheduled maintenance in service, but should be carefully surveyed for deterioration. Some of these hulls have been long stored on land, the inroads of fresh water greatly promoting dry rot. The double-ended motor whale boat is a very able one, but is unsuited to the addition of high cabins due to its slack bilges and can be a dangerous roller unless heavily ballasted. They make fairly acceptable sailing craft but require the addition of a long keel to make them point well. They are never fast boats in any case due to their lack of bearing aft. The naval shore boats in various sizes are also able craft, but because of the hullshape, roll badly if much top hamper is added. They are not fast boats as they have slack bilges to give them an easy motion in harbor chop. They do make fair pleasure cruisers for modest speeds, but are less practical for commercial work since the position of the engine mounting is in the way of the usual hold space. Any changes here involve extensive rebuilding of the shaft log to alter the shaft angle, usually expensive and time-consuming. Perhaps the best proposition for pleasure boat conversions are the officers' gigs, but because of their small original production they are hard to find.

Many landing craft have been converted to various uses, however they are designed for heavy loads, and the high resistance of their broad bows make them uneconomical to power. Assault boats sheathed with armor plate, which may or may not have been removed, are generally badly infected with dry rot from condensation of fresh water under the plating. Not a few landing boats have had their ramps removed and conventional pointed bows added which improves their appearance but does nothing to improve their driving capabilities. Such conversions have figured in not a few marine disasters when the false bows disintegrated as a result of improper structural strength.

Discarded ships' lifeboats are thought to be eminently seaworthy, but their basic form makes them generally unsuitable for other purposes. Older types of lifeboats built of wood are often of good form, but the recently built steel types are generally useless. Their bluff pointed bows make them hard to drive as power craft, and they are very slow due to the lack of bearing aft, the stern sucking down badly at any speed over 5 to 6 knots. They further require much ballast to provide proper immersion of the propeller. As sailing craft they require a long ballast keel to offset their lack of draft. Their high freeboard creates excess windage and they will rarely tack at all unless aided by auxiliary power. They cannot carry the sail area to overcome their shallow hulls, and if heavily ballasted their bluff form makes their overall performance melancholy at best.

In general it may be stated that the usual small boat conversion is only practical where the rare hull can be obtained in very sound condition, the initial cost is small, and for a specialized use where conversion can be accomplished very economically. The dismal prospect of working on an outworn hull and finding successive structural parts requiring extensive rebuilding with constant upward revisions of the original cost estimate is perhaps one of the most disheartening aspects of small boat ownership. As designs of various small craft are available offering the minimum of challenge to those of limited mechanical ability, it is more economical to consider attempting one of these rather than tackle a project fraught with unsuspected and sometimes very bitter disappointments.

14

Engine Installation

The proper installation of an inboard engine in a power launch or auxiliary-powered sailing boat is essential for effective use of the engine power for propulsive efficiency, the maintenance of correct alignment of the drive train and propeller shaft, and to preserve the structural integrity of the hull against the torque thrust of the power plant.

In many boat plans the designer will specify a particular make of engine, and in such cases the installation will be simplified in that all principal dimensions of the ancillary structures will be provided. In the event that the builder wishes to substitute another make of engine, the installation details will be modified to suit. In any case, most manufacturers of either true marine or converted-type engines will supply engineer's blueprints or drawings to various scales to facilitate the work.

The first step in engine installation is to ascertain the position and angle of the propeller shaft. Most designs show a very moderate shaft angle for optimum propeller efficiency, but in converted hulls or empirically built boats, care should be taken to insure that the shaft angle is not over 10 degrees, as the lubrication systems of most four-cycle gasoline or diesel engines will not function properly at angles much greater than this. It is also essential that there be at least 1 inch clearance between the tips of the propeller blades and the bottom plank, and 1½-to-2 inches is better. This cuts down drumming and makes it less likely that small objects will become trapped between the tips of the blades and the hull. After the hull is lofted, the position of the shaft is laid out, carefully noting the position of the crankcase and flywheel in relation to the bottom of the boat or the top of the interior framing. The most effective way to ascertain these dimensions is to make a template from a 10-or-12-inch plank and extend it lengthwise along the centerline of the hull. Strips of light wood or lath are suspended from it at various points to indicate its relationship to the bottom of the hull (Figure 67). A straight edge or string extended from a lath placed on the outside of the stern through the shaft hole will then provide a guide for the necessary clearance around the engine. This template can also be used to indicate the

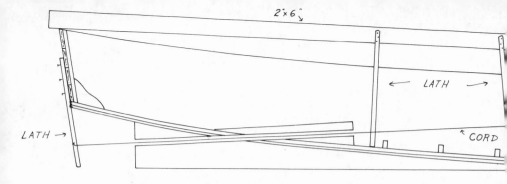

TEMPLATES

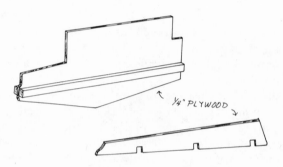

Figure 67　A method of laying out an engine mounting with the use of templates

approximate shape of the engine bearers that will engage the bottom of the lugs. In some installations there will be enough clearance under the crank-case to allow draining the lubricating oil from the drain plug usually pro-vided. If the clearance is small, a sump pump must be provided with which to draw the oil out through the filler pipe. Engine or flywheel cases must never rest on the tops of frames or other hull structures because of the possi-bility of engine vibrations wracking the hull, or even wearing a hole through the casings. There should be a minimum of 1-inch clearance here and at least 2 inches under exposed flywheels. Sometimes shallow pans made up from light sheet metal are fitted to surround the lower arc of such a fly-wheel to prevent bilge water from being thrown upward in case it should rise to the rim while the engine is running.

After all lofting is completed, the shaft hole is bored using a barefoot ship's auger which will allow corrections for misalignment to be made dur-ing the boring. In most cases a pipe handle must be welded to the shank of the auger to give the proper length, together with a cross bar at its outer end of sufficient width to give leverage for turning. The auger should be at least ¼ inch larger in diameter than the hole to be bored. If any ridges re-main inside the hole as the result of directional changes made during the boring process, these can be removed by heating a length of iron pipe or

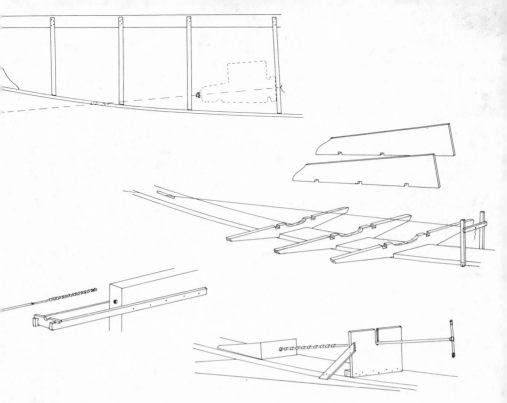

Figure 68 Use of jigs and templates for aligning and boring the propeller shaft alley

drift rod and burning them away. If the hole is to be bored from the dead-wood or skeg, a guide must be made up as shown in Figure 68 to steady the auger. If the hole is bored from the inside, a temporary block must be fastened to the top of the keelson, keel batten, or keel to enable the bit to be started. The handle must be supported by a template as shown. The actual boring should proceed slowly, with frequent checking of proper direction with correction as necessary.

The engine bearers are next gotten out, their approximate shape being determined by the use of the template. In some installations where large or heavy engines are fitted, longitudinal bed logs are often fitted to support the outer edges of the engine bearers, and are usually notched into heavy athwartship bottom framing. The bearers are often notched as well to coincide with these. The fitting of these can be facilitated by the use of a spiling board (Figure 69). It is particularly critical in shaping the engine bearers

Figure 69 Use of a spiling board for laying out engine beds

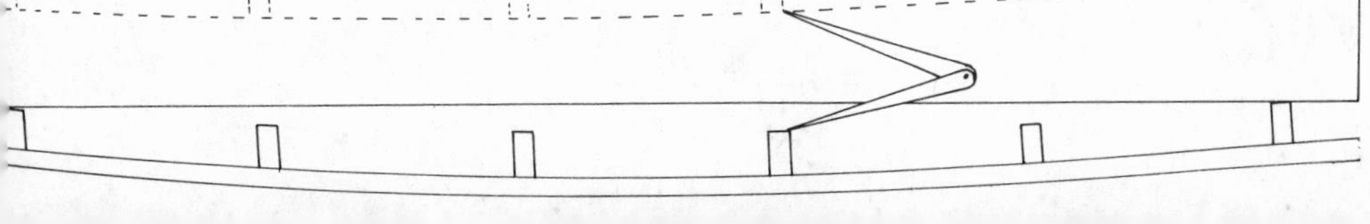

SPILING BOARD FOR ENGINE BEARER

to make sure that their upper surfaces properly coincide with the bottom of the engine lugs to place the center of the shaft in proper alignment with the shaft hole. It is best for initial fitting of the engine to have the tops of the bearers a little high, as it is easier to trim off excess material to fit rather than resorting to shimming with thin sheets of metal.

The hoisting of the engine into the hull must be carefully planned to avoid dropping it or damaging some of its parts. Items such as the carburetor and generator or starter may be removed to cut down on bulk and weight. Very small engines weighing 300 pounds or under can often be manhandled into position by two average men. The engine may be bolted to a short stretcher made up of stout two-by-threes for easier handling. Larger engines may be lifted into place with a small mobile crane. If such is not readily available, a simple derrick arrangement may be set up using two heavy timbers as sheer legs (Figure 70).

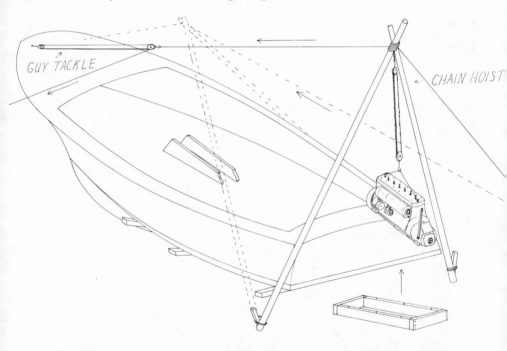

Figure 70   Hoisting gear for the installation or removal of an inboard engine

Once the engine is in place, and if the alignment appears correct, the propeller shaft may be run through its aperture and the inside stuffing box. The self-aligning-type stuffing box with a short length of heavy hose connecting the packing gland with the main bracket is best. The flexibility of the hose connection will compensate automatically with very slight misalignment and the normal vibration of the engine.

After the shaft is run through the stuffing box, the after half of the coupling is securely keyed to the shaft. The shaft is then moved forward so that the engine half of the coupling is in apposition with it. The alignment is then checked again, and three or four thin strips of cardboard may be inserted between the coupling halves around its perimeter to ascertain if all parts of the surfaces are equidistant. If this alignment proves accurate, the coupling halves are bolted together. As a final check on alignment, the engine should be slowly revolved with the spark plugs removed, in the case of a gasoline engine, or the injector pumps removed if a diesel. The lack of cylinder compression will allow any binding to show up readily if present. The apposition of the coupling halves is the best indication of whether the engine is tilting upward or downward, and excess timber on the top of the bearers will be trimmed accordingly. After everything else is in order, the propeller is keyed and locknutted to the shaft taper aft, after properly securing the stern bearing.

The principal problem of engine misalignment in wooden hulls is the shifting of the engine due to its weight, causing compression in the timber of the engine bearers or hogging or sagging of the hull after being heavily loaded or strained in a seaway or upon grounding. After about six months of use after proper alignment, most wooden hulls appear to require another realignment, after which the installation appears to remain in order unless severe wringing of the hull is experienced. In order to prevent the engine from shifting in any case, it is good practice in large installations to fit lengths of heavy angle iron along the inside of each bearer to provide a more rigid foundation that will resist compression (Figure 71). As further

Figure 71   The use of metal fittings for strengthening an engine mounting

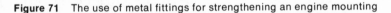

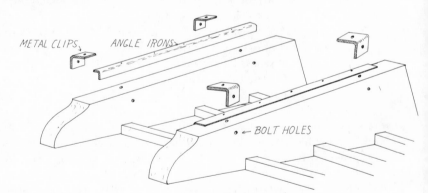

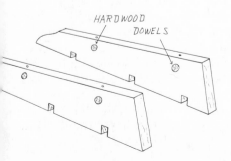

insurance against engine movement, heavy-angle iron braces may be fitted in the way of the hanger bolts securing the engine lugs, and securing these to the sides of the bearers by means of through bolts. This arrangement is also a necessity with powerful engines producing excessive torque, and appears to preclude all movement if kept well tightened.

In smaller installations, the hangers may be more securely fastened into the engine bearers with the use of hardwood inserts or dowels that are let into the sides at a point where the ends of the bolt threads will just pass through them.

Marine engines are cooled mostly by pumping exterior water through their engine blocks from an intake fitting through the hull. A few types of gasoline or diesel engines are aircooled, and require no through hull fittings except an exhaust outlet if a waterline discharge is required. In these cases it is essential to follow carefully the manufacturers' recommendations regarding the size and construction details of the air ducts to the cylinders. Most of these systems are activated by a fan arrangement built into the flywheel.

The disposition of the fuel intake, cooling water, and exhaust discharge are generally indicated on the engineer's installation drawings supplied with the engine. Fuel lines are usually made up from copper tubing of proper length. The last few feet of the line adjacent to the carburetor fittings should be of flexible tubing to avoid engine vibration from fracturing the lines. If flexible tubing is not available, vibration may be dampened by making four or five complete circles of the line, as in a coil spring, just adjacent to the carburetor fuel intake. The same recommendation applies to fuel lines adjacent to the injector pumps of diesel engines.

A diagram of a typical engine installation with all piping in place for a water-cooled exhaust system is shown in Figure 72. The water inlet requires a clamshell-type scoop facing forward to pick up the water, and should be placed well under the turn of the bilge to insure against air entering the system if the hull rolls down in heavy seas. The intake fitting should be securely fitted to the inside of the hull with locknuts over a substantial gasket to prevent leaking. A shut-off valve should be fitted on the inside to allow servicing the system while the boat is in the water. A portion of the intake line near the engine should be fitted with rubber hose well fastened with substantial clamps to dampen engine vibration.

In most small launches, the water is passed out of the engine block and into the exhaust system, functioning both to cool it and to dampen the noise. Some installations have a watercooled elbow at the exhaust manifold outlet; in other cases, the water outlet is fitted directly into a pipe elbow. In any case, the exhaust outlet should drop at a 45 degree angle to insure that no cooling water backs up into the exhaust chamber, as this could readily cause warping of the exhaust valves in the engine. The cooling water should therefore enter the exhaust system about 6 inches below the outlet, and the exhaust pipe itself should drop from 12-to-16 inches before running in a horizontal direction. The exhaust line is generally made up of rubber steam

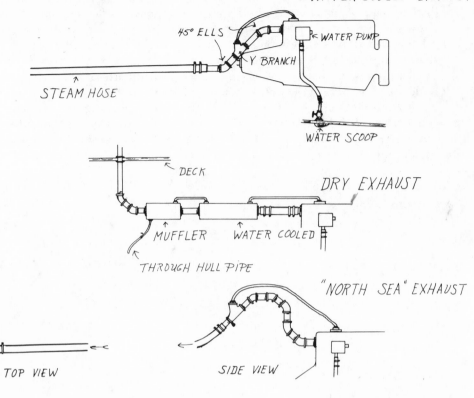

Figure 72 Details of making up wet, dry, and North Sea engine exhaust systems

hose which avoids vibration and should be of the same inside diameter as the manifold outlet to eliminate any back pressure. The line should have a constant fall to the transom, where it is carried off through a fitting that is locknutted and gasketed through the wood. If there is any doubt about any drop in the line, short cleats can be made to support it under the edge of the cockpit coaming or alongside the framing of the hull. Where mufflers are required to suppress the exhaust noise produced in very large engines, these are installed along the exhaust line at any convenient interval. Sometimes two or more are required. The type most used today are ready-made fittings made of neoprene or rubber compounds that resist corrosion more effectively than the older metal types. Some commercial craft or fishing boats employ dry-type exhaust systems that project upward above the decks or steering shelters. These are preferred in some displacement hulls that show a variation in waterline due to loading factors which makes waterline discharging impractical. It is also impractical in some cases to discharge exhaust gases near the waterline where crew members working on deck may be subjected to breathing monoxide fumes. A diagram of such a system is shown in Figure 72. Some seagoing sailing boats with auxiliary power are fitted with North Sea-type exhaust systems which run athwartship with an outlet on either side of the hull. These are preferred to those types which exhaust out under the counter and present problems of flooding if struck by a heavy stern sea. While the pipe passes out on either side near the waterline, one or the other opening will always be clear as the boat heels. A gooseneck pipe is fitted off the engine outlet to prevent water from entering the manifold.

15

Steering and Control Systems

The steering arrangements for power and sailing boats may be divided into four general classifications: tiller steering, mechanical linkage, hydraulic systems, cable and drum.

Tiller steering is the obvious choice in very small sailing boats or inboard powered launches where it is impractical to place the steering station anywhere but in the stern sheets. Rope or lever adaptations are sometimes rigged in somewhat larger power boats. In this arrangement a rope or cable is attached to the end of the tiller and two lines are passed through fairleads fastened to the inside of the cockpit coaming. When loosely fastened with plenty of slack, the line may be grasped at any point, and is very handy to use when the operator is called on to work at various points within the boat. Sometimes the lines are attached to a vertically placed side lever or levers moving within a quadrant set on the inner face of the cockpit coaming. This arrangement is favored in Chesapeake Bay workboats.

Mechanical linkage consisting of rods and levers is sometimes fitted to inboard powered launches and cruising boats. It is less favored in working craft as the rod to the rudder post is often in the way of the cargo space or bait well. These systems usually are fitted in conjunction with geared steering wheels that are set on pedestals. These and the mechanism at the rudder quadrant are manufactured fittings specially made for the purpose but adaptable to various installations. The rods connecting the parts together are usually made up from galvanized pipe to fit the work. The mechanism used in some high-speed launches may be of the cam-and-lever or rack-and-pinion type derived from automotive practice. Various types of available steering mechanisms are listed in leading marine hardware catalogs.

Hydraulic steering systems are becoming increasingly popular, and their initial and installation costs are usually substantially less than the mechanical type, especially in larger craft. Another advantage is that the lines carrying the hydraulic fluid need not be run in straight or arbitrarily positioned lines and can, therefore, be adapted to pass around cargo holds, cabin spaces, or other machinery. Standard fittings are used for the wheel mechanism and at the rudder quadrant, the tubing lengths then being fabricated to suit. Another advantage is that auxiliary steering stations may be let into the lines at any desired location. Manufacturers of this equipment will supply diagrams and installation details for any boat.

Cable and drum steering is fitted to large numbers of small power launches of both pleasure and commercial type due to its low cost and simplicity. Figure 73 shows a typical installation. The cable is usually run through double and single sheaves opposite the rudder quadrant and thence through double blocks along one side of the hull or cockpit coaming to the drum on the steering wheel. In some small open boats, the cable may be run around either side of the cockpit. If any obstructions are in the way of the cable, such as cabin trunks or companion ways, it is best to run the cable through double sheaves along one side. Too many single sheaves and changes in direction may bind the cable and make operation difficult. Specially manufactured steering cable made of stranded wire covered with a smooth plastic cover is available and lasts better than plain rope which may fray or deteriorate from the weather. While the cable is usually prestretched, it is good practice to interpose a tensioning device somewhere along the line to take up the inevitable slack that will occur after prolonged use. This may be either a large turnbuckle or rigging screw, long coil spring, or a double ring with a rope lanyard. The latter is the least costly and is very satisfactory. The rope will have to be renewed from time to time but it is an insignificant item. A similar steering arrangement is sometimes used in large workboats and tugboats, except that a chain is used in place of the cable and wildcat-type fittings are used for the wheel drum and rudder quadrant to give positive control.

Engine control systems used on power launches and auxiliary sailing craft are classified into three types, and for convenience include controls for clutches or reversing gear where fitted.

1. Direct controls fitted to the engine
2. Mechanical type with remote controls through rods and levers or Bowdin wire
3. Hydraulic type with pumps and fluid-carrying lines

Direct controls are found in very small boats where the engine is placed in an open cockpit near the steering station, or in boats where the engine is carried in a pilot house adjacent to the wheel. Many small, heavy-duty engines, such as low-speed diesels or two-cycle gasoline engines with make-and-break or jump spark ignition are supplied by the manufacturers with controls integral with the engine.

Mechanical controls fitted to many small boats include a rod or rope controlled reverse gear and Bowdin wire attachments for the throttle, spark, and choke or air strangler. These latter were a patented device involving a push-pull wire system that has been used for many years in twist-grip throttle and spark controls on motorcycles. This consists of an outer cable laid in

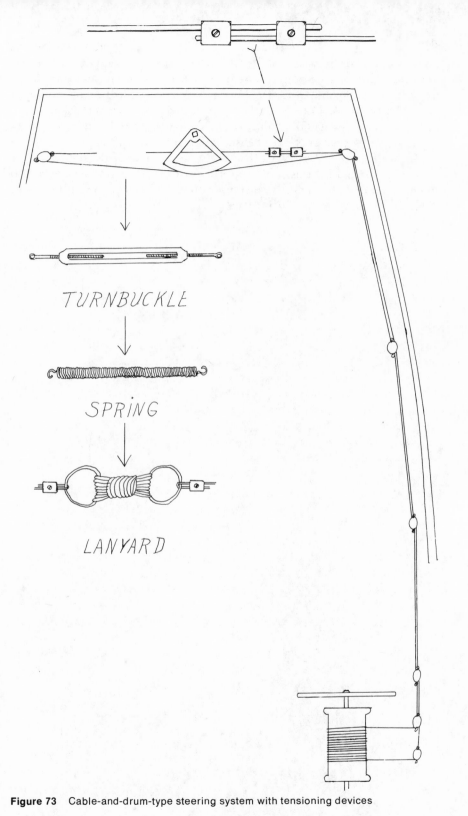

TURNBUCKLE

SPRING

LANYARD

Figure 73 Cable-and-drum-type steering system with tensioning devices

the form of a spring with a stiff inner wire in a single strand. The ends of the outer cover are anchored, but protect the inner wire and allow it to move back and forth in a rather short movement. The levers, control knobs, and all fittings to make up these systems are available from marine supply concerns. Rods for engine controls are seldom used today due to the expense of fitting and problem of installation in small spaces.

Hydraulic systems for reverse gear and engine controls are almost universally incorporated with hydraulic steering systems, as the former are readily included into the control consoles used today in most well-finished boats. Their advantages are as outlined for steering controls.

16

Fuel and Water Tanks

Fuel and water tanks and their location within the hull are an integral part of the boat's design as their weight and bulk are such that they are a factor in weight and balance considerations. This is especially true in high-speed planing or semiplaning launches where loading factors are critical in anticipating performance.

Tanks for both fuel and water are usually identical in construction except that the former are generally of greater capacity and are made from somewhat heavier material. Most are made of metal such as iron, carbon steel, galvanized sheet metal, or from special alloys such as stainless steel or Monel. The latter will last almost indefinitely, but are high in first cost. It must be mentioned that galvanized tanks must never be used to carry diesel fuel as the acid from the oil will attack the zinc and carry particles into the injector pumps and orifices. Tanks in steel vessels are usually built-in as a part of the hull. Some builders have lately favored special materials such as fiber glass or neoprene compounds. Tanks may be either round, oval, or rectangular in shape, and are available in a wide range of capacities from marine supply concerns. These can be bought at much lower cost than having tanks specially made for an individual design, which are sometimes required for specific purposes.

The fabrication of metal tanks is a highly specialized undertaking and a builder seldom makes his own unless he has had training in this work.

The weight of metal used will vary as to the size of the tank. Very large types may be of 3/8-inch material. Medium-sized tanks are made from 16- or 18-gauge metal down to 20 gauge for small launch tanks. An important feature of both fuel and water tanks is the fitting of internal baffles to prevent surging of the contents during violent motion of the hull. These are offered as an option in stock tanks as to presence or number, but any tank of 25 gallons or over should have at least one baffle.

Figure 74 shows typical round and rectangular tanks with two baffles. For fuel tanks, the filler orifice should be fitted with a substantial screw-threaded cap that is attached to a standpipe extending well down to a point

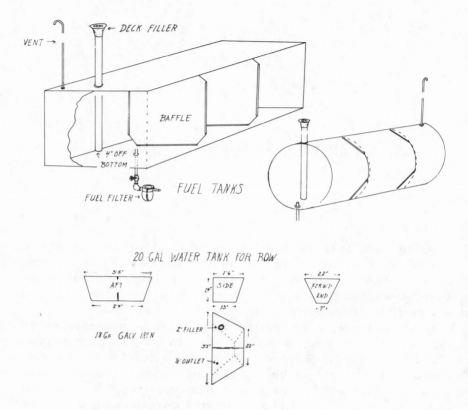

VENT →

← DECK FILLER

BAFFLE

4" OFF BOTTOM

FUEL FILTER →

FUEL TANKS

20 GAL WATER TANK FOR BOW

AFT

3'5"

2'4"

SIDE

1'6"

14"

13"

FCRW'D END

22"

7"

18 GA. GALV IRON

2" FILLER

35"

½" OUTLET

22"

Figure 74 Construction details of fuel and water tanks

near the bottom of the tank. This will prevent excessive fuming when the fuel is added. The inner end of the outlet pipe to the fuel line should stand an inch or so above the bottom to keep any large particles of sediment from entering. A substantial shut-off valve should be fitted just below the outlet as it leaves the tank and adjacent to the fuel filter. This last fitting is absolutely essential to trap water collecting within the tank as there is inevitable condensation of water vapor in both gasoline and diesel fuel. Some experienced offshore cruising men and commercial boat operators fit two or more filters in tandem for added safety. The presence of free water in the fuel can cause immediate stoppage of the engine.

Another essential fitting is a vent pipe or pipes which will equalize the air pressure inside the tank with the atmosphere as the contents are emptied. Unless vented a vacuum will be formed within the tank which will cut off the fuel flow and cause stoppage of the engine. The topside position of the ends of the vents is most critical in gasoline engines due to its volatility and should be positioned somewhere in the upper sheer so as to be discharged outside the hull. If the vents open out onto the deck, the ends should be bent in a circle to keep water out of the system. In very small power launches with small tanks, a hole drilled in the filler cap will serve the same purpose. This should be kept clear at all times to prevent engine stoppage.

All tanks should be securely fastened to the main framing members of the hull in wooden boats, and most designers specify very substantial timbering in the form of beams and upright stanchions to hold them in place. At the same time provision should be made for easy removal for cleaning or servicing. If the tanks are very large or if the design of the boat renders them somewhat inaccessible, large clean-out doors should be fitted. These are usually round, oval, or rectangular pieces of metal secured with cap screws over a heavy gasket. Where the bottom of the tank rests on beams, the contact area should be padded with thick strips of felting or soft rubber. This will prevent possible leaks due to vibration opening the metal. Tanks in very small launches are frequently suspended from the deck beams forward by metal straps held by set screws, and should also be padded. Tanks carried in the stern are often held by a similar arrangement over a low shelf or platform. Most tanks feed their outlets by gravity, but in some cases fuel pumps must be fitted if the tank bottoms are below the carburetor or fuel injectors in the case of diesel engines. For proper gravity flow, the bottom of the tank should be at least 12 inches above the carburetor.

Water tanks are usually of somewhat less capacity than fuel tanks in small cruising launches or commercial fishing boats, although the reverse may be true in sailing auxiliaries carrying very small engines. Many larger craft may be fitted with a ready-made salt water distilling plant, several sizes of which are now available and which materially reduce the need for large storage tanks. The same precautions for the adequate securing of the tanks must be followed as for fuel tanks, with removal or clean-out facilities provided. Venting to prevent vacuum lock is also required.

The water tank of many small power launches and sailing boats is positioned high in the bow. It forms an element of balance here, as well as providing a gravity feed to the galley sink. The dimensions of a small tank for such installations are shown in the drawing (Figure 74).

As a reference guide for various-size round and rectangular fuel or water tanks, the following is a list of various capacities available from marine supply houses:

A. ROUND TANKS

Capacity in gallons	Diameter	Length	Baffles
9	12"	20"	0
14	12"	30"	0
20	14"	30"	1
30	16"	30"	1
39	18"	36"	1
45	18"	42"	2
56	20"	42"	2
64	20"	48"	2
80	20"	60"	3

B. RECTANGULAR TANKS

Capacity in gallons	Diameter	Length	Baffles
55	16″ x 16″	52″	2
70	16″ x 16″	65″	2
80	16″ x 16″	72″	2
16	12″ x 14″	24″	1
24	12″ x 14″	36″	1
32	12″ x 14″	48″	2

For purposes of calculating tank sizes for tanks specially fabricated for individual designs, an Imperial or English gallon (also used in Canada) of fresh water contains 277 cubic inches and weighs 10 pounds. A United States gallon of fresh water contains 231 cubic inches and weighs 8⅓ pounds. A cubic foot of fresh water contains 1,728 cubic inches, 7.40 American gallons, 6¼ Imperial gallons and weighs 62⅓ pounds.

17

Wedges, Trim Tabs, Squat Boards, and Antiroll Devices

The speed capabilities of some planing, semiplaning, and displacement-type power launches can be enhanced by devices that alter the trim or angle of attack or give additional bearing under the stern while the boat is under way.

A notable effect sometimes observed in planing or semiplaning hulls is that the stern is pulled down and the angle of attack of the planing surface is deepened to the extent that the speed is actually reduced as more power is applied. This is usually not a fault in the original design, for the majority of such launches are generally much overpowered. It is possible in some cases to counteract this action (generally referred to as "squatting") by the fitting of wedges under the transom that act to deflect the water flow downward as it passes under the stern and to provide a lifting factor to hold the stern from sinking unduly and consequently maintaining the planing surface at its optimum angle of efficiency. These wedges, as the name implies, are triangularly shaped pieces of wood, or metal fabrications in the case of metal-hulled boats. These sections are approximately 1-to-1¼ inches thick and from 12-to-24 inches long for average power boats of 20-to-35 feet in length. The outer surface is planed at a continuous forward slope to a feather edge as shown in Figure 75. It is customary to fit a number of these across the whole width of the stern with the after edge even with the outside of the transom. The actual size and shape of these wedges can only be determined in actual installations by trial-and-error experimentation; the suggested dimensions are taken from average cases. The wedges are easily fitted by fastening with long screws through the planking, the only complication being that the boat must be hauled out for fitting.

Another variation of this practice is the fitting of trim tabs. These are manufactured metal fittings consisting of two flat plates made up in the form of a common hinge. One plate is securely fastened to the lower edge of the transom, and the other extends out aft, the hinge being set so that the after plate is level with the bottom planking. The position of the lower plate is maintained by an adjustable arm connected with the transom plate

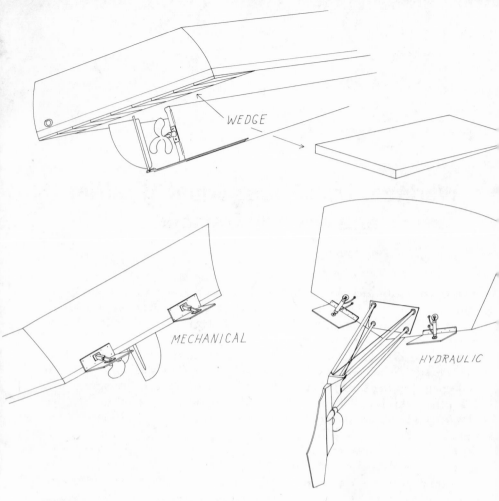

Figure 75 Details of wedges and trim tabs

which can be moved to provide maximum efficiency by trial-and-error experimentation. Due to the rather better efficiency of the rear positioned metal trim tab, usually only one pair of these is required, each at equidistant points from the centerline of the transom.

Trim tabs with hydraulically controlled adjustment of the bearing surfaces are often installed in modern high-speed monohedron or delta-hulled offshore racing launches. Due to the position of the center of balance being placed well aft, and coupled with the high torque of one or more special racing engines, the sterns of such craft tend to squat badly when full power is applied. The manual adjustment allows the helmsman to vary the position of the plates to suit operating conditions.

Squat boards are an empirically developed invention of working boatmen to correct problems of trim and to provide better speed capabilities in power launches that are excessively powered. They are also used in displacement-type launches whose form indicates a low terminal hull speed. These are usually seen in the form of a pair of straight planks, one on either side of the boat, the forward end of which is chocked against the hull somewhat forward of the propeller at the outer edge of the waterline and parallel with it. The after end extends somewhat aft of the propeller and is secured by rods extending upward to the quarters (Figure 76).

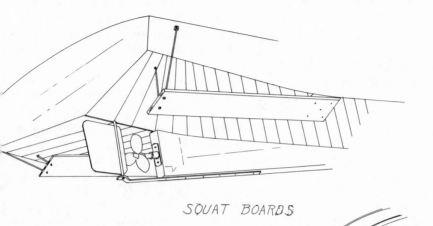

SQUAT BOARDS

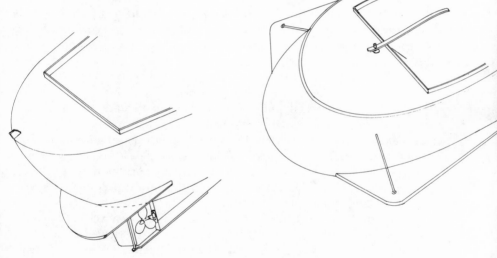

Figure 76   Details of squat board construction for double-ended and fantail-sterned boats

These planks act somewhat like a water ski to support the hull against the thrust of the propeller and are said to add 3-to-5 knots speed in displacement-type boats. They are widely seen on the Chesapeake Bay in converted skipjack hulls which usually have lifted stern sections otherwise much addicted to squatting. Similar devices have been fitted to the sterns of double-ended power boats to provide more bearing aft, or in narrow-sterned launch types, such as the Hooper Island boats which have excessively narrow underwater sections aft of the propeller (Figure 76). The design of such appendages has never received the blessing of professional naval architects who often consider such as a rather crude attempt to overpower boats for speed capabilities at variance with their basic design. As a result there are no known accounts of any formal engineering studies being made of their shape or structure. However, squat boards have been much used in improving the speed of converted or traditional-type hulls that were available for some commercial application at either low first or acquisition cost, and represent an interesting empirical approach on the part of practical boatmen.

A number of devices have been developed to counteract the rather severe rolling which may occur in power boats employed in extensive offshore work where long courses may be run in beam seas. This condition, if prolonged, may bring discomfort to the crew which may be intensified if any are addicted to seasickness. One answer to this problem is the fitting of small steadying sails which provide a stabilizing effect from the wind pressure aloft acting as dampening media. In cases where the fitting of auxiliary sail is impractical, some designers have suggested the fitting of bilge keels outboard and parallel to the keel near the turn of the bilges. Others have designed stabilizers in the form of airfoillike projections which afford lateral resistance to roll. Either of these methods add considerable expense to building, and the latter could cause complications in fishing craft where the airfoil could foul nets and lines. There are also increased resistance factors to be considered where projections of substantial size and area project below the hull.

The most simple and economical of antirolling devices are outboard stabilizers which have come into rather widespread use in recent years. These consist of a pair of metal underwater kites or paravanes which are suspended on either side of the hull and held some distance from it by lines or small diameter wire cable attached to whisker poles rigged amidships or attached to a derrick mast (Figure 77). The kites are fabricated from metal to assure their sinkage, and are shaped so that the forward motion of the boat will keep them headed on course yet exert a downward pressure. The resistance of the horizontal planes will dampen the roll of the boat through keeping tension on the bridles. This device has proven very effective in many types of launches and small vessels. It can be fabricated at moderate cost and can be readily dismantled if not required. Several ready-made types of paravanes are on the market, some of which are covered by patents.

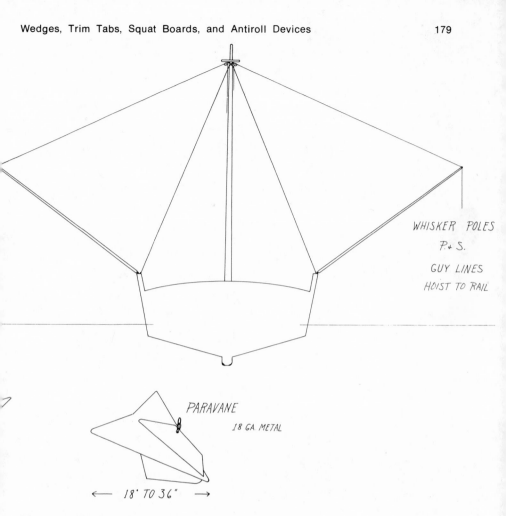

WHISKER POLES
P. & S.
GUY LINES
HOIST TO RAIL

PARAVANE
18 GA. METAL

←— 18" TO 36" —→

Figure 77   Diagram of paravane or antirolling devices

Part
3

The V-Bottom Boat

The V-bottom boat is generally considered to have been developed as an improvement on the flat-bottom boat, and not as a simplification of the round-bottom boat as has sometimes been suggested. The V-bottom boat has many variations, both as to hull form and to construction methods employed. While it is considered an ideal type for amateur construction, such projects should initially be confined to the more simple forms. Generally speaking, prior experience in building simpler flat-bottom boats is strongly advised in order to insure successful execution.

The outstanding construction problem in the V-bottom boat is the fitting of the planking forward in the angle formed between the forefoot, keel, and chine. A high chine line forward allows the bottom planking to be laid on in natural sweeps. A low chine line can impose building complications, as a hard twist is then required to bring the ends of the planking into the stem rabbet. Generally speaking, the chine profile is an indication of the degree of building complication.

An effective method of studying the basic construction of the V-bottom boat is to briefly trace its historical development. As a type it has existed in one form or another since very early times, but its more modern version appears in the Long Island Sound area of New York about 1860. It was developed by professional shipwrights as a cheaper and more easily built version of the so-called New York sloop, a popular type of boat then much used in the local fisheries. These were rather wide and shallow plumb stemmed round-bottom centerboard boats, about 20 to 26 feet in length, with sloop rig. They were good sail carriers and quite fast and weatherly if properly handled. Due to their round bottom form with closely spaced steam-bent frames and fitted planking, a high degree of professional skill was required in their building.

18

High Chine Model
The Northern Skipjack

How the V-bottom versions acquired the name "skipjack" is a matter of conjecture, but it is thought to have been taken from a locally caught type of fish. The appellation "Northern skipjack" was used to differentiate the parent type from subsequent variations that were developed later to the southward on Chesapeake Bay.

The general form of the Northern skipjack is shown on Figure 78. It will be noted that the bottom plank meets the stem in natural sweeps. The curve of the chine line and the general form indicate that the hull can be planked with no hard bends. The lifted chine lines aft show a hull that can be loaded to varying degrees without dragging the stern. As sailing hulls these boats drove easily and were quite stable, as the hard chine contributed good righting moments.

The lines and construction details of several examples of Northern skipjacks have been preserved in the Watercraft Collection of the United States National Museum. Plates 1A and 1B show a popular size of small skipjack much built by the fishermen themselves. Details of its simple construction are shown in Plate 2. The high chine with its bevels are noted, together with a two-piece stem that eliminates rabbet cutting. This was fashioned plumb as in its round-bottom forebear, its heel being fastened to the keel below with either drift rod or long spikes or screws. The keel is formed from a tapered plank, against which the garboard strake is fitted by spiling (see page 113). In some hulls the keel was formed by joining two planks, one on top of the other. The upper or keelson plank, being the wider, forms a rabbet with the lower plank to receive the garboard strakes (Figure 79).

Interior of a Skipjack Hull

Figure 80 shows a diagram of the interior of a skipjack hull. When built with a centerboard as a sailing hull, a locking beam along the lower edge of

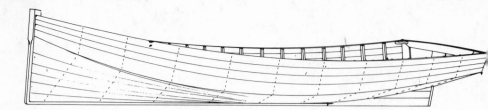

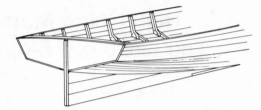

Figure 78   Perspective views of an old-style Northern skipjack

Figure 79   Construction details of frames and keel batten of an old-style
Northern skipjack

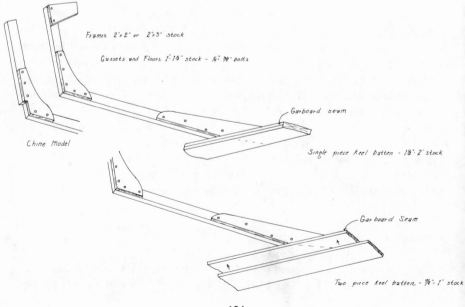

Frames 2"x 2" or 2"x 3" stock

Gussets and Floors 1"-1½" stock - ¼" ⅜" bolts

Garboard seam

Chine Model

Single piece keel batten - 1½"-2" stock

Garboard Seam

Two piece keel batten - ⅞"- 1" stock

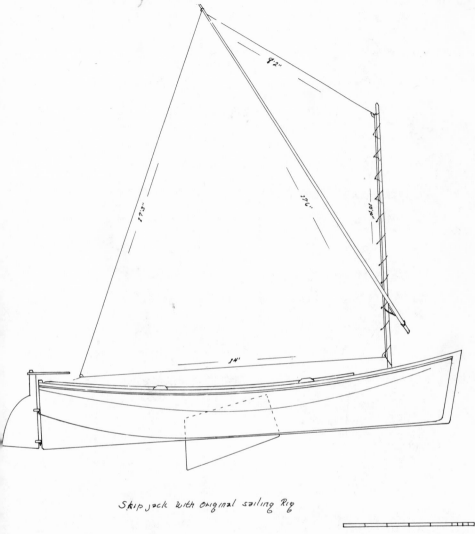

Skipjack with original sailing Rig

Scale ½"= 1'

Plate 1A Old-style Northern skipjack with original sailing rig

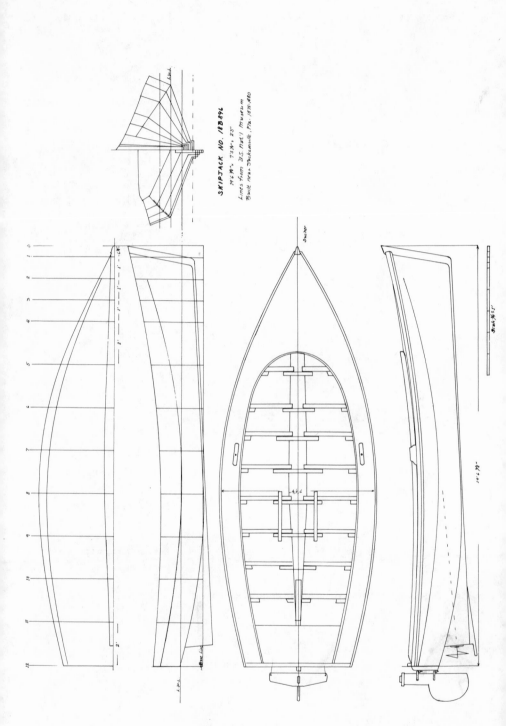

SKIPJACK NO. 18B896

M6#: 734, 23"
Lines from U.S. Nat'l Museum
Built near Jacksonville, Fla. 1875-1880

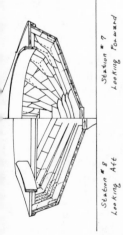

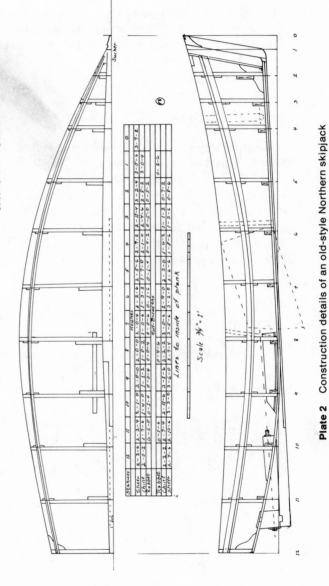

Plate 2 Construction details of an old-style Northern skipjack

the centerboard case was often fitted to prevent the shallow hull from working. Many of the early hulls were built without chines, the plank at the
chine line being merely edge fastened. The inclusion of a chine is advised,
however, for more structural strength and for easier building by boat carpenters of modest skills.

The initial steps for building a V-bottom hull are as described in volume 1,
pages 231 to 233. The frames must be set square with the centerline and
plumbed vertically (Figure 81). It is also good practice to erect the framing
so that the load waterline can be indicated as a datum line in its normal
horizontal position.

22′ Sailing Skipjack

A slightly larger and once popular 22-foot sailing skipjack is shown in
Plate 3. This hull may also be easily arranged as a powerboat (Plate 4).
This hull has a single plank keel, with the garboard seam laid flush along
its upper edge. A lateen-rigged version is shown in Plate 5. While this rig
can be dangerous in unskilled hands, it can offer an interesting alternative
to the experienced sailor. As this rig does not balance well with the mast
offset to clear the centerboard case, the latter is eliminated and the mast is
stepped on the centerline. A false keel is added as shown to give sufficient
lateral plane.

Power Skipjacks

With the coming of power, many of the older sailing hulls were fitted

Figure 80   Interior view of construction details of a Northern skipjack

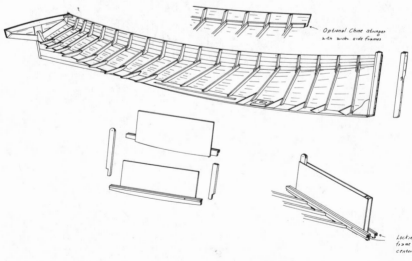

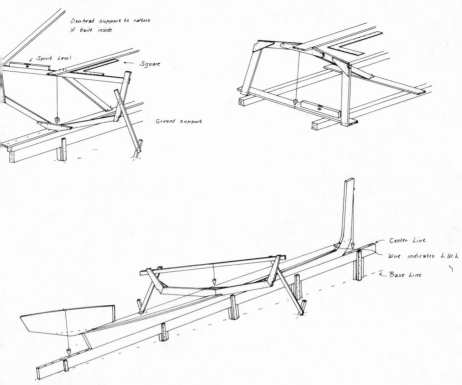

Overhead support to rafters
if built inside

Spirit Level

Square

Ground support

Center Line

Wire indicates L.W.L.

Base Line

Figure 81   Methods of setting up building frames for a Northern skipjack

with engines, and subsequent new ones were built as pure powerboats. The hull lines were well suited as an easy driving displacement launch, the lifted stern sections allowing good load carrying capacity. This fantail effect allows such hulls to be loaded to a negative freeboard amidships when built with tight decks, and appear to be perfectly safe in summer weather. At the same time there is enough bearing aft to prevent any serious squatting. A 36-foot hull on typical skipjack lines designed by the author some years ago showed a top speed of 11 knots when fitted with a 100 hp. medium-speed diesel engine with 2:1 reduction gearing.

The later power skipjacks were often built on the lines of the larger sailing hulls, but with additional length to enhance the speed capabilities and cargo capacity. This is perfectly permissible in a noncritical type of displacement hull, but thought must be given to retaining the original lines. In some cases lengthening is accomplished by adding a certain interval between the original station spacing. In order to avoid fining down the lines forward, some builders add extra stations amidships. These must be lofted in and faired with the original lines, and not built merely as copies of adjacent stations. Otherwise, awkward flat areas will appear in the sides and bottom which would both spoil the appearance and pose difficulties in plank-

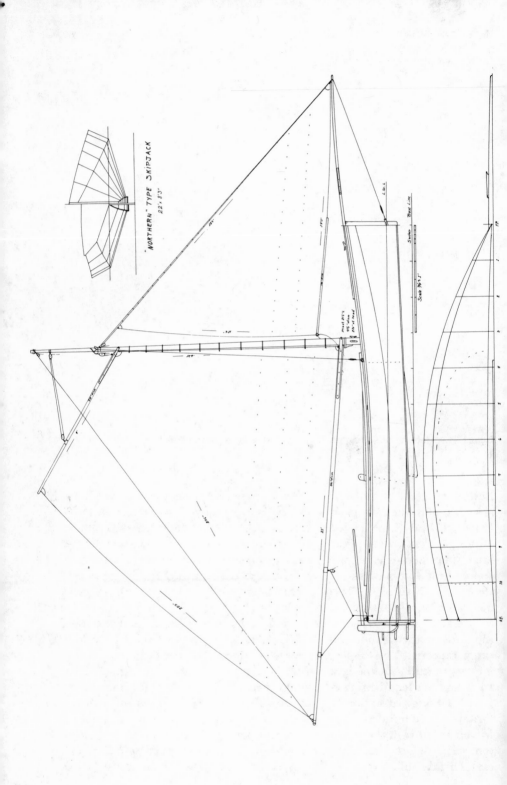

"NORTHERN" TYPE SKIPJACK
22' 8'3"

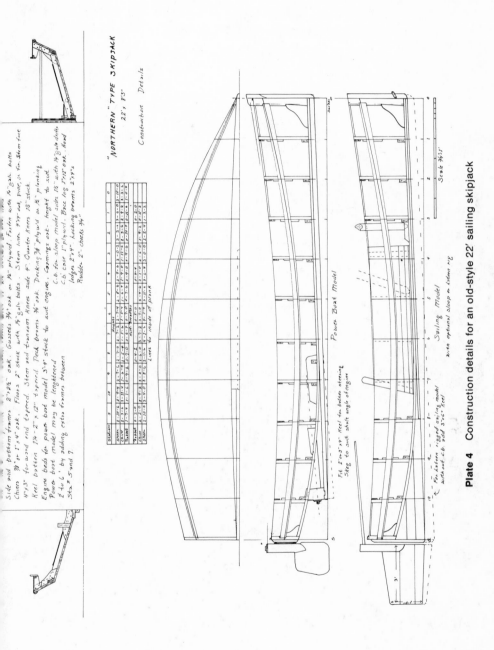

Plate 4 Construction details for an old-style 22' sailing skipjack

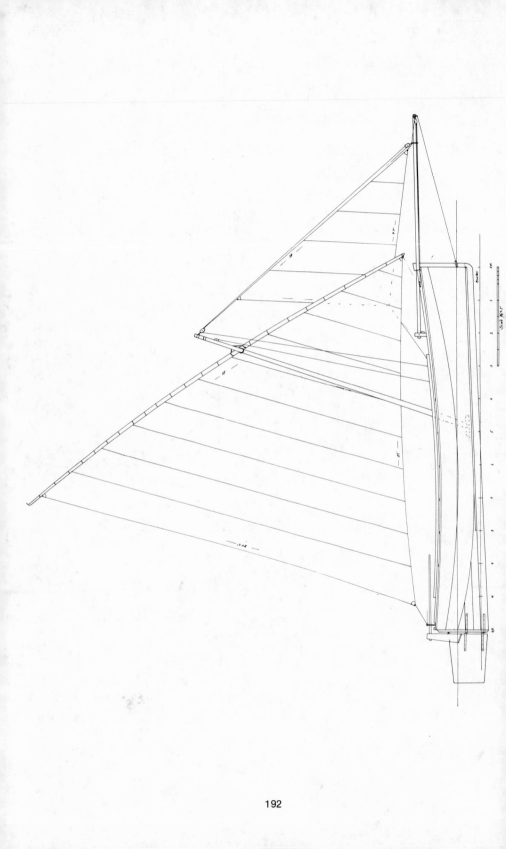

ing. This rule applies to any type of hull and the effect is shown in Figure 82.

Small Skipjack Launch

A small power skipjack launch is shown in Plate 6. Due to the rise in the run aft, various sizes of propellers may be accommodated by adjusting the depth and profile of the skeg.

Magic Sun

Larger hulls built on the skipjack method may require structural modifications to prevent hogging or sagging. An example is *Magic Sun,* whose lines are preserved in the Watercraft Collection (Plate 7). A massive log keelson was substituted for the flat plank type of the smaller hulls. The inner ends of the bottom frames are notched into this, but sometimes a locking beam is fitted (Figure 83). Some of these hulls have conventional scarphed and rabbeted stems as well, although a squared forefoot can be substituted as in the smaller boats.

Fitting Engine Mounting and Propeller Shaft

The construction of the engine mountings forming certain of the floors is

Figure 82   Correct method of fairing extra frames for lengthening V-bottom hull

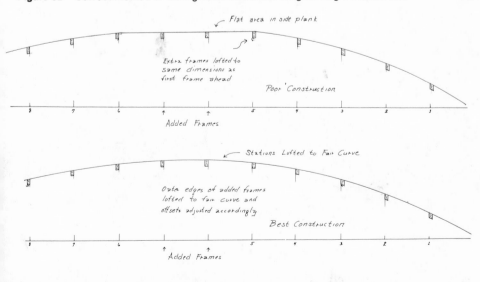

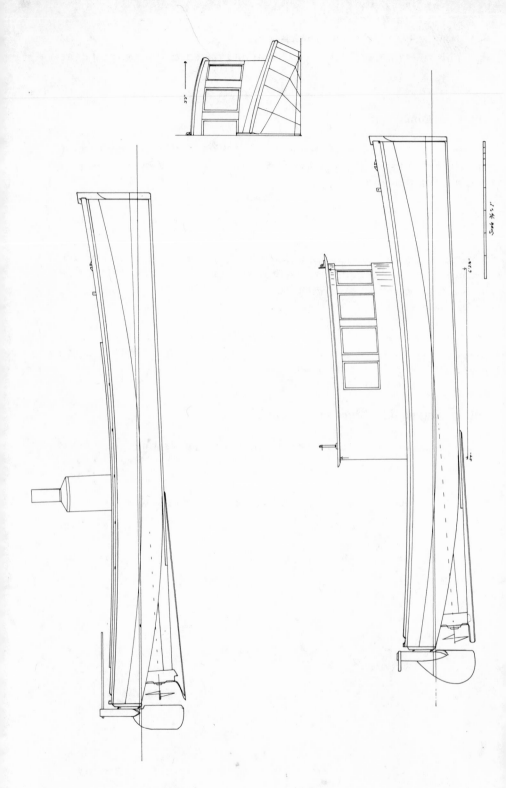

	Heights																					
Sheer	5-1-4	4-11-0	4-10-2	4-9-2	4-8-0	4-7-4	4-6-6	4-6-0	4-5-6	4-6-0	4-7-0	4-7-6	4-9-2	4-11-2	5-0-6	5-4-0	5-6-2	5-10-2	6-2-6	6-8-2	7-1-6	7-11-4
Chine	4-4-6	3-9-6	3-6-2	3-1-2	2-9-4	2-7-2	2-5-0	2-3-0	2-3-0	2-3-1	2-4-0	2-5-6	2-8-0	2-10-4	3-1-2	3-4-4	3-8-4	4-1-6	4-7-4	5-3-0	5-11-6	7-0-6
Rabbet	3-9-4	2-11-0	3-4-6	1-10-4	1-6-0	1-2-2	0-10-6	0-9-4	0-9-4	0-10-0	1-10-4	1-0-2	1-1-0	2-1-6	1-2-4	1-3-4	1-4-0	1-4-6	1-5-6	1-7-4	1-9-4	
	Half-Breadths																					
Sheer	5-11-0	6-2-0	6-4-0	6-5-0	6-7-2	6-7-6	6-8-4	6-9-4	6-9-6	6-10-6	6-9-6	6-9-2	6-8-2	6-5-6	6-3-0	5-10-4	5-4-0	4-6-6	3-7-4	2-8-2	1-8-2	
Chine	5-9-0	5-11-0	6-1-0	6-2-0	6-4-2	6-6-0	6-6-4	6-7-4	6-8-0	6-7-6	6-7-0	6-6-0	6-4-6	6-2-6	6-0-0	5-6-4	5-0-2	4-0-0	3-4-2	2-6-4	1-5-4	

lines to outside of plank

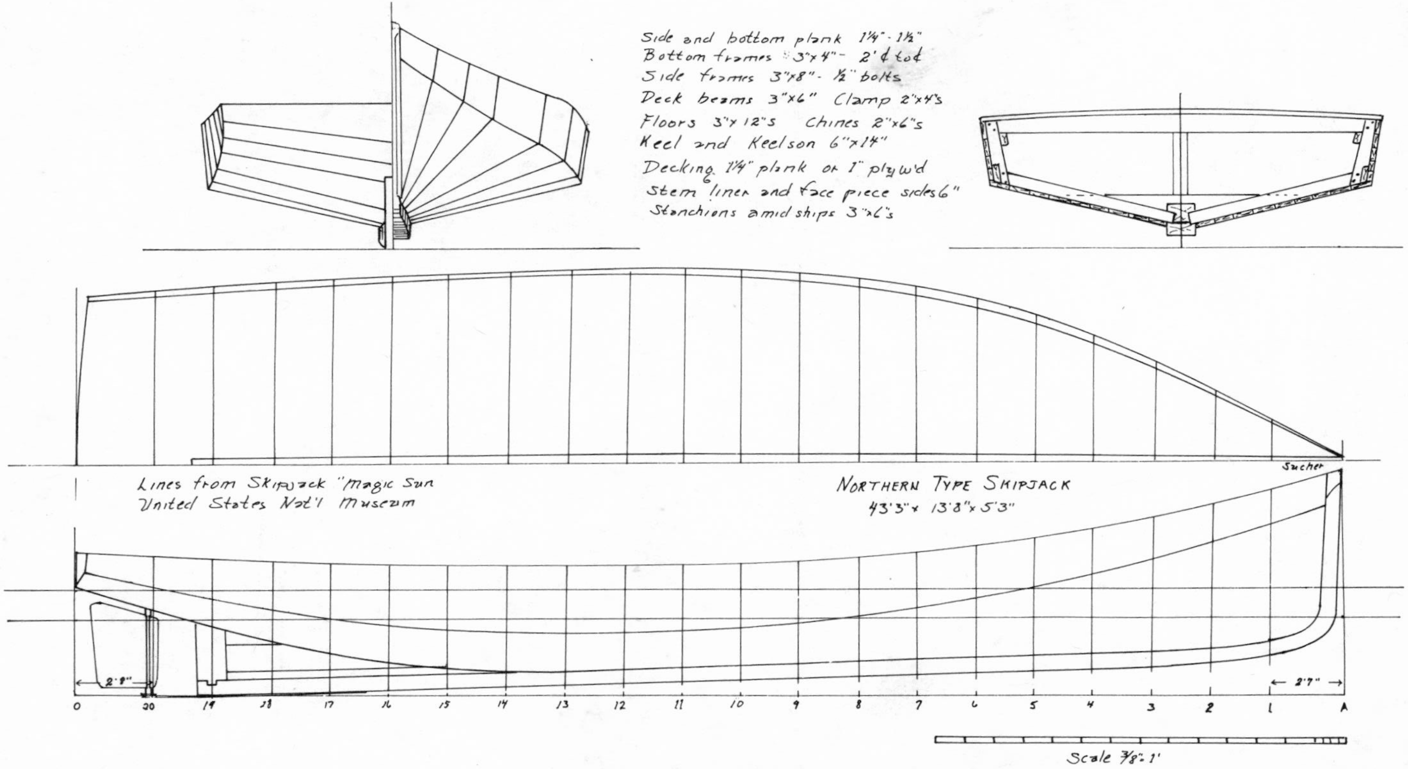

Side and bottom plank 1¼" - 1½"
Bottom frames 3"x4" - 2' ¢ to ¢
Side frames 3"x8" - ½" bolts
Deck beams 3"x6" Clamp 2"x4"s
Floors 3"x12"s Chines 2"x6"s
Keel and Keelson 6"x14"
Decking 1¼" plank or 1" plyw'd
Stem liner and face piece sides 6"
Stanchions amidships 3"x6"s
Sucher
Lines from Skipjack "Magic Sun
United States Nat'l Museum
NORTHERN TYPE SKIPJACK
43'3" x 13'8" x 5'3"
2'8"
2'7"
0
20
19
18
17
16
15
14
13
12
11
10
9
8
7
6
5
4
3
2
1
A
Scale 3/8" = 1'

Plate 7 Construction details for a 43′ Northern skipjack converted to power

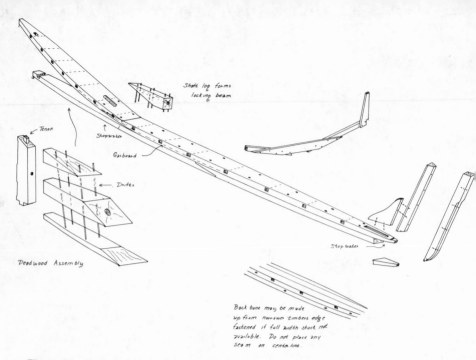

Shaft log forms locking beam

Tenon

Stopwater

Garboard

Drifts

Stop water

Deadwood Assembly

Back bone may be made up from narrower timbers edge fastened if full width stock not available. Do not place any seam on centre line.

Figure 83   Exploded view of the keel and stem timbers of a Northern skipjack

Figure 84   Details of engine mounting and keel construction of a Northern skipjack

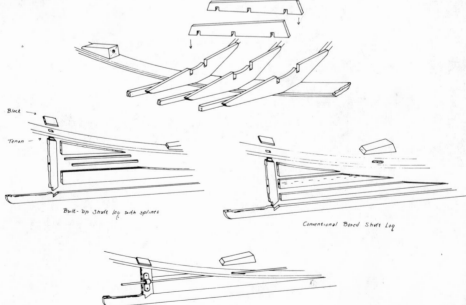

Block

Tenon

Built-up Shaft log with splines

Conventional Bored Shaft Log

Side Mounted Shaft

shown in Figure 84, along with optional methods of building the skeg and propeller shaft bearings. Figure 85 shows the shafting through the interior of the hull with an alley built over it in the way of the hold space. An inspection door should always be fitted over intermediate shaft bearings and couplings to give access for servicing and repair.

Optional Arrangements for a Large Skipjack

As a heavy displacement hull, the large skipjack may be built with a number of optional arrangements. Plate 8 shows a Great Lakes gillnet tug, a freight or cargo launch with the engine aft, and a western-rigged combination boat with engine forward. Plate 9 shows a steam-powered skipjack launch with a deep skeg to accommodate the unusually large, slow-turning propeller required with such installations.

A somewhat smaller launch on these lines may be laid out by reducing the scale to ½ inch–1 foot, with a corresponding reduction in the size of the

Figure 85 Details of fittings for an intermediate propeller shaft bearing

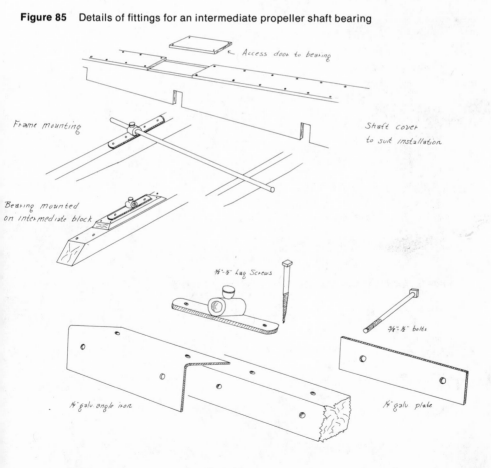

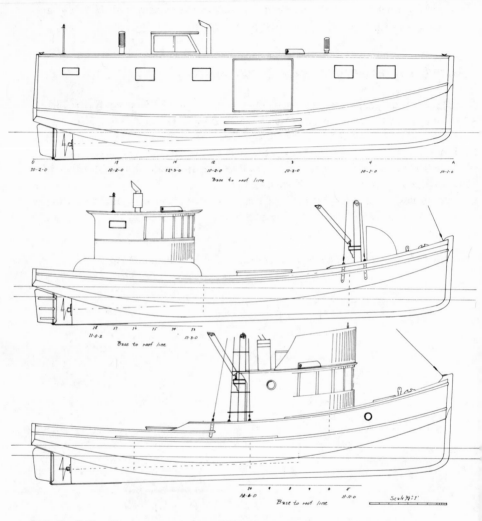

Plate 8   Optional arrangements for a 43' Northern skipjack

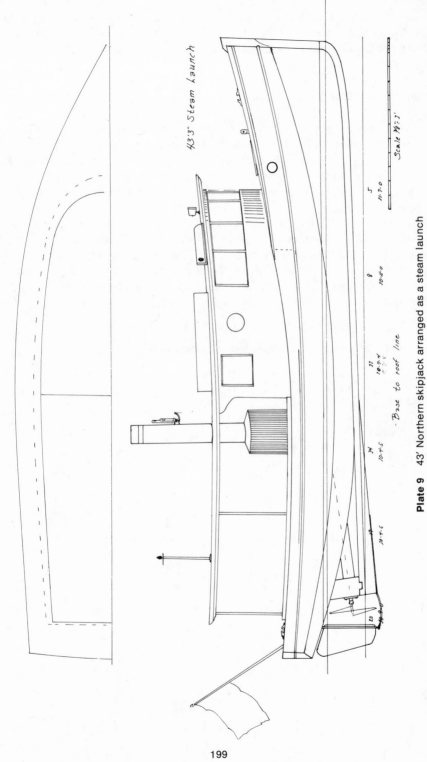

43'3" Steam launch

Scale 3/4":1'

Base to roof line

Plate 9 43' Northern skipjack arranged as a steam launch

scantlings. As this scale reduction results in a lowered freeboard, the addition of a raised deck forward and substantial railings aft will make for a dryer boat and provide useful cabin space forward (Plate 10).

Rail Stanchions

Where the sides of a raised deck show the same flare as the forward sections of the main hull, the basis of the former is merely an extension of the tops of the side frames. The sides may be planked up with material of the same or slightly less thickness. As the flare decreases toward the midship section, stanchions that bolt to the tops of the side frames are substituted (Figure 86).

In fishing boats and small cargo vessels subject to working around docks or other craft, a "breakaway" type of rail stanchion is preferred to extended side frames. The stanchion is made somewhat lighter than the frames and is fastened to them with large diameter bolts. In case of a strong impact, it will then fracture in the way of its fastenings, the side frame usually remaining intact.

Figure 86   Details of rail stanchions and rail construction

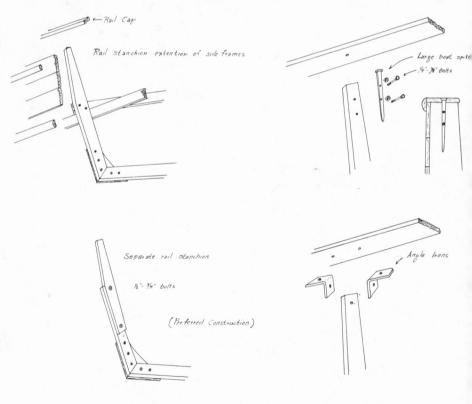

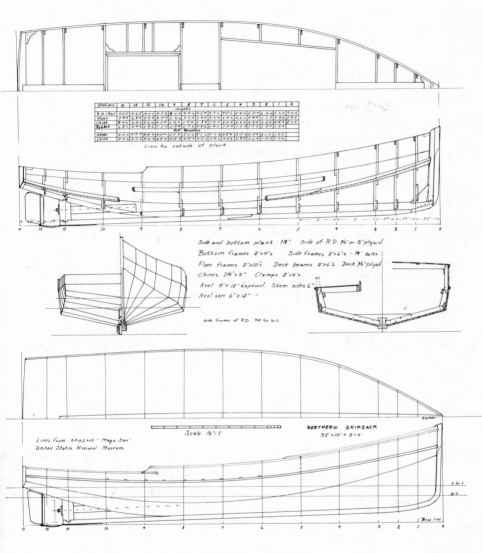

Plate 10 Construction details for a 32′ Northern skipjack

Methods of Fitting Stern Transom

Alternative methods of fitting the lower transom frame to the horn timber are shown in Figure 87. The fitting of the transom frame over the top of the horn timber makes a stronger structure and is preferred in larger hulls.

Optional Interior Arrangements

As with most hulls of generous displacement, a number of alternative interior arrangements are optional. Plate 11 shows the 32-foot model rigged as a western-style combination boat. Plate 12 shows a heavy-duty trawler-type cruiser and a small shrimping or cargo launch.

Rudders

Economies in powerboat construction can be effected by the selection of a simple type of rudder that can be fabricated by the builder. While plate-type rudders with blades of cast naval bronze are available as fittings from marine hardware manufacturers, the cost is high due to the cost of the noble metal. It is possible to build up rudders with wooden blades at substantial savings. The rudder stock may be fashioned from a short length of discarded propeller shaft with its upper end squared to receive the steering quadrant. The blades are fastened to the stock by means of bronze drifts,

Figure 87   Optional methods of fitting a stern transom to the horn timber

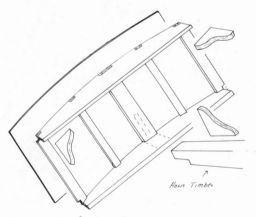

Horn Timber

notches for chine + clamp

Lower Transom frame lapped

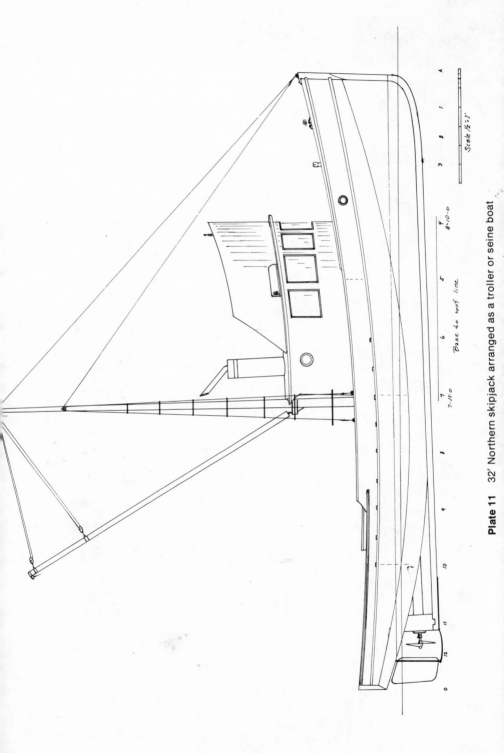

Plate 11 32′ Northern skipjack arranged as a troller or seine boat

Scale ½″=1′

Base to roof line

8-0-0

7-0-0

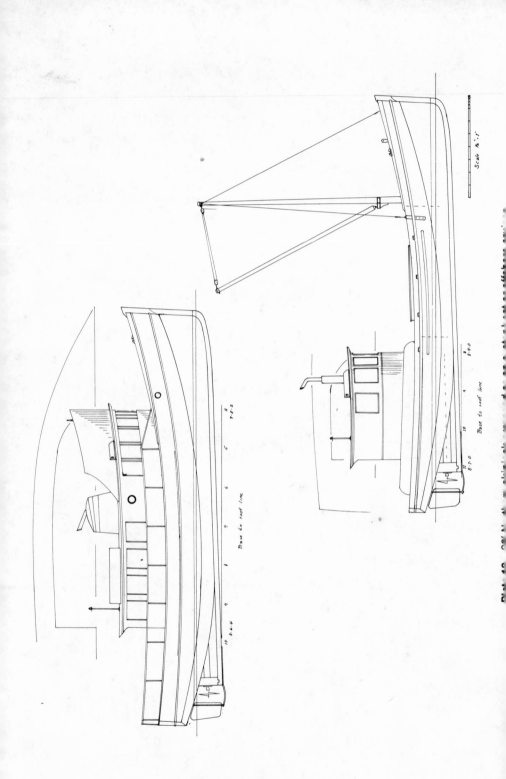

Scale ⅛ = 1'

Base to roof line

8·7·0

8·4·0

Base to roof line

7·8·9

Base to roof line

8·6·4

and braced with oak cheek pieces mortised into the sides (Figure 88). A rudder for a small launch is shown in Figure 89.

The most simple rudder stay is made by extending the lower keel section aft to the heel of the rudder post. In cases where this is not possible due to considerations of minimum draft requirements, a metal stay is then fitted. It is best to use bronze strapping here at the penalty of some extra cost, as a galvanized fitting can lead to electrolysis problems when combined with the bronze rudder, shaft, and stern bearing.

Manufactured fittings for the construction of wooden-bladed rudders for larger vessels are shown in Figure 90. Some of these are available with a channeled metal stay which bolts to the after edge of the keel.

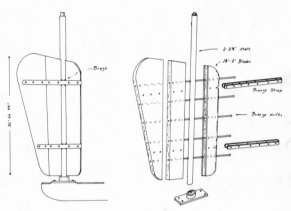

Figure 88 Details of wooden rudder construction for a large power launch

Figure 89 Details of wooden rudder construction for a small power launch

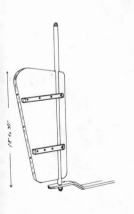

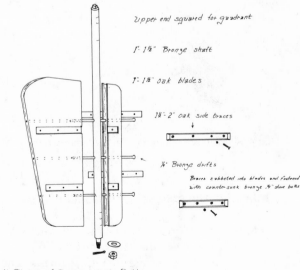

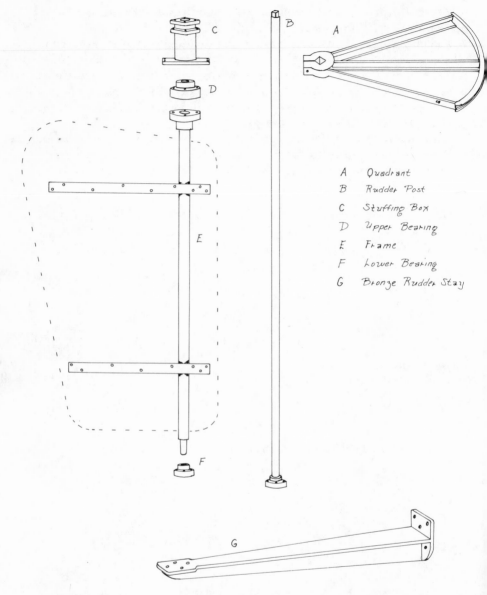

Figure 90   The various parts of manufactured rudder fittings

Cabin and Deckhouse Construction

The construction of cabins and deckhouses for larger classes of power launches is markedly similar in method to land-based structures, with a few special adaptations for marine requirements. The upper perimeter is usually made slightly smaller than the base of cabin structures in order to avoid a boxy appearance.

Deckhouse construction for a trawler-type cruiser or workboat is shown in Figure 91. It will be noted that the lower plate is bolted through the decking and into the deck beams and carlins beneath. If the decks and house sides are to be fiber glass covered, a continuous watertight joint is formed. If this is not the case, a gasket of paint-soaked canvas or felt must be set under the plate to insure a watertight fit.

As the deck line of most launches employing this type of deckhouse is generally curved in profile, the lower plateline is made to conform to this shape (Figure 92). To enhance appearance and to give adequate headroom forward, the upper plate is shaped to a similar profile with rising battens set into the upper plate.

An improvement over the somewhat boxy look of a deckhouse with a squared forward section can be made where the edges are angled (Figure 93).

An even better appearance and somewhat reduced windage is provided

Figure 91 Details of deckhouse construction in a large powerboat

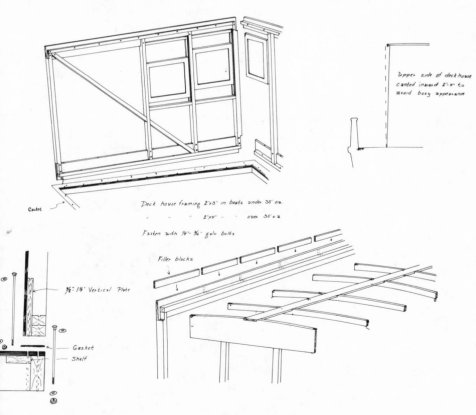

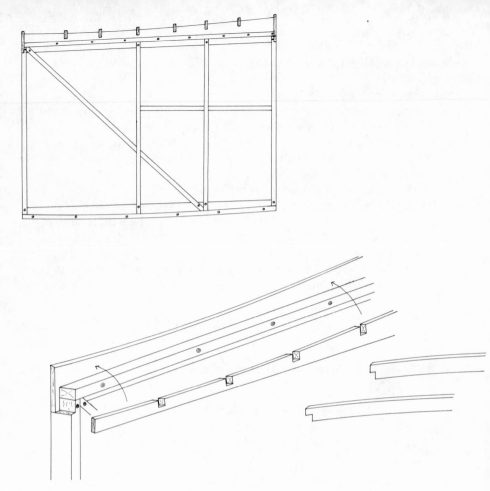

Figure 92 Details of deckhouse construction in a small power launch

Figure 93 Construction details of angular corners on wooden deckhouses

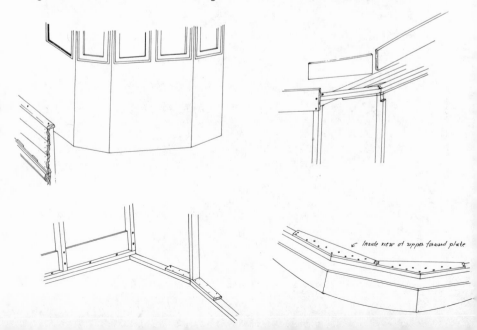

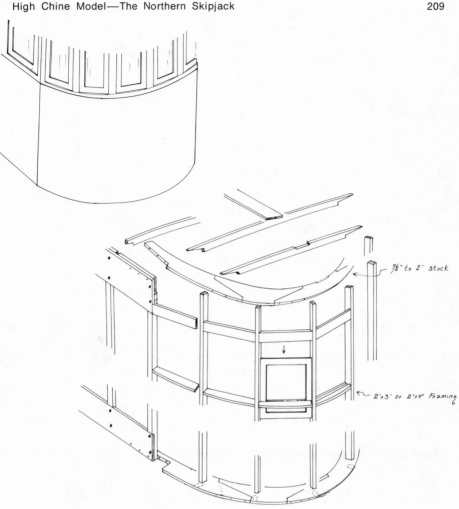

Figure 94 Construction details of a circular front for a deckhouse

by rounding the forward sections of the deckhouse (Figure 94).

Most deckhouses today are built with an outer covering of plywood panels finished with paint or fiber glass. Forward curvatures may be more easily applied if two layers of covering are used in combinations of thickness to correspond to the single layer of paneling used to cover the sides and after end. In older craft or in cases where very hard service is to be encountered, the deckhouse sides are covered with tongue-and-groove staving set vertically (Figure 95). Here the edges of the tongues and grooves must be planed in the way of the curve as shown to make a close fit.

Most deckhouses have interior ceiling of plywood panels. These may have special surfaces to conform to specific requirements. In craft used in very hot or cold climates the spaces between the studding should be filled with

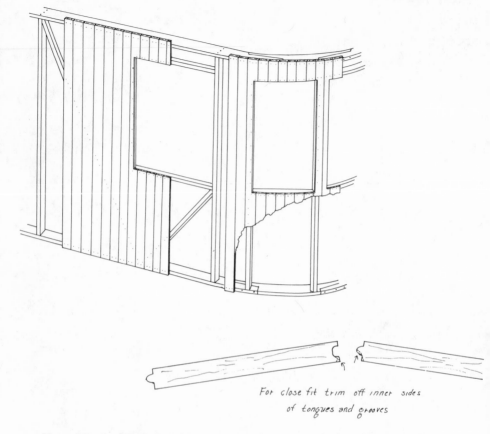

For close fit trim off inner sides
of tongues and grooves

Figure 95   A method of applying tongue-and-groove vertical staving to a deckhouse

insulation material. In extremes of temperature, additional insulation may be obtained by applying sheets of tar paper or felt under the exterior covering.

A few small launches of utility or antique style are built with the so-called glass cabins. The framing here may be a combination of methods previously shown, but the window sash itself may form an integral part of the structure to maintain its rigidity (Figure 96).

Methods of Building Frames for Flying Bridges

The construction details of various types of flying bridges are shown in Figure 97. The framing here should be of lightweight wood to cut down on unnecessary top hamper, the requisite structural strength being gained from careful joinery. Most flying bridges are covered with plywood panels. Vertical staving is sometimes used in larger vessels subject to hard service.

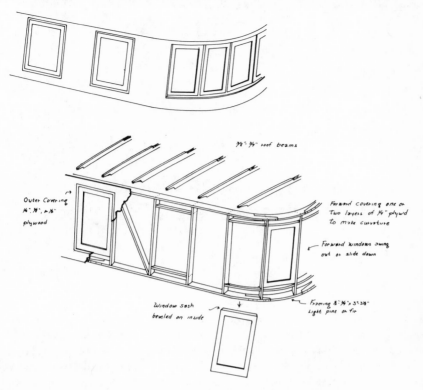

Outer Covering
$\frac{1}{16}$", $\frac{3}{8}$", or $\frac{3}{8}$"
plywood

$\frac{3}{4}$"~$\frac{3}{4}$" roof beams

Forward covering one or
Two layers of $\frac{1}{8}$" plywd
to make curvature

Forward windows swing
out or slide down

Framing $\frac{5}{8}$"~$\frac{3}{4}$" x 3"~3$\frac{1}{2}$"
light pine or fir

Window sash
beveled on inside

Figure 96 Construction details of an old-style "glass cabin" deckhouse

Figure 97 Methods of framing flying bridges

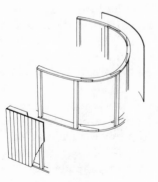

19

High Chine Model
The Chesapeake Bay Skipjack

The easily built Northern skipjack found good acceptance in its native Long Island Sound waters, and later found favor to the south in the northern Chesapeake Bay region. As this area was the largest and most significant inland waterway on the eastern seaboard, those of its inhabitants engaged in commercial fishing and waterborne commerce were logically attracted to simple types of small craft that could in many cases be built by the watermen themselves.

At first widely built in its original form, a simplification in its construction was seen after 1880. In place of the longitudinally laid bottom plank with its attendant full framing system, the Bay builders began substituting diagonally laid or herringbone type of plank that consisted of short strakes on either side of the bilges.

This plank extended from keel or keelson to chine and was applied at an angle of about 15 degrees. Its diagonal application compensated for the slight variation in angle between the rabbet line and chine in most hulls, and allowed for the use of mostly flat pieces of plank. It also made for a stiff enough structure to enable the elimination of the bottom framing, except in certain cases where strongbacks were fitted to provide extra bracing in large hulls.

A slightly different condition existed at the angle in the bow, however, due to the rather abrupt change in the chine line as it flared outward from the stem piece. To form the necessary close fit at both rabbet and chine, a somewhat hard twist was worked into the forward strakes. This was actually built into the plank by hewing and planing, and to allow for this the bow staving was in many cases up to 40 percent thicker stock than the balance of the plank where a hard twist was not required.

The first Bay skipjacks were mostly small sloops like their Long Island forebears. Later on, larger and more substantial craft were built, especially after the coming of power.

45' Power Skipjack

Plate 13 shows a 45 foot power workboat of type and size that has been widely built on the Bay for commercial fishing and freighting. Its very substantial construction and heavy scantlings are typical of this type of craft and enables it to stand up to many years of hard service.

It will be noted that it is the keelson which forms the principal backbone structure rather than the keel, which is merely an adjunct to stiffen the former and to position the propeller shaft and rudder stay. The bottom of the keelson is shaped to the rabbet, with scarphs positioned to form the proper curve. Early builders often used curved tree trunks which were squared with an adz, but these timbers are seldom available today.

The chine logs are also comparatively heavy as these, with the keelson, may form the structural attachments of the bottom plank in lieu of any other framing. Large hulls also carry sister keelsons which give additional support to the bottom plank, and may form a partial foundation for the ceiling required in cargo carrying vessels.

Use of Strongbacks

To prevent wringing in a rather wide and shallow hull, strongbacks are fitted which act as trusses. These may be full frames, but more usually are built up with a heavy timber extending across the hull and kneed into a heavy set of side frames. This is braced against the keelson by means of two or more short blocks which are through fastened with a couple of heavy drifts. Two or three conventional frames are often fitted near the bow which give additional support to the bottom and aid in positioning the chine logs when setting the hull up for building. Additional stiffening is provided by two or more bulkheads of vertical staving or heavy plywood fastened to a heavy sill laid across the bilge and bearing against a deck beam above. In some cases the strongbacks are further braced by heavy galvanized tie rods that pass through the outer plank or "wale" at the sheerline. Tie rods are usually placed near the derrick mast to help to brace the hull against spreading when heavy loads are hoisted.

While some Bay-built craft are virtually frameless, some hulls, notably of smaller size, carry a few frames that are actually used as molds in the building of the hull (Figure 98).

Chesapeake Bay Hulls Built With Frames

The procedure for shaping the forefoot staving of a cross-planked Bay hull is shown in Figure 99. The square or original edge of the staving is set against the lower edge of the keelson, which has been previously beveled to approximate the bevel in the lower edge of the chine above. The lower edge

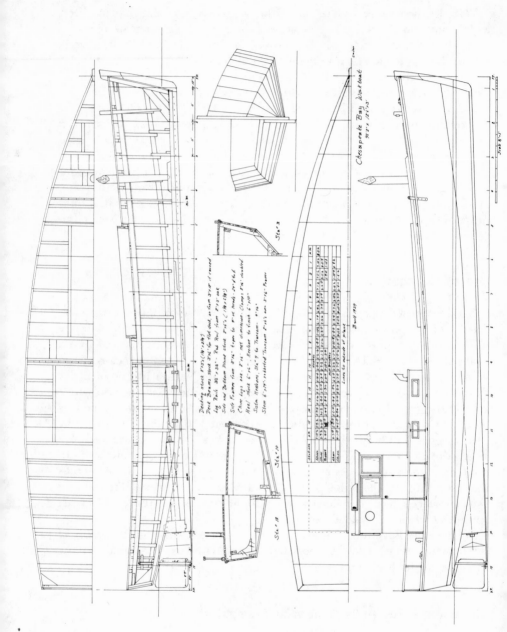

Chesapeake Bay Workboat
50' x 12'-3"

Built 1939

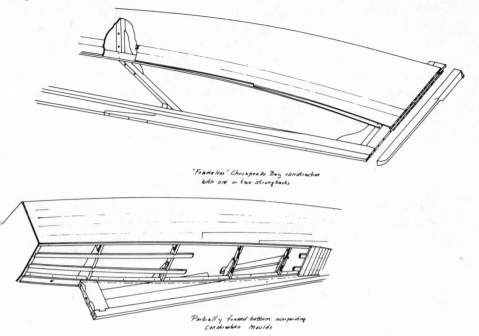

"Frameless" Chesapeake Bay construction
with one or two strongbacks

Partially framed bottom incorporating
Construction moulds

Figure 98   Framed and "frameless" types of bottom construction used in cross-planked
Chesapeake Bay hulls

Figure 99   Method of shaping forefoot planking in Chesapeake Bay construction

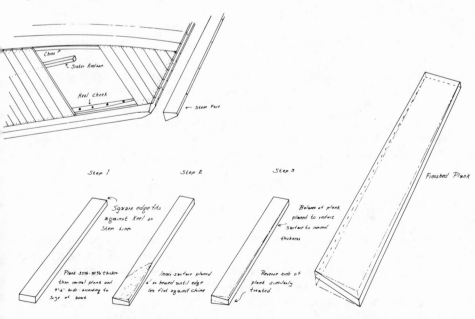

Chine

Sister Keelson

Keel Cheek

Stem Face

Step 1   Step 2   Step 3   Finished Plank

Square edge fits
against keel or
Stem liner

Balance of plank
planed to reduce
surface to normal
thickness

Plank 33%-40% thicker
than normal plank and
4"-6" wide · according to
Size of boat

Inner surface planed
& on hewed until edge
lies flat against chine

Reverse side of
plank similarly
treated

of this strake will bear against the keel itself. The angle of the strakes is determined by trial, the pieces being fitted in a manner which requires the least beveling. They may be straight up and down in plumb-stemmed designs, or set fanwise in a rounded forefoot. The latter are usually rabbeted, but with straight plumb or raking stems, a two-piece liner and face timber are generally fitted to avoid rabbet cutting. In this case it is a simple matter to bevel the stem liner to bring the bottom staving to its outer edge. The hood ends of the plank are then covered by the stem face.

Changing Angle of Bottom Plank Attachment at the Bow

In this type of construction, the joining of the bottom and side plank at the chine must receive special consideration (Figure 100). As the forward strakes of the bottom planking are nearly upright, their upper ends will bear against the lower edge of the first strake of the side plank, but are fastened only to the chine stringer. As their angle increases in relation to the side plank, the nailing surface against the chine decreases. To effect this directional change in the bottom plank, and to allow its outer fastenings to be let into the bottom edge of the side plank for adequate structural strength, the latter must be notched. This is done at some arbitrary point a few feet abaft the bow, the position of the bottom planking strake governed by the angle of the chine as it leaves the stem. This condition exists of course, whether the forefoot is square or rounded.

Methods of Setting Up for Building

In setting up for building, small hulls are put together in the upside-down position, with either temporary molds or several strongback frames which may be left in the boat as structural members. Larger craft are generally built right side up, and are then tilted from one side to the other after the side planks are fitted to facilitate planking up the bottom. In cases where larger hulls are put together in the inverted position, the upper strakes of the side plank may be omitted until after the hull is righted to keep the weight as low as possible.

Hull Variations Possible Using This Method

It will be noted that with this type of construction there is considerable latitude as to the forms of hull to which it may be applied. Varying angles of the bows can be compensated for by adjusting the degree of fanning that is built into the staving, and the angle at which it diverges from the rabbet line. Early empirical builders were quick to visualize the many variations

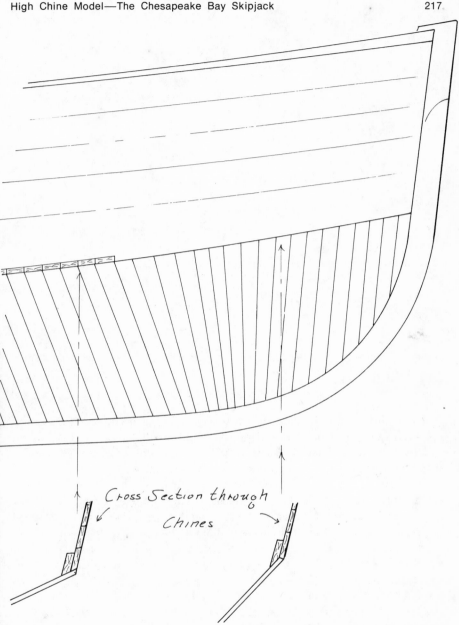

Figure 100   Method of applying forefoot planking to the chines in Chesapeake Bay
construction

possible in utilizing the cross-planked bottom, and adapted it to several distinct types of small craft. In recent years the Bay builders have modified numerous types of modern hull forms of both round- and V-bottom types for
the application of the cross-planked bottom (Figure 101).

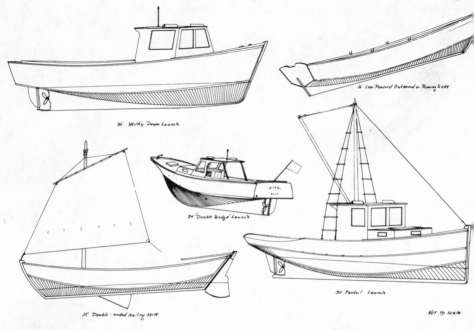

Figure 101   Various types of hulls which may be planked by the Chesapeake Bay method

While this unique method of construction has been employed mostly in its area of origin, it has received much attention from naval architects and practical builders generally for its obvious advantages of economical building. Some authorities have claimed that certain structural weaknesses may be inherent in this system, citing cases where leaks were induced by flexing of the frameless bottom. Proponents of the Bay system have pointed out that careless fitting and inferior joinery together with insufficient attention to proper fastenings have been responsible for the more glaring failures, and hold that poor construction has been the result of a total lack of understanding of the method. As an admittedly controversial method of boatbuilding, the prospective builder must himself view it in the light of his own inclinations and mechanical abilities. Those interested in actual building are advised to construct a model hull, or at least one side of the bow angle to test their understanding of it in a practical sense before attempting a full sized building project.

The Fantail-Stern Power Launch

A useful type of small boat form that is readily adaptable to the cross-planked bottom is the fantail power launch. If a displacement-type hull is required and moderate speeds are acceptable, this type of craft has much to recommend it. The combination of a narrow entrance angle at the bow, gently curving chine lines, and lifted stern sections makes for an easily driven hull that requires but modest power to bring it to its terminal hull speed. These launches are very good performers in rough or choppy waters, and due to the lack of bearing aft are difficult to broach or capsize even with their normally shallow draft, provided top hamper and high deck-house structure are kept in moderation.

Perhaps the most useful attribute of the fantail launch is its ability to carry very large loads. Due to the rise in the stern sections it can be subjected to varying conditions of loading or overloading without dragging the stern or absorbing excess power. In fact, as commercial fishing craft or small freight boats these craft may be safely loaded to a negative freeboard amidships in summer weather, provided high hatch coamings and deckhouse door sills are fitted to keep solid water from penetrating the hull proper.

The noncritical factors of the fantail's loading, weight, and balance characteristics allow for optional positioning of the engine and cargo space. Also, the builder has rather wide latitude in the weight of scantlings employed—very light construction for pleasure boat use, or medium to massive to rigorous commercial service requirements. As a simplified V-bottom, a launch of this type can offer a useful replacement for the older type of round-bottom fantail hull much used by commercial operators or sought after by traditional boat enthusiasts, as building in original form is now prohibitive because of high costs and the lack of carpenters with the manual skills necessary to build them.

A Medium-Sized Fantail-Stern Power Launch

A popular-sized example of such a launch is shown on Plate 14. Its construction is somewhat simpler than the 45-foot freight launch, and the fitting of the full framing sets forward and bulkheads is optional. The scantling sizes shown in the plans may be varied to suit individual conditions. While the transom may be made square, the round or eliptical type gives a much more attractive and shipshape appearance and is less likely to foul nets and lines. It is framed with upper and lower rim logs, and its construction is as described for the sharpie (see volume 1, pages 330–332, Figure 133).

Power Plants Adaptable to Fantail-Stern Hulls

A wide variety of power plants are suitable, low power only being required for its terminal hull speed of 6½–7 knots. Heavy duty two-or-four-cycle gasoline engines of 6–10 hp., or sailboat auxiliary types of small 15 to 20 hp. diesels would offer the most economical power. Automobile conversions

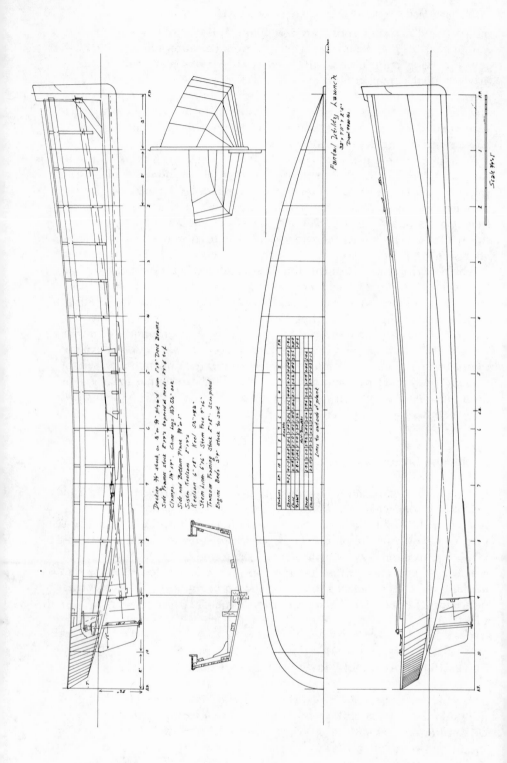

Fantail Utility Launch
32' x 7'10" x 2' 0"
Drawn 1960-61

Decking ¾" stock on 8" in 9° plywd ... on 1½" Deck Beams
Side Frames stock 1½"x¾" tapered at head: 2" x ¾" ...
Clamps 1¼"x¾". Chine logs 1¾"x¾". oak
Side and Bottom Plank 9/16".
Sister Keelson 2" x ¾"s
Keelson 6" x ¾". Keel 5¼"x¾".
Stern knee 6" x ¾". Stem Face 1" x ¾".
Transom Framing Stock 1"x¾". Sculptured
Engine Beds 3½" stock to suit

Lines to outside of plank

or marine type multicylinder engines of up to 200 cu. in piston displacement could be used if able to turn a propeller of at least 16-inch diameter. Such engines should be somewhat detuned to allow low speed running without fouling the spark plugs.

Optional Interior Arrangements in a Fantail-Stern Hull

Optional interior arrangements for various uses include an open launch, combination gillnet boat, or as a pleasure cruiser (Plate 15).

Scale Changes for Various Hull Sizes

Translating this hull form into one of somewhat larger size, the lines may be scaled to ½ inch to 1 foot to make a 48-foot launch for many uses (Plate 16). Practical arrangements include that of a small snapper or halibut schooner or cabin utility launch (Plate 17). This hull could be lengthened 10 to 15 feet to advantage for greater cargo capacity and slightly better speed by lofting in some additional stations amidships.

Minimal Practical Size of Fantail Skipjack Hull

A useful fantail launch of perhaps the minimum practical size is shown in Plate 18. This 26-foot hull may be arranged as a working or toy tugboat or as a utility launch. It will be able enough for offshore use as a raised deck model with tight decks and substantial cargo hatch coamings and with a self-draining trolling cockpit if built for this use (Plate 19). This launch may be powered with a 6–10 hp. heavy-duty, single- or two-cylinder engine, or small four cylinder type such as the Universal Atomic Four, or 22 hp. Palmer.

Use of Single Rim Logs to Make Up a Fantail Stern

A variation in the previously described (volume 1, pages 330–332) construction of round or eliptical sterns for small fantail launches is shown in Figure 102. In this type of stern a single rim log is used, where in a hull of low freeboard a thin profile is required to allow for the correct upsweep of the bottom lines. The size of the timbers used may be from 3 inch stock in very small launches, up to 10 or 12 inch timbers in larger types. The fitting of short blocks by means of long bolts or drifts continues the profile line from the chine as shown. These blocks are shaped after the main frame is assembled, edge-scarphed, and bolted together.

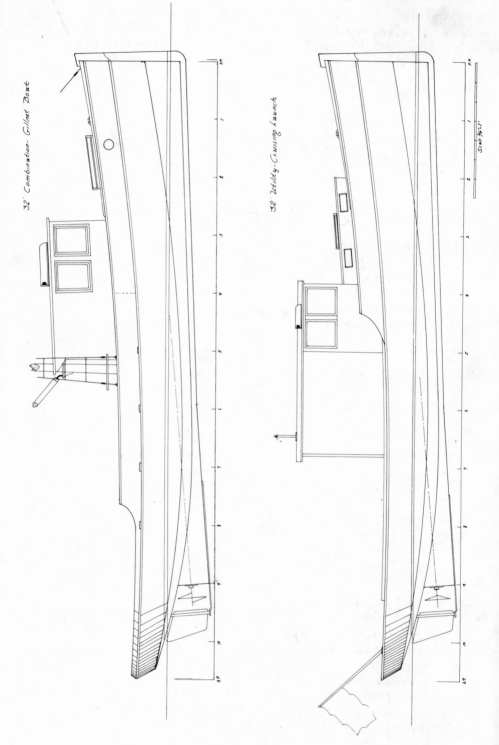

32' Combination-Gillnet Boat

32' Utility-Cruising Launch

Scale ¾"=1'

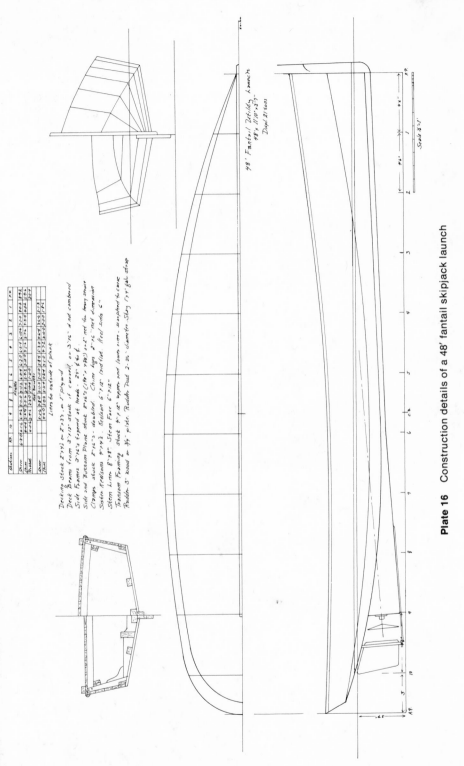

Plate 16 Construction details of a 48' fantail skipjack launch

223

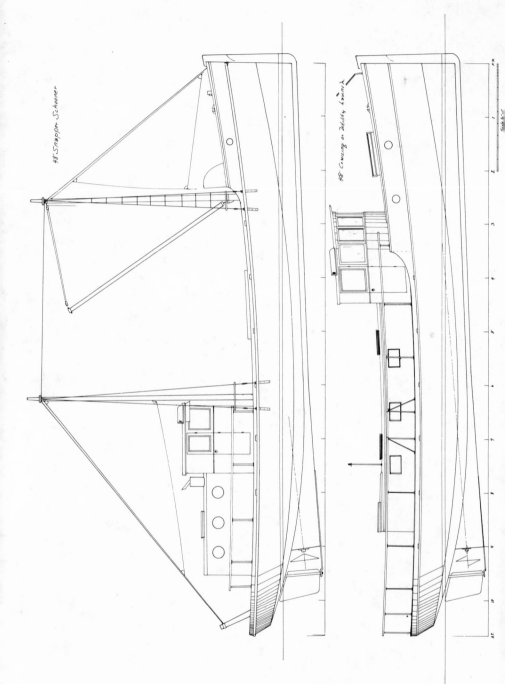

48' Snapper Schooner

48' Cruising or Utility Launch

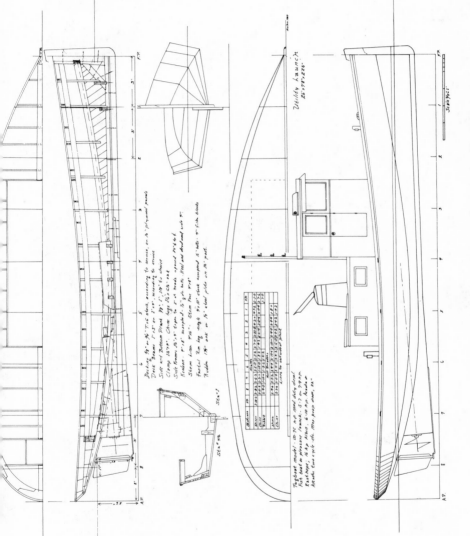

Plate 18 Construction details of a 26' fantail skipjack utility launch

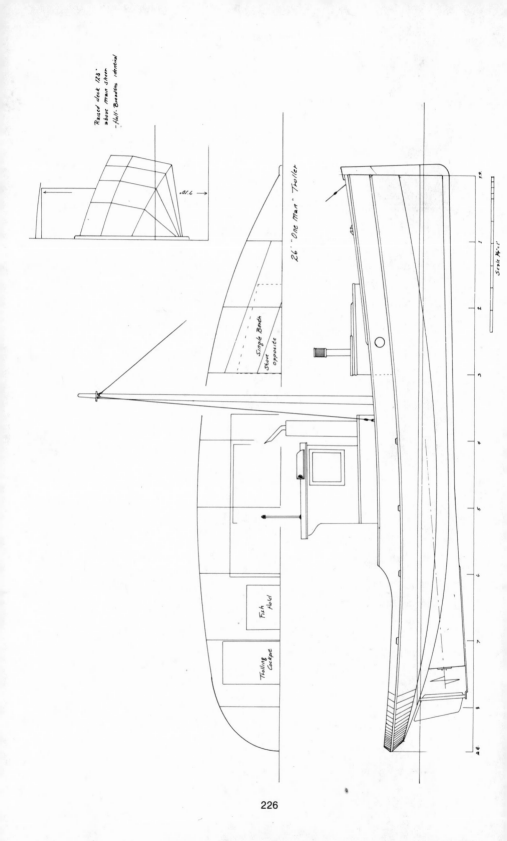

Raised deck 12½" above main sheer
-Half Breadths identical

.01.6

26' "One Man" Troller

Single Berth
Stove opposite

Fish Hold

Trolling Cockpit

Scale ¾"=1'

F.P.

1

2

3

4

5

6

7

8

A.P.

226

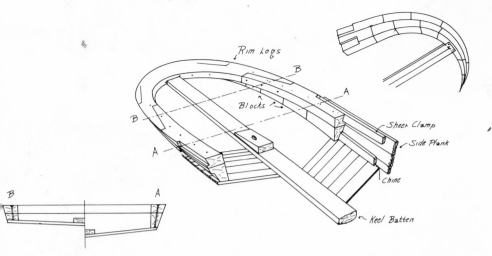

Figure 102 Construction details of rim logs used in making up the stern framing in fantail hulls

An Enlarged Version of the Small Fantail-Stern Hull

An enlarged 39-foot version of the 26-foot model is shown in Plate 20, drawn to a scale of ½ inch to 1 foot. The construction is similar with a moderate increase in the size of the scantlings. This hull may also be arranged as a pleasure launch or commercial fishing boat (Plate 21).

Chesapeake Bay Launch With Transom Stern

A Bay launch with a transom stern is shown in Plate 22. In this case the horn timber extends aft horizontally to form the flattened run. The overall construction is almost identical to the fantail models except for the after detail of the log keelson. The example shown is a moderate-speed launch, due to the slight reverse camber in the after rabbet. This places the center of gravity well aft, and in combination with the easy lines forward gives the hull a comfortable motion in rough water. Due to the support afforded by the after sections, speeds up to about 11 knots are possible without much squatting. These launches are widely used in the Bay fisheries, and are often built or converted to pleasure craft with longer cabins and deckhouses for interior accommodation.

High-Speed Planing Model With Lowered Chine Line

A high-speed planing version of this type of launch is shown in Plate 23. The broad stern sections and shallow flat underbody allow for high speeds with a powerful engine. The nearly flat bottom aft is not as able or comfort-

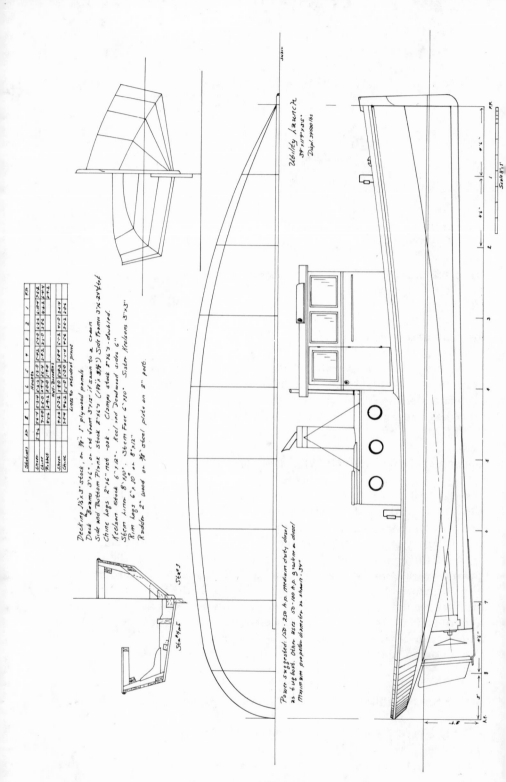

Decking 1½×3" stock on ⅜·1" plywood panels
Deck Beams 3×6" on c.c. from 3"×12"if sawn to a crown
Side and Bottom Plank stock 2"×6's (Pfi 3½") Side from 3"×2½×4 toe
Chine Logs 2"×6" -oak . Clamps stock 2"×6's -doubled
Kcclson stock 6"×12". Keel and Deadwood sides 6"
Stem line 8'×10'. Stem Face 6"×10" Sister Kcelsons 3"×3"
Rim logs 6"×10" or 8"×12"
Rudder 2" wood or ⅜" steel plate on 2" post

Power suggested. 150 - 250 h.p. medium duty diesel
as tug boat. Other uses 50 -100 h.p. 3 water a diesel
Maximum propeller diameter as shown 3'4"

Utility Launch
39'11"×11'×3'
Dspl 34000 lbs

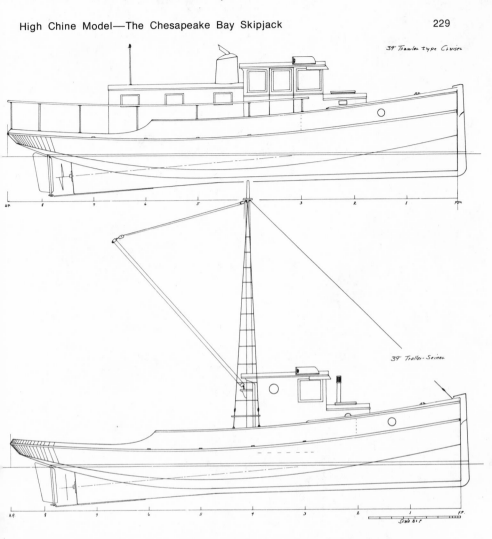

39' Trawler type Cruiser

39' Troller-Seiner

Scale 3/4"

Plate 21 39' fantail skipjack launch arranged as a trawler or cruising boat

able in rough water as the preceding type, but it fulfils the demand for high-speed capabilities in certain commercial fisheries. It is also widely used as a pleasure boat. The flare and flam in the forward sections give a modern pleasure craft appearance that is admired by some, but contributes nothing to the performance while adding to material costs and labor time.

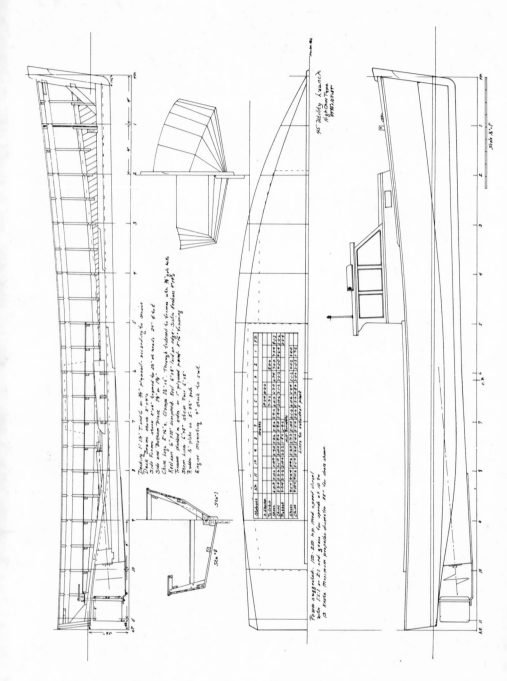

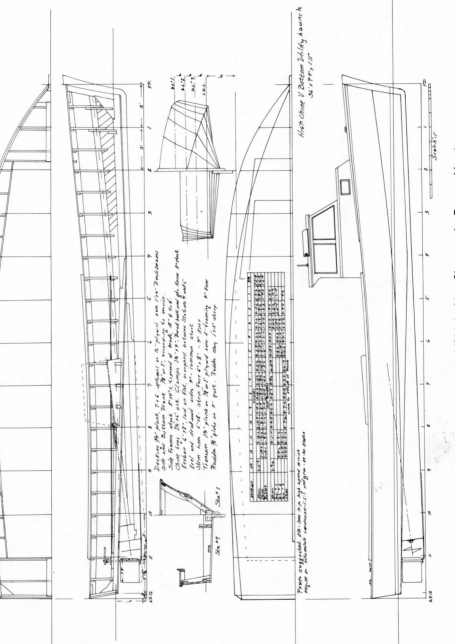

Plate 23   Profile and plan of a 36′ high chine Chesapeake Bay workboat

231

Long Island Scallop Launch

Another variation of the Bay skipjack is the V-bottom scallop launch shown in Plate 24. These boats are used for commercial fishing on Long Island Sound and other parts of the eastern seaboard where the waters are shallow, and are built with little draft. Most of these hulls are built with a slight reverse in the rabbet aft to reduce pitching, and are not ordinarily thought of as being unduly fast. Many of them are overdriven at speeds up to 30 knots or more with powerful engines.

These boats are frequently built with no bottom framing except for a few strongbacks in the way of the bulkheads that subdivide the hold space, and a pair of frames under the engine mounting. Figure 103 shows this type of construction, with the hull placed in an inverted position. The stem liner, stem knee, keelson, and transom stern are assembled and the chine stringers positioned and held by temporary bracing. One or two of the side planks are fitted to help hold the shape and to establish the outer landing points of the cross-planked bottom. Bevels to carry the bottom staving are also shown.

Light-Displacement Pleasure Launches Built to Chesapeake Bay Method

The Chesapeake Bay method of building has sometimes been suggested as suitable for amateur construction where lightly built pleasure launches are offered as a design (Plate 25). This light-displacement hull is of very shallow draft and is well suited for gunkholing in protected waters. Due to this, full

Figure 103   The method of applying a cross-planked bottom to high chine hulls

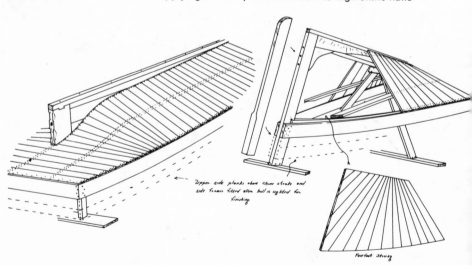

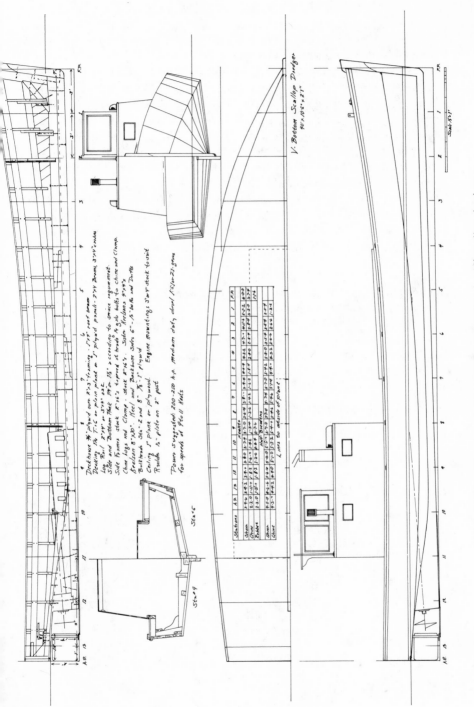

Plate 24 Profile, plan, and construction details of a 40′ scallop dredger

233

headroom should not be expected in the trunk cabin, and the standing top should be rather lightly constructed. This design is simple enough for an amateur builder with a fair knowledge of boat carpentry, who has gained a working familiarity with the Bay system.

It will be noted (Plate 26) that the forefoot and keel construction differs somewhat from traditional Bay skipjack practice. Much lighter scantlings are fitted, with the keel forming the principal supporting member. The inside edges of the bottom staving are fastened to a keel cheek which is bolted to each side of the upper edge of the keel. This is set in a waterproofed gasket, as described in the sharpie section (volume 1, page 329). In some cases a keelson may be fitted, but it is more of a batten than a heavy log type as previously described (page 232). In fitting the staving at the forefoot, the keel is often rabbeted to receive the first few strakes, which then is faired into the underside of the keel cheeks or keel batten as the case may be. Two rather light sister keelsons are fitted into the bilges rather than one heavy member, the former affording more fastening area for the bottom planking.

Chesapeake Bay Building Method Adapted to Heavy-Displacement Hulls

An example of the adaptation of a hull type not native to the Chesapeake Bay area for cross-planked construction is shown in Figure 104. This is a heavy displacement trawler type cruiser that has lately become popular with

Figure 104   Optional keel and bottom plank arrangements in small Chesapeake Bay hulls

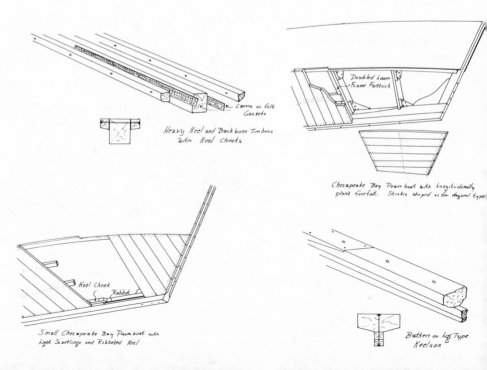

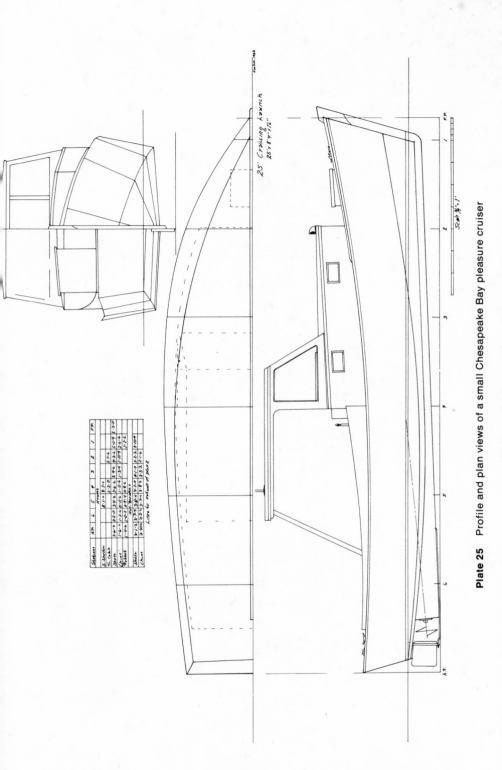

Plate 25 Profile and plan views of a small Chesapeake Bay pleasure cruiser

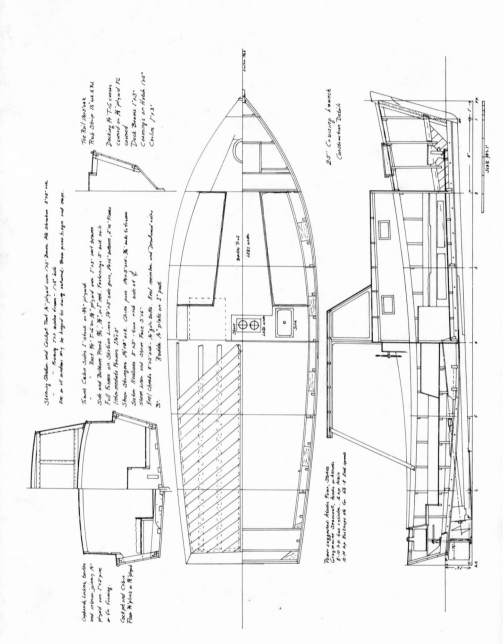

many experienced offshore yachtmen who prefer a wholesome, sea-kindly craft of better-than-average ability (construction details in Figure 105).

Most of these heavy-displacement boats will show speeds of 7–9 knots in cruising trim, but this hull has been designed for higher speeds and high power. Due to the broad stern sections, moderately narrow entrance angle, and straight buttock lines, this hull can be driven up to 16 or 17 knots with a large diesel engine.

Plate 27 shows the principal construction details, and the use of fanned staving to conform to the rounded forefoot.

Plywood Planking Adapted to Chesapeake Bay-Type Hulls

While both the Northern- and Chesapeake Bay-type skipjacks have been shown with traditional planked construction, their simple hull forms and easy lines could be readily covered with plywood by an experienced builder who has a working knowledge of this type of construction. Only slight changes in framing methods are needed to give adequate structural support.

To those experienced in steel fabrication, the larger skipjack hulls offer a simple form that would present few difficulties in fitting the shell plating. Angle iron or bars could be used as framing and chine stringers, with heavier bar stock forming the stem, keel, and deadwoods.

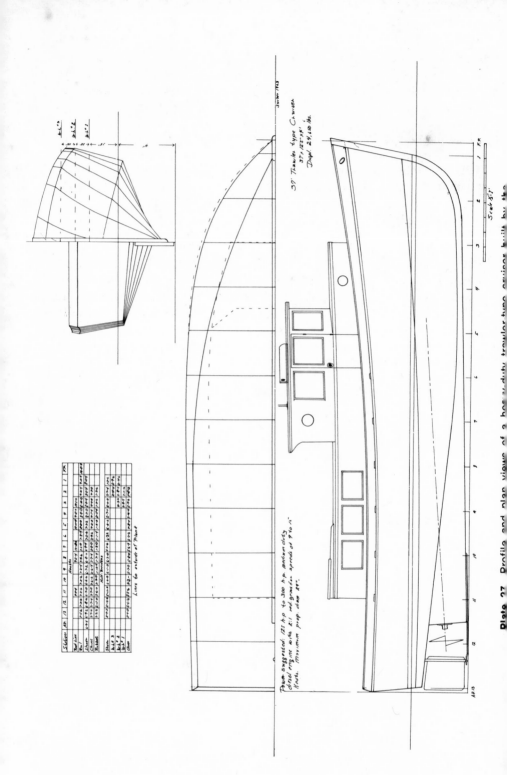

Plate 27. Profile and plan views of a heavy-duty trawler-type cruiser built by the

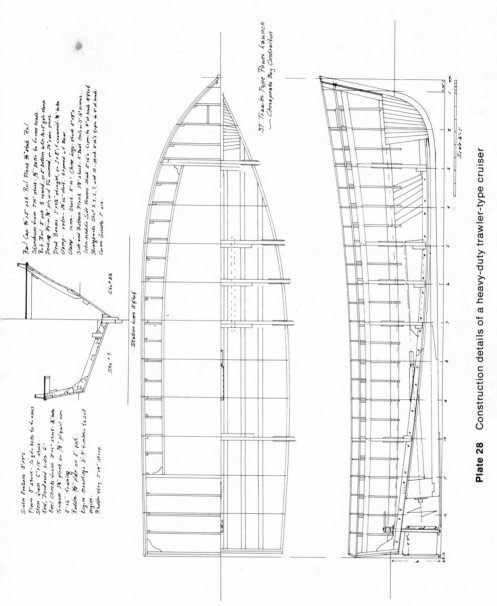

Plate 28 Construction details of a heavy-duty trawler-type cruiser

239

20

High Chine Model
Yamato Boats and Sampans

The Yamato boats of Japan, and the Sampans of the Hawaiian Islands and the South Seas that are derived from them, have many useful characteristics that could be of interest to practical boatmen of the Western world. Developed by practical boatmen and empirical builders through a trial-and-error process dictated by the stern demands of hard service, these launches represent an excellent compromise of both economy in building and upkeep, and in seakeeping ability.

The primitive origin of the Yamato boat was a dugout canoe fashioned from large trees which were once plentiful on the islands of Japan. These craft were built in various sizes from 14 to 26 feet in length, the beam or girth varying as to the diameter of the log selected. The smaller canoes were propelled by sculls or paddles, but the larger types were often fitted with one or two masts carrying lug-type sails of woven matting. The rig was made readily demountable, as the canoes were used as beach boats and were launched through the surf.

In the fourteenth century, the supply of large trees became exhausted and the native builders subsequently developed a canoe of similar size made from thick planks. The form of these hulls was at variance with the trough-like dugouts, as the thick plank could not be worked into sharp bends. The result was a rather spindle-shaped hull of narrow beam. The V-bottom form was no doubt selected as being more able for offshore work than a simpler flat-bottom type, and more suitable for handling through the surf. Its ultimate shape was, of course, determined by the developed form of its planking.

The actual form of these boats was determined by the use of five very wide single planks that varied in dimensions of 1¼ to 2 inches net thickness and 18 to 24 inches in width, according to the size of the hull, which was built in similar sizes as the parent Yamato dugout. Each side has a sheer plank that stands nearly vertical, with a wing plank below that forms the turn of the bilge (Figure 105). The keel plank is common to both sides and laid on the flat, its forward end tapering to a point where it engages the heel

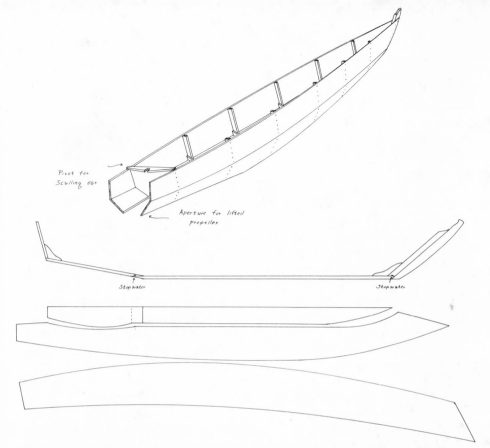

Labels on figure:
Pivot for Sculling oar
Aperture for lifted propeller
Stop water
Stop water

Figure 105 Diagram of expanded plank shapes for a small Japanese Yamato boat

of the stem. The latter is straight and set at a strong rake, accommodating the developed shape of the side and wing planking in a natural sweep. The similarity here to the American Northern skipjack form is notable, except that the Oriental builders fashioned an even easier bend by the sharply raked stem, although the beam forward is much more narrow than when formed with a plumb stem. Both of these forms impose a high chine configuration.

A distinctive feature of the Yamato boats is the structure at the transom. In the traditionally built hulls, the side and wing planks are extended aft of the transom some 18 to 24 inches on the average, according to the size of the boat. As the bottom plank ends at the bottom of the transom, an aperture is left through the bottom to accommodate a sculling oar which has its fulcrum in a notched beam across the top of the transom. The inner edges of the wing plank are usually cut away somewhat to widen the opening, and the after end is left open.

Another characteristic feature of the Yamato boat is the fitting of three or four or more heavy thwarts across the beam that extend outboard from 12 to 24 inches on either side. These appear to have been fitted to carry the poles used in the pole and line fishing these boats principally engaged in, and compensate somewhat for the narrow beam of the boats in providing useful storage space. The thwarts are fitted with short upright pegs at their outer ends to keep the poles from falling off. In most cases the thwarts are tapered or rounded to a smaller diameter at their outer ends from about the edges of the gunwales to lower their outboard weight and for better appearance.

While the older types of planked Yamato boats were fitted for sculling, the larger types were fitted with one or two short masts and lug sails of woven matting as in the case of the earlier dugout canoes.

In building, the hulls are set up in an upright position on a heavy building form, and the heavy planks are sprung into position with the aid of props, stays, and chains which are used in conjunction with levers. The keel is fashioned first, and is actually in two pieces, the after section being set at a shallow angle to rise toward the transom. This produces an easy driving hull as there is little drag in the stern sections even under varying conditions of loading. A stopwater is required in this joint, but sometimes where very heavy plank is used a mortise joint is formed in place of any fastenings. A similar condition exists forward, where the heel of the stem may have a like fitting. As the heavy plank possesses great longitudinal rigidity, most builders dispense with a full framing system. A few floors were placed at intervals in the bottom to act as braces for the wing planks, and a few side frames are fitted in the form of cleats to brace bulkheads that subdivide the interior into fish holds and storage spaces. A fair degree of manual skill is required in edge-fastening the outer planks, as no chine stringers appear to have been fitted in either the older examples or contemporary craft.

The Yamato boats have been built to this system for centuries, with but slight variations on the part of individual builders or perhaps to the dictates of local areas. In recent years a growing shortage of the wide planks formerly used has necessitated the incorporation of somewhat narrower stock. This entails cleating or edge fastening to build up the material to the correct width, the construction then proceeding in the usual manner. The heavy construction results in a very durable and long lasting hull, and many of the boats have been in constant use for 100 years or more, finally having been converted to power. The native builders do not appear to wish to compromise the excessive weight in the hull to easier beaching that a light hull could afford.

With the coming of power in the twentieth century, many of the old hulls were fitted with engines. After 1920, most new boats were built as power launches. As a fine-lined displacement hull with a lack of bearing aft, the speed capabilities are moderate, and low powered, single cylinder engines are sufficient to drive them up to their terminal hull speed of 5-to-7 knots.

Modern Yamato Boat

Plate 29 shows the plans of a modern Yamato boat that is typical of many

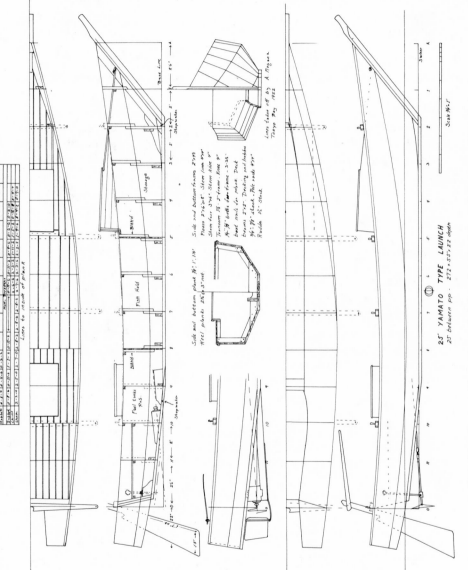

Plate 29 Plan, profile, and construction details of a small Japanese Yamato boat

243

thousands of similar launches that are being used along the coasts of Japan. The engine is placed well aft and is almost always of the kerosene or diesel type for reasons of safety and operating economy. To facilitate beaching, most launches carry a retractable propeller mechanism as described in the section on the power dory (volume 1, page 389). The lifted propeller rises into the well aft formed by the extended side and wing plank extensions, and the shaft follows the upward slope of the after portion of the keel plank. The distinctively shaped rudder is quite deep and is said to be an aid against the shallow hull yawing excessively in following seas. It is also used to scull the boat in shallow water after the propeller is retracted, and is fitted to be unshipped when the boat is beached.

While the small Yamato boat may have a somewhat limited appeal, it might well be suited to certain areas of the world where elaborate boatbuilding facilities are lacking, but where local timber is readily available and where workmen of acceptable skills could be recruited for building. As an alternative to the usual construction at the transom, an optional conventional type is shown (Plate 29) in cases where a retracting propeller is not required.

Larger Modern Yamato Boat

In the early 1920s a larger, modified Yamato boat type, which closely followed the original hull form, was developed for longlining. Such a launch is shown in Plate 30. In this somewhat enlarged type, tight decks are added for offshore use, and the builders utilized the Yamato boats' extended thwarts to support deck extensions at the sheerline. This adds useful deck room, acts to deflect spray, and gives additional buoyancy factors under conditions of heavy loading. The hull form is one easily driven at acceptable speeds with moderate power. The construction details are shown in Plate 31.

For the benefit of professional shipwrights who might be interested in the type for adaptation for general uses, the lines of a 48-foot model are shown in Plate 32. This type of vessel is currently being built in Japan in various sizes up to 70 or 80 feet in length. Many of the smaller boats up to 50 feet are also built with retractable propellers for beaching in areas where harbor facilities are lacking.

Early Hawaiian Power Sampans

The power sampan originated in the Hawaiian Islands during the period of the First World War. It was developed by native builders of Japanese descent who were familiar with the Yamato type of hull form. As the islands of Hawaii possess sheltered harbors and anchorages, beaching craft were not

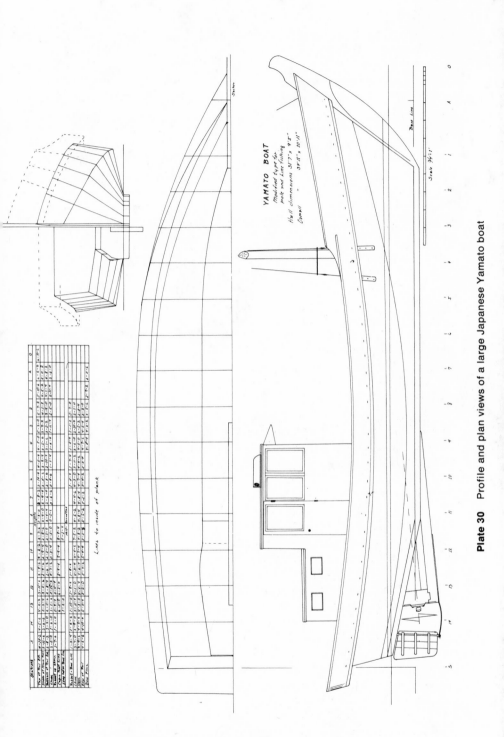

YAMATO BOAT

Modified type for
pole and line fishing

Hull dimensions 31'7" x 9'5"
Overall " 39'11" x 10'1"

Lines to inside of plank

Plate 30 Profile and plan views of a large Japanese Yamato boat

245

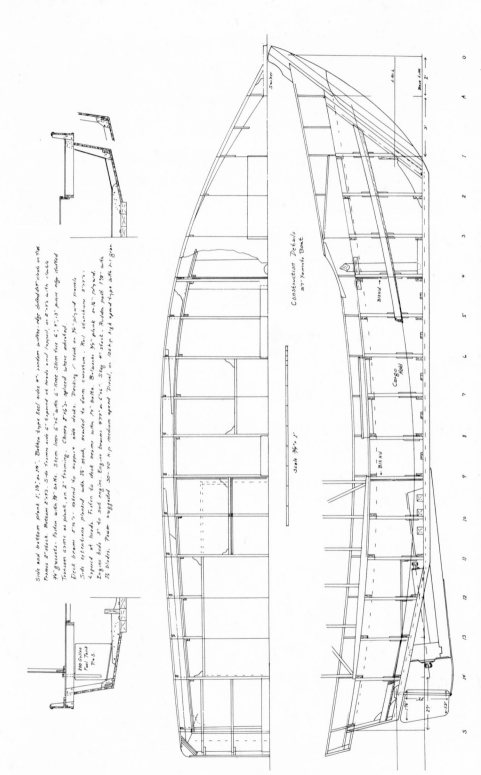

Construction Details
317' Yarmila Boat

Scale 3/8" = 1'

Side and bottom plank 1 1/4" on 1 1/4". Batten type keel sided 4", sided 6" width-edge slotted 3/8" close on flat. Frames 2" sided. Bottom 2"×3". Side frames sided 6" tapered at heads and topsail, or 2"×3" with double 3/4" gussets. Fasten with 3/8" bolts. Stem line 6"×6" with 6" knee. Stem line 6"×9"×13" piece edge slotted. Transom same as plank on 2" framing. Chines 3"×6", spliced where indicated.

Deck beams 3"×4", extend to support side decks. Decking / steak on 3/4" plywood panels. Side extensions planked with 3/4" steak, scarfed to form curvature. Rail stanchions 2"×3", tapered at heads. Fasten to deck beams with 1/4" bolts. Bulwark 3/4" plank on 8" plywood. Engine beds 3" to suit engine. Engine bearers 4"×9" on 6"×6" stock. Skeg 4" stock. Rudder pack 1 1/2" with 3/4" blades. Power suggested 30-40 hp medium speed Diesel, or 100 hp high speed type with 2:1 gear.

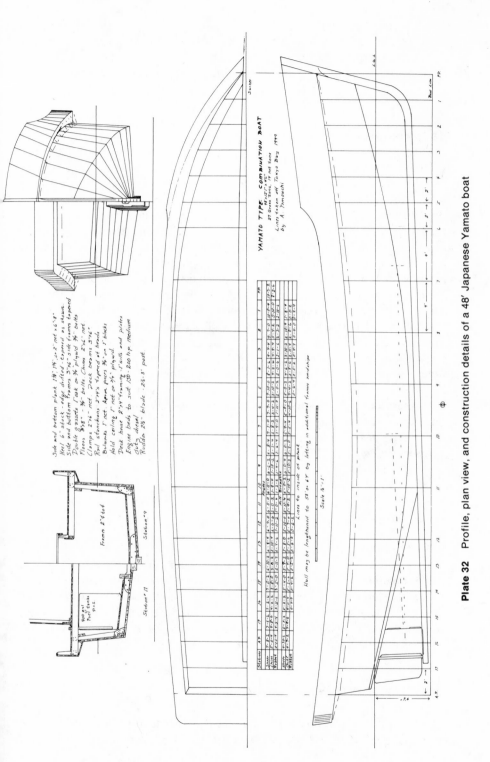

Plate 32 Profile, plan view, and construction details of a 48' Japanese Yamato boat

247

required and sampans have always been built with conventional powerboat sterns. In the quest for better speed, the angular keel batten of the Yamato boat was replaced by the straight-sectioned underbody of the western power launch.

Early Hawaiian Sampans

The early sampans were built in sizes of about 25 to 30 feet between perpendiculars. Their upper works were in the form of a modified Yamato boat, with tight decks for offshore use and extended deckline with substantial railings. In deference to the narrow beam, freeboard and top hamper were kept to a minimum for reasons of stability, and trunk cabins when fitted offered only sitting headroom. The engine was carried well forward, was usually protected by a trunk, and the exhaust system was usually of the dry type. The muffler, if fitted, was protected by a sheet iron stack that was usually set at a sharp rake. The fish hold was generally aft of amidships, with the fuel tanks carried in the stern. Most of the launches had a light mast set in a tabernacle, and it was usually carried in the rigged-down position on a gallows frame set on the after end of the trunk cabin. In case of engine failure, it was raised by hauling on a forestay; sometimes shrouds were also provided. The sail was usually cut from a heavy piece of tarpaulin. With this arrangement the hull could be driven before the wind. In later years and with more dependable engines, the mast arrangement became more rudimentary, and seems nowadays to be used only to hang lines and fishing gear on. In any case the decks and cabin roof are almost always painted orange to facilitate spotting by air-sea rescue units in case of engine failure.

Early Hawaiian Sampan Built in Oahu

An example of an early type of small sampan built on Oahu in 1922 is shown in Plate 33. The typical modified Yamato boat features may be noted, together with rather low freeboard. As this hull was built for a small 10 hp. marine engine, the chine line aft was raised above the waterline aft to avoid dragging the stern when under load. Such a hull cannot be made to plane and is capable of speeds up to 7 knots. Excessive power will only cause squatting without a noticeable increase in speed.

Hull Form and Construction Details

In the study of the hull form and construction details of sampans it must be mentioned that, as they are empirically developed boats, no original

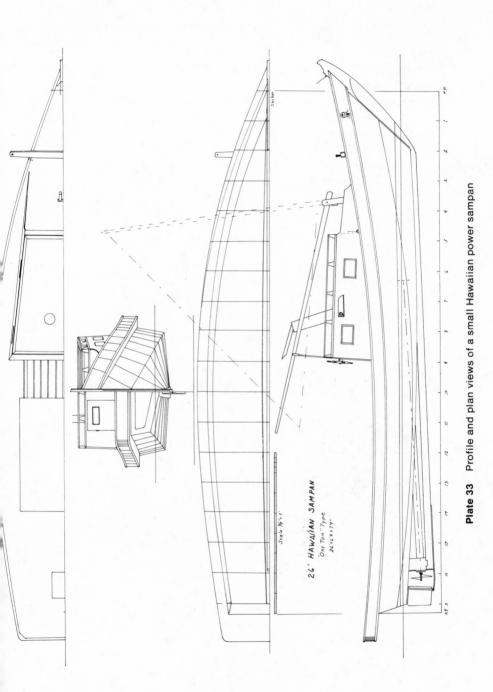

Scale ¾ = 1'

26' HAWAIIAN SAMPAN
"One Ton" Type
26'4" × 7'4"

Plate 33 Profile and plan views of a small Hawaiian power sampan

249

building plans have ever existed. At the same time contemporary craft are built as copies of existing boats usually following the "eyeball" method, together with such individual modifications as the builder deems necessary to carry out his own ideas. Any marine historian or naval architect desiring to develop a set of formal plans for these craft must measure hauled out examples and otherwise examine a number of boats to arrive at a definitive conclusion concerning their ultimate form. In drawing up a set of building plans, the original form of the hull must be closely adhered to, but at the same time certain inequities such as lopsidedness in the topsides and questionable structural features must be corrected. While the sampan is basically an uncomplicated boat, prospective builders should have had some prior experience in boatbuilding as a certain amount of improvisation and interpolation is required.

Construction Details of Oahu Sampan

Turning to the building plans of the Oahu sampan in Plate 34 it will be noted that the hull structure closely follows conventional V-bottom practice except for minor variations to incorporate the distinctive features that these craft possess. The builder has the choice of either lapped or gusseted frame joints at the chine. Due to the very sharp rake of the stem, an extra frame is usually worked in bearing on the stem liner itself to support the forward strakes of the side plank. The floor is set into the liner by means of a notch, and is through-bolted from below and reinforced by a block on its forward side which is also through-bolted (Figure 106).

Details of Bow Construction

The details of the construction at the bow is shown in Figure 107. While a few sampans show rabbeted stems, most utilize the simpler two-piece stem with an inner liner and outer facing. The inner liner is beveled to receive the side plank, with the face piece shaped to cover their hood ends. The outer stem may be a straight timber with its lower forward edge shaped to a cutwater, but in most cases is fashioned to a curve with a characteristically Oriental shaping at the top. The builder uses his own ideas here, and sometimes a carving or other decoration is worked in. It will be noted that an extra rabbet is usually cut into the stem piece somewhat forward of the main rabbet in order to accommodate the end of the railing that follows the edge of the extended deckline.

Details of Extended Deckline

The extended deckline is supported in various ways as shown in Figure

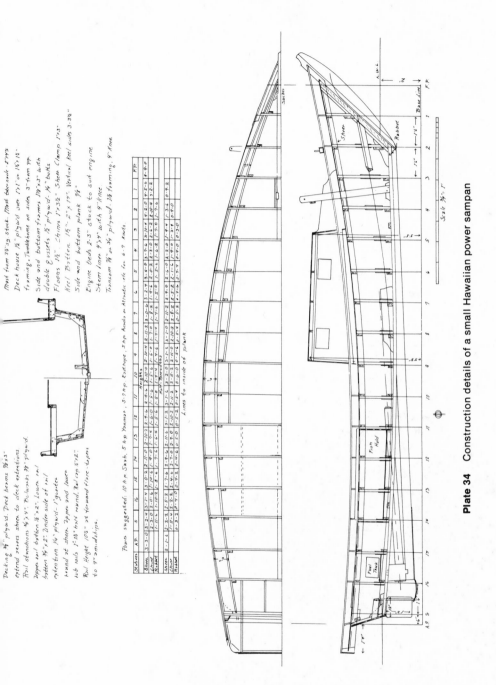

Plate 34 Construction details of a small Hawaiian power sampan

251

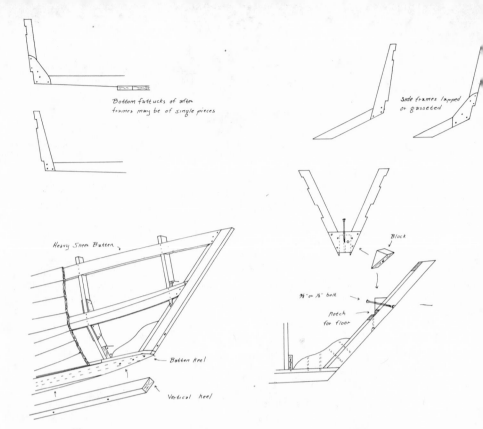

Bottom futtucks of after frames may be of single pieces

Side frames lapped or gusseted

Block

3/4" or 1/2" bolt

Notch for floor

Heavy Sheer Batten

Batten Keel

Vertical Keel

Figure 106 Details of framing and bow construction as used in small Hawaiian sampans

Figure 107 Details of stem construction used in large Hawaiian sampans

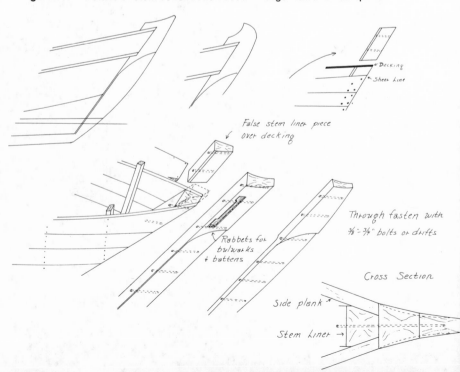

Decking

Sheer Line

False stem liner piece over decking

Through fasten with 3/8"- 3/4" bolts or drifts

Rabbets for bulwarks + battens

Cross Section

Side plank

Stem Liner

108. The side frames may be extended a short distance above the sheerline, where they engage the deckbeams which may be laid either on the flat or set edgeways. In other cases the side frames are cut off at the sheerline and short blocks are then through-fastened with bolts through the tops of the frames. In larger hulls the deck extension may be built up from longitudinally laid timbers that are scarphed to form the curve along the sheer and edge bolted.

The attachment of the outer rail stanchions will vary with the type of deck framing selected (Figure 109). In large sampans or in modified Yamato boat types built in lengths over 40 feet, the underside of the deck extension is sometimes sheathed and its lower framing extended to the hull at an angle.

Use of Plywood and Fiber Glass

Most of the smaller sampans built in recent years have marine plywood deckhouses, steering shelters, decking, and rail structures covered with fiber glass. This offers less building time and results in desirable weight saving. Figure 110 shows a popular method of this construction. Figure 111 shows the stern framing of a plywood-covered sampan, along with various methods of working a rounded angle where the side and stern railing are joined. This entails some extra building time and expense over the use of a square angle, but affords a slightly more pleasing appearance.

Figure 108 Optional methods of building sponson supports for a Hawaiian sampan

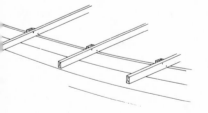

Deck beams set on edge

Deck beams laid on flat

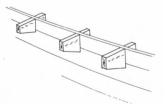

Blocks through bolted to frames

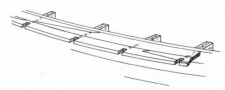

Scarphed planks edge fastened

A few small sampans have been built with plywood-covered hulls, although the basic design benefits from the original heavy plank construction due to the desirability of substantial hull weight for stability factors with narrow beam. Due to the straight-sided sections in the midship and after body, the plank may be laid on in panels. Approaching the bow, ripped out panels backed by battens may be required to follow the framing, although angularly cut pieces may be sprung into place as shown in Figure 112.

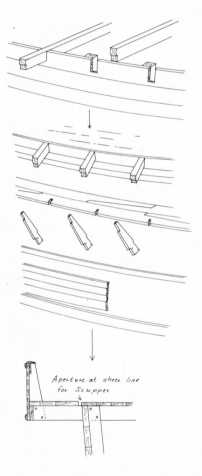

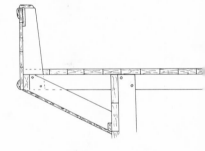

Apron under deck extention
on larger vessels

Aperture at sheer line
for Scupper

not to Scale

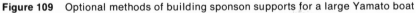

Figure 109 Optional methods of building sponson supports for a large Yamato boat

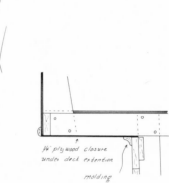

TYPICAL SCANTLINGS

Deck beams 7/8" to 1¼" x 4"   Decking ¼" 5/8" or 3/4" plyw'd
Rail stanchions 7/8" x 5½"   Bulwarks 3/8" plyw'd
Upper sheer batten 5/8" - 3/4" x 2½"
Lower sheer batten 7/8" x 4"
Moldings 1" 1 1/8" oak half-round
Rail cap ½" 3/4" oak

Not to scale

¼" plywood closure
under deck extension

molding

Figure 110   Scantling guide for building plywood-covered sponsons as used in small Hawaiian sampans and Japanese Yamato boats

Figure 111   Optional methods of sponson construction at the transom of a small Hawaiian sampan or Japanese Yamato boat

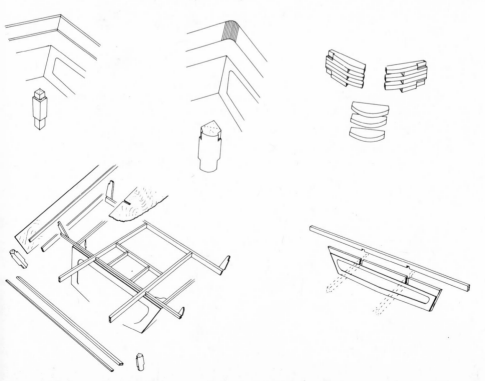

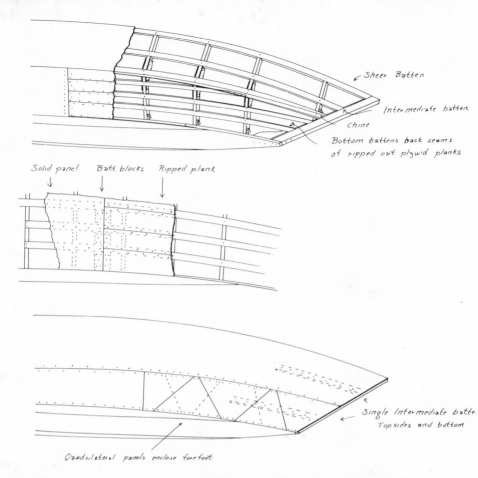

Sheer Batten

Intermediate batten

Chine

Bottom battens back seams
of ripped out plywd planks

Solid panel   Butt blocks   Ripped plank

Single Intermediate batte
Topsides and bottom

Quadrilateral panels enclose fore foot

Figure 112   Optional methods of planking a small Hawaiian sampan with plywood

Sampans Built as Semiplaning High-Speed Launches

The construction details of the mast with its tabernacle and the outboard mooring bitts are shown in Figure 113. Some of the launches built before World War II have substantial masts, but many of the more modern examples carry a rudimentary pole mast. The curious mooring bitt that extends across the gunwales forward obviously follows the fitting of the extended thwarts of the parent Yamato boats. The upright pegs at the ends sometimes have decorative carvings.

Small Sampans Used as Pleasure Launches

In recent years many sampans of the smaller class have been built as pleasure boats with open cockpits to accommodate a number of passengers or for pleasure fishing purposes. Many have been built as water taxis, ship

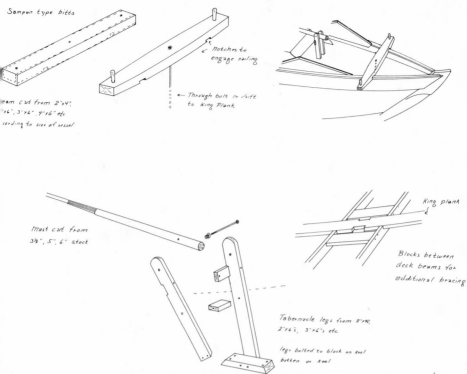

Figure 113 Construction details of sampson posts and mast tabernacles as fitted to small Hawaiian sampans

chandler's launches, or as bumboats in the ports of Southeast Asia (Plate 35).

32′ Working Sampan

A popular 32 foot size of working sampan is shown in Plate 36. The curve of the chine line indicates a burdensome hull and a good load carrier. The raised profile aft allows for variations in loading without dragging the stern. Possessed of moderate speed capabilities, such a hull can be economically driven with a low-powered diesel engine at about 7 knots. Some of the launches of this form have straight-sided hulls that create a pontoon effect, with little, if any, flare to the sections. Such hulls are more prone to rolling for lack of righting factors, but appear to be popular with some builders.

Construction Details

In this larger model a steering shelter is usually fitted, with a forward

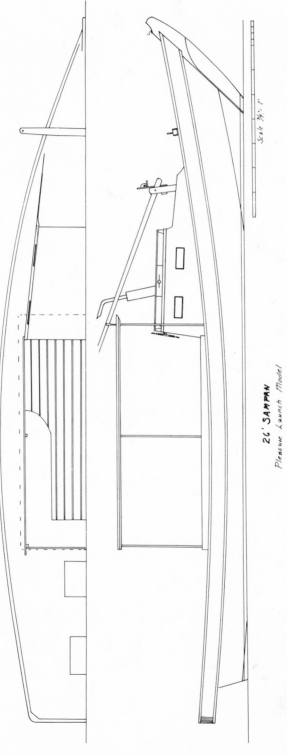

26' SAMPAN

Pleasure Launch Model

Scale 3/4" = 1'

Plate 35 Small Hawaiian sampan arranged as a pleasure launch

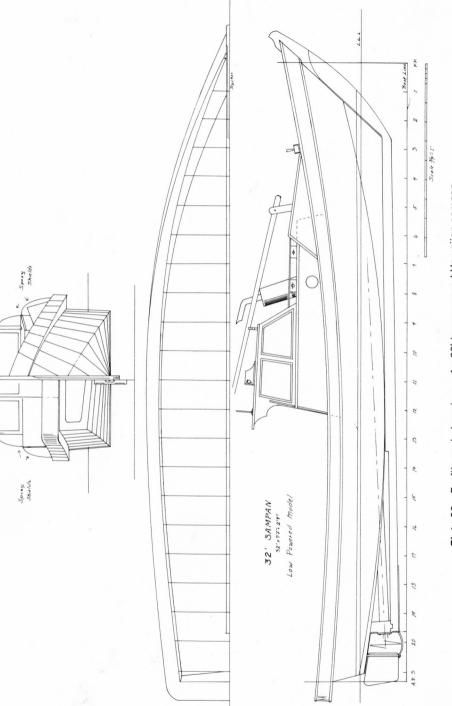

32' SAMPAN
32'x9'6"x2'4"
Low Powered Model

Spray Shields

Spray Shields

Plate 36   Profile and plan views of a 32' low-powered Hawaiian sampan

259

slope to the roof line of both it and the cabin trunk which carries a muffler in a sharply raked funnel. Spray rails are generally fitted forward. Nowadays they are triangularly shaped plywood panels with the outer edges protected by moldings and are bolted to the inside of the railings. As the extended deck usually eliminates spray or green water from coming aboard, these structures may well be an Oriental idea of ornamentation. No two ever appear to be quite the same shape, each being an expression of the builder's originality (Figure 114).

Most of the sampans also carry spray shields on either side of the after end of the steering shelter. These gatelike structures are now made of plywood panels trimmed with moldings and are hinged at their inner edges. This allows them to be opened for access forward, and under way they are carried in the closed position and bear against a stop on the inside of the railing.

A decorative effect on the transoms of many sampans is made by routing out the inner portion, leaving a raised margin around the outer edges. While this is seen on many older boats, most modern types fit a cut out plywood panel that creates a similar effect.

The construction details (Plate 37) show the various parts and average scantling details, and are self-explanatory. If a somewhat larger hull is required, it is possible to add either two, four, or eight feet in the midship section by lofting in extra frames.

Figure 114   Construction details of spray rails and transom decoration as seen in Hawaiian sampans

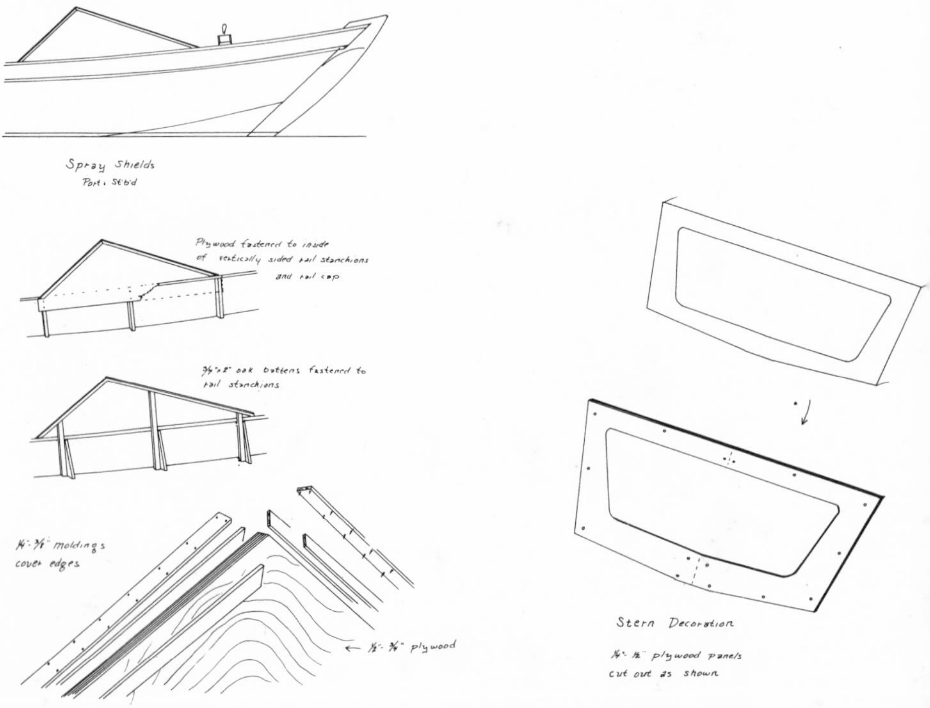

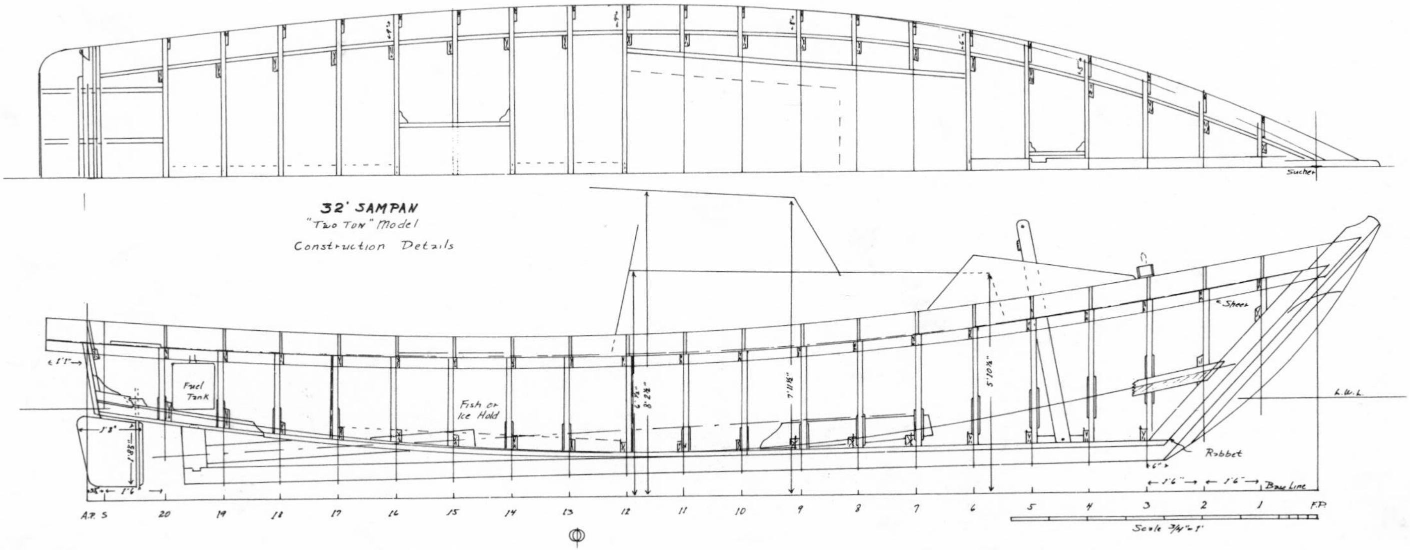

Plate 37 Construction details of a 32' low-powered Hawaiian sampan

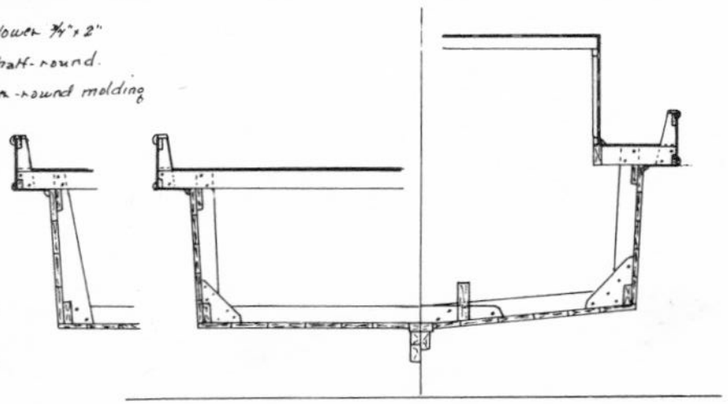

32' SAMPAN
"Tao Tow" Model
Construction Details

Steering Shelter Details

The steering shelters on most of the sampans and in many cases the trunk cabins are built with the roof line slanting slightly forward. This imparts a somewhat rakish appearance and in the case of the steering shelter, has a practical value in leveling the profile of the boat when under way at speed. Most of the sampans of medium and larger sizes carry railings around the roof lines of the trunk cabins and sometimes the steering shelters as well. These function to hold lines, floats used in longlining, and other fishing gear. These vary from about 6 inches to a foot or more in height and the supporting blocks or stanchions are carved in decorative patterns at the option of the owner or builder (Figure 115).

A few sampans have been built with the trunk cabin, steering shelter, and engine room aft, and the cargo hold forward. The fuel tanks are then carried forward. Plate 38 shows the 32-foot low-powered sampan with this arrangement.

Figure 115 Optional types of decorative trim applied to steering shelters and deckhouses of Hawaiian sampans

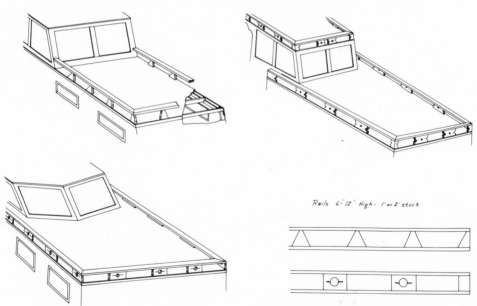

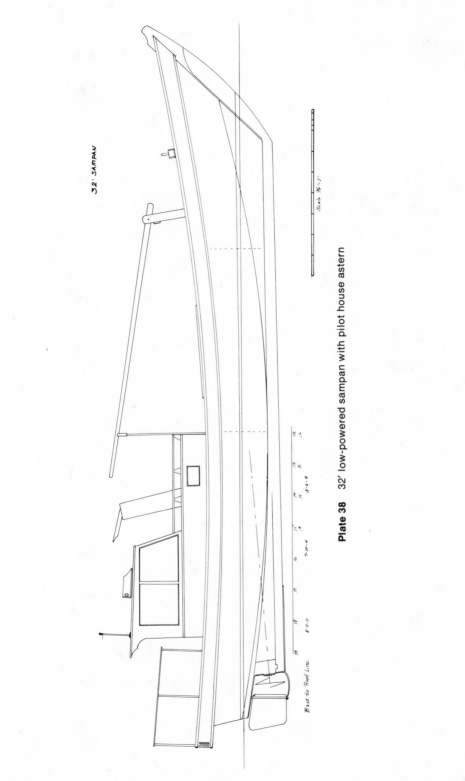

32' SAMPAN

Scale ⅜"=1'

Base to Roof Line.

Plate 38 32' low-powered sampan with pilot house astern

High-Speed Sampans

In recent years large numbers of small sampans have been built as semiplaning launches with light car-type marine engines or automobile conversions. These offer better speed capabilities than the older displacement types, and are in some cases used as sport fishing boats. Plate 39 shows one of these in the 30-foot class. It will be noted that the bottom lines are identical to many Western launches, except for the sharp sampan bow with its raked stem and high chine line. The construction details in Plate 40 are self-explanatory, except for a description of the flat keel batten. This appears to help the speed capabilities, as when the hull rises the flat keel acts as a water ski and the displacement and wetted surface is further reduced by the vacuum formed as the water is deflected from its outer edges at speed.

Flat Keel Construction

The construction of the flat keel is shown in Figure 116. In its building, the vertical keel members are assembled and its top is sawn to the profile of the rabbet. The planks for the flat keel are gotten out and held edge to edge by cleats while being cut to shape. In most cases the keel batten must

Figure 116 Construction details of batten-type keels and garboard planks used in Hawaiian sampans

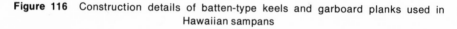

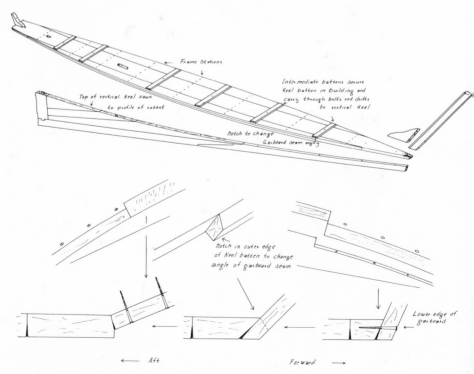

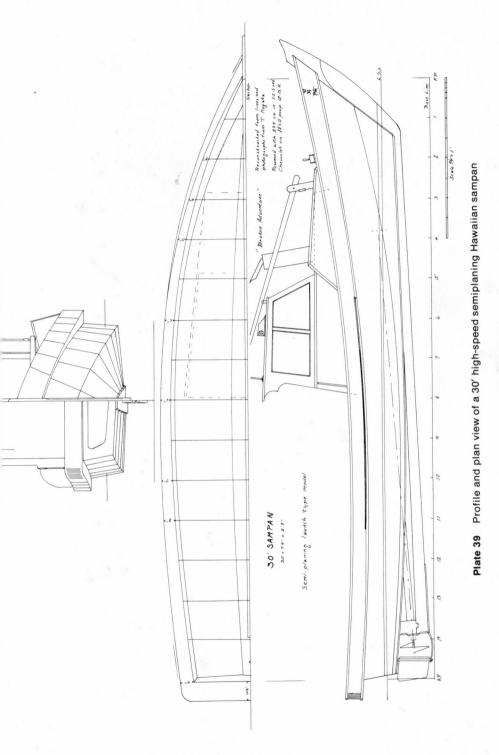

30' SAMPAN

30' × 9'9" × 2'8"

Semi-planing launch type model

"Broken Adventure"

Reconstructed from lines and photographs from T. Nagata

Powered with 25V car in 1951 and Chevrolet in 1952 gave 12.5 K.

Plate 39   Profile and plan view of a 30' high-speed semiplaning Hawaiian sampan

265

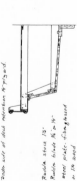

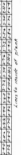

Decking 7/8" or 1/2" plywid. fiberglass covered
Deck beams 1"x4". King plank 7/4"x6" or 8"
Headers 1 1/4"x4" at deck openings
Under side of deck extention 1/4" plywid.

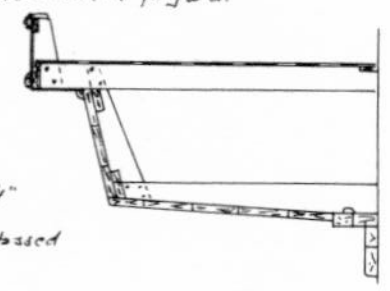

Rudder stock 1 1/2"
Rudder blade 7/16" or 1/4"
steel plate- fiberglassed
or 1 1/4 wood

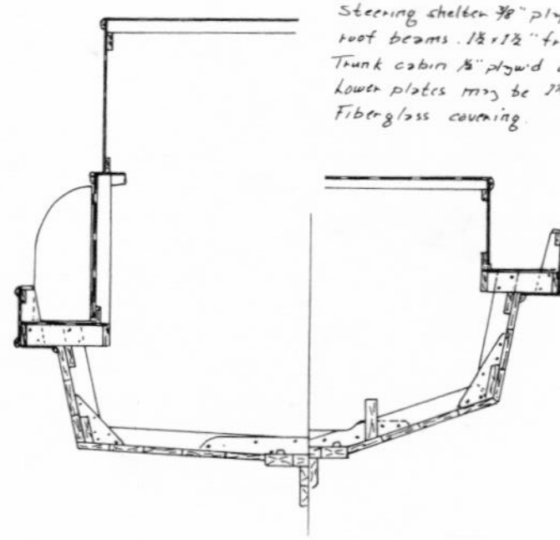

Steering shelter 3/8" plywid - roof and sides - 3/4"x2" roof beams. 1 1/8 x 1 1/2" framing. Windows to suit
Trunk cabin 1/2" plywid over 1 1/8 x 1 1/2" framing
Lower plates may be 1 1/4"x4" rabbeted.
Fiberglass covering

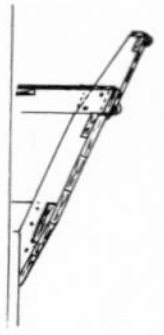

Rail cap 1/2"x2" oak. Upper sheer batten 7/4"x 2". Rail stanchions 7/4"x 4". Lower sheer batten 7/4"x4". Bulwarks 3/8" plywid.
Moldings 1-1/8 oak half-round.
Sheer clamp 1 7/8"x4". Chine 1 1/4"x6 Forward, 4" aft.
Side and bottom frames 1 1/4"x 3 1/2". Frames lapped or gusseted with 1/2" oak or 1/2" plywid- doubled - 1/4" galv. bolts
Floors 2" stock. Frames aft of Sta. 8 have single bottom futtocks lapped to 1 1/4"x6" side frames tapered to 3" at heads.
Side and bottom plank 1" or 1 1/8" stock - F.h. #14 screws or nails
Keel batten 2"x8" with 1 1/4" cleats between stations
Vertical keel from 4" stock. Stem liner 4"x6 on flat
Stem and stern knees - 4" - quarter knees 2"

Stations	A.P.	14	13	12	11	10	9	8	7	6	5	4	3	2	1	F.P.
	Heights															
Sheer	3-7-4	3-6-0	3-5-6	3-4-4	3-4-0	3-4-0	3-4-6	3-5-0	3-6-6	3-8-6	3-11-4	4-3-0	4-6-6	4-11-6	5-4-2	5-9-0
Chine	2-2-2	2-0-6	1-10-6	1-9-0	1-8-4	1-8-0	1-8-2	1-8-4	1-9-6	1-11-2	2-2-0	2-5-4	2-10-0	3-3-6	3-9-6	
Rabbet	1-11-4	1-10-0	1-8-4	1-7-0	1-6-4	1-5-4	1-5-2	1-5-4	1-5-6	1-7-0	1-8-2	1-9-0	1-9-6	1-10-6		
	Half- Breadths															
Sheer	2-11-0	3-2-4	3-5-2	3-7-0	3-9-0	3-10-0	3-10-4	3-10-6	3-9-0	3-8-6	3-5-6	3-1-6	2-7-2	1-11-4	1-1-4	
Chine	1-9-0	2-11-6	3-2-2	3-4-4	3-6-0	3-7-2	3-7-4	3-7-6	3-7-2	3-5-6	3-3-0	2-11-0	2-3-6	1-6-0	0-5-4	
Rabbet	0-5-2	0-6-0	0-7-0	0-8-2	0-9-0	0-10-0	0-10-2	0-10-2	0-9-2	0-8-6	0-7-6	0-6-4	0-5-0	0-3-0		

Lines to inside of plank

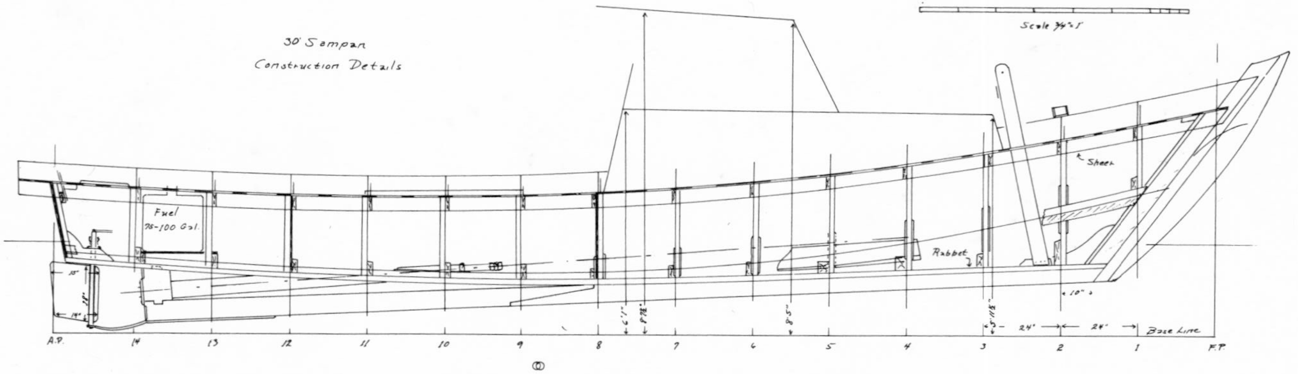

30' Sampan
Construction Details

be assembled over the vertical keel, as the finished structure would be too stiff to be bent into position if first assembled as a complete unit. A notch must be fitted at its forward edge on either side to allow for a change of direction when fitting the garboard strakes. While this type of hull construction adds somewhat to the building time required, it allows the bottom plank to be laid on in natural sweeps, and in most cases spiling of the garboard is not necessary.

If a slightly longer boat is required, from 2–6 feet of added length can be lofted into the hull amidships.

Plate 41 shows a somewhat larger launch in the same class that can be powered for speeds of 18-to-20 knots. Its construction is as described in the previous model (pages 265–266). It is also capable of being lengthened by respacing the frames.

Variations in Underwater Form

A study of the lines of various sampan-type hulls will indicate that the waterlines can be manipulated to produce other characteristics, such as widened beam for added speed with more power, or even modern monohedron forms. While such changes can add to the performance in smooth water, it can be clearly evident that a price must be paid in increased initial building and later operating costs. On the other hand, mandatory running at displacement hull speeds will show reduced performance in rough water, together with hard steering and the possible danger of broaching in steep stern seas.

45' Hawaiian Sampan

Plate 42 shows a 45-foot sampan of the type most used by the commercial fishermen of the Hawaiian Islands for extensive offshore work. Most of these are fitted with diesel engines and have a long cruising range, remaining at sea until a full catch is loaded. The length and beam afford substantial deck and hold space, together with Spartan accommodations for a crew of two or three men.

In recent years a few of these larger launches have been rebuilt with large, Western-type, combination boat deckhouses placed well forward, some being fitted with a flying bridge. Such modifications have not proved entirely satisfactory, as the sharp forefoot and lack of bearing forward is insufficient to offset the weight and windage of the excessive top hamper forward, and the boats roll excessively. As traditionally conceived boats, they are at their best when built as originally developed.

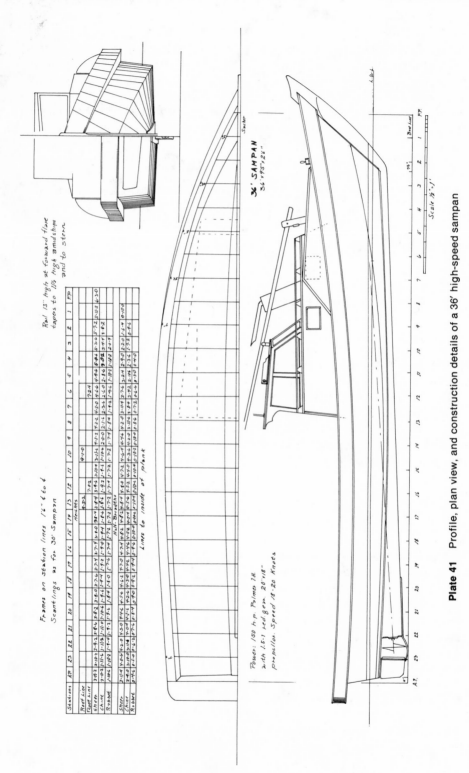

Plate 41   Profile, plan view, and construction details of a 36' high-speed sampan

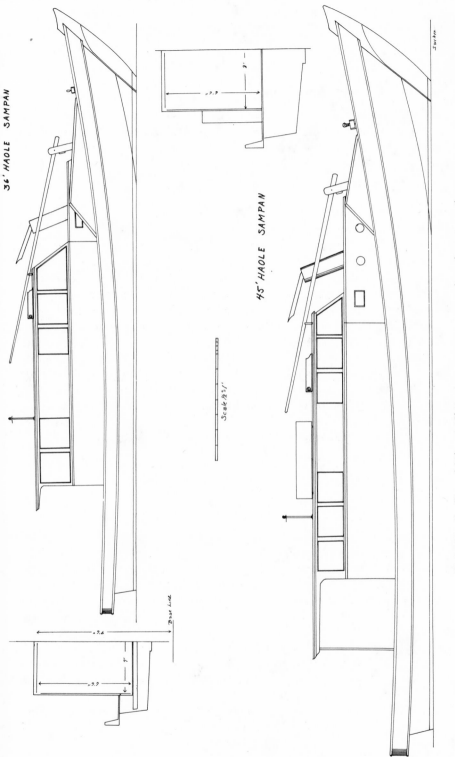

Plate 42 Profiles of 36′ and 45′ Haole sampans arranged as pleasure cruisers

36′ HAOLE SAMPAN

45′ HAOLE SAMPAN

Scale ½=1′

Base Line

"Haole" Sampans, or Pleasure Cruiser Adaptations

A few medium- and large-type sampans have been built or converted for use as pleasure cruisers or sport fishing craft. In these cases plywood-covered deckhouses have been built aft without other significant changes in the basic arrangement of the hull (Plate 43). Although they add somewhat to the top hamper and windage, the hulls are generally of the semiplaning type, are used mainly inshore, and can usually outrun anything they cannot weather.

Large Sampans Used for Longlining

Large, heavy-duty, offshore displacement-type sampans of substantial cargo capacity are built in Hawaii as well as in the South Seas and along the Asian Coasts. These are mainly used as longliners, and can remain at sea for two or three months. Many of these larger vessels are built with straight-sided pontoon-type hulls, but fit a distinctive type of spray rail to dampen the rolling. These are made up of heavy timbers set edgeways and scarphed to the curve of the hull, being through bolted just at or slightly below the light load waterline. In some boats the forward end is raised somewhat, the local theory being that some lift is imparted to the hull when running light. In view of the weight of these heavily built craft, capabilities of such performance is debatable. A riding sail is often carried aft. Plate 44 shows a well-designed example of an offshore sampan.

A Modified Sampan Launch

The modified sampan launch shown in Plate 45 was designed by the author some years ago as a compromise between the best features of the sampan hull and Western launch types to produce a good performing low-cost boat that could be economically built by carpenters of modest skills. The flat keel batten as previously described (page 264) is fitted and appears to help the speed capabilities. A top speed of 21 knots in roughish water may be obtained with a 230 cu. in. six-cylinder engine with a 1:5-1 reduction gear and a 17-inch diameter propeller. The boat performs well as a displacement hull in rough water at lower speeds. The boat has been variously built as a lobster boat, cruising launch, sport fisherman, and utility launch. About 200 hulls have been built to date.

Plate 46 shows the construction details, which are conventional for a modern-type plywood-covered launch. Most of the pieces are common run mill cuts with no special dimensions required.

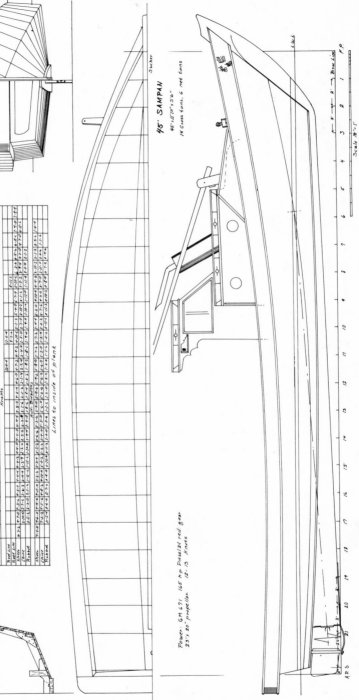

45' SAMPAN

Plate 43   Profile, plan views, and construction details of a 45' Hawaiian sampan

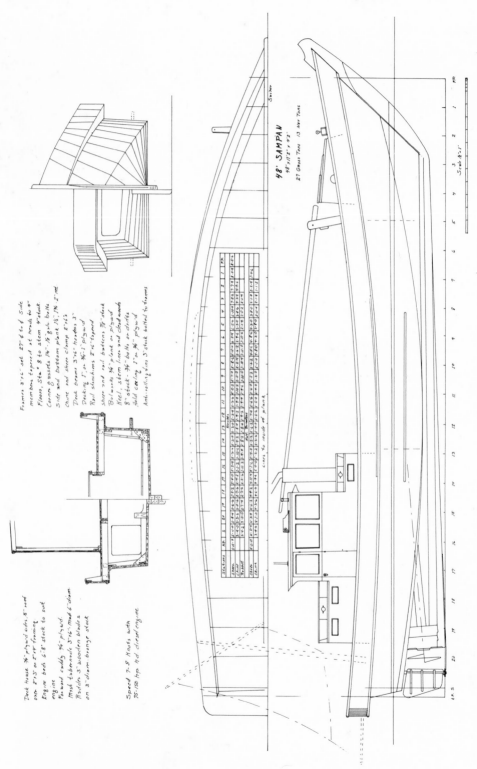

48' SAMPAN

48'x11'2"x4'2"

27 Gross Tons 13 Net Tons

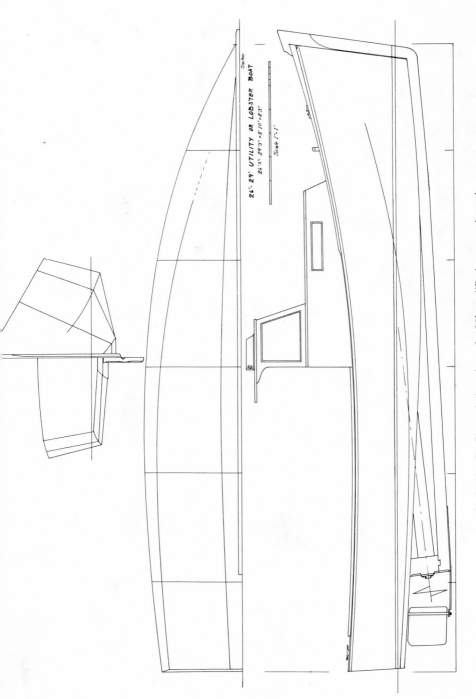

26'-29' *UTILITY or LOBSTER BOAT*

26'3", 29'3" × 8'10" × 2'3"

Scale 1"=1'

Plate 45 Profile and plan view of a 26' modified sampan launch

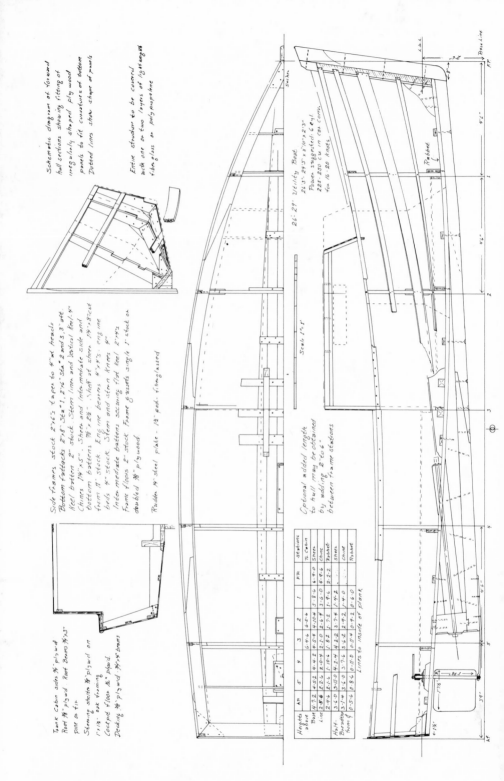

Beveling the Edges of the Flat Keel for Garboard Plank

The only special consideration is the beveling of the edges of the flat keelson to receive the lower edges of the bottom panels. Figure 117 shows one method of continuously beveling the garboard seam to the curve of the side panels from bow to stern. Figure 118 shows another method of making this bevel, with a notch cut into the edge of the keel batten to aid in making the directional change of the bottom plank. In any case it is best to fit a batten along the inner edge of the garboard seam to give additional fastening area for the lower plank panels.

Optional Arrangements for Modified Sampan Launch

The trunk cabin and steering shelter are optional, and several arrangements are possible, but only lightweight structures are permissible. The engine must be placed where shown. The boat may be built in various lengths of 26 to 29 feet by spacing the frames to suit each size as shown.

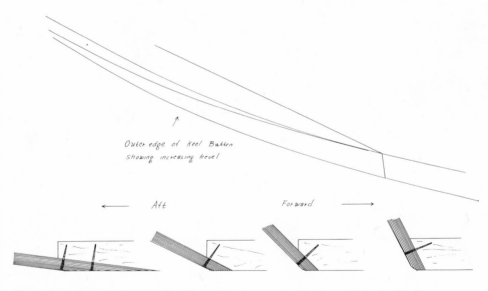

Figure 117 Construction details of a garboard seam used in plywood-planked hulls

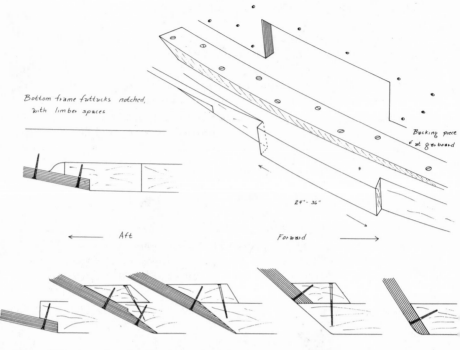

Bottom frame futtucks notched,
with limber spaces

Backing piece
£ at garboard

24" - 36"

Aft   Forward

Figure 118   An optional method of garboard seam construction used with plywood plank

21

Low Chine Model
The Modified Sharpie

A short time after the flat-bottom sailing sharpie came into general use in the Chesapeake Bay area, following the American Civil War, practical sailors and empirical builders discovered that the boats performed much better if a slight V-shape was worked into the bottom aft. This modification added somewhat to the displacement, with consequent enhanced interior space and slightly increased sail carrying capacity. It also enabled the boats to come about on a new tack more quickly, especially in light airs.

Chesapeake Bay Double-Ended Crab Skiff

The early builders incorporated this improvement into various small types of sharpies without otherwise deviating markedly from established methods of flat-bottom skiff building. Plate 47 shows a small double-ended crab skiff formerly much used on the Bay which had a well deserved reputation for speed and good handling qualities, and which is typical of the modified V-bottom type in construction details.

Construction Details of Double-Ended Skiff

In building, the hull is put together in the upside-down position over temporary molds. The usual plank keel batten is fitted, but is cut slightly longer so that springing it between the heels of the stem and stern posts will allow for a slight bow in the middle. Its forward and after ends are cut off at angles to fit inside the chines at their outer ends. The centerboard case is fitted in the usual manner, and the outer edges of the keel batten are beveled to form a close fit for the herringbone bottom planking that extends from the center to the chine lines. Many of these small hulls with narrow beam have no interior framing. The hull is stiffened somewhat by short for-

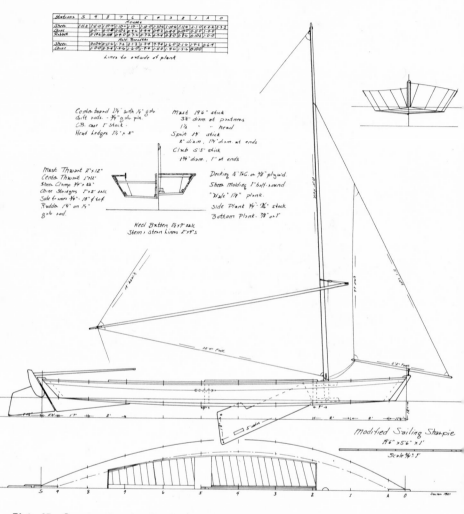

Plate 47   Construction details of a modified V-bottom sailing sharpie

ward and after decks and washboards supported along the gunwales by short side frames set on edge between sheer and chine.

Chesapeake Bay Type V-Bottom Sailing Skiff

Figure 119 shows a somewhat more burdensome type of small sailing skiff with a square stern and consequent broader beam. These types usually carried a strongback amidships which materially strengthened the hull and prevented it from working near the centerboard case when sailing hard. Sister keelsons were generally fitted which gave extra support to the bottom plank between chine and keel. Also shown is a log-type keelson which is frequently fitted to skiffs of this size as well as larger examples that have lifted stern lines that enable them to carry heavy loads without dragging the transom.

Modified V-Bottom Sharpie Power Launch

Plate 48 shows a simple modified sharpie-type hull arranged for outboard power. The shallow V-bottom is carried aft to the transom which will allow

Figure 119 Construction details of a small modified V-bottom sharpie

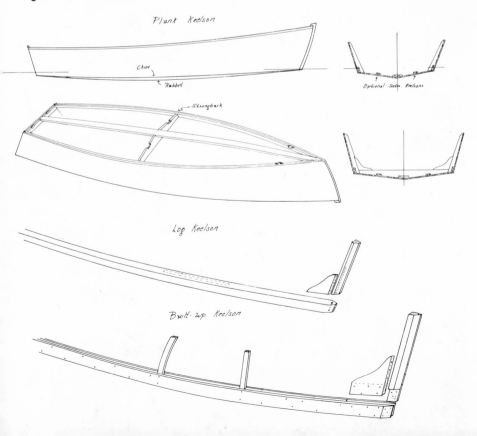

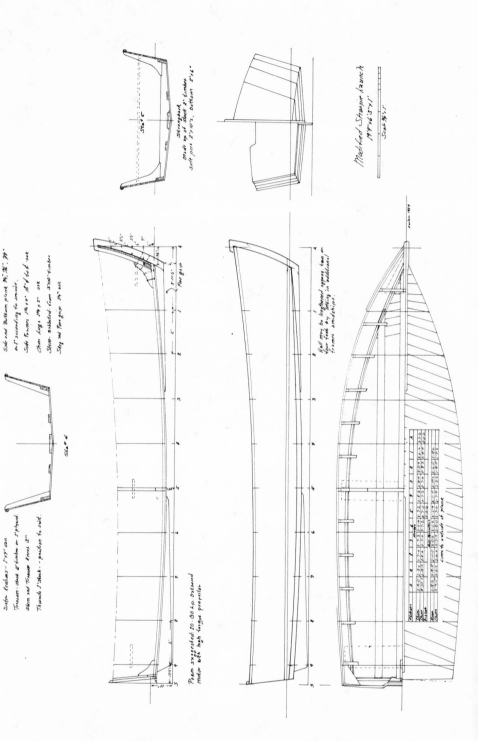

Modified Sharpie launch

280

a medium-sized 15–20 hp. engine to be fitted for fairly good speeds without undue squatting. It will be noted that a false keel or vertical fin known as a foregripe is fitted under the stem to aid in steering, as this type of underbody otherwise has but slight grip on the water forward. As with other noncritical hulls, the boat may be lengthened somewhat if more carrying capacity is desired. While shown as a conventionally planked model, this hull could be covered with either ⅜ inch or ½ inch plywood panels and then covered with fiber glass, if appropriate battens are fitted at the sheer and midship sections of the sides together with an extra sister keelson on each side in the bottom.

Large V-Bottom Chesapeake Bay Sailing Skiff

In larger sailing skiffs, particularly in the square-sterned types intended for substantial load carrying, a somewhat different type of bottom is employed. An example of this is shown in the large Bay crab skiff in Plate 49. In these models the stern sections are raised well above the waterline to avoid dragging under load. Most of these skiffs have a simple forefoot with the keel batten attached directly to the heel of the stem. Some of the hulls have a slightly deeper forefoot which is made from a single block fastened with drifts into the stem liner. The outer edges are then planed down into a V shape which fairs into the first strakes of the bottom planking.

Construction Details of Large Chesapeake Bay Sailing Skiff

The construction details of this skiff are similar to others of the sharpie type except for the keelson aft which is made from a heavy timber and shaped to the curve of the rabbet. Figure 120 shows its construction, with the use of scarphs to make the curve and its joining with the plank type keel-

Figure 120 Construction details of the keel and centerboard case of a small modified V-bottom sharpie

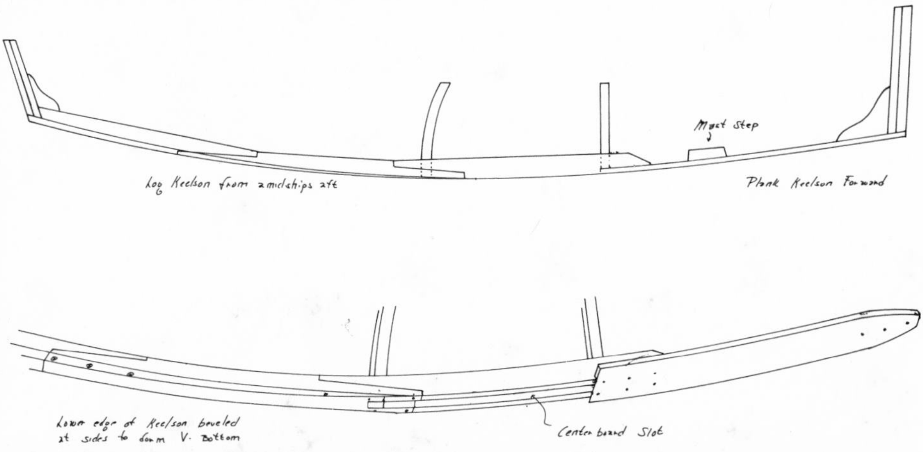

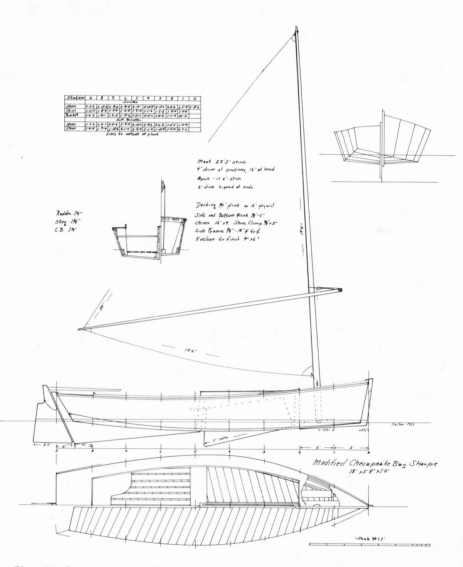

Plate 49   Construction details of an old-style V-bottom Chesapeake Bay sailing sharpie

son forward. The outer edges of the whole structure must be carefully beveled along each side of the bottom to make a close fit with the herringbone bottom plank. Sister keelsons are optional, but if the bottom plank is over 1 inch of net thickness they are sometimes omitted.

In some types of modified sharpies the forward to midship sections were made flat, with the V-bottom being worked into the after sections only. This was done to preserve the high speed capabilities of the parent type which in some cases could be made to plane under favorable conditions. At the same time, the V sections aft allowed for a somewhat wider hull coupled with the ability to come about more quickly.

33' Modified Sharpie Terrapin Schooner

Such a craft is shown in Plate 50, and is a 33 foot modified sharpie for the benefit of experienced builders who might require a low-cost sailing boat with some cruising accommodations. This boat is based on the so called "terrapin schooners" of similar size developed in the 1880s and employed well into the present century for turtle fishing along the Florida and Gulf coasts. These small sharpies, many with a schooner rig like the one shown, were built in lengths of from about 30 to 36 feet and were constructed with cabin accommodations to allow the crews to stay out until a full catch was loaded. Most of the boats were fitted out as smacks, with live baitwells fitted on either side of the centerboard trunk.

Many of these small schooners had flat, skifflike bottoms, but the better and more seaworthy examples were built as shown (Plate 50). While this type of craft is not generally considered suitable for blue water work, these boats ventured all along the Florida Keys and into Caribbean waters. While shallow draft was necessary for their area of employment, they were said to be able enough, in competent hands, to ride out hurricanes.

Construction Details

Prospective builders must be satisfied with sitting headroom in the trunk cabins, as the otherwise excellent sailing qualities of these boats will be spoiled if the roof lines are raised any higher than shown on the plans. An alternative could be lifting cabin tops for standing headroom while moored in protected anchorages. The construction plans shown in Plate 51 are self-explanatory. About a ton of ballast will be required, and should be stowed on either side of the after end of the centerboard trunk. Inboard auxiliary power in the form of a small, heavy duty motor could be fitted, but a simpler and cheaper installation would be a heavy duty type 20–30 hp. outboard set on a bracket on the transom.

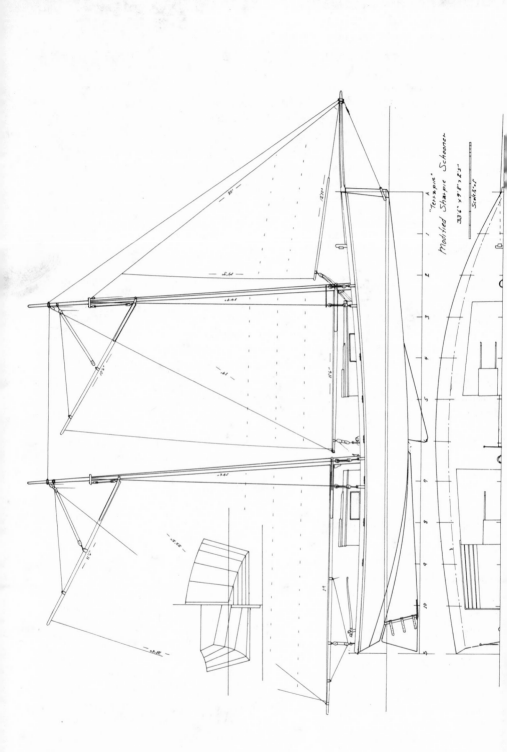

"Terrapin"

Modified Sharpie Schooner

33'6" x 9'8" x 2'5"

Scale 1/4"

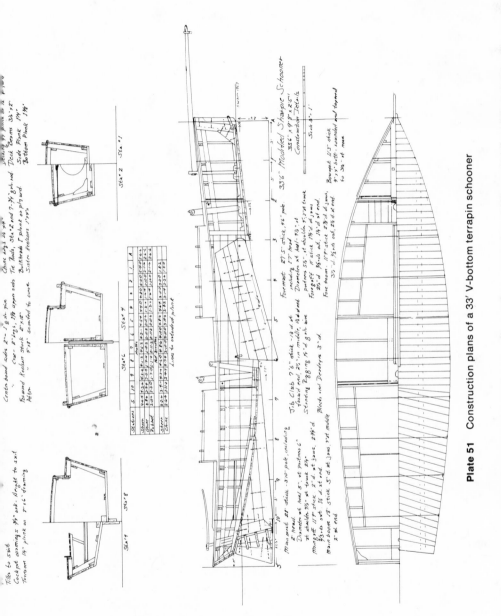

Plate 51   Construction plans of a 33′ V-bottom terrapin schooner

Modifications for Installation of Power

Various types of sailing sharpies on the Chesapeake Bay were fitted with power after the coming of the gasoline engine. Some were fitted as auxiliaries, and many new types were built as out and out powerboats. The initial drawback to this type of powerboat was its tendency to pound when driven into choppy water. One obvious remedy was to build power sharpies with very narrow forefoot sections somewhat immersed below the waterline, driving them as displacement craft short of planing speed. This resulted in a somewhat narrow hull of rather light displacement and restricted interior room.

The next obvious step was to work in V-shaped underwater sections forward to keep the underbody somewhat immersed even when the hull lifted somewhat in the planing attitude. The use of flat sections from the midship section aft was an advantage, as this helped the speed by providing a hull that would plane, and gave the builder some latitude as to the power requirement and load carrying capacity for a given size of boat.

Power Mullet Skiffs

While various types of modified sharpies appeared on Chesapeake Bay, a definite and distinctive type of power launch soon developed along the Carolina coast and sounds and shortly afterward spread to Florida and along the Gulf coast. As these boats were first used in the mullet fisheries, they became known as Mullet skiffs. A simple flat-bottom hull of conventional construction, they were characterized by a rather pronounced V-section in the forefoot, definite curve in the chine line, and a strong sheer. A further difference from most Bay-built craft was the use of longitudinal bottom plank and the required full framing system to support it, in contrast to cross planked bottom and frameless construction.

Early Florida Mullet Skiff

An example of one of the earliest known Mullet skiffs was built in Florida in 1906, and its lines are shown in Plate 52. The drawing was provided by Charles W. Bond, a naval architect and marine historian who has made a lifetime study of early small boat types of Florida and the Gulf regions. It will be noted that its general construction is that of a simple flat-bottom boat except for the V-shaped sections forward. A distinctive feature is the termination of the chine stringer at a point just forward of amidships where the bottom becomes flat. The side plank was then fastened to the bottom plank by edge nailing aft of this point.

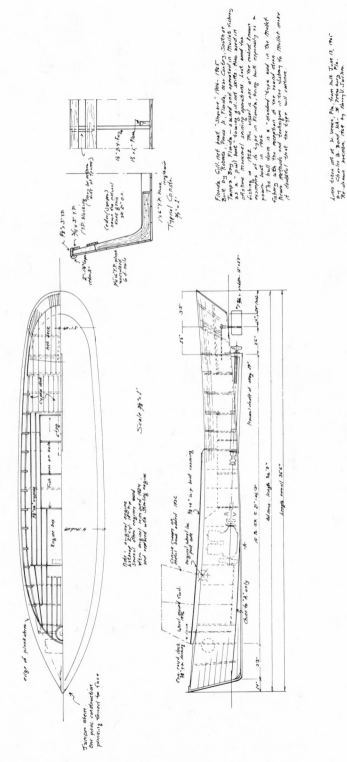

Plate 52   Construction details of an old-style modified V-bottom power sharpie

287

Stern Construction of Florida Mullet Skiffs

Many of the early hulls, like the one shown, had round sterns which offered less resistance to a following sea and gave a somewhat better appearance. A flat transom with a pronounced rake was also seen, and offered somewhat cheaper and easier construction—the choice was up to the builder and both types are to be seen in contemporary launches.

Bow Construction of Florida Mullet Skiffs

The bow construction details are shown in Figure 121. The stem piece is built up and scarphed in the usual manner, the forward planks ending in a rabbet cut to the indicated profile. The lower and after end of the stem is notched to fit the keel batten, which is tapered in plan view to coincide with the stem rabbet. The bottom plank is laid over this, and the vertical keel is added after the hull is planked up. The bottom plank is either steamed or boiled to make the required twist in the forward sections to engage the rabbet.

Interior Construction of Florida Mullet Skiffs

The simple interior framing is also shown in Figure 121. The builder has the choice of either lapped or gusseted frame members where they join at the chine angle.

Figure 121   Construction details at the forefoot of a longitudinally-planked Florida Mullet skiff

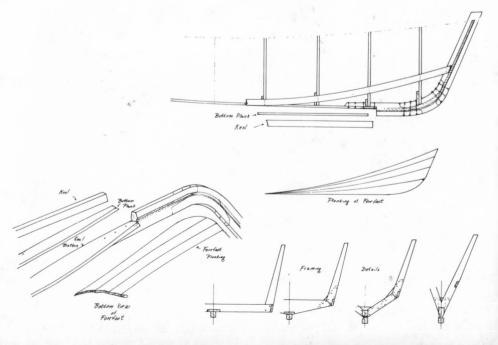

Framing and Planking Details of Florida Mullet Skiffs

The Mullet skiffs are built in lengths of from 25 to 45 feet, the most popular size being of 30 feet and upwards. They are simply and cheaply constructed of common lumber yard materials. The frames are generally made up from stock 2" x 6"s with the upper ends of the side frames tapered somewhat. In the absence of gussets at the frame corners, the pieces are usually fastened with two or three ½ inch galvanized bolts. The frames are usually spaced at 18–24-inch intervals, the lesser dimension being seen in the larger hulls. The planking may be ⅞ inch, 1 inch net, or up to 1¼ or 1½ inches in hulls above 40 feet in length. In recent years many of the skiffs have been planked with plywood panels covered with fiber glass, with no change in the basic framing other than the addition of the usual sheer and intermediate battens in the topsides and one or two on either side of the bottom. While flat panels are used on both sides and bottom from amidships aft, the bow sections due to their shape require ripped out plywood plank of narrow width backed by battens.

Early Types of Florida Mullet Skiffs

The actual form of the boats has been varied by empirical builders to suit the speed desired and the conditions of use. The earlier types as shown in Plate 52 had rather moderate beam for easy driving characteristics made mandatory by the early low-powered engines—often single-cylinder two-cycle models. After the First World War, converted automobile engines of higher power were fitted, which brought the building of hulls with wider beam to enable them to plane efficiently.

Variations in Chine Profile

In this regard the chine profile becomes critical. The most seaworthy types require moderate beam with a pronounced rocker which gives them an easier motion in a seaway when run at displacement boat speeds. The broad-beamed heavily-powered examples at their best in smooth water benefit from a flattened chine line for proper angle of attack for the most efficient planing characteristics.

Fitting of Skegs

Another critical consideration is the fitting of a proper skeg. The V sections in the forefoot of some boats make the forward sections the deepest part of the hull. As the hull rises forward when reaching planing speed, a part of the forward keel is still immersed which cuts down on pounding. When running at lower speeds as a displacement hull in rough water, the forward sections in this attitude could then root and make for hard steering or even broaching if caught by a stern sea. A substantial skeg is then required to offer lateral resistance to such yawing.

As these launches are used in areas where much shallow water exists, the draft is kept as small as possible. The long skeg may be made quite shallow. In some cases primitive tunnel sterns have been fitted to raise the propeller. Another and much cheaper method is to fit a propeller of smaller than usual diameter but with greatly increased pitch which also reduces the draft.

High-Speed Florida Mullet Skiffs

The Mullet skiffs received some dubious notoriety during the prohibition era of the 1920s to the 30s when many of them were used as high-speed contact boats to bring liquor cargoes ashore from the schooners and freighters that brought these cargoes to the coastal waters off the twelve-mile limit. Most of these were of the broad-beamed flat chine models in the 30-foot class which were powered with large automobile engines or in some cases converted airplane power plants. As craft captured by the Coast Guard were subject to confiscation, these launches were cheaply and quickly built as expendable entities.

Optional Forms of Stern and Hull Construction

Plate 53 shows a drawing by Mr. Bond of a contemporary Mullet skiff of good form with building options of both round and square sterns. Plate 54 shows a popular 30-foot model with a square stern which indicates easy building. Plate 55 shows a hull drawn to a larger 39-foot size which is fully capable of serious offshore use. Plate 56 shows a 40-foot hull with a low deckhouse and light flying bridge as used in Caribbean waters for wreck diving. Due to the moderate beam and light draft of these skiffs, high cabin or bridge structures will seriously affect stability, and heavyweight structures here should be avoided for any erections above the sheerline.

Florida Mullet Skiff Adapted to Gillnetting

Mr. Bond has designed many small power launches for various purposes based on the simple Mullet skiff. One of these is the 30-foot gillnet skiff for use in Alaskan waters. Its profile and building plans are shown in Plates 57 and 58. It will be noted that he has lifted the forward sections of the under-

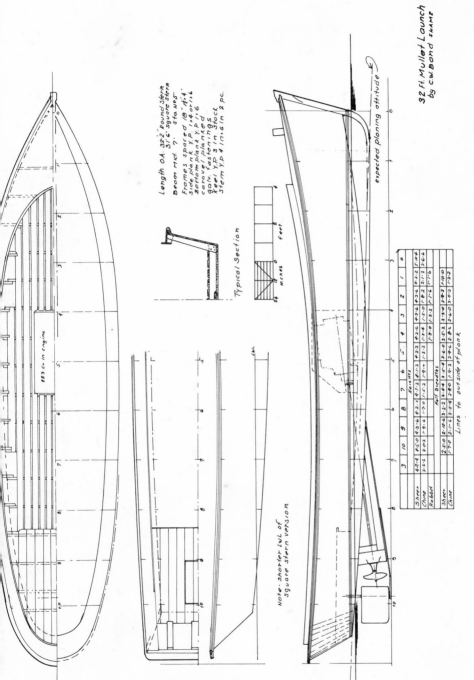

Plate 53 Profile, plan, and construction details of a 32' Florida Mullet skiff

32 ft. Mullet Lounch
by C.W.Bond SHMME

expected planing attitude

Typical Section

Length O.A. 32'2" Round Stern
                31'6" square stern
Beam Mid 7' . sta. No.5
Frames spaced 18"-4"
Side plank Y.P. 1½ or 1⅝
Bottom plank Y.P. 1⅝
carvel planked
galv. fastenings
keel Y.P. 3"7" stock
stem Y.P. 4" mid in 2 pc.

Note- shorter LWL of
square stern version

223 cu in engine

Lines to outside of plank

	3	10	9	8	7	6	5.	4	3	2	1	0
Heights
Sheer	4'9-4	4'5-0	4'3-6	4'2-4	4'1-2	4'1-2	4'2-2	4'2-6	4'3-6	4'3-6	4'4-2	5'n4
Chine	3'1-2	2'0-2	1'9-6	1'7-0	1'5-2	1'4-7	1'3-2	1'2-4	1'3-0	1'8-2	2'1-2	2'6-6
Rabbet							1'3-0	1'2-2	1'1-6	1'1-6
Half Breadths
Sheer		2'5-0	2'10-4	3'2-2	3'4-4	3'5-4	3'6-0	3'5-2	3'3-9	2'8-2	1'1-0 0
Chine		1'7-0	2'1-6	2'5-4	2'8-0	2'9-2	2'9-6	2'9-2	2'6-0	2'0-2	1'2-2

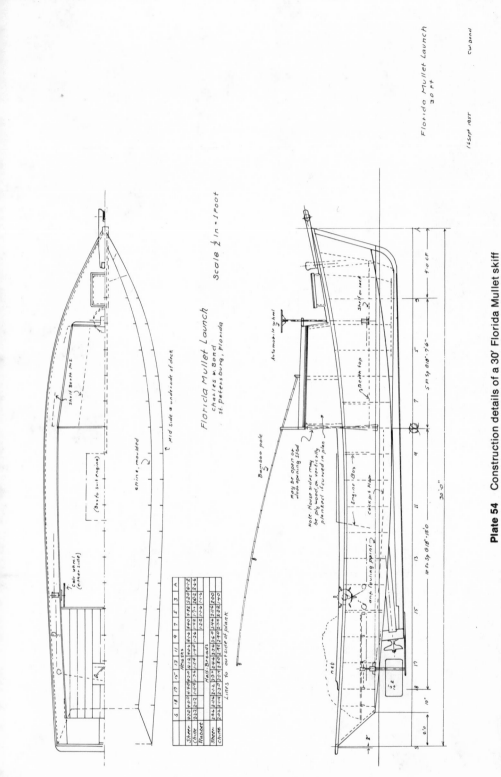

Florida Mullet Launch
Charles W. Bond
St. Petersburg, Florida

Scale ½ in = 1 Foot

Florida Mullet Launch
30 ft

16 Sept 1957   CW Bond

Plate 54 Construction details of a 30′ Florida Mullet skiff

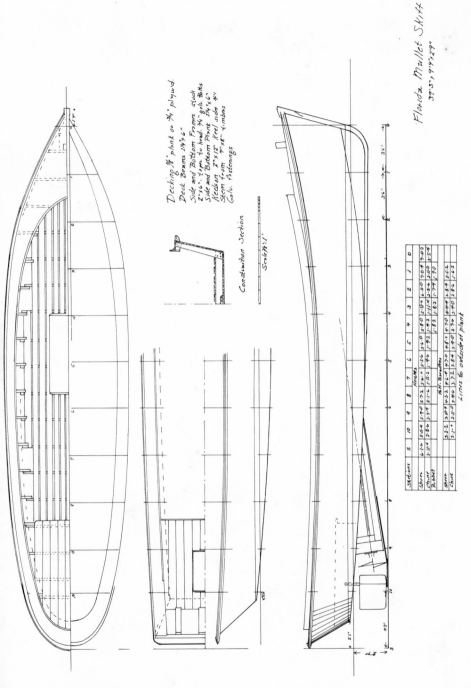

Plate 55 Construction details of a 39' Florida Mullet skiff

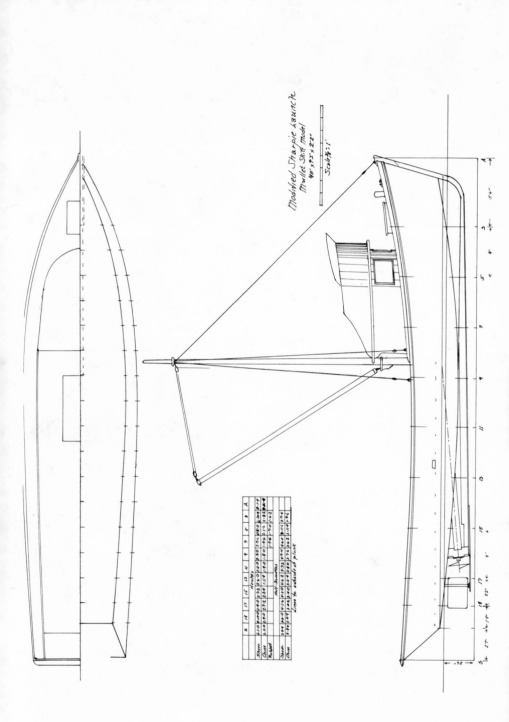

Modified Sharpie Launch
Mullet Skiff Model
40' x 7'3" x 22"
Scale ¾":1'

	5	14	17	15	13	9	9	6	3	A

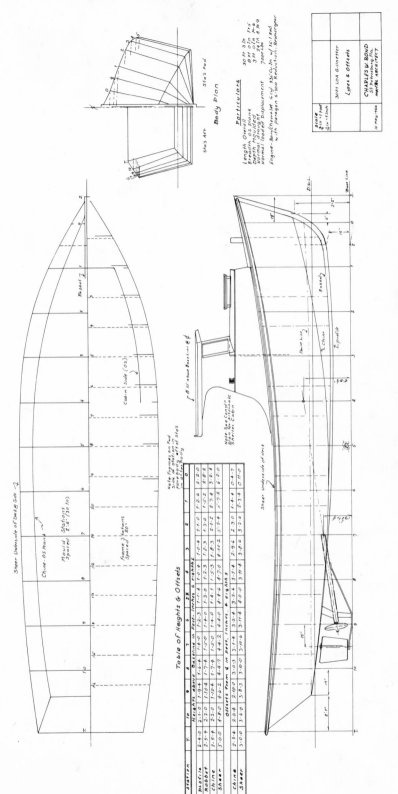

Plate 57 Profile and plan views of a 30' Mullet skiff adapted for seining

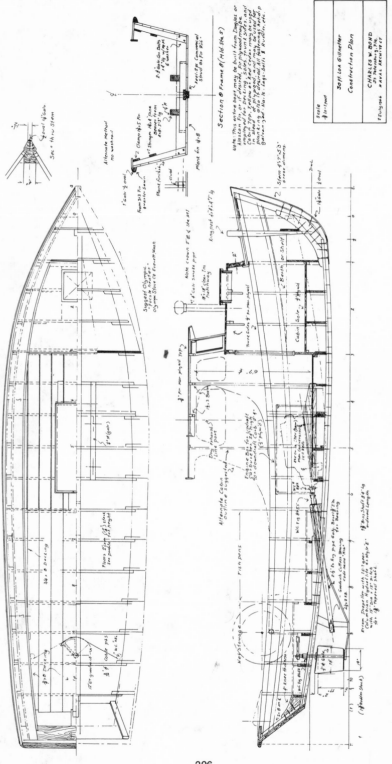

Plate 58 Construction details of a 30' Mullet skiff adapted for seining

296

body to keep the bow from rooting, and the large rudder and skeg offer sufficient resistance for good steering and safety in stern seas. This boat could also be used as a utility skiff, sport fishing launch, or cabin cruiser if the aft cabin bulkhead were at forward end of the engine case.

26' Florida Mullet Skiff

Plate 59 shows a small 26-foot Mullet skiff hull adapted for sport fishing. Its lines were taken from an actual boat by the author on a trip to the Florida Keys. Both conventional plank or plywood covering are shown as construction options. With the latter type of planking, the boat would be light enough to be transported on land by trailer.

Lafitte-Type Mullet Skiff

Plate 60 shows a specialized version of a Mullet skiff designed for a specific purpose, this example being a typical Lafitte skiff as used in the Louisiana bayou country for commercial fishing. As these launches fish over wide areas, high speed is an economic asset. Add the fact that the boats are subject to very hard service, and the result is a massively built high-speed hull very heavily powered. This boat is very similar to the flat-bottom Lafitte skiff except for the V sections forward. These launches are not as fast as the flat-bottom type, but pound less in a chop and are more suited to open water. Note the flat chine line for optimum planing efficiency.

Modified Mullet Skiff as a Seagoing Launch

The lines of the modified sharpie have been adapted for the design of rather large seagoing launches. Such craft perform satisfactorily if the hull is designed as a moderate-speed medium-powered vessel with moderate beam and sufficient rocker in the chine to give an easy motion in rough water. For the interest of experienced builders, the profile and building guide for a 60-foot utility launch are shown in Plate 61. The lines of this hull were slightly refined from those of a similarly sized launch of the same hull type in Subic Bay in the Phillipine Islands. The launch was used for interisland passenger and light freight service. While flat sections of the bottom are somewhat more prone to induce rolling than if the sections had a slight V shape, the moderate beam in this case combined with adequate flare appear to overcome this difficulty. In any case the simplicity of this hull form and its economy of building can offer a useful compromise as a low-cost large boat.

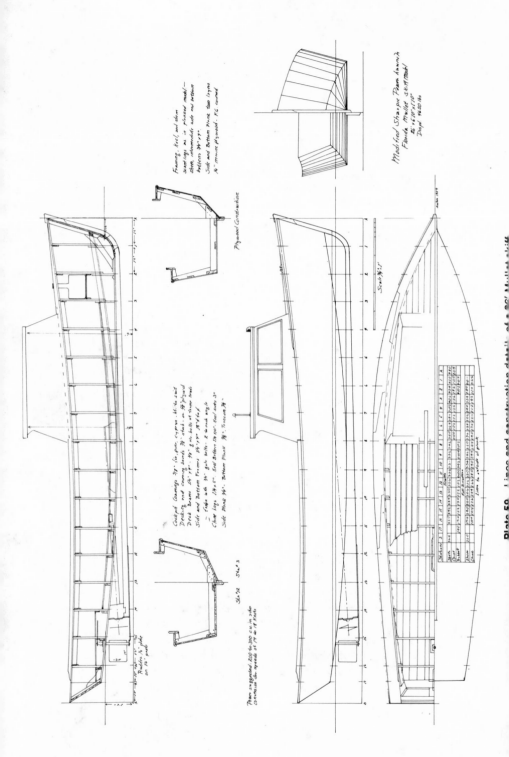

Framing, keel, and stem
scantlings as in printed model—
stem, intermediate side and bottom
battens 3/4"×3".
Side and Bottom Plank two layers
1/4" marine plywood. FG covered.

Plywood Construction

Modified Sharpie Power Launch
Florida Mullet Skiff Model
25'×6'10"×1'10"
Displ. 4,520 lbs.

John 1979

Cockpit Coamings 3/4" fir, pine, cypress oak to suit
Decking and coaming boards 3/4" steel or 1/2" plywood
Deck Beams 2 1/2"×3", 1 1/2" g in bulb at frame levels
Side and Bottom Frames 3/4"×3", 2 1/2"×3"×4" fwd
Frame to be 3/4" g in botts—2 in mid angle
Chine Logs 1 3/4"×3". Keel Bottom 3/4"×10". Keel sides 3"
Side Plank 3/4". Bottom Plank 3/4". Transom 3/4".

SK 42   Stat 3

Power suggested 200 to 300 cu in inbo
conversion for speeds of 14 to 18 knots

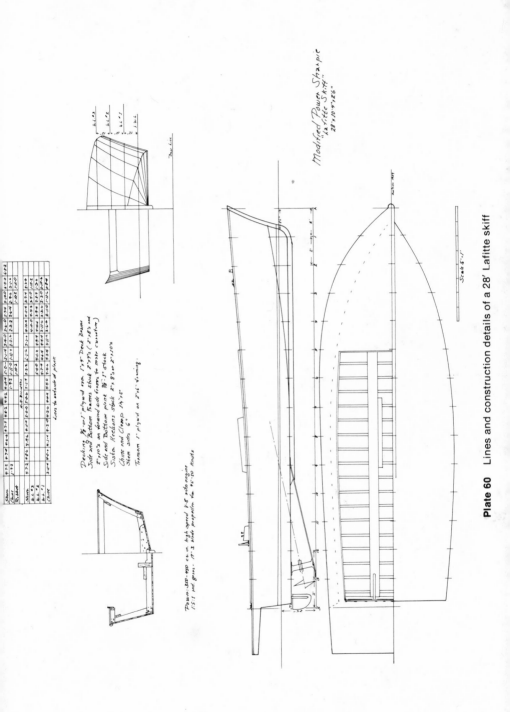

Modified Power Sharpie
"Lafitte Skiff"
28' x 10' 4" x 26"

Decking ³⁄₄" x 1" plywood over 1" x 4" Deck Beams
Side and Bottom Frames stock 2" x 9"s (2" x 8") and
2" x 10"s on athward side frames to mate curvature.)
Side and Bottom plank ⁷⁄₈"-1" stock
Sister Kitchens stock R's 8"3 or 2" x 10%
Chine and Clamp 1⁄4" x 5"
Stem sides 6"

Transom 1" plywood on 2" x 6" framing.

Power: 350-450 cb in high speed V-8 auto engine
15:1 red. gear. 17-3 blade propeller for 12-20 knots

Plate 60 Lines and construction details of a 28' Lafitte skiff

Scale 5/8-1'

299

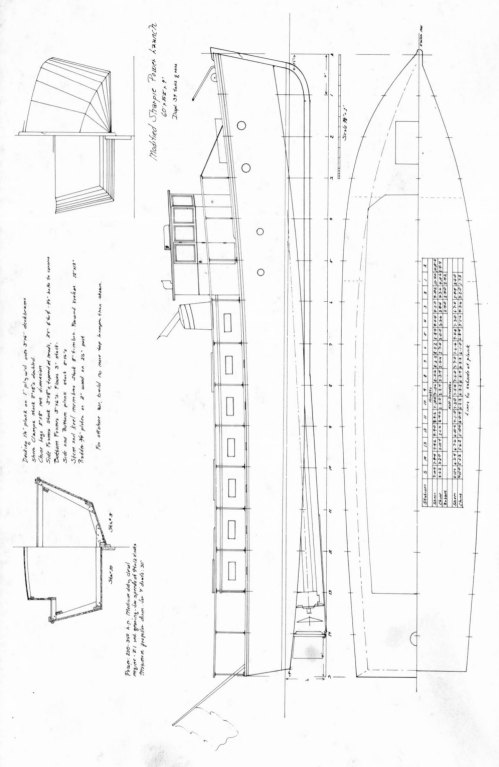

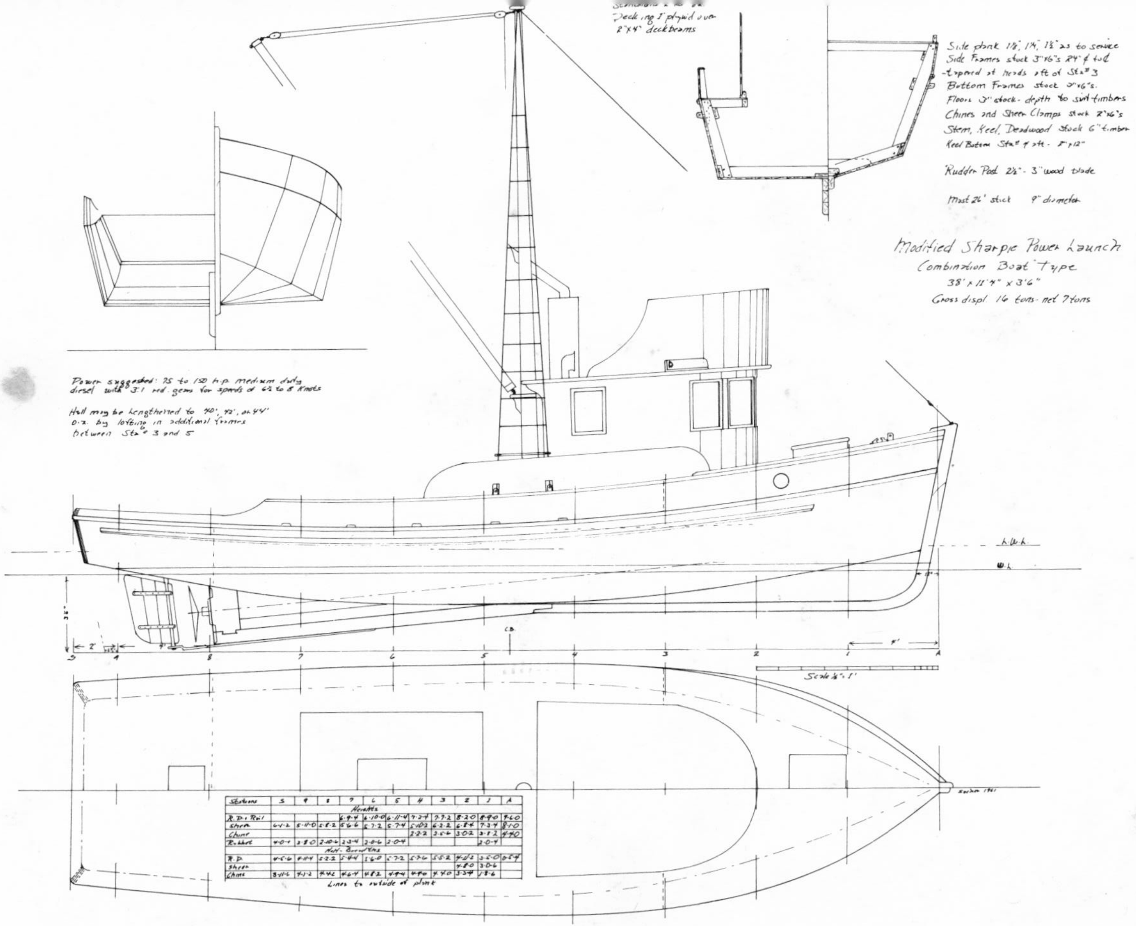

Plate 62 Lines and construction details of a 38' modified sharpie workboat

Modified V-Bottom Sharpie With Fantail Stern

While the usual flat-bottom hull or slightly modified sharpie variation is
not generally considered to be suitable for offshore use, there is a fantail-
sterned type of sharpie that has long been used as a deepwater vessel. An example of such a craft is the 38-foot combination boat shown in Plate 62. In
this modification the forefoot is given a rather deep V shape which is afforded by a high chine line. This reduces the displacement forward to lessen
pitching, and at the same time results in a hull form that cannot pound and
offers low resistance for easy driving with moderate power. The strong curve
or rocker in the chine positions the center of balance just aft of amidships
and gives an easy motion in rough water. The pronounced chine curve rises
to the fantail stern, which is noted for extra buoyancy and flotation factors
that keep the stern from dragging under varying conditions of loading or
overloading. The moderate slope or flare in the sides of the hull affords
good righting moments and helps to dampen the roll. These somewhat opposed factors designed into this hull form produce a stable vessel that is
very able and difficult to capsize even with a moderate draft—if top hamper
is kept to sensible proportions.

Fitting of Long Cargo Holds to Enable Proper Trimming

In small fishing vessels like the one shown, the hold space is generally extended well forward under the after end of the deckhouse, putting the engine well forward. This allows for trimming the cargo under varying conditions of loading to keep the load waterline in a more or less level condition.
The fuel tanks are carried well aft to balance the boat when running out
light to the fishing grounds. The buoyancy factors of this type of hull are
such that many are seen to be loaded to a negative freeboard amidships in
good weather without any seeming risk of foundering.

Planking and Framing of Large Modified
V-Bottom Sharpies

While these hulls may be constructed conventionally with a full framing
system, considerable saving in cost and building time may be effected by
utilizing a cross-planked bottom. A schematic diagram of its application to a
modified sharpie is shown in Figure 122. The main supporting member is
the heavy keelson forward. This is faired into a plank keelson at about the
midship section where the bottom becomes flat. Two or three full frames
are erected near the stem to give additional stiffness to the forward plank
strakes and to act as a building mold which is then left in the hull. The
shaded areas in the drawing indicate the bevels.

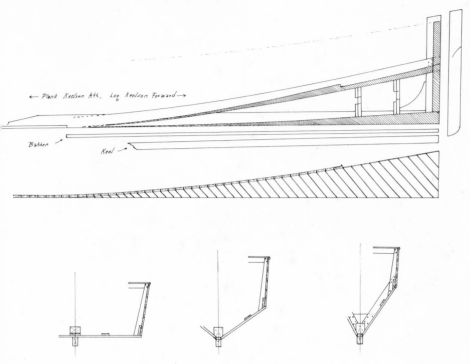

← Plank Keelson Aft. Log Keelson Forward →

Batten

Keel

Figure 122 Construction details of a cross-planked forefoot as used in modified
V-bottom sharpies

Optional Round, Elliptical, or Square Sterns

The transom of the 38-foot combination boat is shown as the square type.
If more deck room or a more pleasing appearance is desired, a round or
elliptical stern may be lofted in. If a long ellipse is projected, the framing
will be made up of single rim logs. If a somewhat larger hull is required, six
or eight feet of length may be added by respacing the stations.

Small Offshore Sharpie Launch

As in the case of the Mullet skiff, the lines of the fantail-stern-type modified sharpie may be manipulated to gain certain desired characteristics. The
plans of a modified sharpie fantail launch adapted for a specific purpose are
shown as a small offshore swordfish launch in Plate 63. Here a boat of large
cruising range is desirable, along with easy driving characteristics that will
enable the fitting of a low-powered engine for good fuel economy. The
lines of this hull have been drawn out for a fine waterline entrance angle to-

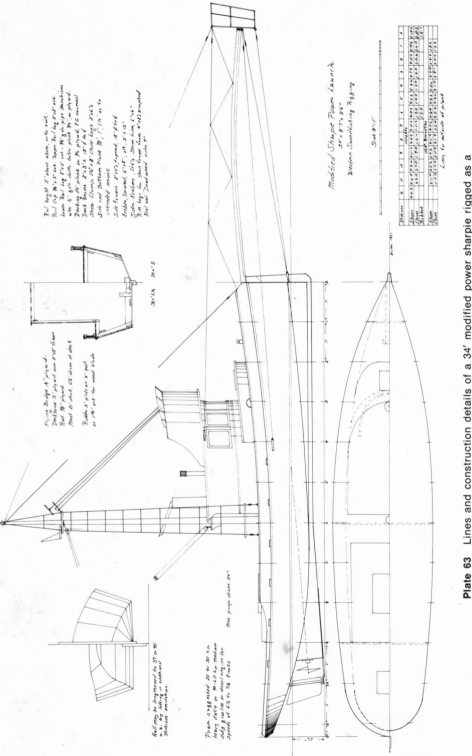

Modified Sharpe Power Launch
34' x 8'7" x 24"
Western Smontboating Rigging

Scale 3/8" = 1'

Plate 63 Lines and construction details of a 34' modified power sharpie rigged as a

304

gether with a very moderate beam-length ratio. To balance this latter characteristic, the sides have been given a marked flare to give adequate righting moments and to enhance load carrying ability. Stability factors are here well in hand, if the deckhouse and flying bridge are rather lightly constructed. The swordfish pulpit and boom shown are typical of such fishing craft. The details are rather general in scope, as experienced swordfishermen incorporate their own individual ideas in the rig of their boats.

Hull Modifications of Sharpies for Specific Uses

The lines of the fantail-stern sharpie may be adapted to very small hulls, as in the 26-foot launch shown in Plate 64. Such a boat could serve usefully as a troller, gillnetter, working or toy tugboat, boatyard service launch, or harbor or fuel service craft, as it is capable of carrying large loads for its size. If a somewhat larger or longer hull were required, the lines could be drawn out to 28 or 30 feet by respacing the frames. This would help the speed somewhat, but it must be remembered that such launches have speed capabilities in direct ratio to their waterline length, and are suited only for low-powered engines.

46′ Modified Sharpie as a Shrimp Trawler

The majority of launches built to this hull form have been commercial fishing vessels of substantial size, where the builders required a burdensome boat that could be economically constructed. An example of this type is the 46-foot shrimp trawler shown in Plate 65 whose lines were taken off when hauled out in Ensenada, Mexico. These boats are somewhat roughly but strongly built and appear to stand up well to their hard usage. The boat shown has a square stern, which offers cheaper building than the round or elliptical type which could be substituted if desired. The large hold extends well forward under the deckhouse. Access to the engine is provided through the deckhouse, and minimal crew accommodations are placed in the forepeak. As with the previous boats shown, the hull could be lengthened up to about 60 feet by respacing the stations. This hull form is advantageous in areas of large tidal variations, as the boats, if grounded out, will rest in a nearly upright position due to the flat bilges.

Construction Details of Large Modified Sharpie Launches

The large fantail-stern modified sharpie can offer very definite economies in construction to the experienced builder who might require a really large

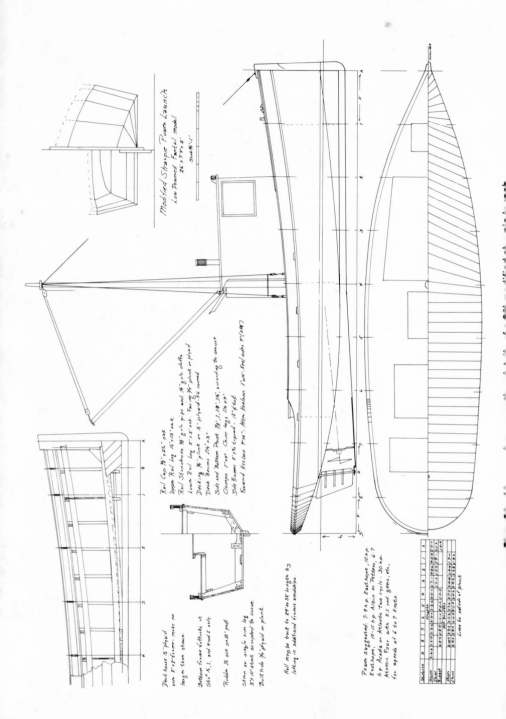

Modified Sharpie Power Launch
Low Powered Fantail Model
26' x 7' x 2'
Scale ¾" = 1'

Rail Cap ⅞" x 2½" oak
Upper Rail log 1½" x 1½" oak
Rail Stanchions ⅞" galv. pipe and ⅞" galv. chalks
Lower Rail log 2" x 3" oak. Facing ¾" plank or plywd
Decking ⅜" plank on ⅜" plywd. 'G' covered
Deck Beams 1½" x 3"
Side and Bottom Plank ⅞"; 1'; 1⅜"; 1⅝" according to service
Clamps Rises. Chine logs 1½"
Side Frames 2" x 1½" spaced 10" apt.
Forward Keelson 3" x 4" Aft'n Keelson 1 ½" x 3" secured x" (9 ½")

Deck house ⅜" plywd
over ½" x ½" frames matr. no
large than shown.

Bottom frame V.butts at
Sta's A, 1, and 4 and 5 only.

Rudder ½" oak or ⅜" pad

Stem on single rim log
3" x 10" stock scorphod to curve.
Bulkheads ⅜" plywd or plank.

Hull may be built to 29' or 32' length by
lofting in additional frames amidships.

Power suggested: 7-9 h.p. Eastharpe, 10 h.p.
Easthope, 10-15 h.p. Albin or Petters, 6-7
h.p. Acadia or Atlantic Two cycle - 30 h.p.
Atomic Four with 2:1 red. gears. etc.
for speeds of 6 to 7 knots

306

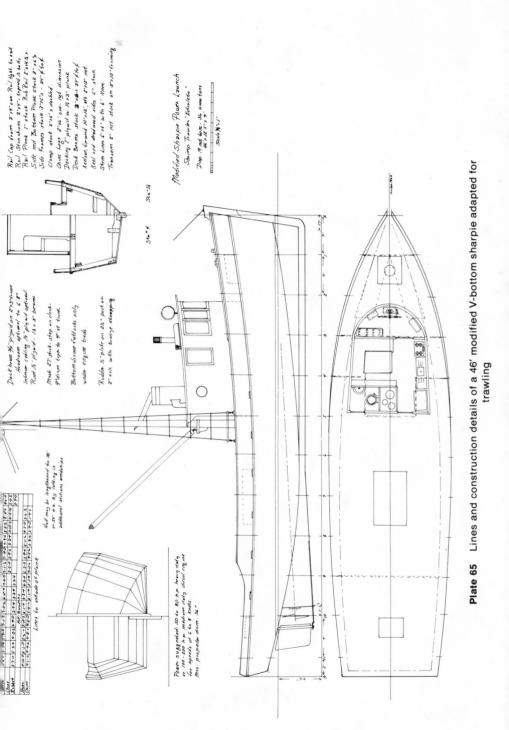

Plate 65 Lines and construction details of a 46' modified V-bottom sharpie adapted for trawling

307

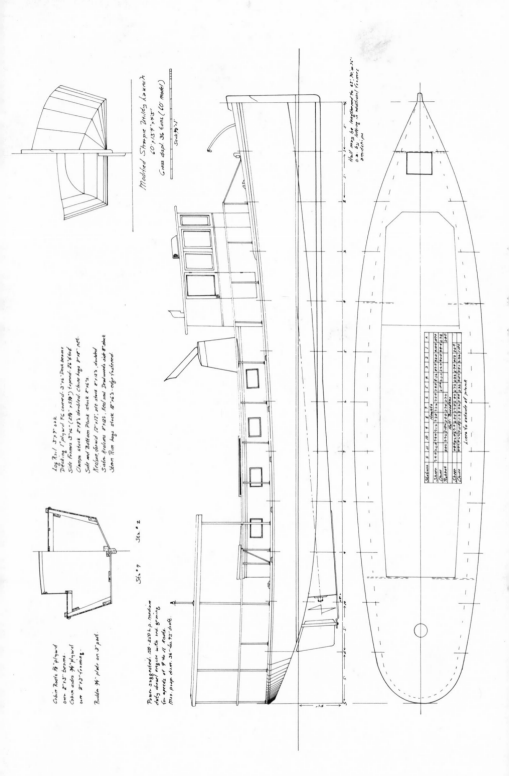

Modified Sharpie Utility Launch
20' × 13'4" × 13"
Gross displ 3½ tons (10° model)

launch. Such a craft is shown in Plate 66. The profile shows a utility launch or cruising boat, but many other arrangements are possible if the top hamper is kept to reasonable proportions in deference to the shallow draft. The hull may be lengthened up to about 75 feet by respacing the frames. It could also be used as the basis for a party fishing boat with high railings all around the decks if the freeboard were reduced about 24 inches all along the sheerline.

22

Low Chine Model
The Double Wedge Power Launches

The "double wedge" power launch, so called because its form presents a wedge shaped appearance in both profile and plan view, represents the first small boat type that was specifically developed for mechanical propulsion. While in its early form it is generally considered to be obsolete today, it is significant that modern power boat hulls based upon it are considered by many naval architects and knowledgeable boatmen to be among the best all-around performers of our contemporary designs.

The double wedge hull had its origin in both the efforts of professional naval architects and empirical builders to produce the highest possible speeds in a displacement-type hull. Its lines therefore were projected to lower resistance factors and to spread the weight of the boat over as long a waterline length as was practical. The result was a rather long and extremely narrow hull of very light displacement. It was this very narrowness that put its form into the category of the fast contemporary steamship, and it is therefore the only small powerboat type whose low resistance factors approach the low resistance ratings of large ships.

Form of Early Double Wedge Launches

In form, the early launches showed beam-length ratios of from six to ten, with very sharp forward sections, usually with a rounded or semicircular forefoot that produced a knife like entrance angle at the waterline. In some cases this was narrow enough to make the station lines nearly straight from rabbet to sheer, which imposed a rather deep rabbet line in the forward third of the hull. The hull then became more shallow with the rise of the rabbet line in the after sections; it was usually straight until it reached the region of the rudder post, and flattened under the transom. This latter feature was critical for supporting the stern sections against the thrust of the large high torque propellers to prevent the hull from squatting at speed.

The principles and theories underlying this type of hull form were well known to designers and shipbuilders as early as 1850, who then as now were constantly searching for greater speed. Actual development was not possible until the advent of the lightweight high-speed steam turbine engine which was perfected by 1880.

Steam-Powered Double Wedge Launches

The first steam-powered launches were expensive novelties, mostly built at great cost for people of wealth who fancied something faster than the then-fashionable fantail steam yacht whose hull form was based on the racing sailboat or clipper ship. A number of steam launches were built in England and in the United States, the famous Nathaniel Herreshoff being the principal American innovator.

These early yachts were built in lengths of 65 to 90 feet, but due to the extreme beam-length ratio they had Spartan interior accommodations. These were probably far less than seen today in hulls of half the length, because of the space demands for the engine and boiler room plus the coal bunkers. Their high-speed capabilities caused them to gain great notoriety in both the nautical and daily press. One of them, the English yacht *Turbinia,* launched in 1885, astounded Queen Victoria, her naval aides, and visiting dignitaries of other nations, when it dashed through the Royal Fleet, assembled at Spithead in 1887 for the Golden Jubilee Naval Review, at 34 knots.

Double Wedge Launches Adapted as Torpedo Boats

Naval constructors of the leading maritime nations were quick to adapt this new hull form for a torpedo boat to carry either the old-type spar-mounted torpedo used in the American Civil War, or the latterly developed Whitehead-type that could be launched to run under its own power. High speeds for this use were important for both surprise and withdrawal, and the torpedo boat opened up a new phase of naval warfare. Marine engineers set about improving the reliability and lowered fuel consumption of the steam turbine engines. Naval architects concerned themselves with improving the seaworthiness of the narrow hulls which in their early forms rolled excessively and were very wet due to their sharp forward sections. Bilge keels were introduced to steady the hull, and flare and flam were worked into the bow sections to give increased righting moments. The first serious use of torpedo boats of this improved form was during the Spanish American War of 1898, where they figured prominently in several naval engagements.

Variations in Hull Form of Double Wedge Launches

The actual hull form of both the early and later improved versions varied from round- to V-bottom and combinations of both types. Most of the early craft were rounded in the forward sections, but showed a chine knuckle from amidships aft where the sections flattened to support the stern. It also became quite apparent that a hard chine line was a prominent factor in giving some resistance to rolling, the curse of the earlier naval types in anything like a rough sea.

Torpedo Boat Form Adapted for Small Power Launch

At the beginning of the twentieth century, small boat designers and builders turned their attention to the torpedo boat hull form as a small power launch, attracted by both the wide publicity given to the type during the Spanish conflict and the increasing reliability of the newly developed gasoline engine. Most of the early launches were built as racing craft, and contemporary photographs show them as scaled down replicas of torpedo boats with a rather straight sheer and rounded or canoe-type sterns. Some of these were built as round-bottom craft, with light carvel planking and closely spaced steam-bent frames.

Fairbanks No. 2

An historic example of a V-bottom racing launch was *Fairbanks No. 2* built by Captain Charles W. Langdon of Oxford, Maryland, in 1902. It was 37 feet long with a beam of 4 feet 2 inches, and was very lightly built, showing a total displacement of 1,900 lbs. Its beam-length ratio, profile, and rounded stern were almost an exact copy in reduced scale of the earlier steam yacht and torpedo boat types. Powered with a heavy duty 12–15 hp. Smalley engine manufactured by the Fairbanks Scale Company, it regularly made 26 statute miles per hour.

As the fastest launch of its day on the Chesapeake, it received much publicity, both locally and in the yachting press, and its lines were published in the *Rudder* magazine in 1903.

A half model of the hull is preserved in the Watercraft Collection of the United States National Museum, and the drawing in Plate 67 is copied from a set of lines made from it by Howard I. Chapelle, Historian Emeritus, U.S. Museum of History and Technology, Smithsonian Institution.

While a powerboat with such an extreme beam-length ratio is obviously impractical for ordinary use, the form of the *Fairbanks* is significant from an historical point of view as being the direct ancestor of a subsequent group of fast displacement type powerboats closely based on its lines with somewhat wider beam. It is also a good illustration of the effect of resistance factors governing speed capabilities in relation to shaft horsepower.

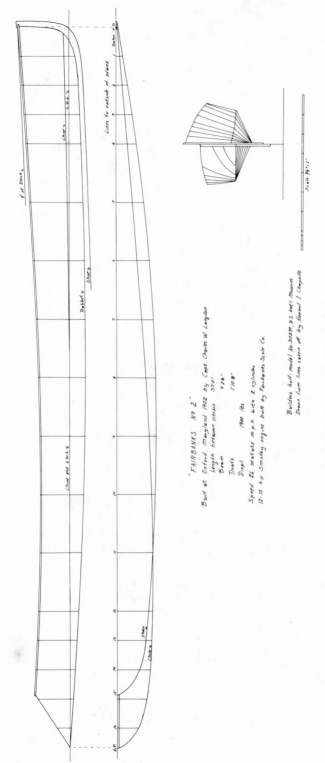

"FAIRBANKS No 2"

Built at Oxford, Maryland 1902 by Capt. Charles W. Langdon
Length between perps.   37'0"
Beam   4'2¾"
Draft   1'10⅜"
Displ   1900 lbs
Speed 8½ statute m.p.h. with 2 cylinder
12-15 h.p. Smalley engine built by Fairbanks Scale Co.

Builders half-model No 311239, U.S. Nat'l Museum
Drawn from lines taken off by Howard I. Chapelle

Plate 67   Lines of Fairbanks No. 2

313

Racing Boat Designs Adapted to Small Launches

At any rate, the publicity attendant to the *Fairbanks* and other contemporary round- and V-bottom racing launches stimulated much experimentation by practical boatbuilders. By 1910 the double wedge hull form had been developed into a very practical small power launch for both work and pleasure. The beam, while somewhat narrow by modern standards, had been increased to sensible proportions, and a deep skeg was commonly fitted which made for more accurate steering and balanced the hull against broaching in stern seas.

Ability of Double Wedge Launches in Rough Water

Perhaps the most useful and attractive feature of these launches was their ability to maintain good speed and to handle well in rough or choppy water without pounding or undue spray throwing, and being of light displacement, they were buoyant and lively in a seaway. While the hull speed was obviously not nearly as high as that of the narrow beamed racing hulls, it was still almost double that of contemporary displacement powerboats based on sailing boat hull forms. Because of its easy driving characteristics it was particularly suited for use with the heavy duty single and twin cylinder two-cycle engines of the period, and they were most efficient with their high torque capabilities turning large propellers of generous pitch.

Double Wedge Launches as an Alternative to Power Dories

The fishermen of New England and the Maritime Provinces of Canada were at once attracted to these launches as an alternative to the power dory, which was the first small powerboat used in significant numbers when gasoline engines began to replace working sailing craft. While the double wedge launch lacked the supreme seaworthiness of the dory, it was fully capable in the same 24 to 26-foot lengths of cruising at 9 to 11 knots with the same 5 or 6 hp. single cylinder two cycles that had formerly had such widespread employment as to be called "dory engines." As the loaded dory in most cases could not exceed 5 knots, it suffered greatly in comparison.

While the light displacement double wedge obviously lacked the great load carrying capacity of a dory of similar length, it found almost universal acceptance among the lobster fishermen. Its speed allowed doubling the length of the trapline, and it was fully capable of hauling the few hundred pounds or less of weight that made up a day's catch.

Construction Variations in Double Wedge Launches

While following the general hull form of the *Fairbanks* and other contemporary racing launches in most respects except for the beam, the actual construction methods used varied as to the ideas of the builders and were particularly influenced by their locale. The New England and Canadian builders favored lightweight round-bottom hulls with shaped planking and light, closely spaced, steam-bent frames. In some cases the deadwood was planked up "schooner fashion." The Chesapeake Bay builders favored the V-bottom type, and generally employed the heavy construction and cross planked bottoms that were already widely used in their sailing skiffs and bateau.

The launches here shown for purposes of illustration and possible reproduction are all of the V-bottom type. The double-wedge Hooper Island boats of the Chesapeake are shown in their original and traditional form. The round-bottom New England launches are offered as modified V-bottom types using modern building materials. These versions are more practical for today's building where the generally high degree of manual skill required to construct closely fitted planking and steam-bent frames is not needed, not to mention the cost factors in inflationary times.

V-Bottom Variation of Early New England Launches

An example of an early-day New England launch in V-bottom form is shown in Plate 68. Its 26 feet of length and 6 foot beam represents the smallest type commonly used in the lobster fisheries. Moderate beam hulls of this size are not suited for fixed steering shelters, particularly when used offshore, but the fisherman-type spray hood shown will give some protection to the forward part of the cockpit. While its general appearance is somewhat old fashioned, it could find useful application today for the reasons previously discussed and can be built and powered at moderate cost. The power plant shown is a 5 or 6 hp. single cylinder Acadia or Atlantic two-cycle engine which will drive the boat at a maximum of 10 or 11 knots. Small modern multicylinder engines are also offered as an option. In powering these old-style launches, excessive power is not advised, as the hulls are incapable of planing and will merely squat and wallow if overdriven. Launches of this form in sizes up to about 30 feet have a terminal hull speed of about 13 knots.

Use of Modern Materials in Double Wedge Launches

The construction details (Plate 69) show suggested simplified methods of building and the use of modern materials. The framing is of light weight as befits a hull of light displacement, but is strong and is well braced by a full plywood bulkhead at either end of the cockpit. The hull abaft the stem is further braced by a single wide plank that extends clear across and acts as a side frame for both sides.

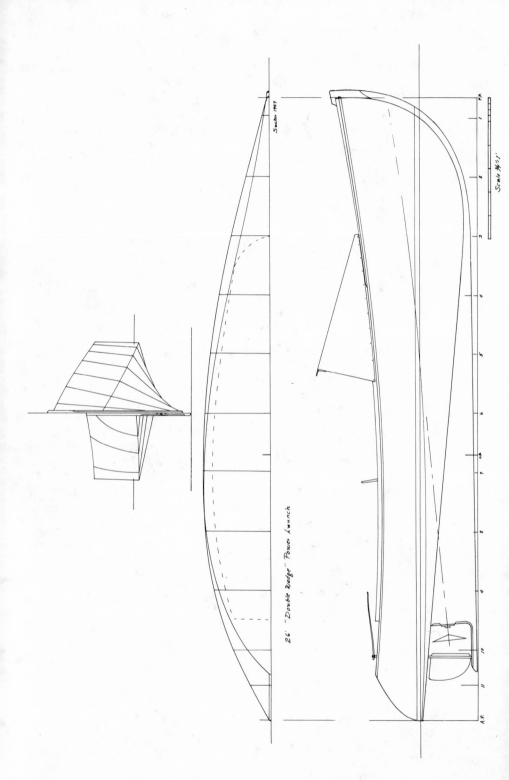

26' "Double Wedge" Power Launch

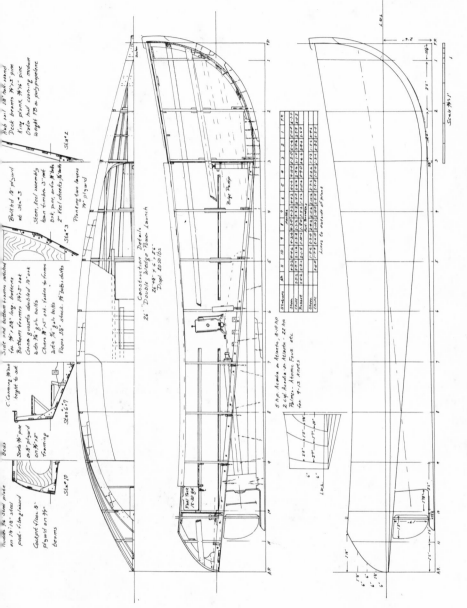

Plate 69 Construction details of a 26′ double wedge launch

317

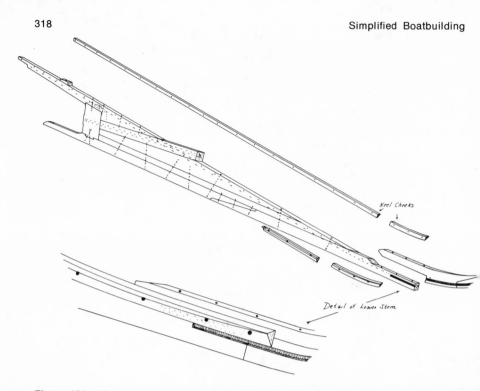

Figure 123   Keel and backbone construction of a light-displacement V-bottom double
wedge launch

Keel and Backbone Construction of Double Wedge Launches

The keel and backbone layout for this and similar types of double wedge
launches is shown in Figure 123. To keep the overall weight low, most of the
launches under 30 feet of length utilize timbers of 3 inch section, which is
amply thick for drifting with ¼-inch rod and allows for the boring of a shaft
log up to 1¼-inch diameter. As the rabbet line in these hulls is in most cases
a straight line from the forefoot to the transom, keel cheeks to back the garboard offers the most simple type of construction here.

Stem Construction of Double Wedge Launches

The stem of these launches is usually semicircular in profile, and is gotten
out of straight pieces and scarphed in the usual manner. Attention is called
to the point where the after end of the stem piece joins the keel timbers—
the forward ends of the keel cheeks have their lower edges beveled to coincide with the slope of the bottom frames, and this must be carefully faired
into the stem rabbet to form a continuous backing for the garboard seam.

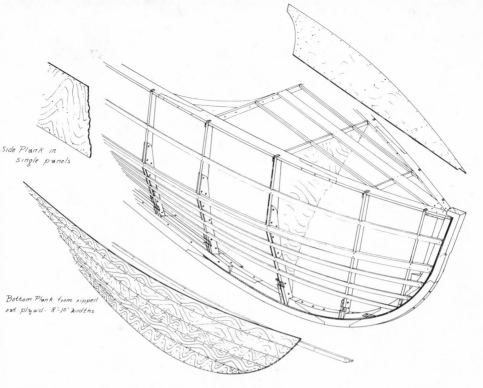

Side Plank in single panels

Bottom Plank from ripped out plyw'd - 8"-10" widths

Figure 124 Construction details of a double wedge plywood-planked V-bottom launch

Framing and Planking Details of Double Wedge Launches

The details of the framing and planking are shown in Figure 124. The upper ends of the side frames are let into a horizontal sheer shelf that is gotten out of straight planks and scarphed to the curve of the sides. This makes a very strong structure that effectively braces the hull against changing shape. As the sides of this style of launch are usually straight enough to allow the fitting of plywood panels for the planking, an intermediate batten need be fitted midway between chine and sheer to supply additional bracing and to act as a fastening piece. On the bottom approaching the forefoot, the plywood will have to be ripped into 8-inch or 10-inch planks to accommodate the compound curves, the seams being backed by battens. An alternative to this is shown in Figure 125, which is the use of irregularly

Figure 125 Optional methods of applying plywood bottom planking to a V-bottom double wedge launch

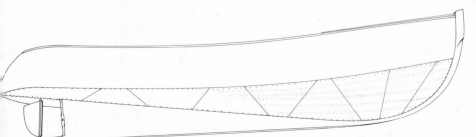

Bottom of double wedge hull planked with irregularly shaped panels

shaped plywood panels which can be more readily sprung to the shape of the bottom. As in the ripped out planking, this type of bottom should also be backed by battens set 8-to-10 inches apart to give adequate strength to the bottom. If the hull and deck are covered with two layers of lightweight fiber glass or polypropylene compound, a very rigid and long lasting structure will be achieved.

Construction Details of Torpedo Boat Stern

The framing details of the canoe or "torpedo boat" type stern are shown in Figure 126. The sheer shelf aft is shaped to the indicated curve, and a similar shelf is made up for the bottom, its forward ends being notched to fair into the chine stringers. A plywood bulkhead should be fitted either just forward or aft of the rudder post for added stiffening of the hull, but is not shown in the drawing. In the case of the 26-foot launch, the curve of the sides and the profile of the stern liner will allow the fitting of solid plywood panels which will follow their developed shape. A metal band should be fitted around the lower edge of the after planking to protect the structure from blows.

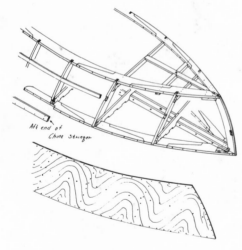

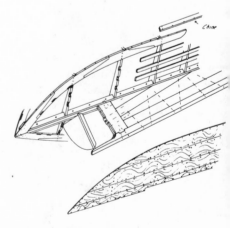

Figure 126 Framing and planking details of a torpedo-boat stern double wedge V-bottom launch

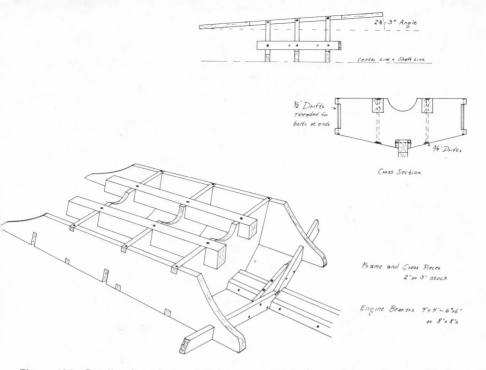

Figure 127   Details of engine mounts to accommodate heavy-duty engines as fitted to some double wedge V-bottom launches

Heavy Engine Mountings for Use With Heavy-Duty Engines

In cases where heavy-duty engines, particularly of the two-cycle or small sailboat auxiliary diesel type, are fitted in these lightly built hulls, special attention should be given to the construction of the engine mountings. Any of these types of engines can produce very severe vibration in a light hull unless anchored to a substantial foundation. Figure 127 shows a type of engine mounting which has proved satisfactory in such instances. In addition to the usual heavy engine bearers, two deep longitudinal timbers are notched over heavy floor pieces and spread over as many bottom frames as is practical. If the lower stringers are splayed out at a slight angle from the centerline, the dampening effect of the structure is augmented by giving a better bearing surface.

Importance of Proper Skeg Area in Double Wedge Launches

The lines of the double wedge hull are capable of being manipulated into various alternatives or variations as to length, beam, and displacement, but a word of warning is in order concerning the reduction of area or possible omission of the long skeg. As an appendage of rather large area, there are significant resistance factors or drag involved in its application. In the earlier days of this hull's development, some builders seeking the highest speeds possible eliminated the skeg entirely, or at best fitted a rudimentary

321

one. The results were sometimes fatal. Such early speedboats showed a very sharp wedge- or pie-shaped bow in plan view to give a very fine waterline entrance angle for the lowest possible resistance factors. Without the presence of much flare above the waterline with attendant reserve buoyancy, such hulls show a marked tendency to root and dive when driven into a head sea. If the boat was tripped or broached by a steep stern sea, the hull could be swung around and capsized without the balancing factors of a skeg. An example of one of these "autoboats," as they were sometimes called, is shown in Plate 70. As low-cost launches capable of fairly high speeds with low-powered engines, they enjoyed a brief vogue among pleasure boatmen between 1909 and 1915. Aside from their capsizing proclivities, they were at their best when run on a straight course, as the lack of a skeg made them very difficult to steer, particularly in choppy water. The type happily lost favor before World War I.

Fitting of Steering Shelters and Trunk Cabins

Reverting again to the development of the early practical double wedge launches, larger versions of 30 feet length and upwards came into being that offered more carrying capacity and interior accommodation. The increase in size and beam encouraged the fitting of trunk cabins and steering shelters for better weather protection for the occupants. An example is shown in Plate 71. Boats of this type were widely used in the lobster fisheries where longer traplines and greater carrying capacity were an advantage. A riding sail aft was frequently fitted which helped to dampen the roll in beam seas.

Construction Details of Round Sterns

Some of these launches were built with round sterns as shown (Plate 71) in preference to the canoe or torpedo boat type stern. As far as performance is concerned, there is little to choose from in comparing both types, although the round sterns were said to offer a bit more speed through the slightly increased bearing area at the waterline. Figure 128 shows the framing details

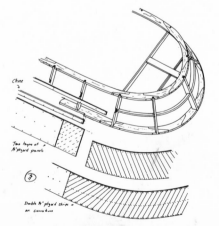

Figure 128   Construction details of a round stern as fitted to a V-bottom double wedge launch

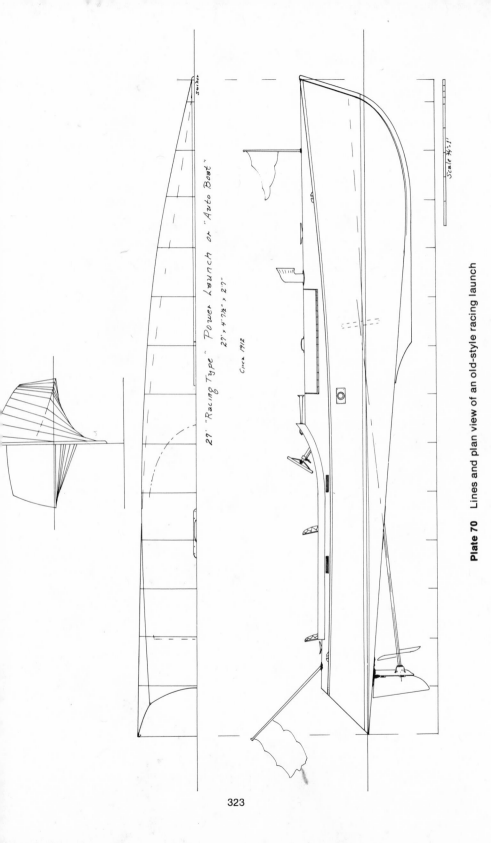

27' "Racing Type" "Power Launch or "Auto Boat"

27' x 4'2½" x 2'2"

Circa 1912

Plate 70 Lines and plan view of an old-style racing launch

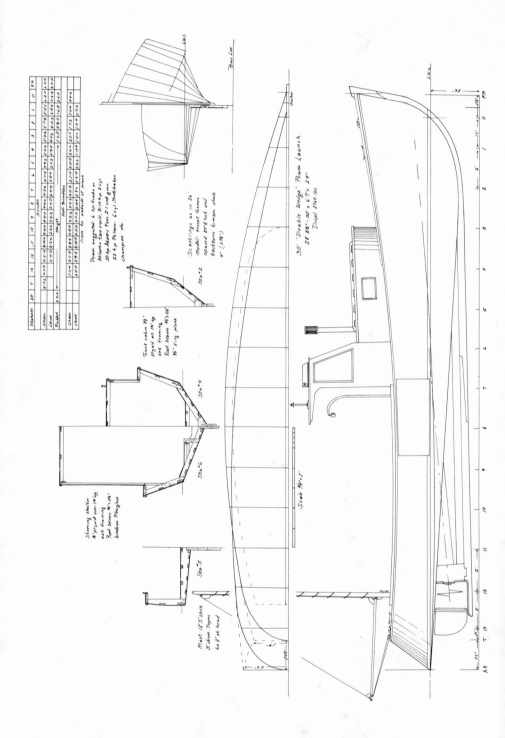

324

of the round stern. It is framed with horizontal upper and lower shelves as in the case of the canoe type, the only difference being in the shape. An intermediate batten or false frame was usually fitted midway between sheer and chine to give extra bracing to the light planking. The lower rim was protected by a galvanized iron rub rail to prevent denting of the sharp edge if struck.

Many builders did not favor contoured sterns due to the costs and building time involved, and often substituted the conventional flat transom shown in Figure 129. In some cases these were canted forward so as to approximate the profile of the torpedo boat type stern. As the position of the transom is not critical to performance, it may also be set plumb or raked aft at the option of the builder.

The 30-foot launch shows the same construction features as described for the 26-foot model, and can be built with the same procedures and scantling dimensions.

Importance of Lightweight Deck Erections

In the matter of steering shelters and cabins for the double wedge launches and other lightweight hulls of modest beam, care should be taken

Figure 129 Construction details of a flat or raking transom-type stern as fitted to a V-bottom double wedge launch

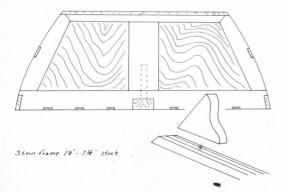

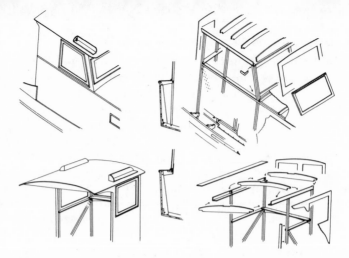

Figure 130 Construction details of steering shelters fitted to light-displacement double wedge launches or conventional launches of narrow beam

to make certain that top hamper weights and windage do not reach excessive proportions. The framing should be made up of light materials, the requisite strength being obtained by careful joinery and proper fastenings. Figure 130 shows various types of framing options for steering shelters of light weight.

Construction Details of Lightweight Trunk Cabins

Some experienced small boat sailors have improved their launches by the addition of trunk cabins made of very light framing over which canvas or

Figure 131 Construction details of lightweight trunk cabins or bow shelters as fitted to light-displacement launches

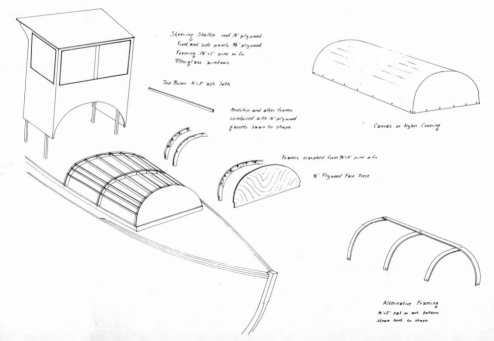

nylon covers have been fitted. If the framing is made circular in section, there is very little windage as the shelter presents a streamlined form to beam winds. Another method used is to make up a framing of light ash bows steam bent to the required shape to hold the cover. Diagrams of these structures are shown in Figure 131. They can be made in suitable dimensions to fit any small launch that is used in offshore work.

Plate 72 shows a double wedge launch with a canoe stern fitted with a lightweight steering shelter and canvas-covered trunk cabin on a semicircular frame. This type of arrangement has been much used on lobster boats. Plate 73 shows a double wedge launch with a canvas awning.

Type and Position of Engine in Double Wedge Pleasure Craft

Many rather small power launches were built in the double wedge principle as pleasure or day fishing craft. Due to the very light displacement resulting from reducing the size of the hull, the engine was placed toward the bow to balance the boat when three or four passengers were carried. A 4 or 5 hp. engine will drive this boat at 7 or 8 knots. A small four-cylinder engine such as the Universal Atomic Four or 22 hp. Palmer will give 10 to 11 knots. Due to the small beam-to-length ratio, this is about the smallest practical size that can be built. The construction method follows that as previously described (page 317), except for reduced weight of the scantlings.

Steam Power for Double Wedge Launches

Due to their easy driving capabilities, small double wedge hulls perform well with light steam power. The large diameter high torque propellers that are used with these power plants are particularly efficient in these light displacement hulls. One of these modernized hulls might be of interest to steamboat enthusiasts who could find their speed capabilities advantageous over the usual 5-or-6-knot speeds of the more common fantail or conventional displacement hull that is more often fitted with such power. For best results, the power plants should be of the lightweight type, and the engine and boiler mountings should be carried on long stringers to distribute the weight over as many frames as possible. Figures 132 and 133 show the 23 and 26 foot launches arranged as steamboats.

The Hooper Island Launch

Another and perhaps best known example of the double wedge power launch is the Hooper Island boat of the Chesapeake Bay, so named for the

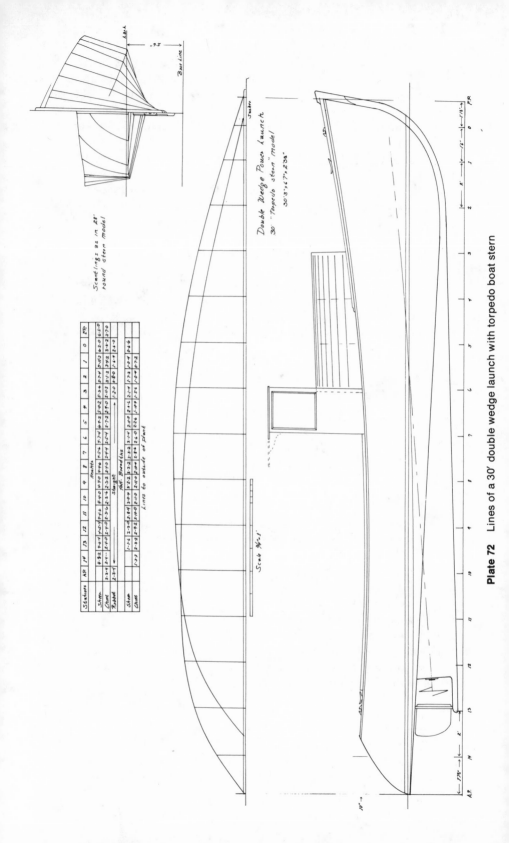

Plate 72 Lines of a 30' double wedge launch with torpedo boat stern

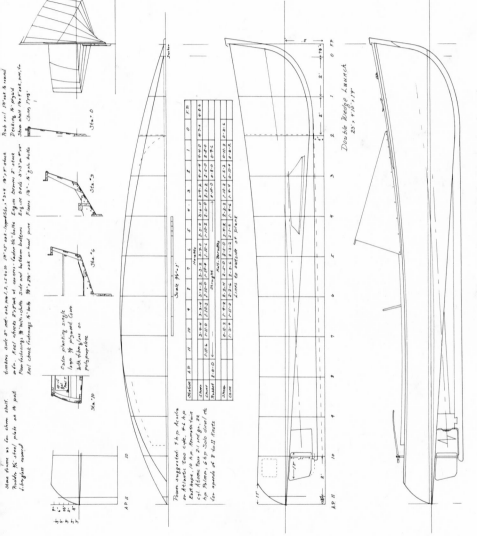

Plate 73 Lines and construction details of a 23' double wedge launch

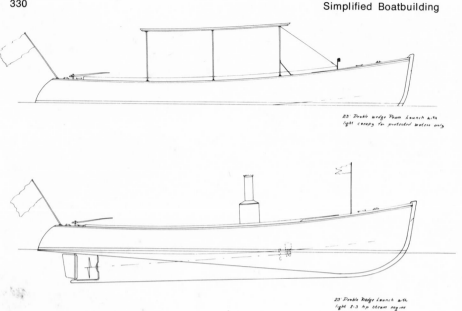

Figure 132   Optional arrangements for a 23' V-bottom double wedge launch

area of its early development. These boats in their traditional form are direct descendants of Captain Langdon's early racing boat. As this launch was well known on the Chesapeake for its speed capabilities, it is logical that the Bay builders seeking an efficient type of power boat based their experiments on this model.

Figure 133   Details of skeg arrangements to accommodate large diameter propellers as required in small steam-powered launches

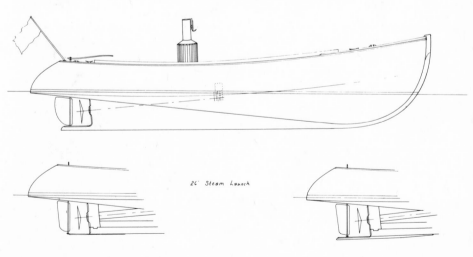

Development of the Hooper Island Launch

The first consideration for developing a launch for practical use was to widen the beam to provide adequate interior room, but not to the extent that the low resistance factors inherent in the basic hull form would be appreciably increased. The subsequent increase in displacement permitted the use of heavy scantlings which enabled the boats, as working craft, to stand up to the demands of hard usage.

Seaworthiness of Hooper Island Launch

The Hooper Island launches in their individually developed form proved to be singularly able boats in rough water, and handled well in the often steep chop encountered throughout the shallow reaches of Chesapeake Bay. Their good steering qualities made them useful craft in the crab fisheries, for they ran straight with the unattended helm lashed while running a trot line. The round stern was of particular advantage in working over the oyster beds, as the operator could more easily work the tongs around the after quarters without fouling.

Various Sizes of Hooper Island Launches

The launches were built in various sizes from 25 to 50 feet in length, to a more or less fixed set of proportions, the most popular length being of 30 feet and upwards. Plate 74 shows a widely built 34 foot 6 inch example with 6 foot 6 inch beam, which was constructed throughout the Bay region between 1910 and 1925. The lines of this hull are typical of the best examples of these boats, with the chine line paralleling the load waterline, and with the familiar rounded stern. As with many empirically developed craft, no original line drawings or plans ever existed, each builder following his own individual ideas as to overall dimensions and detail finish.

The construction detail illustrates how the Bay builders adapted their own distinctive methods of heavyweight construction in these launches, which were markedly similar in detail to those employed in various previously developed sailing boats.

Backbone and Stem Construction of Hooper Island Launches

The main supporting member of the hull was the heavy keelson, which in some cases was hewn from a grown tree that showed the proper curve. In most cases the keelson was made up of two or more separate pieces that were scarphed to form the correct shape.

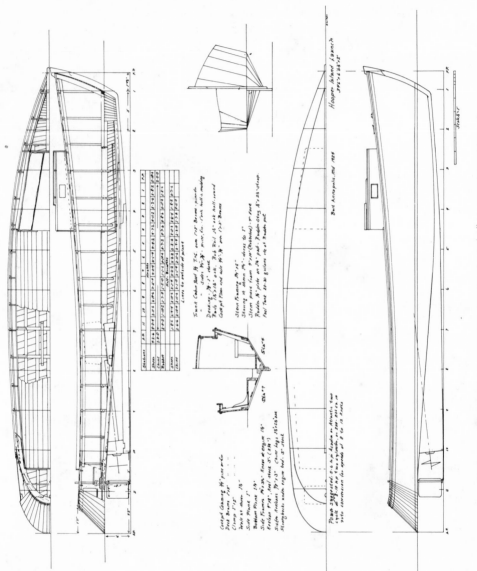

Plate 74 Lines and construction details of a 34′ 6″ Hooper Island launch

The stem was usually fashioned from a single timber, as the rabbet showed but a slight curve, but sometimes a two-piece type was fitted. In both cases the forward edge of the liner was beveled to receive the side plank which extended flush with plank's forward edge, and a steam-bent strip of oak was fastened over the hood ends of the plank to make the cutwater.

General Construction Details of Hooper Island Launches

The hull was frameless except for a couple of strongbacks worked in under the engine bearers, and sometimes another was placed forward near the after end of the trunk cabin. The bottom plank was laid on herringbone fashion, the forward strakes being hewn from thick pieces as described previously (pages 215 and 303). The chine, being parallel with the load waterline, was actually S-shaped in its expanded form, and was cut from a wide board. Due to its length, it was usually in two pieces spliced together. The round stern was framed by an upper and lower rim log, as previously described and was planked up with vertical staving that was planed off in finishing to make a smooth outer surface.

Method of Building the Hooper Island Launch

In building, temporary molds were set in the upside-down position, and the log keelson and stem piece were joined together and set over them. The chine stringers and sheer battens were temporarily fastened into the mold notches, and the side plank was applied. This was rarely shaped, with the upper strakes allowed to die out under the covering board. Due to the increasing height of the plank surface at the bow, extra strakes here were merely let into the longer planks of the middle topsides. The side frames were then fitted and the bottom plank applied. The strongbacks and stern framing were generally fitted after the hull was righted, a few molds being retained to maintain the shape until all framing structures were finished. The skeg was drifted to the keelson just before the bottom plank was laid on.

The Bay builders often fitted a type of stern bearing that was peculiar to the region, but which could be used to advantage on any type of powerboat employing medium-speed engines. A short length of steam hose, of inside diameter that was a loose fit on the propeller shaft, was obtained. The after end of the shaft hole was reamed out to a depth of 6–8 inches and the hose was inserted into it. The outer end of the hose was split, and the tabs were nailed above and below the shaft opening to the upper and lower edges of the back of the skeg. The tabs were then covered by a cleat, with a hole bored in its middle to pass the shaft through. The result was a cheap but effective bearing that lasted for years. The device was cooled by boring a small hole through the sides of the skeg into the shaft alley at the forward end of the hose.

The launches were built as open boats in most cases, but the forward end was usually fitted with a low trunk cabin that offered little windage. The raised deck was seemingly not favored by the Bay builders, as few if any were ever observed.

Larger Types of Hooper Island Launches

Plate 75 shows a slightly larger 38-foot model of the Hooper Island launch, which was a popular size for oyster tonging where a crew of two worked the boat. It is said that to obtain a slightly longer boat, molds coinciding with this beam were spaced to make hulls up to 40 or 45 feet, the longer waterline length offering an easier motion in choppy water when at anchor over the beds. The steering shelter erected over the companionway opening of the trunk cabin should be noted. This offered an enclosed station for the helmsman in winter weather, when a stove was set up in the cabin. The small size of the structure made for economical building, and presented little windage due to its small outside dimensions.

25′ Hooper Island Launch

The 25-foot model shown in Plate 76 is typical of the smaller size of Hooper Island launch, and due to the characteristic small beam-length ratio, it represents about the minimum size that is of practical use. While resembling a powered canoe with somewhat restricted interior room and carrying capacity, it was of a type used as a handy utility boat that was cheap to build and which would make very good speed with a small, economical engine. Most of these small hulls were built as pleasure fishing boats.

Powering Hooper Island Launches

The early Hooper Island boats were powered with one or two cylinder two-cycle engines of 5 to 15 hp. with which they made speeds of about 7 to 12 knots, according to the installation. The large high torque propellers turning at moderate speeds were very efficient here, and the launches could be driven into a chop without any noticeable loss of speed over free running in smooth water. With the advent of the high-speed car-type marine engines and the conversion of automobile engines in the 1920s, many of the old-style boats were fitted with these, either in new construction or in repowered older boats. Due to the narrow beam and lack of wide stern sections, the hulls would squat and wallow if driven at speeds much over 13 knots. In

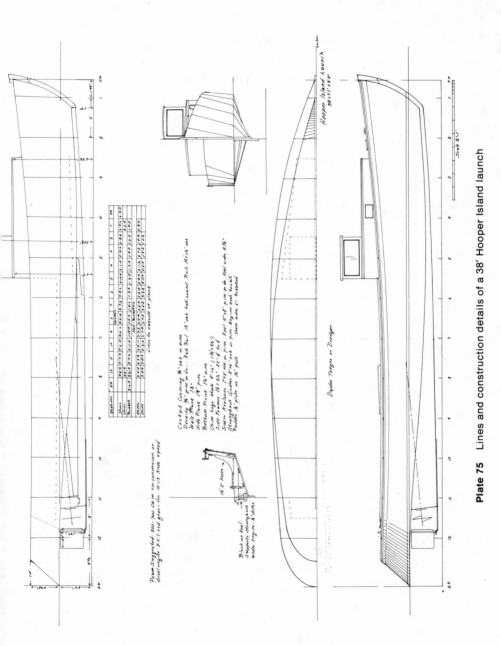

Hooper Island Launch
38' × 7'7" × 2'3"

Dyton Tingre or Designer

Plate 75 Lines and construction details of a 38' Hooper Island launch

335

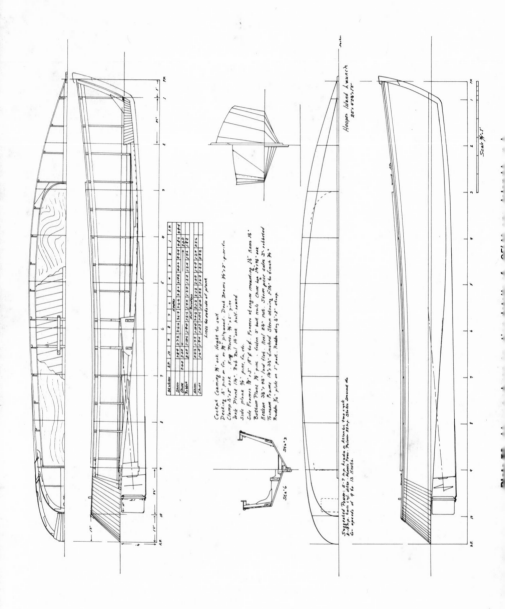

Hooper Island Launch
28' × 7' 10"

Scale 3/4" = 1'

many boats these larger modern engines are detuned for running at low engine speeds, and under continuous use last very well.

Later Modifications of Hooper Island Launches

In the constant search for speed, a modified Hooper Island launch of wider beam was developed that was better suited to the more powerful engines. As a result, few if any of the old-style hulls were built after 1930. The older boats of heavy construction lasted very well, however, and many still survive in the Bay region. Because of their rough water capabilities, many owners of modern-type craft retain an old Hooper Islander for winter use.

Modifications to Hull Form

The need for modification existed also in the case of the original New England type of double wedge launch, when larger and more powerful engines created the demand for faster hulls. Reverting to the V-bottom versions of this type as previously discussed (pages 317–330), a somewhat revised example of a useful 38-foot launch is shown in Plate 77, a hull form that came into general use about 1925. The widened beam will be noted, and the overall appearance does not greatly differ from modern practice.

With the increase in beam for greater speed, the hull will lift to a semiplaning attitude as the power is applied, with acceptably low resistance factors for economical running due to the sharp forward sections. While the deep forward section cannot lift from the water as is the case with hulls with cutaway underbodies, the fact that contact with the water is maintained even at top speed does much to eliminate pounding. While the speed is not as great as with the modern monohedron-type hulls that carry proportionally much greater power, the launch will perform well as a displacement hull and steer accurately at reduced speeds required in heavy going. Launches of this type were widely built during the two decades following the First World War, and offered very satisfactory performance as both pleasure cruisers and light-duty commercial boats. While the beam is somewhat less than is generally seen today in hulls of comparable length, the overall seakeeping ability is infinitely better, not to mention operating economy possible with engines of more moderate horsepower.

Plywood and Fiber Glass Construction

The construction details in Plate 78 show the use of plywood and fiber glass for the hull covering, the general details being as previously described (page 317). The hull may be planked conventionally at the cost of some

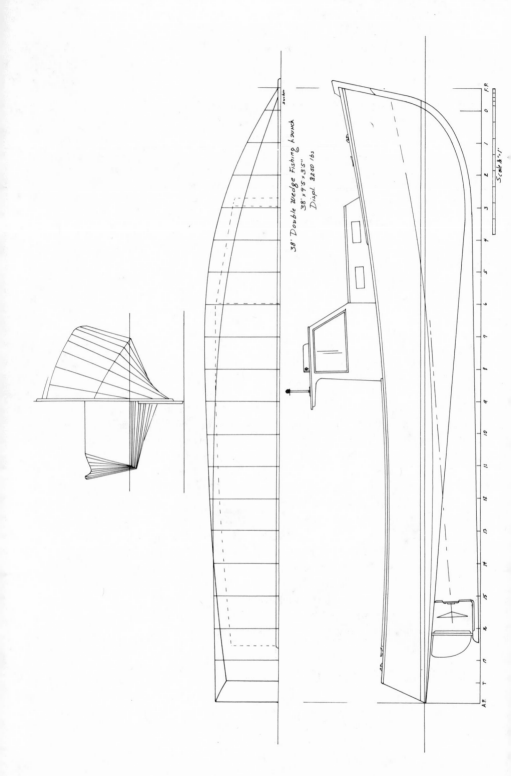

38' Double Wedge Fishing Launch
38' x 9'5" x 3'5"
Displ. 8280 lbs

Scale 3/8" = 1'

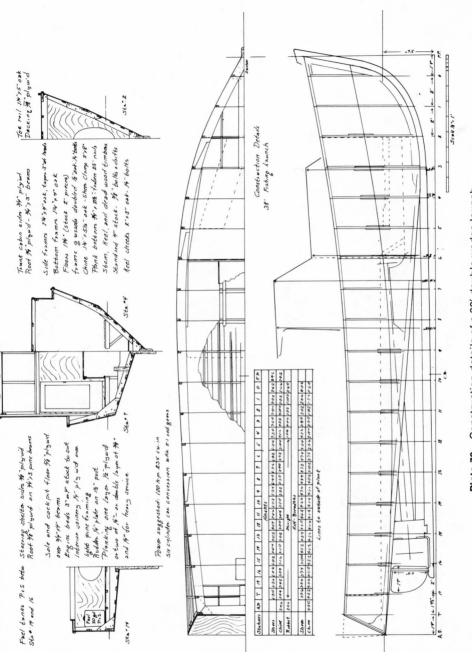

Plate 78 Construction details of a 38' double wedge launch

339

added weight. Plate 79 shows this boat arranged as a pleasure cruiser. The forward canting transom shown is like those fitted to the earlier hulls, no doubt to carry out the aspect of the old torpedo boat stern, but this may be set plumb or raked aft at the option of the builder.

Present-Day Revival of the Double Wedge Hull Form

The double wedge hull has enjoyed a revival in recent years, as some naval architects and knowledgeable boatmen have sought a type of power-boat that could be an improvement over some of the rather hastily contrived designs that were rushed into production to fill the shortage of new boats after World War II. These postwar types were often designed around spacious interior accommodations to the neglect of proper hull form. Carrying excessive beam-length ratios, they were generally prone to pitch badly in rough water. As many were designed for mass production utilizing full panels of heavy plywood bent around a building form for quick building, the bluff bows and cutaway forefoot imposed by the limitations of shaping the material showed many undesirable characteristics. Large, expensive engines were required to drive them, the wide chine sections forward caused much pounding when driven into head seas, and the inordinately wide sterns were a source of weakness when combined with a very shallow forefoot that made for hard steering.

Modifications of Double Wedge Hull Form for High Speeds

An example of a recent attempt to utilize the double wedge hull form to suit high-powered engines is the 26-foot launch in Plate 80. It well illustrates the problem of trying to incorporate a number of opposing factors into a single design. The generous beam and wide stern are necessary to provide planing characteristics for high speeds with a large engine. The deep and sharp forefoot is intended to neutralize pounding, and to form a narrow waterline entrance angle that fairs into a narrow chine line in the forward sections for low resistance factors. The chine line is carried in a nearly straight sweep aft to the broad stern to provide enough bearing to prevent squatting.

Manipulation of Hull Lines to Counteract Broaching

The principal potential weakness in hulls of this form is the broad stern which could be struck by a stern sea, so the bow sections must be given considerable flare for reserve buoyancy in case the forward part of the boat is forced down in the water in an impending broach. The long skeg is an im-

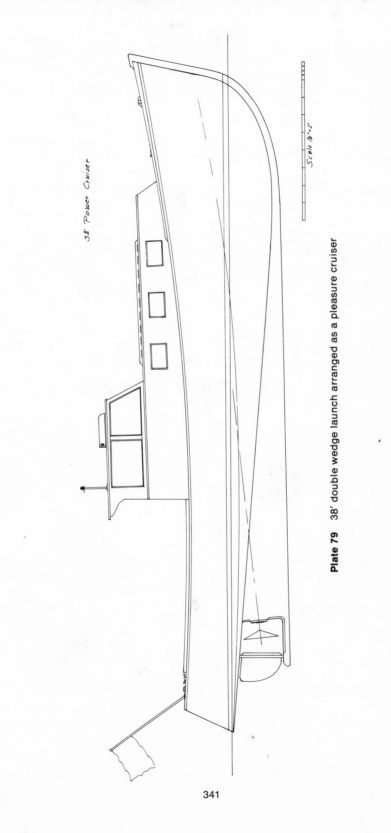

38' Power Cruiser

Scale ⅛"=1'

Plate 79 38' double wedge launch arranged as a pleasure cruiser

341

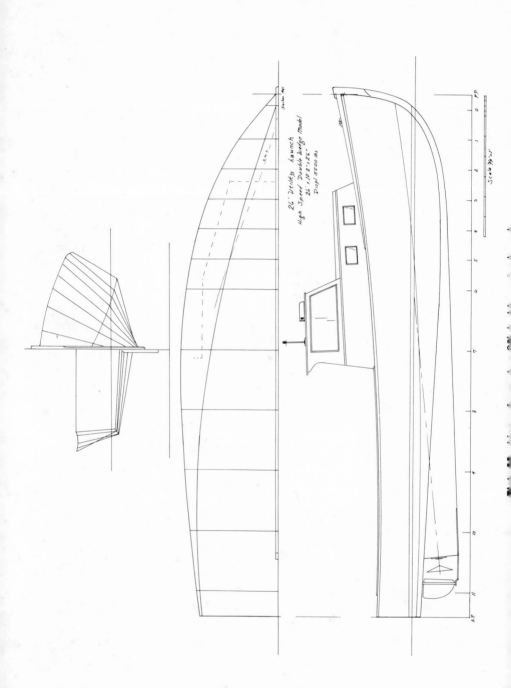

26' Utility Launch
High Speed Double Wedge Model
26' × 10' 2" × 26"
Displ 5500 lbs

portant feature in offering resistance against the bow acting as a pivot, as well as providing directional stability and accurate steering. As in the case of the narrower beamed double wedge launches, the presence of the skeg is a critical factor of the design and must not be omitted or reduced in area.

Optional Planking Methods

The hull may be planked conventionally, or covered with plywood and fiber glass as previously described (page 319). The latter method is preferred as the reasonably light but very strong structure provided is desirable in a heavily powered hull intended for high speeds. This launch may be arranged as a utility boat, sportfisherman or cruiser, or for light commercial fishing or lobstering (Plate 81).

A Large Modified Double Wedge Launch

The 37 foot modified double wedge launch shown in Plate 82 is an example of some recent attempts to produce a larger type of boat with substantial carrying capacity that can be economically driven at good speeds with moderate power. In this case the boat is considered as a displacement-type craft with moderate power installed for this mode of operation. The easy driving characteristics of the double wedge hull allows a speed of 12 knots with a 100 hp. six-cylinder diesel engine of 365 cu. in. displacement, which is much faster than could be obtained in a more conventional displacement hull with similar power. The boat is capable of planing at higher speeds, but for this work the power output would have to be tripled.

Construction Details of Large Double Wedge Launch

The construction details in Plate 83 show plywood and fiber glass cover with the option of conventional planking. If the latter is used, an extra frame must be placed between each of those shown on the drawing.

This boat could also serve equally well as a pleasure cruiser or sport fishing boat (Plate 84).

A Light-Displacement 25' Modified Double Wedge Launch

A useful 25 foot light-displacement-type launch is shown in Plate 85. This boat is designed for seaworthiness and ability in rough water rather than for high speed, and it can be transported by trailer. The deep forward sections and generous skeg will allow it to handle well in choppy water. It would be

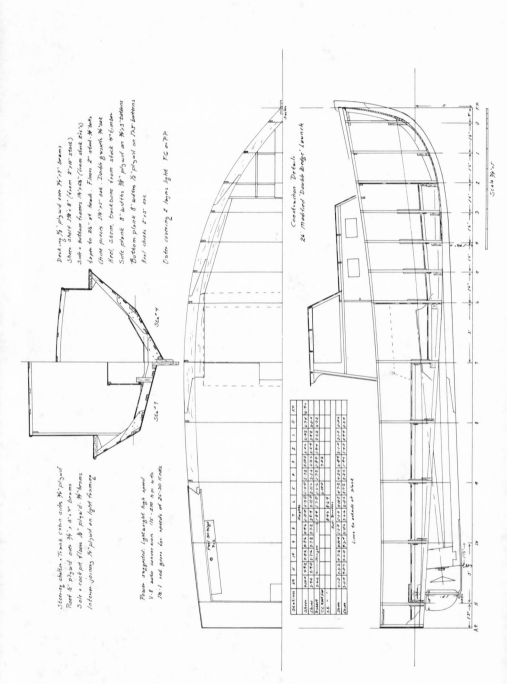

Construction Details
26' Modified Double Wedge launch

Steering shelter - Trunk cabin sides ¾" plywd
Roof ⅜" plywd over ¾" × 3" × 4" beams
Sole + cockpit floors ⅜" plywd - ¾" beams
Interior joinery ¼" plywd on light framing

Power suggested: lightweight high speed
V-8 auto conversion 155-250 hp with
1½:1 red gears for speeds at 20-30 knots

Decking ½" plywd over ¾" × 4" beams
Sheer shelf 1⅜" × 8" (from 2" × 10" stock)
Sole + bottom frames 1⅜" × 3" (from steel 2½")
Apron to 23° at head. Floors 2" steel ⅜" bolts
Chine pieces 1¾" × 5" oak. Double gusset ⅜" oak
Heel. Stem, backbone from stock 4" timber
Side plank 8" widths ⅜" plywd on 1½" × 3" bottoms
Bottom plank 8" widths ½" plywd on 1" × 3" bottoms
Keel chests 2" × 3" oak

Outer covering 2 layers light FG or PP

Lines to outside of plank

Sections	AP	11	10	9	8	7	6	5	4	3	2	1	0	FP
Sheer	4·0·0	4·9·2	4·9·4	4·9·6	4·9·6	4·9·2	4·0·4	3·9·2	2·9·7					
Chine	2·1·4													
Rabbet	2·1·4													
T.C. baseline														
SS														
Sheer														
Chine														

Sta. #9

Sta. #4

Scale ¾"=1'

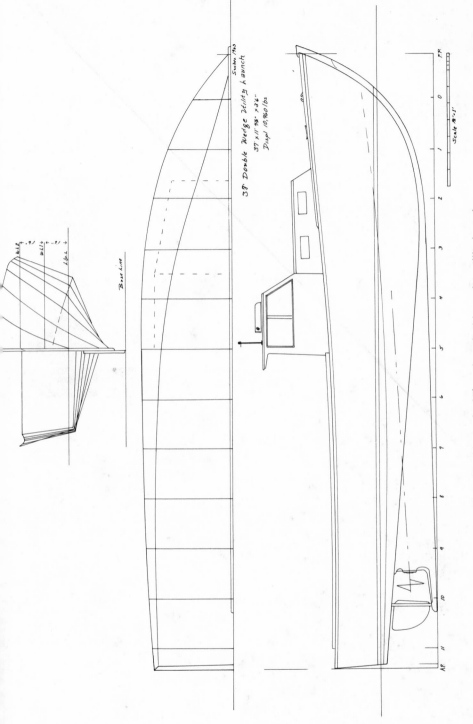

37' Double Wedge Utility launch
37' x 11'7½' x 3'6"
Displ 10,960 lbs

Sucbm 1963

Base Line

Plate 82 Lines of a 37' modern double wedge utility launch

Scale ¼"=1'

F.P.

0   1   2   3   4   5   6   7   8   9   10   11   A.P.

345

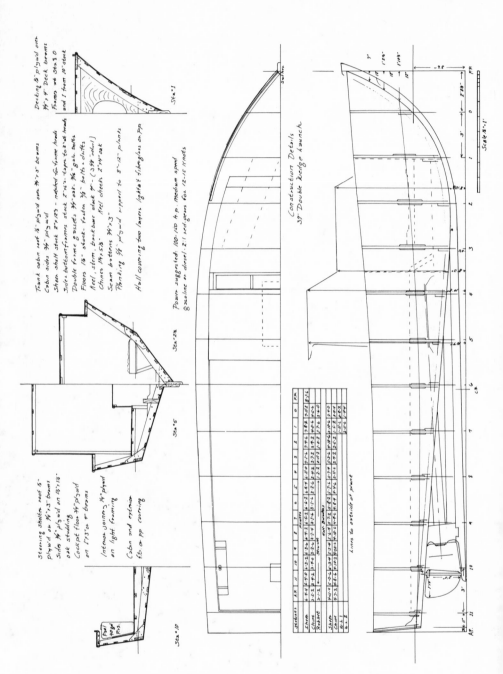

Construction Details
37' Double Wedge Launch

346

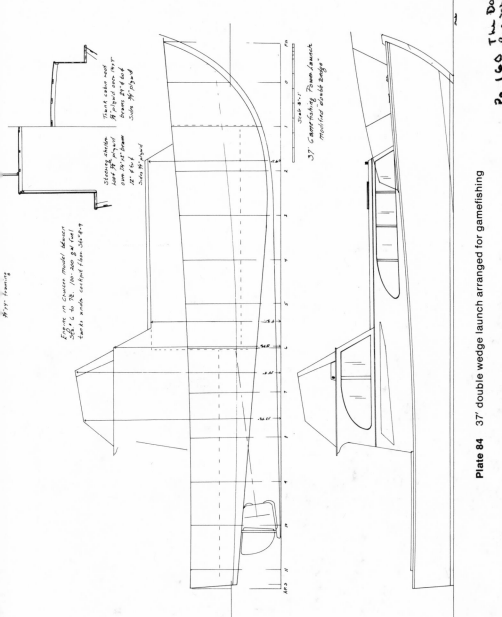

Plate 84 37′ double wedge launch arranged for gamefishing

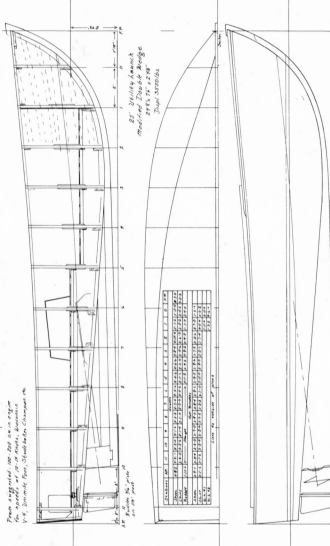

25' Utility Launch
Modified Double Wedge
24'8" × 7'1" × 2'4½"
Displ. 3550 lbs

Decking ¾" plywd. Deck beams ¾"×8"
Coamings 1½" oak, height to suit.
Sheer shelf 1¼"×8". Bilkhd ¾" plywd
Side and bottom frames 1¼"×¾" taper to 2½"
at head. Double gussets ¾" oak ¼" bolts
Chine ⅞"×8¼" oak. Bottom fore seams ¼"×3"
Floors 1½" oak. Keel checks 1¾"×3" oak ¾" bolts
Stem keel, back bone stemford 4" oak
Cockpit floor ⅞" plywd over 1¼" beams
Planking ⅜" plywd 7'8" widths, outer
covering 2 layers lightweight FG or PP

Power suggested 180-200 cu in engine
for speeds of 20-24 knots, Wisconsin
V-4, Universal Four, Studebaker Champion etc.

Base Line

Scale ¾"=1'

Lines to outside of plank

well suited for use as an inshore lobster or bass boat. Optional arrangements are shown in Plate 86 including a trunk cabin model. For best results this launch should be built of light materials.

A Double Wedge Launch Designed for Chesapeake Bay-Type Construction

Another variation of a double wedge hull is the 32-foot model shown in Plate 87. The sections below the chine are straight, as modified by Chesapeake Bay builders for fitting a cross-planked bottom. The five full frames shown are set up for building molds and are left in the boat. Plate 88 shows the typical Bay construction. This launch may also be built and planked conventionally, or ripped plywood plank can be substituted at the option of the builder. The hull form indicates good performance in rough water.

Plate 86 Optional arrangements for a 25' modified double wedge launch

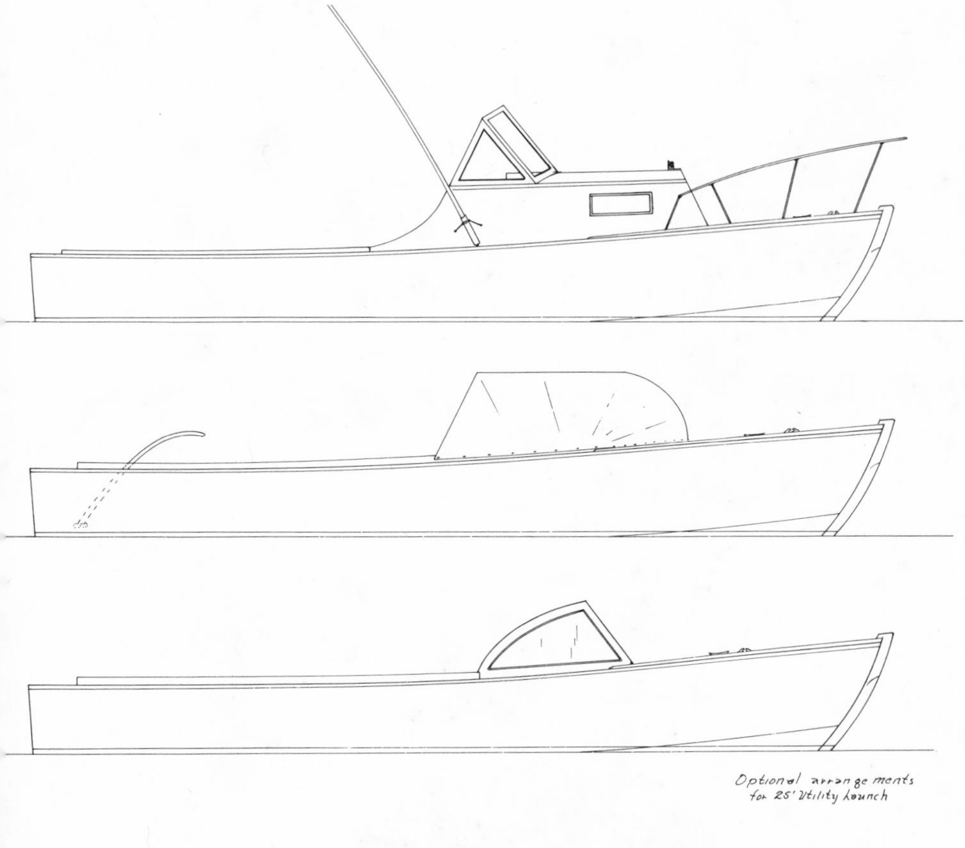

Optional arrangements
for 25' Utility Launch

Scale 3/4"=1'

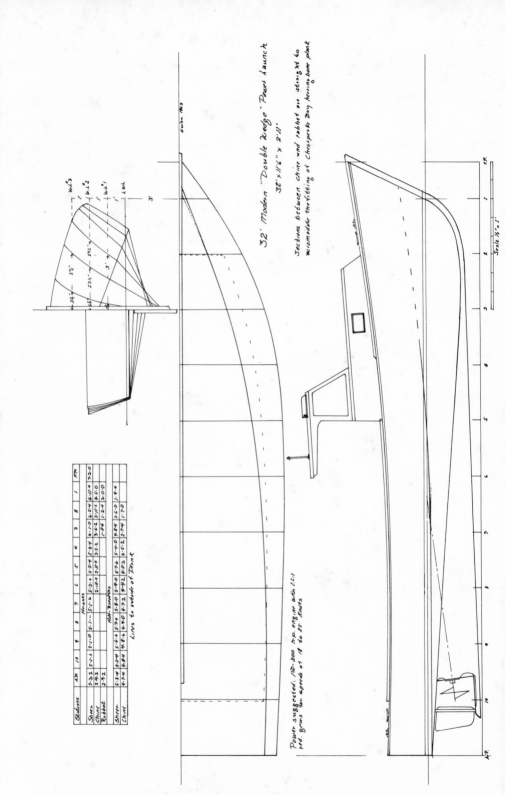

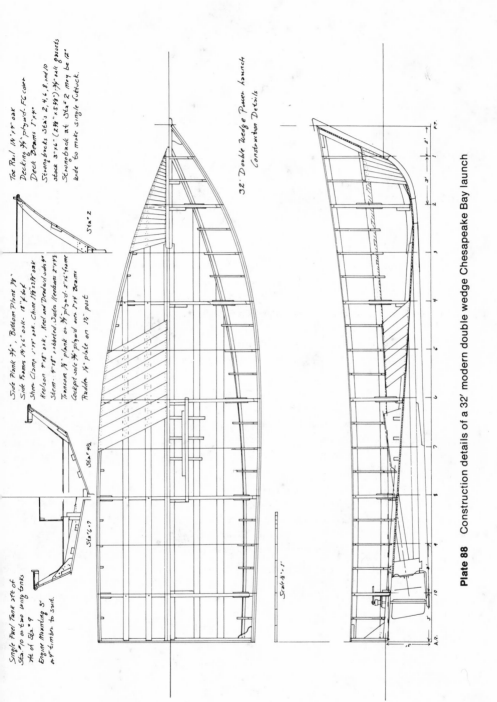

Plate 88 Construction details of a 32' modern double wedge Chesapeake Bay launch

351

23

Low Chine Model
The Chesapeake Bay Skipjack

In the second decade following the development of the Northern skipjack in the Long Island Sound area and its appearance in the upper reaches of the Chesapeake Bay, another form of V-bottom boat came into being to the south. While this newcomer showed the hard chine and straight hull sections of its northern counterpart, it was proportionately wider and more shoal and had a number of characteristics already seen in Chesapeake Bay craft. The frameless construction with the cross-planked bottom of the Bay skiffs and sharpies was incorporated in this new hull form, and the low-chine configuration at the bow terminated into a forefoot that was formed from heavy baulks of timber.

With a V bottom, a central backbone member was required to support the hull longitudinally, and in this case it was in the form of a very heavy keelson extending from the stem to the transom. In order to compensate for the angle of divergence between the rabbet and chine lines, the strakes of the cross-planked bottom were laid on at an angle of about 15 degrees. The short heavy blocks forming the angle in the forefoot were a triangular structure that were drifted into each side of the end of the heavy keelson and were in effect an extension of the bottom planking.

The use of logs in boatbuilding was not new to the Chesapeake Bay. The log canoe itself, a long narrow hull laboriously carved from a single large tree, had been built by the aborigines of the area. Dugout canoes were also built by the early English colonists in the absence of trained shipwrights to construct conventional hulls, but their construction was facilitated by the use of tempered steel tools not possessed, of course, by the natives. As larger craft were ultimately developed, some had log bottoms formed by carefully edge fitting several straight tree trunks together and fastening them with heavy iron drifts. The bottom side was hewn to a shallow arc. The topsides were formed by fitting heavy longitudinal plank around the upper edges of the logs, which were supported by short, vertical side frames notched or kneed in position.

The famous log canoes of the Bay, noted for their good sailing qualities, were built in this manner. The rather extreme racing versions built in the early years of this century received wide publicity in the contemporary yachting press, and a few examples still exist. Another well-known type of Bay craft, the "brogan" was a two-masted sailing boat from 35 to 45 feet in length that also had a log bottom.

At any rate, the use of logs was quite common among Bay boatbuilders, and the presence of large numbers of shipwrights skilled in their fitting allows us to assume that the use of a log forefoot was to them a simple method of forming the forefoot of a boat's hull.

"Corner Boats," "Bateau," or "Chunk Boats"

The first V-bottom craft, known locally as "corner boats," "bateau," or "chunk boats," were rather small sloops 25 to 30 feet in length. They carried a rather large rig, with a low leg-o-mutton mainsail and a large foresail set on a sharply raking mast. As the hulls were very shoal, a large centerboard was fitted to give sufficient lateral plane. In spite of their skimming dish aspect, these boats were very smart sailers, being fast and weatherly. With the balancing effect of the distinctive rig, the boats appeared singularly able in the steep and often vicious chop of the open Bay. Large numbers of these boats were built after 1890 for various uses in the Bay fisheries, and found wide employment until 1915 when gasoline power began to replace working sail. While boats of this general classification were known as "skipjacks," this term appears to have been applied more by people other than the local sailormen, who had their own names for them, as above.

The *Jesse Willard*, a Small "Handscraper"

An example of this unique method of construction in a small working skipjack is shown in Plate 89. This 25-foot boat is based upon a model currently on view in the Watercraft Collection of the United States National Museum. This was an actual boat named *Jesse Willard*, in honor of the heavyweight boxing champion of the day, and was built in 1915. It represents the final development of this class of hull in rig and fittings. It was locally known as a "handscraper" and was used in crabbing in summer and as an oyster tonger in winter. The low trunk cabin was made demountable and was removed for summer use.

In order to provide a comprehensive description of the construction details of these craft, a cutaway view is shown in Figure 134.

Importance of Keelson as Supporting Member of Keel and Backbone

The principal supporting member of the hull structure is a heavy keel-

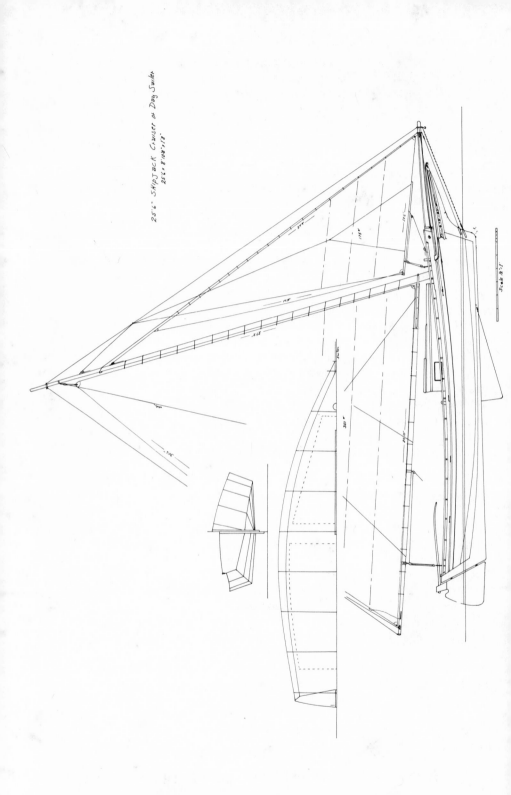

25'6" Skipjack Cruiser or Day Sailer
25'6" x 8'10" x 1'8"

Scale ¾"=1'

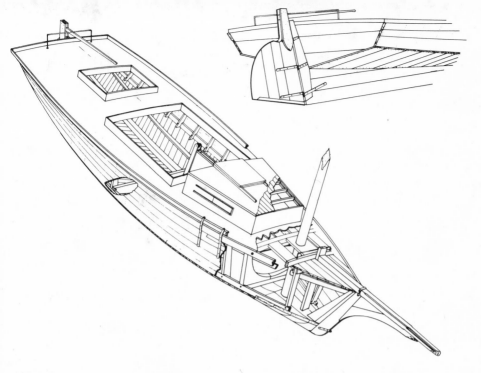

Figure 134   Construction details of a small Chesapeake Bay skipjack or bateau

son, which forms the central fastening piece for the bottom planking and which carries the skeg secured below. Figure 135 shows a typical keelson, with alternative methods of construction. In some cases a grown tree was used, if a bole of the proper curve could be found. In most instances a built-up type was fitted, being formed of straight pieces hewn to the proper curve and scarphed together. In some later boats, the keelson was built from

Figure 135   Construction details of the stem, backbone, and transom of a typical Chesapeake Bay skipjack or bateau

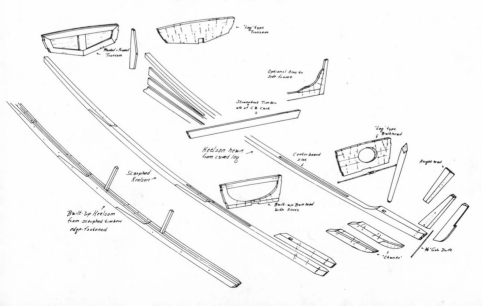

heavy planks set on edge and bolted together, leaving an aperture for the centerboard as shown.

Details of Stem Construction

The stem was usually of the two-piece type, with internal liner and a face timber forward shaped to a cutwater and covering the hood ends of the side planking. The principal fastening of the liner was usually a large diameter drift driven into it from the end of the keelson. Knightheads to give extra support to the stem and side planks were fitted in the better built hulls. The tenon for the mast step was cut in the proper place, and a heavy bulkhead was fitted near the point where the mast emerged from the deck. These were generally made up of heavy baulks of timber edge set and drifted together. In smaller or lighter hulls, the bulkheads were built up as an extra heavy frame, with two pair of heavy knees worked into the angles at the top and bottom. In any case a heavy iron tie rod with a turnbuckle was fitted across the hull at this point to secure the sides against working, as the thrust of the heavy mast was considerable.

Details of Centerboard Case Construction

The centerboard case was built up in the usual way from heavy plank, and just aft of this a heavy strongback extended across the hull, bearing against both the chine logs and side planking. In some boats this was a thick plank set on edge with knees fitted so as to form an additional side frame. An examination of the plan view of some older skipjacks suggests that in building, the side plank were bent around this central strongback without the use of any other temporary framing, the side plank being allowed to form their own natural curvature.

Details of Transom Construction

The transom in the smaller skipjacks was usually built conventionally, with horizontal plank laid over a frame. In some of the larger hulls it was built up of edge fastened baulks or logs without any other framing. The after ends of the side planks were fastened with large spikes which appeared to have held well in the end grain of the logs.

Construction Details of Bow Logs or "Chunks"

The shape of the keelson forward and the disposition of the bow logs or "chunks" on either side are shown in Figure 136. The outer edges of the lat-

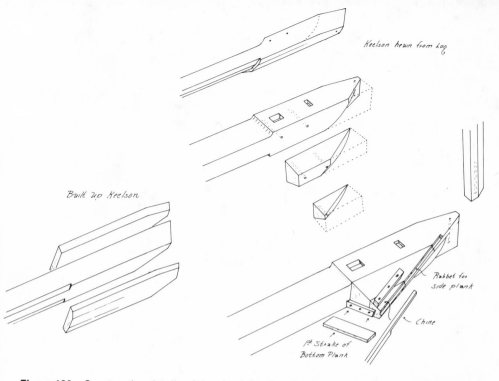

Figure 136　Construction details of the chunk forefoot fitted to a small Chesapeake Bay hull

ter were carefully shaped with plane and adz to make a close fit, but most builders added a piece of heavy paint-soaked canvas between the timbers to insure watertightness. The chunks were edge fastened with long drifts positioned at various angles to jam the pieces together when driven home. In some cases where a very heavy timber was selected for the keelson, its lower edge where it engaged the bow logs was hewn to project a little below the rabbet line. This lower edge then represented the outside of the plank surface in the forefoot. The outer sides of the bow logs were shaped to coincide with this contour. In other cases a short piece of plank was spiked to the bottom of the keelson at the forefoot to create the same effect.

Method of Fastening Chine and Forward Plank at Bow

The forward end of the chine stringer was notched in its lower edge as it joined the top of the bow logs. Its inner side was then fastened to a heavy cleat nailed on the tops of the bow logs at an angle that coincided with that of the chine line. The first strake of the bottom had its forward edge supported by a cleat fastened to the after edge of the bow logs, where it began the sequence of the cross-planked bottom. The first three or four strakes of

357

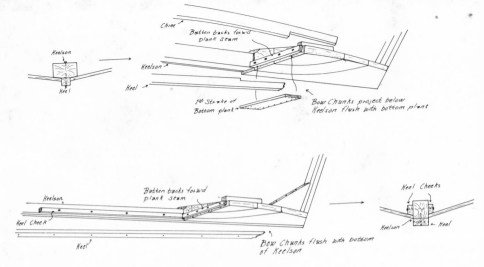

Figure 137 Construction details of the chunk forefoot fitted to a small Chesapeake Bay hull

the bottom plank were usually fan shaped to initiate the correct angle of application for the balance of the bottom strakes.

In some of the smaller and often more lightly built hulls, keel cheeks were frequently fitted to form the inner or garboard landing for the bottom plank. A comparison of this method with the single-log type construction is shown in Figure 137.

Variations in Bow Log Construction

Another variation in the log bow construction of skipjacks is shown in Figure 138. In this method the forward ends of the chine planks are fas-

Figure 138 Construction details of the bottom and stem assembly of a small Chesapeake Bay skipjack

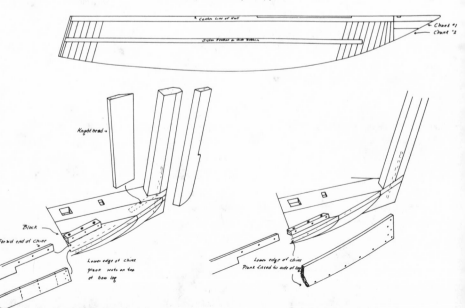

tened to the outer edges of the bow logs, rather than resting on the upper edges of the bow logs as previously shown (Figure 136). In this case the bow logs do not represent the entire outer surface of the forefoot. The positioning of the heel of the stem liner is also shown.

A Small 25' 6" Skipjack

The construction details of the small 25 foot 6 inch skipjack are shown in Plate 90, and follow the data given in the preceding illustrations. This boat could well serve as a distinctive day sailer or weekend cruiser, particularly on large bodies of water where shallow draft would be an advantage. The roof line of the trunk cabin, if one is fitted, should not be raised higher than shown on the plan, as the boat's good sailing qualities can be spoiled by excessive windage and top hamper.

Individual Variations in Skipjack Design

As could be expected, these small empirically developed skipjacks were built in many variations of rig and hull form, according to the ideas of the builder or the locale of origin. A somewhat simplified model of a small skipjack is the 32-foot boat shown in Plate 91. It was built on the Little Choptank River in 1897, and its lines were taken off its hulk in 1942 by Howard I. Chapelle and are now a part of the Watercraft Collection of the United States National Museum. It will be noted that the bottom in the midship section is flat, with a shallow V in the sections in the bow and stern. The mast is very heavy and without stays, the only shroud being the forestay to support the foresail. This boat was reported to be a very smart sailer, being both fast and weatherly. Its massive construction enabled it to last under very hard service for more than four decades, which is typical of most of the old working skipjacks.

40 to 60' Working Skipjacks

The larger 40 to 60 foot skipjacks still to be seen working on the Chesapeake are quite naturally the size with which contemporary boatmen are most familiar. Long-standing conservation laws concerning the preservation of the oyster beds limit dredging work on large areas of the Bay to sailing craft. The only power permitted is the use of a push boat when not working the beds. For this reason the working skipjacks in their original form are still operating, although in slowly decreasing numbers. The last two examples known to be built were in 1955.

These craft reached their final form about 1900, and some of them have

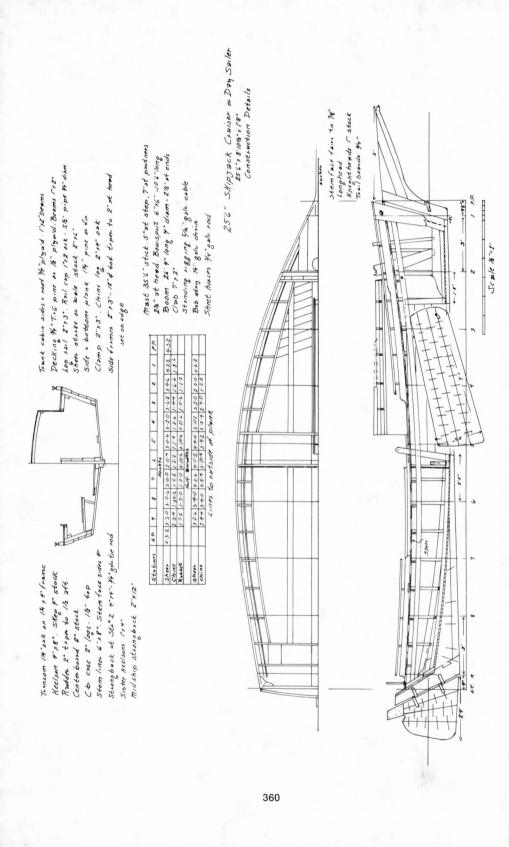

25'6" Skipjack Cruiser or Day Sailer
25'4" x 8'10½" x 18"
Construction Details

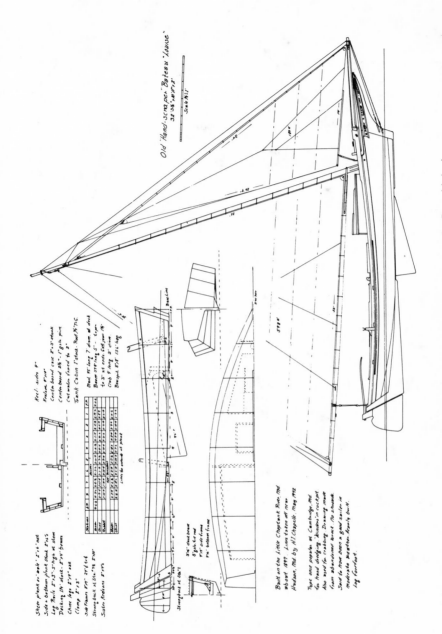

Plate 91 Lines and construction details of a 32' Chesapeake Bay skipjack

361

lasted to this day. Their very longevity helps to perpetuate the type, as the newer boats have the hull form, fittings, and details of rig of their predecessors.

The *Carrie Price*

An example of a working skipjack typical of its class was the *Carrie Price,* built by James Price in 1897. A detailed set of plans has been made of this boat, and is preserved in the Watercraft Collection. A profile and sail plan are shown in Plate 92. The hull lines and offset tables are in Plate 93. A building guide for the hull and its scantling details are shown in Plate 94. Deck details and hull arrangement are shown in Plate 95. The dimensions of the spars and their iron fittings are shown in Plate 96. The details of the rudder and centerboard and their fittings are in Plate 97.

The *Cannon*

Some skipjacks in this class were built to a rather yachtlike form by builders of exceptional skills, or were produced in small yards with reputations for turning out fine work. An example is *The Cannon* (Plate 98), whose lines were taken off by Howard I. Chapelle and Marion V. Brewington, and whose plans are also included in the Watercraft Collection.

The scantlings, as well as the general features of construction, are similar in dimension to those of the *Carrie Price.* The sail and rigging plan (Plate 99) are shown in complete detail, and can serve as a guide to those sailormen interested in this type of rig. A few of these types were converted to yachts in their old age, with a trunk cabin built in the way of the main hatch. Not a few of these boats had their sailing qualities impaired by excessive top hamper when the cabins were built with excessive height.

The Large Skipjack as Pleasure Cruiser

The advocacy of the sailing skipjack for today's pleasure-boat use is debatable. Due to their shallow draft they are not suited for blue water voyaging, but could be safe enough for summer coastal use in skilled hands. Their sail plan and rig is noteworthy both for its efficiency and economy in all weather conditions. Considerable manual skill is required to build a skipjack hull, yet the use of modern power tools and most particularly the power plane could somewhat simplify the shaping and finishing of the various heavy timbers and the log forefoot. As the last surviving example of working sail in North America, the type as a whole is of more than passing interest to students of naval architecture and those with an interest in marine history. Perhaps the class of skipjack for most practical modern use as

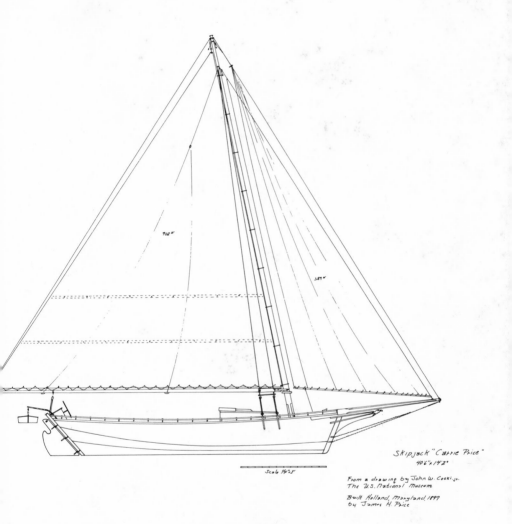

Plate 92 Profile and sail plan of the 46' skipjack *Carrie Price*

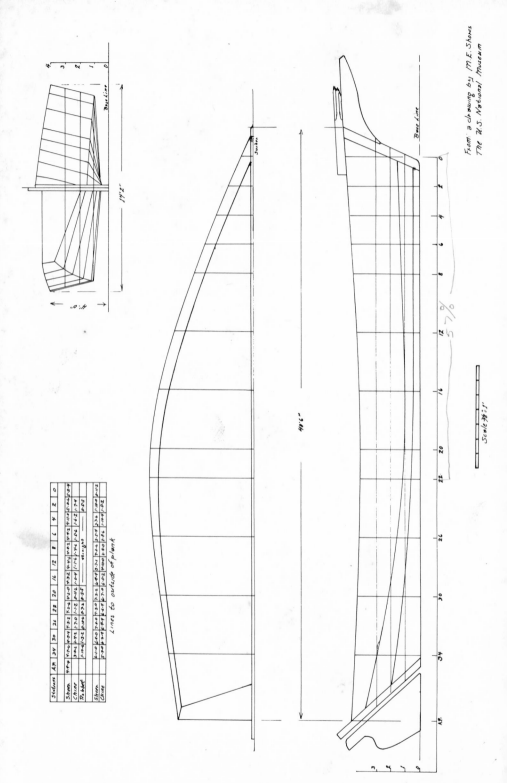

From a drawing by M.E. Shores
The U.S. National Museum

Lines to outside of plank

Scale ⅜" : 1'

Stations	A.P.	34	30	24	22	20	16	12	8	6	4	2	0
Sheer	4-4-4	4-3-4	4-2-1	4-2-4	4-2-0	4-2-2	4-4-4	4-4-2	4-1-1		4-2-4	4-2-4	4-2-4
Chine	3-0-4	2-9-2	1-7-0	1-1-2	0-0-2	1-0-4	1-1-4	1-4-4	1-4-2		1-7-4		
Rabbet	1-10-4	1-3-2	0-10-4	0-7-2	0-5-4		straight				0-5-4		
Sheer	4-1-0	6-4-0	7-8-0	7-9-0	7-10-6	7-11-4	7-9-4	7-3-2	7-1-4	7-3-6	7-10-6	7-10-4	
Chine	5-10-0	2-5-4	6-8-4	6-7-4	6-7-0	6-3-2	4-0-2	3-0-0	2-6-0	2-2-6	1-10-4	1-0-2	

364

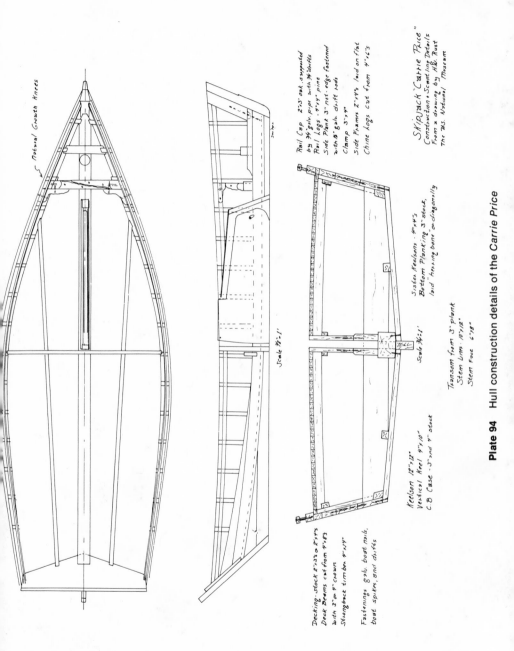

Natural Growth Knees

Scale ⅜"=1'

Scale ⅜"=1'

Decking: stock 2"x3"x 8'x4's
Deck Beams cut from 4"x4's
with 3" or 4" crown
Stringback timber 4"x14"

Fastenings galv. boat nails,
boat spikes, and drifts

Keelson 12"x12"
Vertical Keel 4"x10"
C.B.Case - 3"and 4" stock

Sister Keelsom - 4"x4's
Bottom Planking 3" stock
laid herring bone on diagonally

Transom from 3" plank
Stem Limb - 10"x12"
Stem Face 6"x8"

Rail Cap 2"x3" oak, supported
by ¾" galv. pipe with ½" drifts
Rail Logs - 4"x4" pine
Side Plank 3" nat. edge fastened
with 15" galv. drift rods
Clamp 3"x9"
Side Frames 2"x4"s laid on flat
Chine logs cut from 4"x6's

Skipjack "Carrie Price"
Construction & Scantling Details
from a drawing by H.I. Chapelle
The M.S. National Museum

Plate 94   Hull construction details of the *Carrie Price*

365

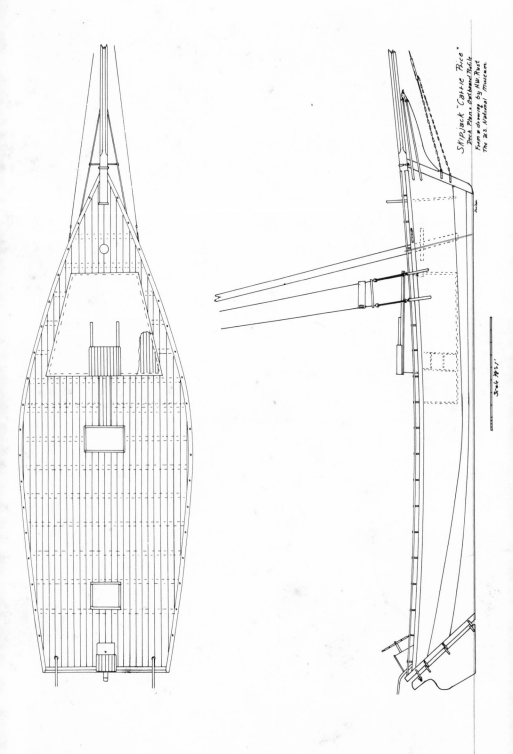

Skipjack "Cattie Price"
Deck Plan & Outboard Profile
From a drawing by H.W. Rust
The U.S. National Museum.

Scale 3/8 = 1'

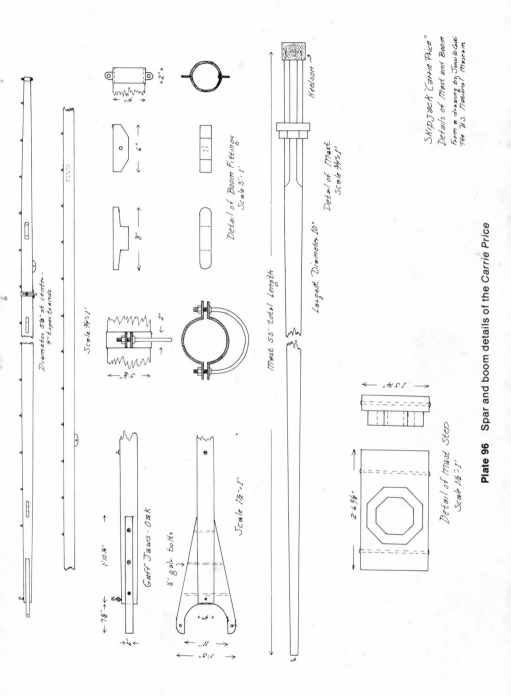

Diameter 5½" at center -
4" at each ends

Scale ¾"=1'

1:0.¾"

Gaff Jaws - Oak

7½"

2"

1"-8 galv. bolts

Scale 1½"=1'

11"

1:8"

4"

2"

6"

8"

5½"

2"

Detail of Boom Fittings
Scale 3"=1'

Mast 55' total length

Longest Diameter 10"

Heelson

Detail of Mast
Scale ¾"=1'

1.4.5.1"

2.6⅝"

Detail of Mast Step
Scale 1½"=1'

Skipjack "Carrie Price"
Details of Mast and Boom
From a drawing by John W. Goti
The U.S. National Museum

Plate 96   Spar and boom details of the *Carrie Price*

367

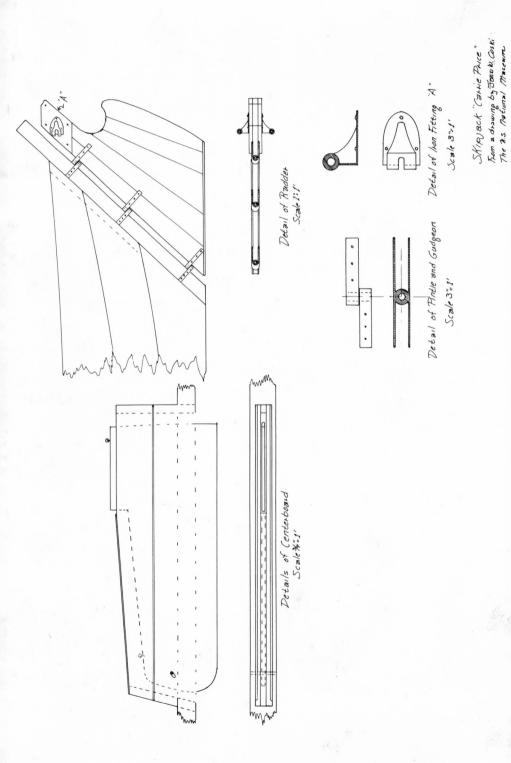

Detail of Rudder
Scale 1"=1'

Detail of Iron Fitting "A".
Scale 3"=1'

Detail of Pintle and Gudgeon
Scale 3"=1'

Details of Centerboard
Scale ¾"=1'

SKIPJACK "Carrie Price"
From a drawing by John R. Coski.
The U.S National Museum

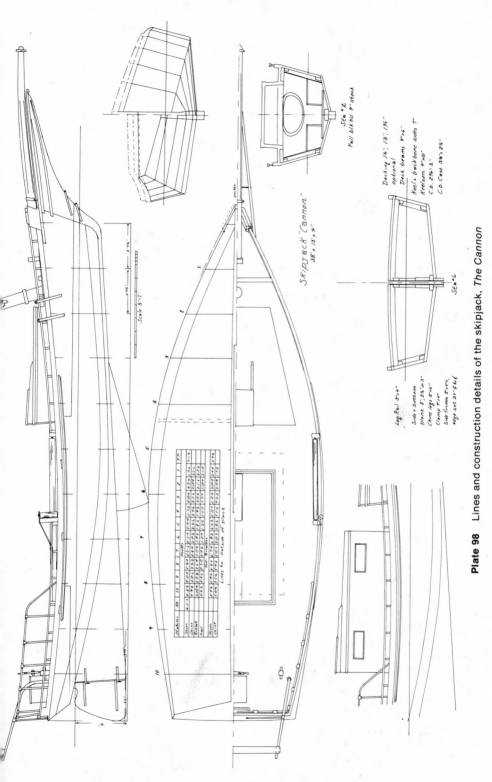

Plate 98 Lines and construction details of the skipjack, *The Cannon*

369

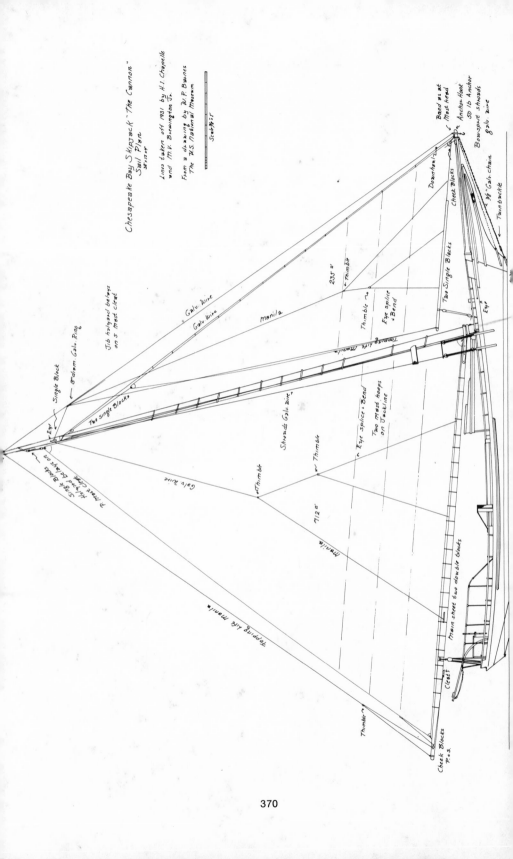

Chesapeake Bay Skipjack "The Cannon"
Sail Plan

Lines taken off 1931 by H.I. Chapelle
and M.V. Brewington Jr.

From a drawing by W.P. Barnes
The U.S. National Museum

Scale 3/32" : 1'

Band as at Mast head
Anchor Hook
50 lb Anchor
Bowsprit shrouds
8 Galv wire
3/8" Galv chain
Turnbuckle

Downhaul
Cheek Blocks
Two Single Blocks
Eye

235 0"
Thimble
Thimble
Eye splice & Bend
Topping Lift (Manila)
Eye splice & Bend
Two mast hoops on Jackline
Thimble
Shrouds Galv wire
7 1/2 0"
Manila

Galv. Wire
Galv. Wire
Manila
Jib halyard belays on s mast cleat

Eye
Single Block
8 strand Galv. Rivet

Eye
Two single Blocks
Single Blocks
Hoisted Blocks on
B-hast Cleat

Galv Wire
Thimble

Main sheet two double blocks
Topping lift Manila
Cheek Blocks
Cleat
Thimble
Cheek Blocks
P.+S.

day sailers and weekend cruisers for those not inclined to deep water voyaging, would be the smaller "handscrape" types. At any rate the basic features of skipjack hull construction are important in that they are employed up to the present time in many types of small and economically built launches. The Bay mode of cross-planked hull construction is still a rather controversial form of small boat construction, and must be evaluated in the light of individual inclinations and interest.

Conversion of Skipjack-Type Hulls to Power

With the coming of power, many types of skipjacks not directly concerned with oyster dredging itself were fitted with gasoline engines, mostly the heavy-duty single and twin cylinder two-cycle types. The shaft was usually placed off center along the side of the skeg, because the many heavy drifts through the skeg's centerline and into the keelson made shaft boring impractical without the considerable expense of rebuilding the entire deadwood. In some cases the engine was fitted as an auxiliary to the sails, but not a few models were cut down to pure powerboats, with the mast used to support a derrick boom and winch.

As a powerboat conversion, the result was not too satisfactory. The wide and shoal hull with shallow forefoot was prone to pound when the boats were driven into a head sea or chop. The lack of bearing aft over the propeller held the top speed down to 6 or 7 knots, as higher speeds produced squatting and wave making that absorbed extra power. Without the balancing effect of the sailing rig, the wide beam led to much pitching.

In subsequent new construction, the lines of skipjacks intended for power were subject to substantial modification, and by 1910 a very satisfactory hull form came into general use. A 45-foot example (Plate 100) which is representative of a size and general arrangement much used on the Bay, was widely built until quite recently. These launches were used mostly for freighting, either as fish or oyster carriers or for carrying general cargo into remote areas of the Bay.

Modification of Skipjack Hulls for Installation of Power

It will be noted that the beam has been decreased, the bottom sections deepened, and the rabbet line aft carried downward to give sufficient bearing against the thrust of the propeller. The depth of the hull was increased to add cargo capacity, and attention was given to a moderately fine waterline entrance angle and easy underwater lines for efficient use of power. The result was a burdensome vessel that appeared to emulate its sailing ancestor in being very able in the often rough and stormy waters of the open Bay. As the flare in the sides of the hull gave great reserve buoyancy, they could be loaded to a condition of negative freeboard amidships.

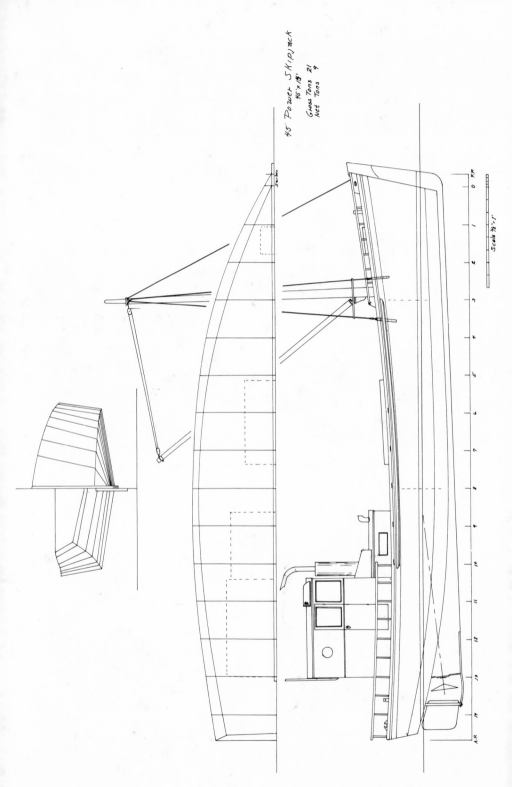

45' Power Skipjack
45' x 13'
Gross Tons 21
Net Tons 9

Scale 3/8" = 1'

45' Power Skipjack Construction Details

The construction details of the 45-foot power skipjack are shown in Plate 101, and closely follow those of their sailing counterparts except for the construction of the skeg. The same heavy scantlings are employed, and the derrick mast is additionally supported by a heavy bulkhead with a tie rod which stiffens the hull against working. Other bulkheads subdivide the hull into cargo hold and engine spaces.

The keel and backbone structure of a typical power skipjack are shown in Figure 139.

Small Power Skipjacks

Many small power skipjacks are built for various uses on the Bay. An example is the 36-foot model shown in Plate 102 which is often used for oyster dredging in areas where conservation restrictions against powerboats do not apply. The building plans in Plate 103 show typical small skipjack construction. Plate 104 shows three optional arrangements possible with this hull, a gillnetter, pleasure cruiser, or ferry launch. If a somewhat larger boat is required, the hull may be lengthened from four to eight feet by lofting in extra stations amidships.

The general characteristics of these smaller power skipjacks are similar to the larger models. The slight reverse in the rabbet puts the center of gravity

Figure 139   Construction details of stem, backbone, and transom of a small Chesapeake Bay power skipjack

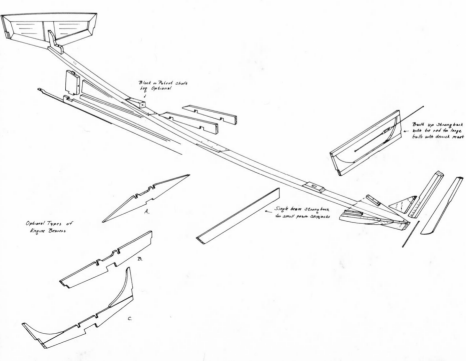

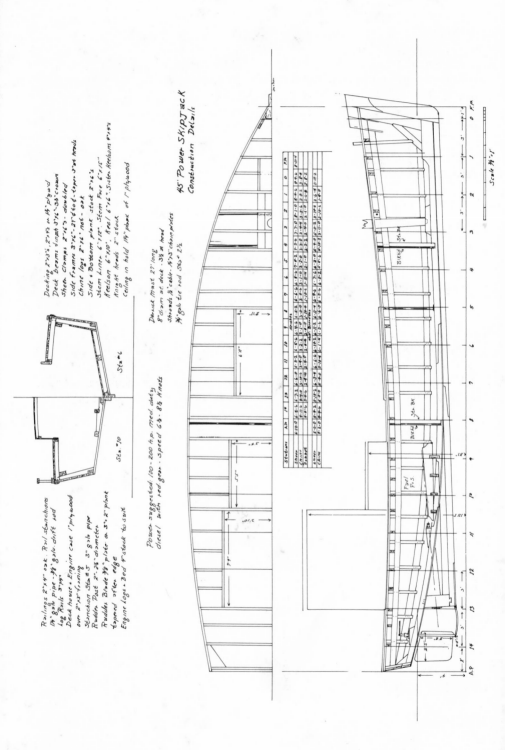

45' Power Skipjack Construction Details

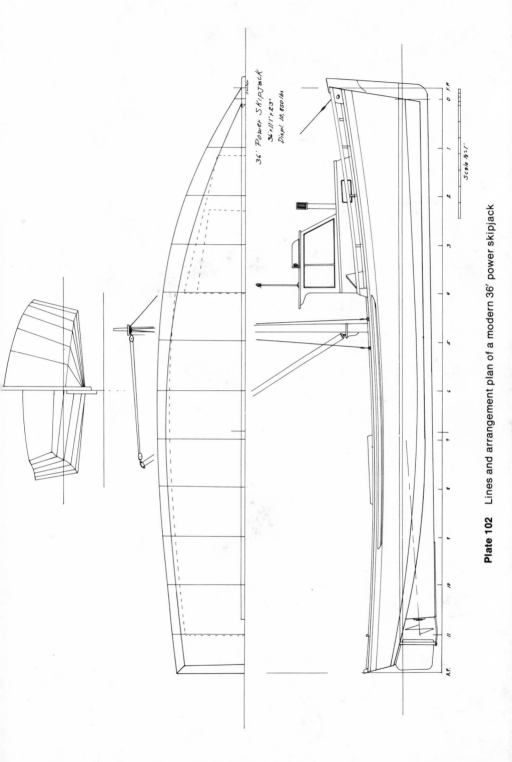

36' Power Skipjack
36'×11'3"×23"
Displ. 10,850 lbs

Scale ½"=1'

Plate 102 Lines and arrangement plan of a modern 36' power skipjack

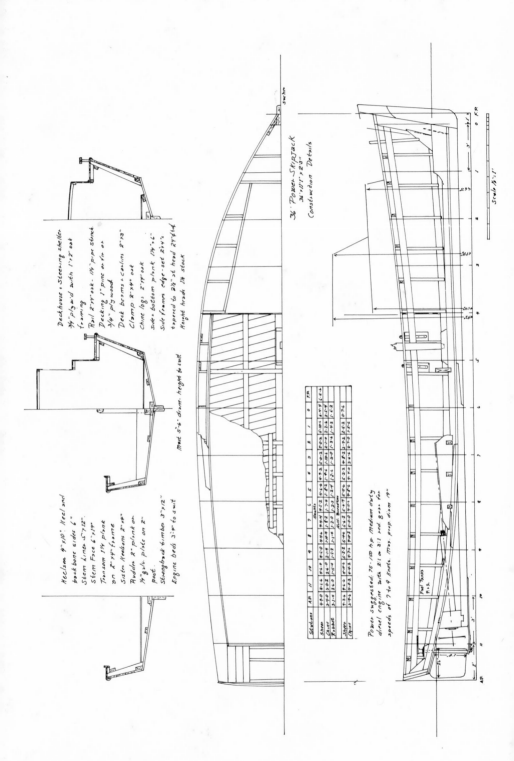

36' "Power Skipjack"
34'-10" x 23"
Construction Details

Scale 5/8"-1'

Power suggested. 75-100 h.p. Medium duty diesel engine with 2:1 or 3:1 red. gear. For speeds of 7 to 9 knots. Max. prop diam. 19"

Keelson 4"x10". Heel and back bone sides 6".
Stem Lines 5"x12".
Stem Face 6"x14"
Transom 1¼" plank on 2"x4" frame
Sister Keelsons 2"x4"
Rudder 2" plank on 2" post.
¼" galv. plate on 2" post.
Strongback timber 3"x12"
Engine beds 3"x to suit

Deckhouse & Steering shelter
¾" plywd with 1"x2" oak framing
Rail 2"x4" oak. 1¼" pipe stanch
Decking 1" pine on fir or ¾" plywood
Deck beams & carlins 2"x3"
Clamp 2"x4" oak
Chine logs 2"x4" oak
Side & bottom plank 1¼"-6"
Side frames edge-set 2¼"x4" tapered to 2¾" at head 2"x4"x4
Might heads 1¾" stock

Mast 5'-6" diam. height to suit

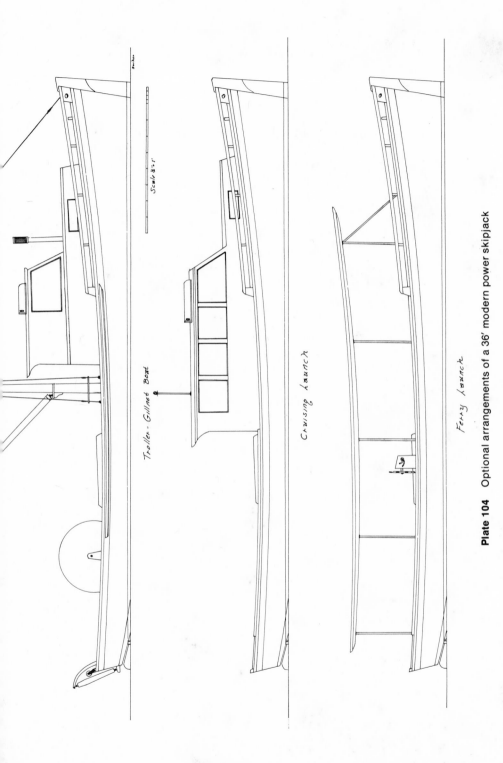

Troller - Gillnet Boat

Cruising Launch

Ferry Launch

Scale ⅜"=1'

Plate 104 Optional arrangements of a 36' modern power skipjack

well aft, and if the hull is so loaded, an easy motion in rough water is the result. These launches also drive easily up to displacement hull speeds with moderate power.

Variations of Small Power Skipjacks

Very small hulls on the skipjack model show a wide variety of optional uses, such as the 30-foot launch in Plate 105. Boats of this type are well suited for rigging as swordfish boats or other applications where derrick masts are fitted. The substantial skipjack construction combined with the heavy backbone timbers help to counteract the thrust of the mast and keep the hull from working (Plate 106).

Many very small power skipjacks have been built on the Bay, such as the 24-foot model in Plate 107. It finds wide use as a pleasure cruiser or fishing launch, as shown in Plate 108.

The Virginia Bateau

A variation of the power skipjack is the Virginia bateau shown in Plate 109. While generally following skipjack lines, the hulls are somewhat more shallow and less beamy. They are built in sizes of 35 to 50 feet, the 40-foot length appearing to be the most popular. They are economically driven up to about 9 knots with converted automobile engines or medium sized truck-type diesels. These hulls show a very marked reverse in the rabbet line aft, and while shallow, appear to be very able in rough water. The square stern is sometimes seen, but the favored configuration is round or elliptical, which gives a more pleasing appearance. An upper and lower rim log forms the framing. The keel and backbone structure that is typical of these launches is shown in Figure 140. Keel cheeks to support the inner ends of the cross-

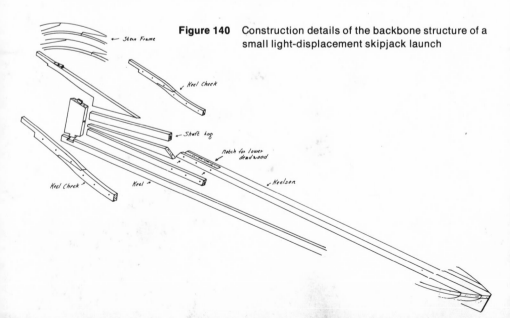

Figure 140   Construction details of the backbone structure of a small light-displacement skipjack launch

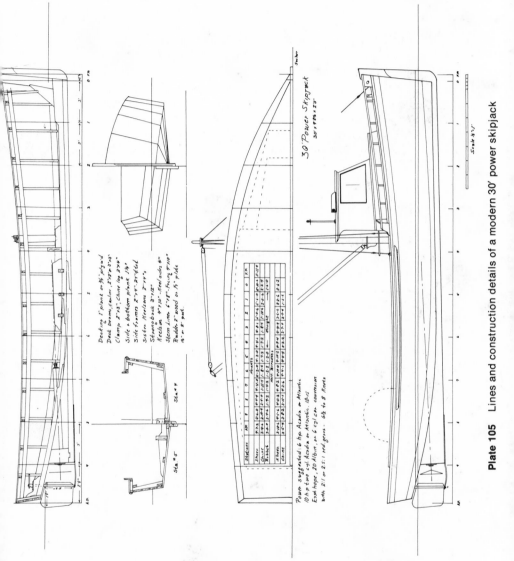

Decking 1" plank or ¾" plywood
Deck beams, Saslon, 2"x2" 3"x3"
Clamp, 2"x3", Chine log 2"x6"
Side & bottom plank 1¾"
Side frames 2"x4", 2"x6" oak
Sister Keelsons 2"x4"'s
Steamoback 3"x12"
Keels 4"x10" steel sides 6"
Stem Linen 6"x8" facing 4"x10"
Rudder 2" wood or ½" plate
¼" or 3" post.

Power suggested 6 hp Acadia or Atlantic.
10 h.p. two cyl. Acadia or Atlantic. (D-6
Easthope, 20 Albin, or 6 cyl. car. conversion
with 2:1 or 2.5:1 red. gears - 6½ to 8 knots

Stations	AP	1	2	3	4	5	6	7	8	9	0	KR
Sheer	7-2½	6-6-0	6-1-4	5-8-4	5-4½	5-0½	4-8½	4-6-0	4-4½	4-3-6	4-3-6	4-3-6
Chine	3-9-6	2-11-4	2-1-0	1-5½	1-0-4	0-9-0	0-6-0	0-4-0	0-3-4	0-3-6	straight	0-4-0
Rabbet	3-0-4	2-1-6	1-4½	0-11-2	0-8-1	2-2½	2-3-0	–	–	straight	1-4-0	
Sheer		4-9-4	4-0-3	4-8½		not brackets						
Chine		4-7½	4-0½	3-2½	3-0-0	2-8-3	2-5-1	2-2-2	3-1-1	3-2-2		
		3-2½	3-1½	3-0-4	2-9½	2-6-0	2-3-6	2-1-4	2-1-4	1-14		

Sta = 0

Sta = 4

30' Power Skipjack
30' x 8'4" x 2'0"

Scale ¼" = 1'

Plate 105   Lines and construction details of a modern 30' power skipjack

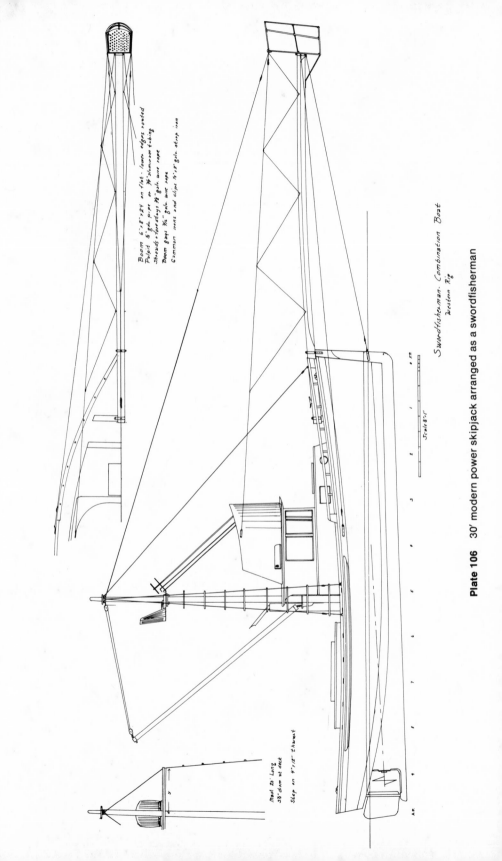

Boom 6'x8'x24 on flat. lower edges routed
Pulpit 8' galv. pipe on 7/8" aluminum tubing
Shrouds + forestays 7/8" galv wire rope
Boom guys 7/6" galv. wire rope
Common iron: sand clips 4'x8" galv. strap iron

Swordfisherman. Combination Boat
Western Rig

Mast 26' long
3⅝" diam. at deck

Step on 4'x12' thwart

Plate 106 30′ modern power skipjack arranged as a swordfisherman

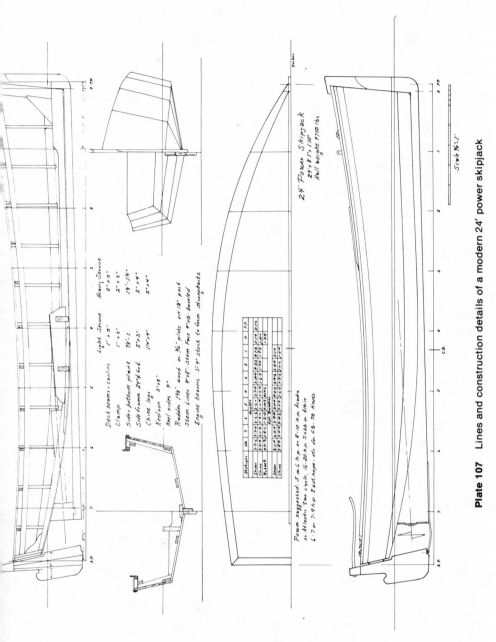

Plate 107 Lines and construction details of a modern 24' power skipjack

24' Power Skipjack
24' x 8'-1" x 1'10"
Hull weight ±750 lbs.

Power suggested, 5 or 6 h.p. or 8-10 h.p. Honda
or Atlantic two cycle, 16-20 h.p. Sabb or Albin
6-7 or 7-9 h.p. Easthope- etc. for 6½-7½ knots

Deck beams & carlins
Clamp
Sides: bottom plank
Side frames 24" c-c
Chine logs
Keelson
Keel sides 4"
Rudder 1¼" wood on ¾" plate on 18" post
Stem Liner 8"x8". Stem Face 4"x12 beveled
Engine bearers 3-4" stock to form strongbacks

	Light Service	Heavy Service
Deck beams & carlins	1" x 3"	2" x 3"
Clamp	1" x 3"	2" x 3"
Side: bottom plank	⅞"	1⅛" - 1¼"
Side frames 24" c-c	2" x 3"	2" x 4"
Chine logs	1¾" x 4"	2" x 6"

Stations	A.P.	7	6	5	4	3	2	1	0	F.P.
Sheer										
Chine										
Rabbet										

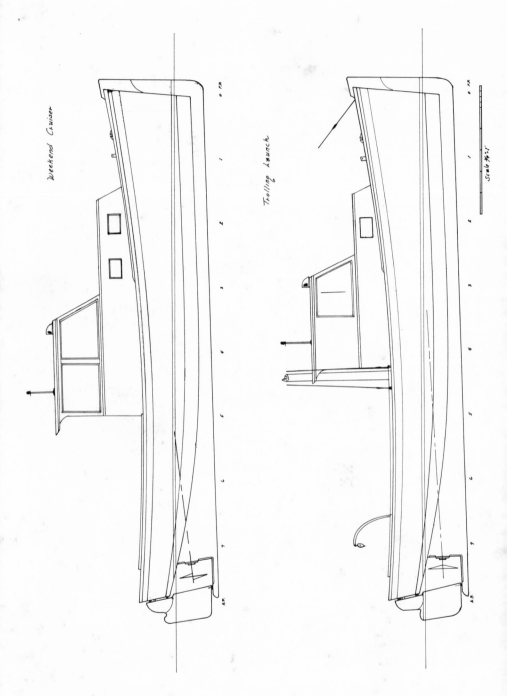

Weekend Cruiser

Trolling Launch

Scale ⅜"=1'

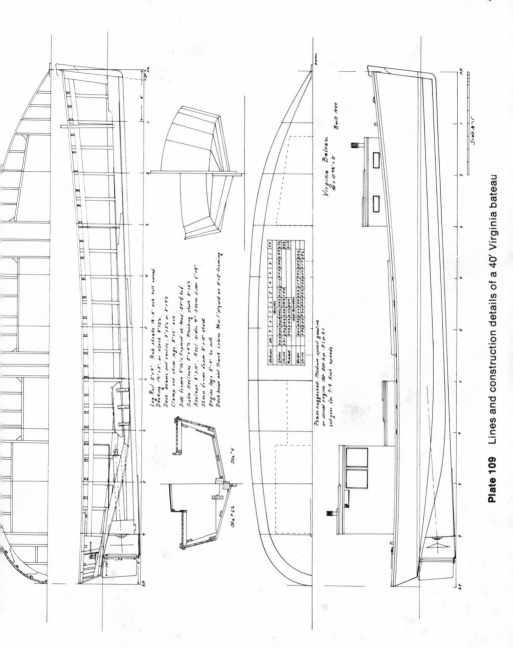

Leg Rail 2 × 9". Rub strake 1½ × 2". oak half round.
Decking ¾ × 1½". or about 1½ × 2½.
Deck beams and ceiling 2 × 2½" or 1½ × 2½.
Clamp and chine logs 2 × 1½" oak
Side frames 2 × 1½"s spaced at front 2 × 1 × 6 oak
Side keelson 2 × 9"s Planking stock 1½ × 8's
Keelson 8 × 10". Keel sides 4" Stem line 6 × 9"
Stern frame from 2 × 12 stock
Engine logs 2 × 1" to 2 × 6
Deck house and Trunk cabins ¾ × 1" plywd on 1½ × 1½ framing

Power suggested. Medium speed gasoline
or diesel engine 100 200 h.p. 2½ to 3:1
red gear for 7 9 knot speeds

Virginia Bateau
40 × 10 × 3. 3'

Built 1949

Plate 109 Lines and construction details of a 40' Virginia bateau

planked bottom are favored here, and these are in separate pieces aft and sawn to a curve to make the reverse curve of the rabbet.

Variations in Small Bateau Types

Many smaller editions of these bateau-type hulls have been built on the Bay for various types of individual fishing, such as the 26-foot dragger in Plate 110. Some suggested options for other arrangements are shown in Plate 111. While these are light-displacement hulls with moderate free-board, they appear to be very able in rough water due to the shape of the after sections.

The Cape Hatteras Boat

A launch of somewhat similar form but of a different area of employment is the 30-foot Cape Hatteras boat in Plate 112. While the general aspect of the hull is like the Virginia bateau, the underwater sections are somewhat deeper and the entrance at the waterline is quite narrow. The round stern adds to its ability in rough water to deflect stern seas, and these boats are used offshore in what is probably one of the roughest areas in the world. While some of these launches have been built with a cross-planked bottom, most of the contemporary models are planked longitudinally with a full framing system. Most are powered with medium-sized car-type engines, and make from 8 to 10 knots.

At about the time when the Hooper Island launch was being developed, Bay builders searching for more speed in launches used for carrying light loads evolved the skipjack-type speed launch. While somewhat similar to the Hooper Island type, the log type forefoot was fitted, and the underwater sections forward were much more shallow. While not quite as able in rough water, these launches were much simpler and cheaper to build and were quite fast with low power because of their easy lines and narrow beam.

The Skipjack Launch

An early type of skipjack launch is shown in Plate 113. The logs or "chunks" in the forefoot were generally limited to just one piece on either side, because of the extreme narrowness of the section. In most cases the heavy keelson was left to its original dimension forward to form the central portion of the forefoot. A low chine log was let into the stem knee on either side, and a single block was fitted under each to fill the bow angle, the whole being planed off to form the proper shape. The cross-planked bottom strakes were worked into the after edge of the two side chunks, and the bal-

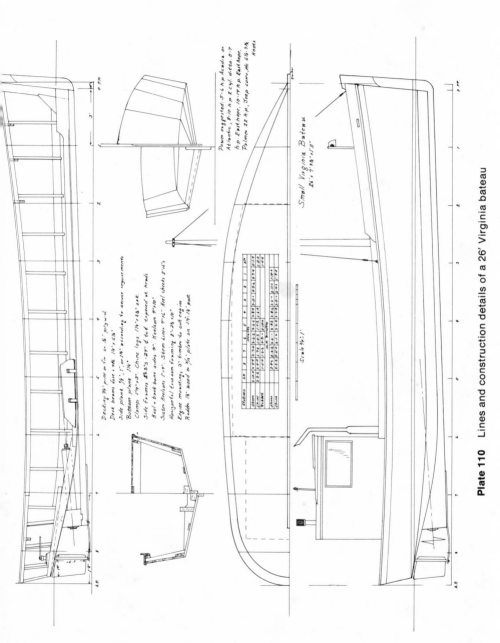

Plate 110 Lines and construction details of a 26' Virginia bateau

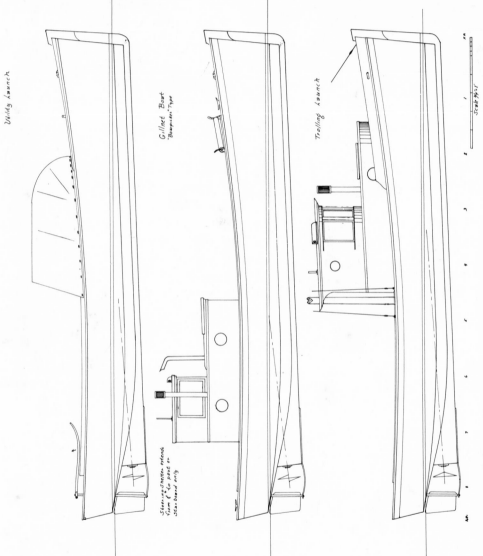

Utility Launch

Gillnet Boat
"Bowpicker" Type

Steering Station extends
from 6" to port or
Starboard only

Trolling Launch

Scale 3/4"=1'

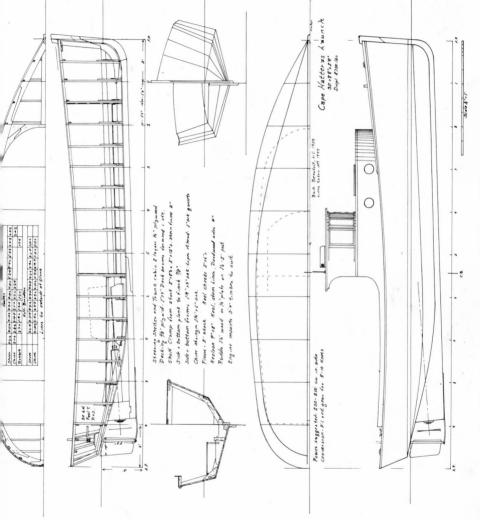

Cape Hatteras Launch
30'-8" x 9'-2"
Displ. 8700 lbs.

Built Beaufort, N.C. 1939
Lines taken off 1947

Power suggested 200-250 cu. in. auto.
Conversion 2:1 red. gear for 8-10 Knots.

Stern shelter and Trunk cabin 2 layers ¼" plywood.
Decking ¾" ply-wd. 1⅞" Deck beams for-ward, aft.
Sheet Clamp from stout 2"x1½"s 2"x1½"s stem from 2"
Side & bottom plank to finish ⅞".
Chine chunga 1¾"x1⅛" oak.
Floors 2" stock   Keel cheeks 2"x1½"s
Keelson 9"x8"   Keel, stem Liveoak, Deadwood white oak.
Rudder 1½" wood or ¼" plate or 1½-2" post.
Engine mounts 3"-4" timbers to suit.

Plate 112   Lines and construction details of a 30' Cape Hatteras launch

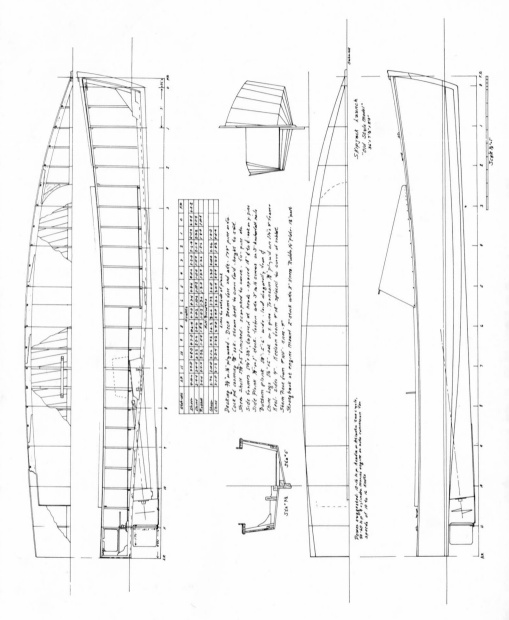

388

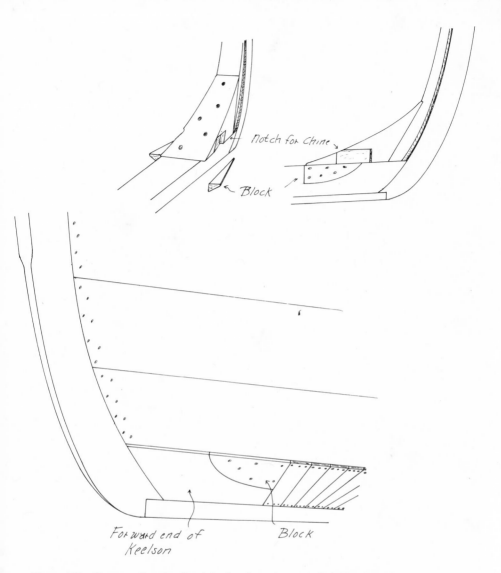

Notch for chine

Block

Forward end of
Keelson

Block

Figure 141 Construction details of the forefoot of a small Skipjack launch

ance of the plank was laid on as previously described (page 358) (Figure 141).

A Small Skipjack Launch

A smaller 26-foot model still seen on the Bay is shown in Plate 114, and is of a later type with slightly increased beam. A useful 30-foot size is shown in Plate 115 with a canvas-roofed trunk cabin and light steering shelter. The small riding sail aft will reduce rolling in a beam sea.

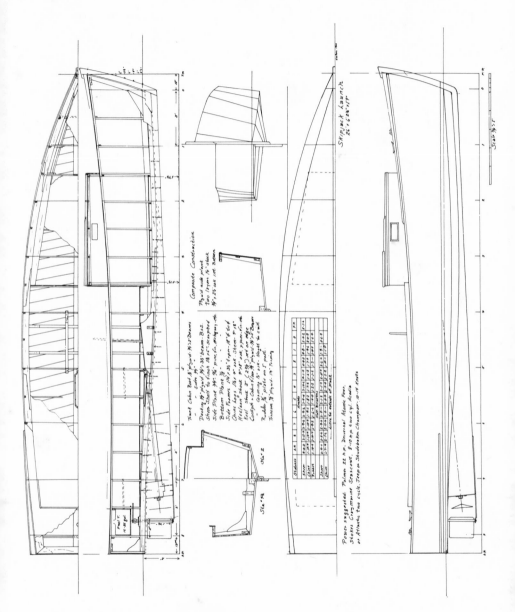

Front Cabin Roof 3/8" ply'd. 3/4" x 2" Beams
" Sides 1/4"
Decking 3/8" ply'd. 3/4" x 3 1/2" beams - B.J.S.
Stem Stenh'd to finish 1 1/2" x 1" Scarphed
Side Plank 3/4" x 3/4" pine fir, mahog., etc.
Bottom Plank 7/8"
Side Frames 1 3/4" x 1 3/4" spar. 1 3/4" x 1 1/2" but
Chine logs 1 3/4" x 2" oak Stem- 3" x 3"
Keel shoe 3" (2 3/4") oak x pine- fir, oak
Cockpit Coaming 3/4" oak House 1/4" x 3/4" Beam
Rudder 3/4" plate on 1" pintl
Transom 7/8" plywd. 1 3/4" framing

Composite Construction
Ply'd. note plank
Two layers 1/4" plank
3/4" x 1 1/2" oak int. Bottom.

Ship jack Launch
21' x 7'4" x 1 1/2"

Scale 3/4" = 1'

Power suggested. Palmer 22 h.p. Universal Atomic Four.
Stokes Gray-marine Seascout. Pick up two cyl. Model
or Atlantic Two cycle. Jeep or Studebaker Champion, with shafts

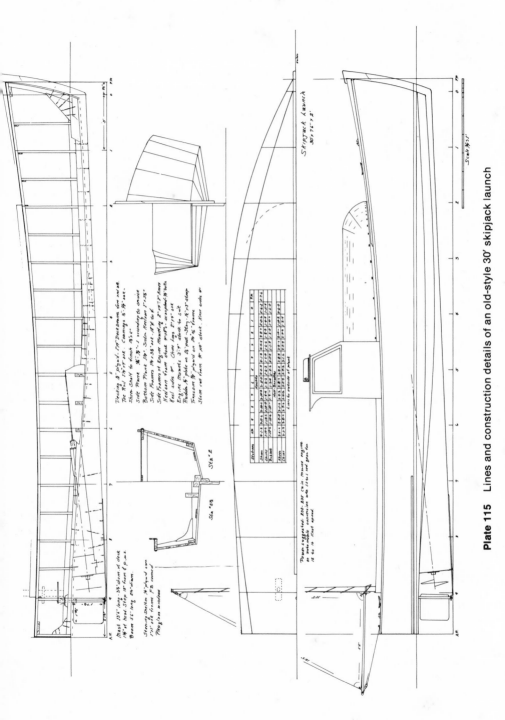

Plate 115   Lines and construction details of an old-style 30' skipjack launch

391

General Construction Details

While these launches were built with rather heavy bottoms supported by a substantial keelson, the upper works were often made rather light to reduce somewhat the overall weight of the hull and to increase the speed capabilities. In modern reproduction plywood panels could be used to advantage for the topsides, stern, and decking. The fitting of light, conventional plank is not difficult here, however, as Bay craft rarely showed fitted planking. Much use was made of stealers and filling pieces, and the top of the strakes aft were allowed to run out under the covering board.

Modern Hooper Island Launches

Referring again to the old-style Hooper Island launches, the type underwent a rather radical change in the late 1920s with the growing popularity of the high-speed car-type marine engine. The beam was considerably increased, the forward underwater sections were made more shallow, and the stern sections flattened to accommodate the high-speed capabilities of the "improved" hull. The low chine profile forward was found to provide the necessarily low angle of attack forward that was essential to semiplaning and planing speeds, and the straight waterlines needed aft. The entrance at the forefoot was found to be of the correct shape for the fitting of a log bow, and the old Hooper Island hull metamorphosized into the "box stern" boat —so-called because of the wide and square-shaped transom that resulted.

Modern Hooper Island Launches Styled from Speedboats

In the early 1930s the Bay builders began incorporating design features of contemporary speedboats, such as excessive flare and flam in the topsides forward and tumblehome topsides aft. While these modifications added some debatable visual appearances, they also added to material costs and building time without otherwise improving the performance. These boats are still being built on the Bay in various sizes for both work and pleasure. Plate 116 shows the hull lines and building outline for a popular size of 32-foot box-stern boat much used in the crab fisheries. A small 24-foot model apparently based on pleasure launch lines is shown in Plate 117.

In order to exploit the best speed potential of this design, many of these launches have been rather lightly built to reduce weight. As in the case of most empirically developed craft, the standard of workmanship and quality of finish varies widely, anything from crude to excellent. In some lightweight construction, a "chunk" bow is fitted that employs some rather intricate joiner work (Figure 142).

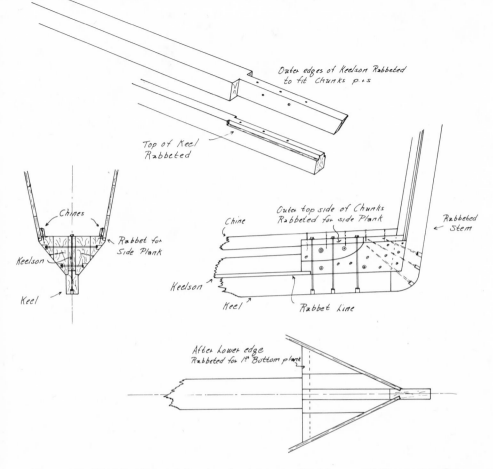

Figure 142　Construction details of a chunk bow as fitted to a small Chesapeake Bay power boat

"Box Stern" Launches

In recent years some rather large box-stern launches have been built on the Bay for commercial fishing, and are often driven at high speeds with large engines. Plate 118 shows a 40-foot model much used for oyster tonging and is of a size often fitted with a mechanical clam dredger where the use of such is permitted. Many of these boats have been converted or originally built for pleasure use with steering shelters and trunk cabins.

Towboat Stern Launches

Another early powerboat development on the Bay was the towboat-sterned launch. These were originally of the round-bottom type, and were

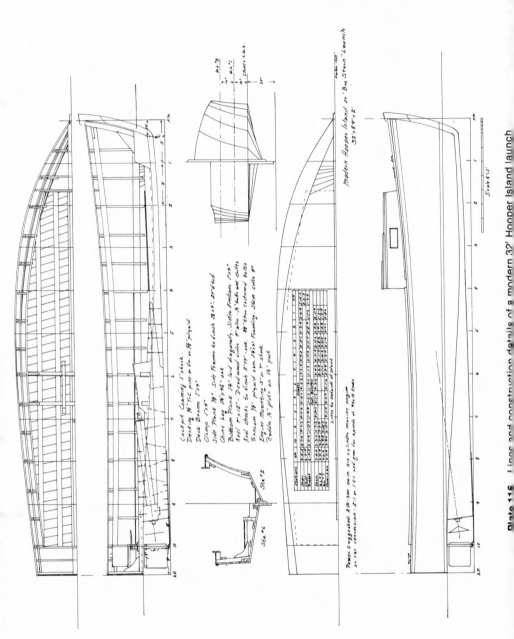

Cockpit Coaming 1" stock
Decking 3/8" T+G. pine or fir or 3/8" plywd.
Deck Beams 1"x9"
Clamp 1"x9"
Side Plank 3/4" Side Frames to finish 1 3/4"x 1 3/8"x 30" oak
Chine keel 1 3/4" x 4 1/2" oak
Bottom Plank 3/4" laid diagonally, Sitka Arlidson 1" x 9"
Keel 7" x 12" - Dead wood sides 3" also - 1/2" bolts and cleats
Keel cheeks to finish 8" x 9" - oak.   1/2" thru fastened bolts
Transom 3/4" plywd or own 1 1/2" x 4" framing. 3/4" cent. sides 3/4"
Engine Mounting 3" x 7" stock
Tandem 1/4" plate on 1/4" pad

Sta #6   Sta #2

Power suggested: 230-300 cu.in. six cylinder marine engine
or car conversion - 2.1 or 1.51 red gear for speeds of 9 to 12 knots

Lines to outside of plank

Modern Hooper Island or "Box Stern" launch
32' x 8'9" x 2'

Plate 116   Lines and construction details of a modern 32' Hooper Island launch

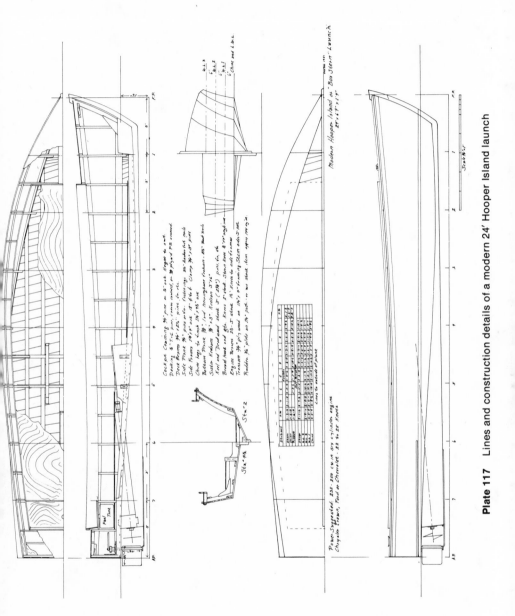

Plate 117 Lines and construction details of a modern 24' Hooper Island launch

395

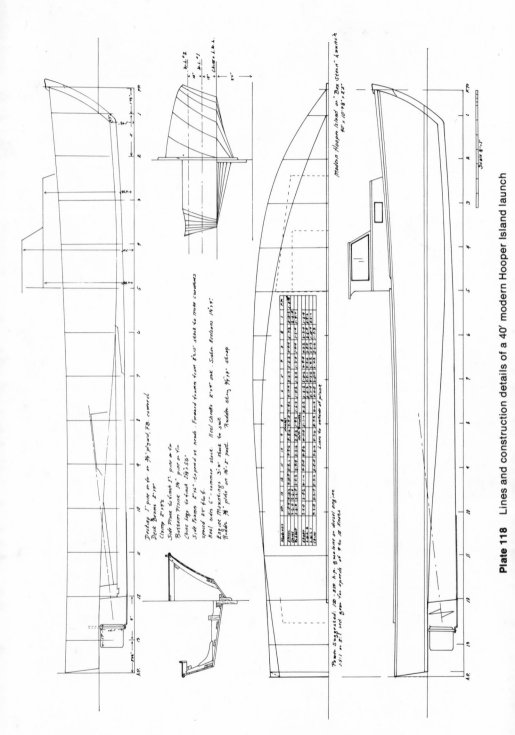

Plate 118 Lines and construction details of a 40' modern Hooper Island launch

396

built as scaled-down replicas of the well-known fantail-sterned steam tugboats that were then extensively used for both harbor and coastal activities,
having become highly developed since the time of the American Civil War.
As small gasoline-powered launches, they were very useful in various commercial and pleasure boat activities—they were able in rough water, had an
easy motion in a seaway, could carry large loads, and were economically
driven at modest speeds with low power. They were particularly adapted for
use as small towboats, as the counter stern permitted the fitting of a large
propeller.

With all their virtues, these round-bottom tugboat replicas were expensive
to build, both for materials and the building time involved, and practical
boat carpenters of the Bay set about devising a lower-priced substitute. The
result was a plumb-stemmed V-bottom skipjacklike hull with a low chine
forward terminating in a log forefoot, together with a usually graceful sheerline and a rather fine counter stern that was generally thin in profile. These
launches were commonly of rather light displacement, and had a much narrower beam than the parent skipjack type. The scantlings were often rather
light, and keel cheeks were favored over a more massive hewn log keelson.

Versatility of Towboat Stern Launches

While few of this style of launch have been built in recent years, the type
has much to recommend it. Aside from being economical to power, its load-
carrying ability and the noncritical nature of its displacement and waterline
immersion factors allow a number of options as to its interior arrangement
and final fitting. As a fantail-sterned boat it could have an appeal to commercial operators for its load-carrying ability, or to those who like a touch
of "character" in a somewhat unusual design. The scantlings may be either
light or heavy at the option of the builder or in keeping with intended service.

26' Towboat Stern Launch

Plate 119 shows the lines and building plan for a 26-foot towboat-stern
skipjack. This hull is based upon a similar launch called *The Only Son,*
whose plans are preserved in the Watercraft Collection. Its general construction details follow those described for previous Bay-type hulls (pages
352–396). It may be lengthened to 29 or 30 feet if a slightly longer boat is
required. Plate 120 shows some optional arrangements—a small salmon
troller, an antique glass cabin launch for protected waters, or a steamboat.

Raised Deck Towboat Stern Launch

Plates 121 and 122 give the lines and building guide for a raised-deck fantail launch with an increased beam for enhanced interior room and possible

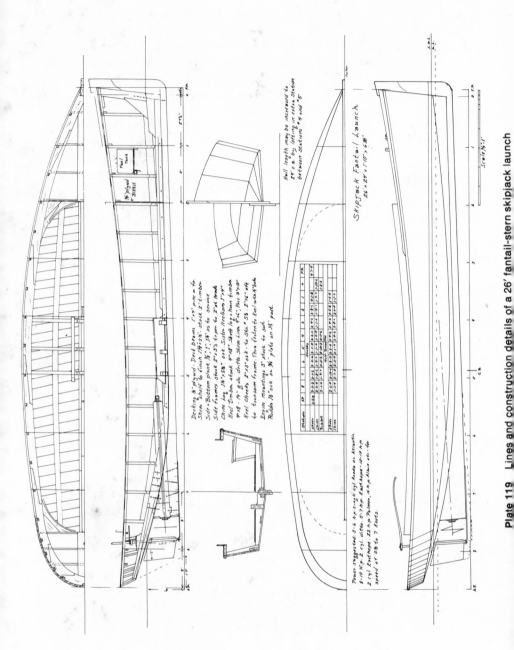

Plate 119   Lines and construction details of a 26' fantail-stern skipjack launch

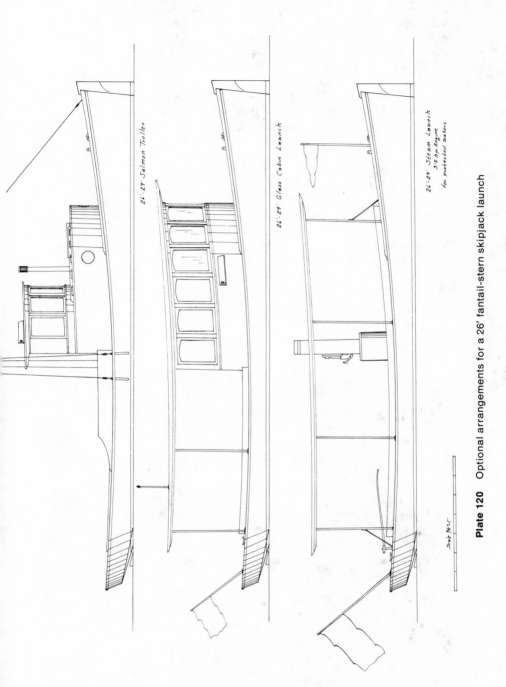

26'-29' Salmon Troller

26'-29' Glass Cabin Launch

26'-29' Steam Launch
3-5 hp Engine
for protected waters

Scale ¾=1'

Plate 120 Optional arrangements for a 26' fantail-stern skipjack launch

399

cargo capacity. It could be arranged as a workboat-type cruising boat, or as a small commercial fisherman.

Towboat Stern Launch as Combination Fishing Boat

Plate 123 shows a somewhat larger skipjack laid out as a small combination boat. This hull has lifted stern sections to enhance its cargo capacity, and will have a single rim log to frame the stern on account of this profile. This hull may also be lengthened.

36' Utility or Cruising Launch

Plates 124 and 125 give the hull lines and building plan for a 36-foot launch arranged as a cabin utility or cruiser with central trunk cabin and forward pilot house.

A light displacement launch of moderate beam is shown in Plate 126. This would be suitable as a pleasure or ferry launch where light loads are to be carried. It drives easily up to about 7 knots with very low power, and would be most efficient with a 5 to 10 hp. steam engine.

19' Fantail Utility Launch

The 19-foot launch in Plate 127 is about the smallest practical size for this style of hull due to the beam-length considerations. As its short waterline length will hold its hull speed down to about 5 knots, it is best suited to some casual or novelty use with a small steam plant.

Ram-Type or Tumblehome Bows in Small Launches

Some early models of the V-bottom versions of the towboat launches were built with tumblehome or "ram" type bows, as in some of their round-bottom counterparts. This profile was copied from some of the large tugboats so constructed, and also simulated the bow form of some contemporary naval warships that carried a ram on the forefoot below the waterline. While it may well be considered as an affectation in a small powerboat, some builders have preferred its somewhat distinctive and jaunty aspect. The construction of this type of stem is as described in the previous skipjacks, except for the raking of the top of the stem somewhat aft of the forward perpendicular in laying out the work.

A 36' Ram-Bowed Combination Boat

Plate 128 shows a ram-bowed 36-foot combination boat. Plates 129 and 130 show the building plan and optional arrangements for a 24-foot model.

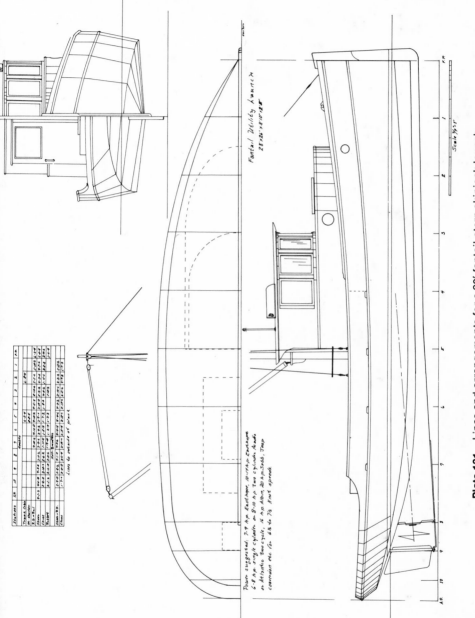

Plate 121 Lines and arrangements for a 28′ fantail-stern skipjack launch

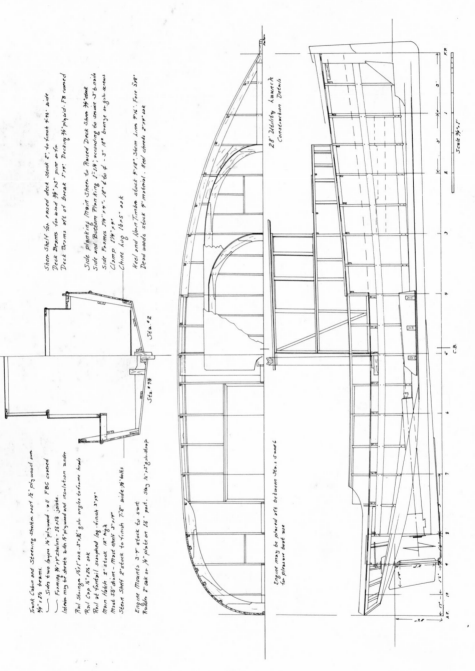

Plate 122 Construction details for a 28' fantail-stern skipjack launch

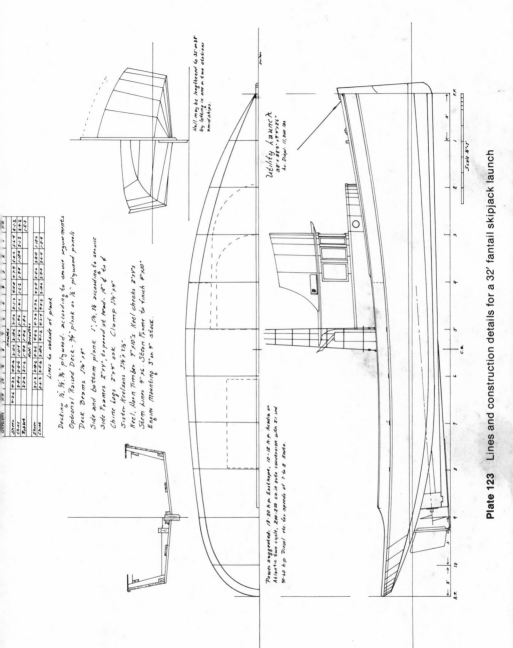

Plate 123 Lines and construction details for a 32' fantail skipjack launch

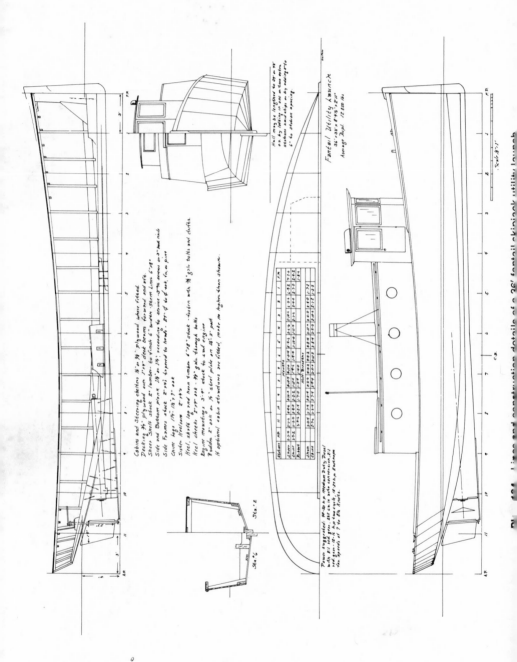

Fig. 404. Lines and construction details of a 26' fantail skipjack utility launch.

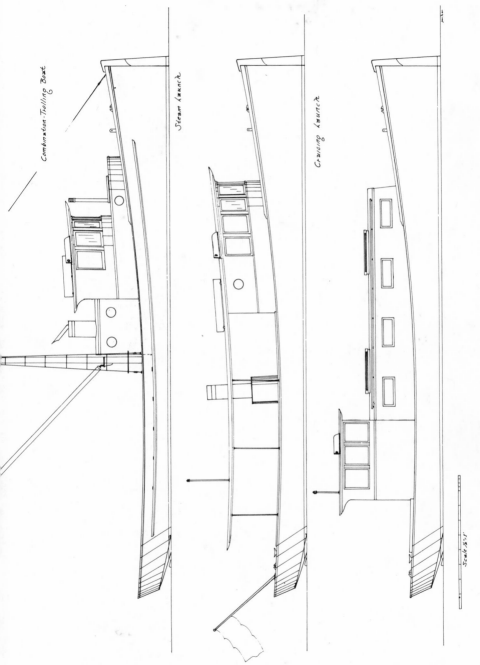

Combination-Trolling Boat

Steam Launch

Cruising Launch

Scale ⅜:1'

Plate 125 Optional arrangements for a 36' fantail skipjack launch

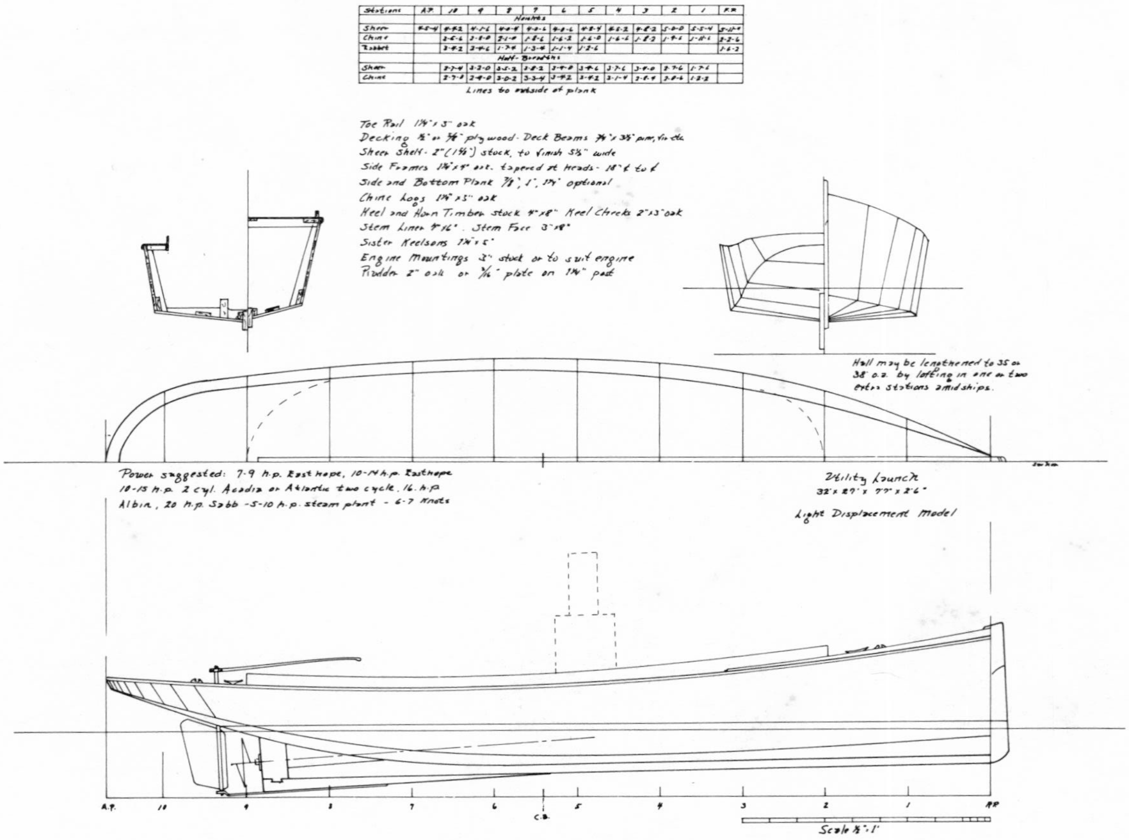

Plate 126 Lines and construction details of a light-displacement fantail skipjack launch

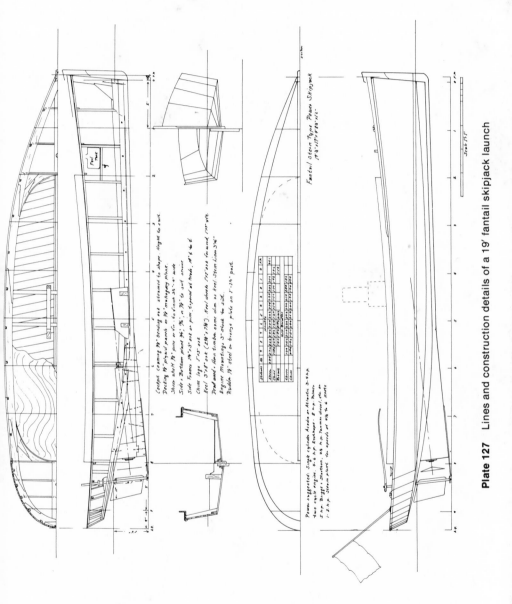

Cockpit coaming ⅞" bending oak steamed to shape. Kept to suit.
Decking ⅜" pcywood panels or ⅜" mahogany plank.
Sheer strake ⅞" pine or fir to finish 3½"-4" wide.
Side ~ Bottom plank ⅞'. ⅞', or ⅞" to suit owner.
Side Frames ⅞"×⅝" oak or pine tapered at heads. № 1" to 6.
Chine logs 1"×2" oak.
Keel 3"×8" oak (2½"×3½"). Keel above 1½"×2½" fwd and 1¼" aft.
Dead wood. Horn timber same dim as keel. Stern Liner 3½".
Engine Mountings 3" oak to side.
Rudder 1⅜" steel or bronze plate on 1"-1¼" post.

Fantail Stern Type Power Skipjack
19'-6"LOA×6'-0"×1'-6"

Stations	18	17	16	15	14	13	12	11	10	9	8	7	6	5	4	3	2	1	0	FP
Sheer																				
Chine																				
Keel Rabbet																				
Buttocks																				
Sheer																				
Chine																				

Power suggested. Single cylinder Acadia or Atlantic 3-4 h.p.
two cycle engine. 6-8 h.p. Kermath. 8 h.p. Palmer.
5 h.p. Briggs + Stratton. 3½ h.p. Yanmar diesel, etc. or
1-2 h.p. Steam plant. for speeds of 4½ to 6 knots.

Plate 127 Lines and construction details of a 19' fantail skipjack launch

Scale Ft.

407

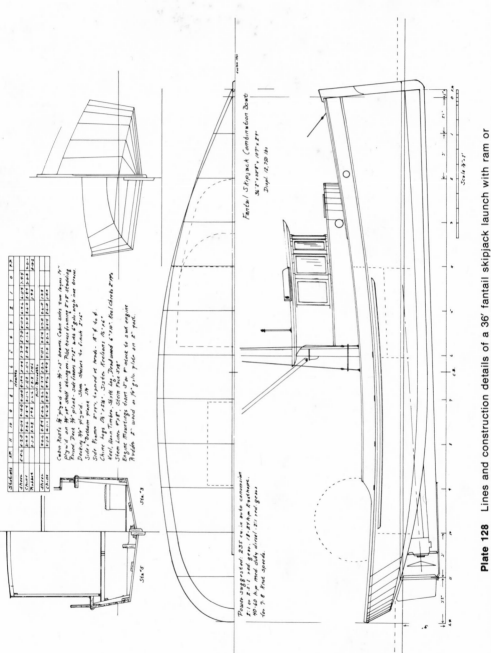

Fantail Skipjack Combination Boat
36'2"×10'7"×2'7"
Displ. 12,730 lbs

Power suggested: 235 cu. in. auto conversion
2:1 or 2.5:1 red. gear. 18-24 hp Easthope.
40-60 hp. med. duty diesel, 2:1 red gear
for 7.8 knot speed.

Cabin Roofs: 3/8" plywd over 1/2"×2" beams. Cabin sides: two layers 1/4"
plywd on 3/4"×1" steel stringers. Pilot house framing 1"×1". Standing
Raised Deck 3/4" plank, sides frames 1"×2" and 5/8" plywd on inner Bureau.
Decking 3/8" plywd. Deck beams to finish 1"×1½".
Side: bottom plank 1¾".
Side Frames: 2"×2½", tapered at head: 1¼" to 2".
Chine logs 1¾"×3¼". Sister Kneelsons 1½"×6".
Keel, Horn Timber, Shaft log, Deadwood 6"×10". Keel/Clamps 2"×6".
Stem Liner 4"×8". Stem Face 5"×8".
Engine Mountings from 3" to finish to suit engine.
Rudder 2" wood or 3/8" galv. plate or 2" pack.

Scale 3/4"=1'

Plate 128 Lines and construction details of a 36' fantail skipjack launch with ram or
tumblehome type bow

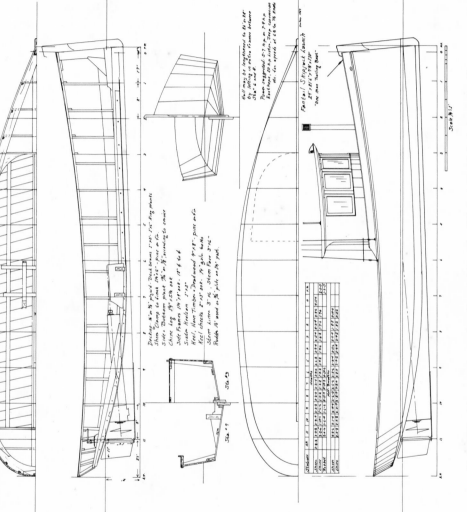

Plate 129 Lines and construction details of a 24′ fantail skipjack launch with ram or tumblehome-type bow

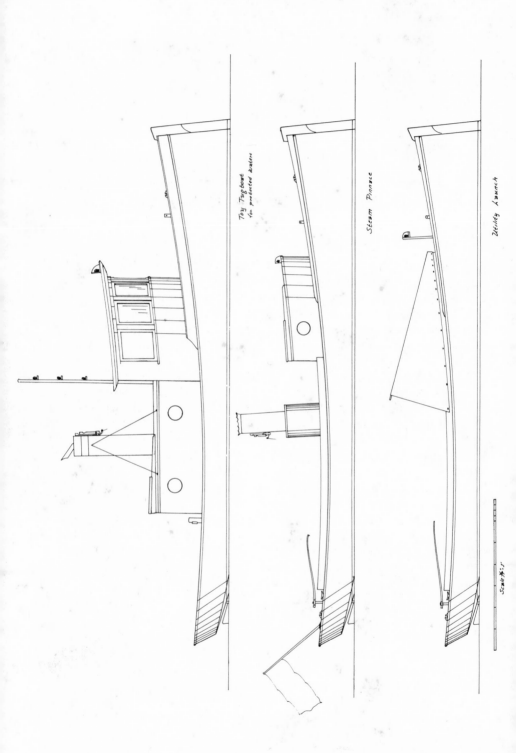

Toy Tug boat
to projected scale.

Steam Pinnace

Trinity Launch

Scale ⅜ : 1

24

Low Chine Model
Plywood Covered Boats

Small boats and launches with plywood hull covering came into widespread use after World War II. The quality and uniformity of commercially produced plywood in all grades had been greatly improved as a result of the accelerated demand for its use in many types of small vessels constructed for the armed forces. Thousands of landing barges, aircraft rescue launches, airplane rearming boats, as well as the famous PT boats, utilized plywood planking.

Both naval architects and practical small boat builders turned increasing attention toward new designs with hull forms suitable for plywood, often with an eye toward the mass production of small craft to fill the large peacetime demand. A further impetus was given to these efforts a decade later when it had been successfully demonstrated that fiber glass hull coverings materially increased the strength of even very light plywood planking and added immeasurably to its longevity. The obvious advantage of this type of construction was that it appeared to be one answer to the centuries old search for a monolithic hull structure.

Aside from the advantages of reduced costs of material and building time, the plywood covered hull offers the designer certain flexibilities in hull forms and displacement options not possible with more traditional construction.

Four principal options in plywood covered hulls are:

1. A fully framed hull with varying weights and/or layers of plywood planking and decking with fiber glass covering.
2. A fully framed heavyweight hull structure with random lengths, or pieces of plywood fastened to heavy battens let into the side frames and covered with fiber glass.
3. The so-called "frameless" or monocoque construction, where spliced or specially manufactured long length panels form the sides and bottom of the hull. These full length panels, combined with the stem, keel assembly, sheer shelves, and sister keelsons, maintain the shape of the hull through longitudinal stiffness without other internal bracing.

4. The lightly framed hull with light plywood planking combined with fiber glass covering, each of these three elements combining to give adequate structural strength.

1. THE FULLY FRAMED PLYWOOD-COVERED HULL

This type of construction can be applied to any hull form with straight sections, as the plywood panels cannot be readily bent into compound curves. It is particularly adaptable to planing or semiplaning launches where low or moderate weight is desirable in order to obtain the best speed capabilities. The builder also has the option, within reasonable limitations, of employing either light or heavy scantlings according to intended service requirements. While a variation in hull weight will, of course, result in a change in the flotation factors in relation to the designed waterline, this condition is not critical, as the ultimate hull speeds in such designs may be controlled by the rather wide choice of power plants available.

60′ V-Bottom Patrol Launch *Cuba Libra*

The 60-foot V-bottom patrol launch shown in Plate 131 is an example of this type of construction. This could well serve as a pleasure yacht, party fishing boat, or personnel or utility craft. While of a size usually considered somewhat above that being suited to amateur or individual construction, its simplicity of form and straightforward construction details are such that a couple of apprentice carpenters with some prior boatbuilding knowledge could put her together within a reasonable time.

This launch was designed by the author some years ago for patrol activities in the Caribbean area. The requirements were for a low cost and possibly expendable craft to be used mostly for personnel carrying, able enough for use on the open sea, and capable of a flank speed of 28 to 30 knots when required. Built with lightweight scantlings and in a light condition of loading with fuel tanks half full, it exceeded 30 knots with two 375 hp. lightweight, high-speed Cummins diesel engines. These turned 26-inch propellers through 1.5:1 reduction gears. The boat was built and fitted out near Vera Cruz by native Mexican shipwrights. It was ultimately sunk by aerial bombardment off the southern coast of Cuba.

Plate 132 shows the hull outline, offset tables, and two cross sections of the hull.

Typical Framing Layout for Plywood-Covered V-Bottom Launch

A schematic diagram of the framing is shown in Figure 143, and is typical of this method of construction for launches of similar form in lengths of 25

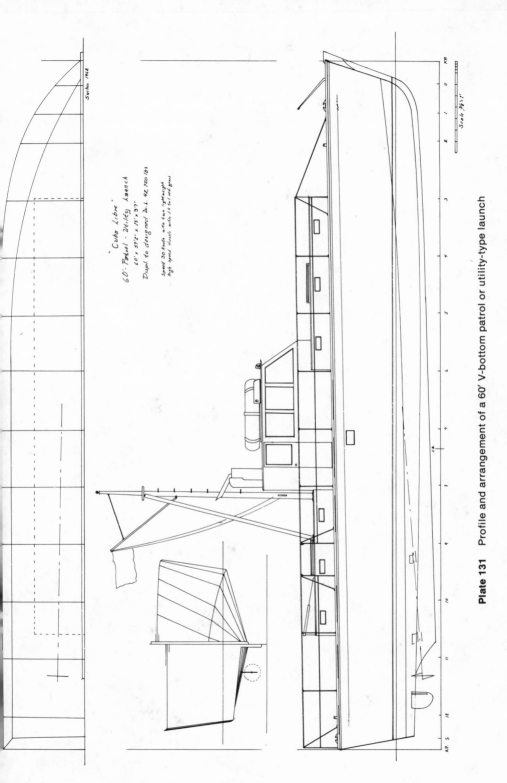

"Cuba Libre"
60' Patrol - Utility Launch
60' x 59" x 15' x 37"
Displ. to designed D.W.L. 42,750 lbs

Speed 30 knots with two lightweight
high speed diesels with 15 tol ied gross

Scale ⅜"=1'

Plate 131 Profile and arrangement of a 60' V-bottom patrol or utility-type launch

413

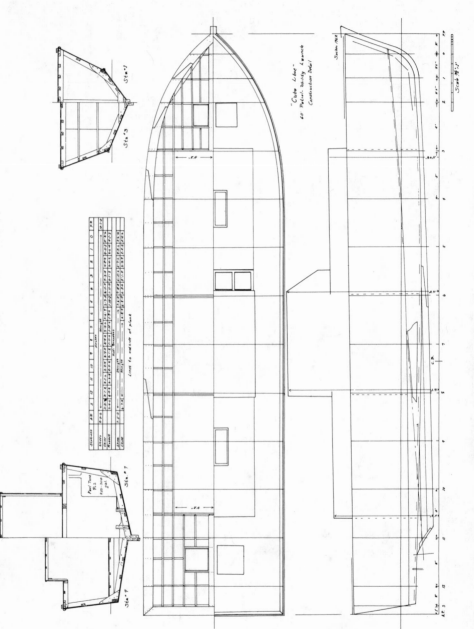

Plate 122. Construction details of a 60′ V-bottom launch.

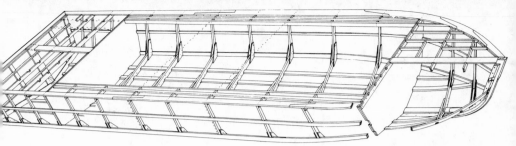

Figure 143 Framing details of a 25' to 75' planing launch to be covered with playwood

to 75 feet with appropriate variation in scantlings. Two full, watertight, collision bulkheads fore and aft are shown. Additional full bulkheads forward and aft of the engine space would add additional safety factors, if added weight were not objectionable. The substantial deck framing does much to add structural strength to a rather wide and shoal hull.

While the straight hull sections will allow the fitting of solid plywood panels the full length of the sides from bow to stern, the usual compound curves in the angle of the forefoot between chine and rabbet will not permit their use on the bottom forward of this point. For closing in this portion of the hull, the panels must be ripped into 6- or 8-inch wide planks which can be sprung easily to the proper curves. These planks are laid diagonally in opposite directions in either double or triple layers, according to the number used on the rest of the hull. This sequence is shown in Figure 144.

Built Up Stem Piece for V-Bottom Plywood-Covered Launch

The stem piece may be either of the laminated or conventionally built-up type of straight or slightly curved timbers scarphed together. As the bow angles are generally rather wide in planing-type hulls, stem cheeks rather than

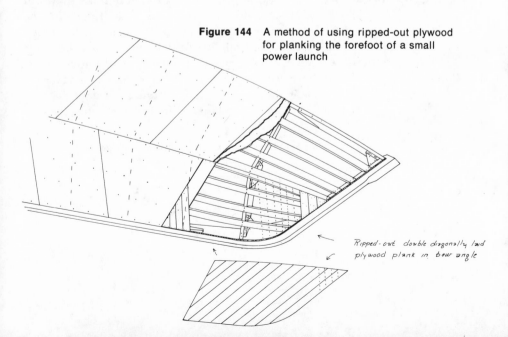

Figure 144 A method of using ripped-out plywood for planking the forefoot of a small power launch

Ripped-out double diagonally laid plywood plank in bow angle

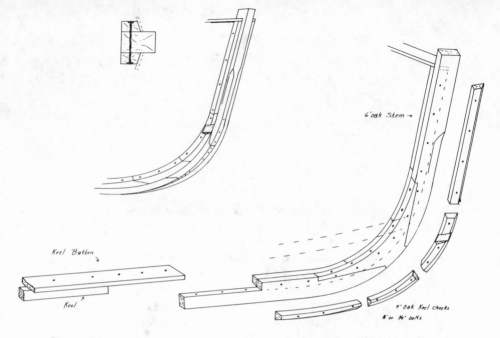

Figure 145 Construction details of a built-up stem assembly as fitted to small launches

a cut rabbet are best fitted to receive the forward ends of the planking. This method of fitting is almost mandatory in such hulls, as the use of a cut rabbet would entail the selection of an inordinately large piece of timber where the bow angle is excessively wide. A diagram of this construction is shown in Figure 145.

Framing Details of Large V-Bottom Plywood-Covered Launch

The framing details of a typical large plywood-covered hull are shown in Figure 146. Notches must be cut into the outer sides of the frames for the keel batten, sister keelsons, chine stringers, side stringers, and sheer plates. In larger hulls, double gussets at the angles of the frames are best fitted for adequate strength. Triangular floor pieces that bear on the tops of the frames amidships may be fitted for some saving of weight and material. These are through bolted as shown. They provide ample strength here, as the hull is otherwise well braced by the longitudinal stringers and the con-

Figure 146 Construction details of frames for V-bottom plywood-covered launches

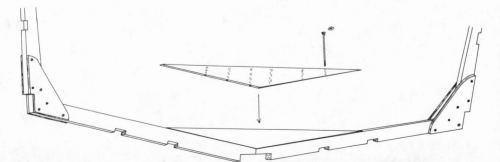

tiguous panels used as planking. The bottom shape of each floor must be taken for its corresponding frame from the loft plan.

Bulkhead Construction in V-Bottom Launches

The construction of a typical bulkhead is shown in Figure 147. The plywood may be either large single panels, or built up from two or three smaller pieces. Watertightness may be achieved by careful joinery and by sealing the edges with glue or fiber glass. In larger hulls and especially those where powerful engines are fitted, large, flat surfaces within the hull may be prone to vibration and drumming unless well braced. In these cases, it is best to fit cross braces consisting of stock 2 x 6-inch planks set horizontally and through bolted to the side frames. This gives better rigidity to the structure than if laid on flat, as it gives the effect of a truss or girder.

Further construction details and a scantling guide for the building of large plywood-covered hulls are shown in Figure 148.

2. HEAVY FRAMING COVERED WITH RANDOM PIECES OF PLYWOOD

Due to the heavy framing used in the construction of this type of hull, these boats are generally of the displacement type and intended for hard service. As the substantial main frames are fitted with heavy battens that are closely spaced to form nailing pieces for the random planking panels, much of the hull weight is represented by these structures. The strength of the planking is augmented, however, by the application of two or three layers of fiber glass or polypropylene covering.

Figure 147   Construction details of bulkheads for V-bottom plywood-covered launches

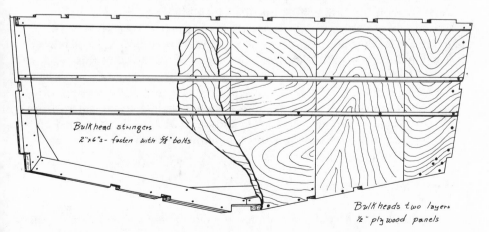

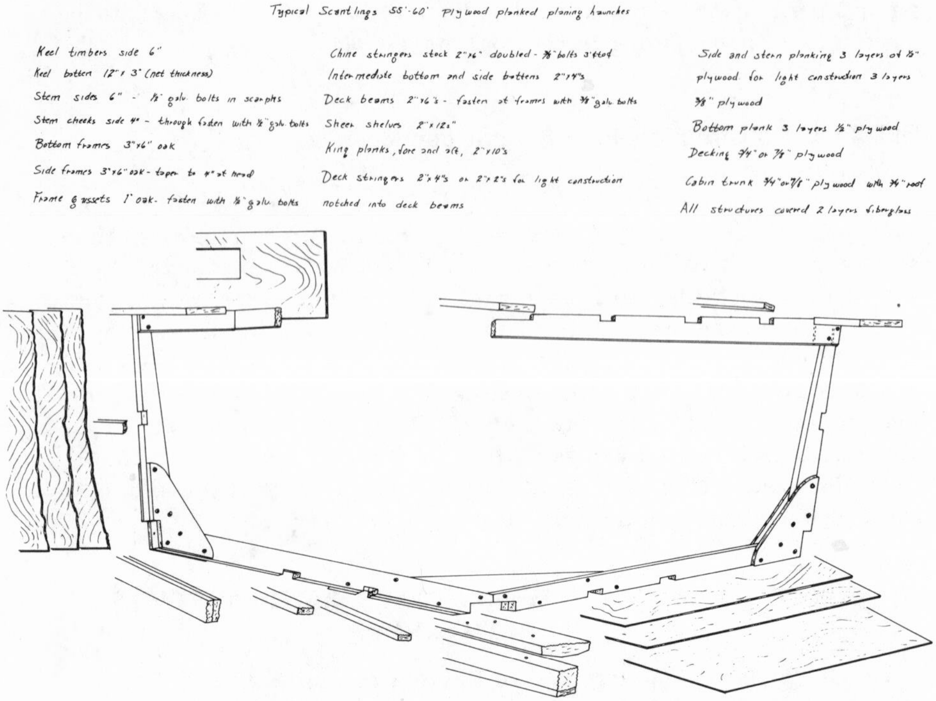

Typical Scantlings 55'-60' plywood planked planing launches

Keel timbers side 6"	Chine stringers stock 2"x6" doubled - 3/8" bolts 3'foot	Side and stern planking 3 layers of 1/8"
Keel bottom 12" x 3" (net thickness)	Intermediate bottom and side battens 2"x4"s	plywood for light construction 3 layers
Stem sides 6" - 1/2" galv bolts in scarphs	Deck beams 2"x6"s - fasten at frames with 3/8"galv bolts	3/4" plywood
Stem cheeks side 4" - through fasten with 1/2"galv bolts	Sheer shelves 2"x12"	Bottom plank 3 layers 1/2" plywood
Bottom frames 3"x6" oak	King planks, fore and aft, 2"x10"s	Decking 3/4" or 7/8" plywood
Side frames 3"x6" oak- taper to 4" at head	Deck stringers 2"x4"s or 2"x2"s for light construction	Cabin trunk 3/4"or 7/8" plywood with 3/4"roof
Frame gussets 1" oak. fasten with 1/2"galv bolts	notched into deck beams	All structures covered 2 layers fiberglass

Figure 148   Typical scantlings for the framing of V-bottom plywood-covered launches

28' V-Bottom Displacement-Type Troller-Gillnetter

A typical example of a launch built to this system is the 28-foot troller-gillnetter shown in Plate 133. As this is a displacement-type hull, the principal weights are concentrated amidships to give an easy motion in rough water. Due to the lifted chine line aft which allows substantial loads to be carried without dragging the stern, the terminal hull speed is limited to 7 or 7½ knots. Low-powered, heavy-duty engines are indicated for maximum economy, and the hull should not be overpowered. Boats of this type are often fitted out as inshore fishermen where the fishing grounds are close at hand and high speeds are not required. This boat could also serve in other commercial or utility capacities, or as a snug, seagoing cruiser for two people. In this case, the steering shelter and deckhouse could be moved aft a few feet to allow more spacious interior accommodation.

Mast Step Construction

The hull outline and offset tables are shown in Plate 134, with a sug-

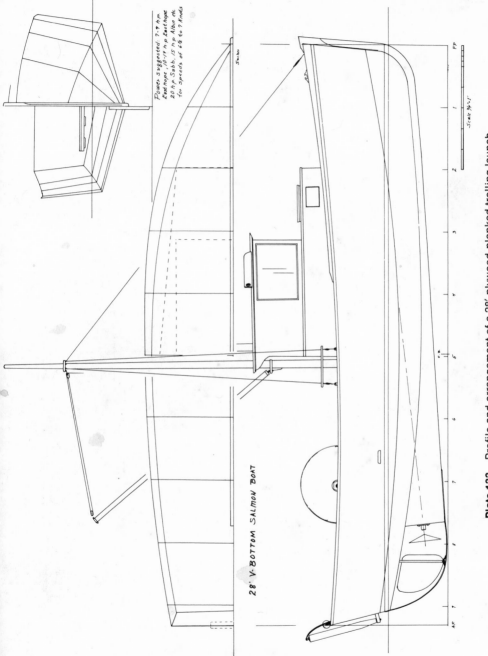

Power suggested, 7-9 h.p.
Easthope, 10-14 h.p. Easthope,
20 h.p. Sabb, 15 h.p. Albin etc.
for speeds of 6½ to 7 knots

28' V-BOTTOM SALMON BOAT

Scale ¾"-1'

Plate 133 Profile and arrangement of a 28' plywood-planked trolling launch

Station	A.P.	9	8	7	6	5	4	3	2	1	F.P.
Sheer	5-1-4	5-9-6	5-7-2	5-6-0	5-6-0	5-6-6	5-8-2	5-10-4	6-2-2	6-6-2	6-10-6
Chine		3-4-2	3-0-0	2-8-6	2-6-0	2-5-2	2-6-2	2-8-6	3-1-2	3-7-0	4-2-2
Rabbet		2-9-6	2-3-4	1-9-6	1-5-6	1-4-2	1-4-0	1-5-+	1-7-4	1-10-6	
Sheer	3-1-2	3-3-+	3-9-0	4-1-4	4-4-2	4-5-0	4-5-0	4-2-2	3-6-6	2-3-4	
Chine	2-10-0	2-10-6	3-4-0	3-8-4	3-11-2	4-0-6	4-0-0	3-7-4	2-9-6	1-7-2	

Lines to outside of plank

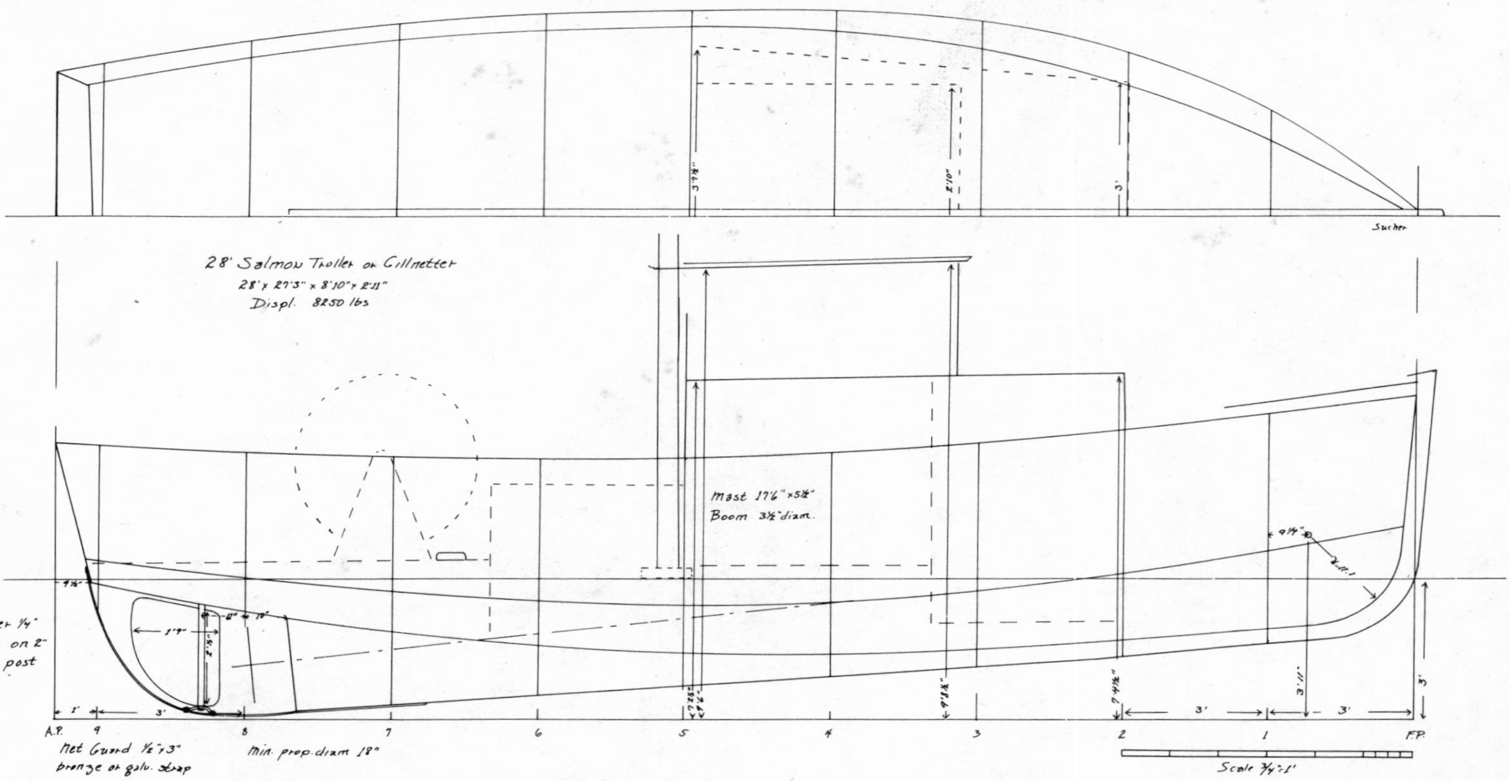

Sucher
28' Salmon Troller or Gillnetter
28' x 27'3" x 8'10" x 2'11"
Displ. 8250 lbs
Mast 17'6" x 5½"
Boom 3½" diam.
Rudder ¼" plate on 2" diam. post
Net Guard ½" x 3" bronze or galv. strap
Min. prop. diam 18"
A.P.
9
8
7
6
5
4
3
2
1
F.P.
Scale ¾" = 1'

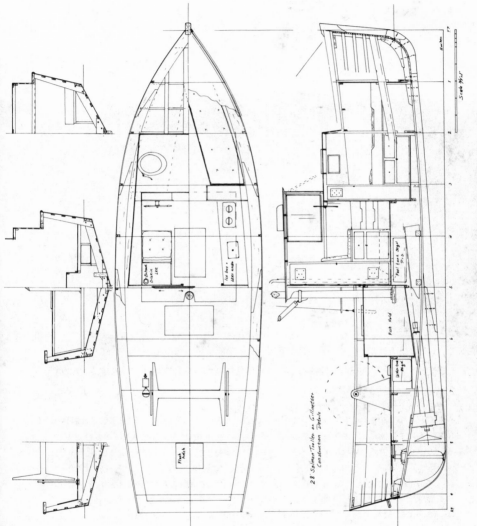

Plate 135 Construction details of a 28' V-bottom trolling launch

28' Salmon Troller or Gillnetter
Construction Details

Flush Hatch

Fish Hold

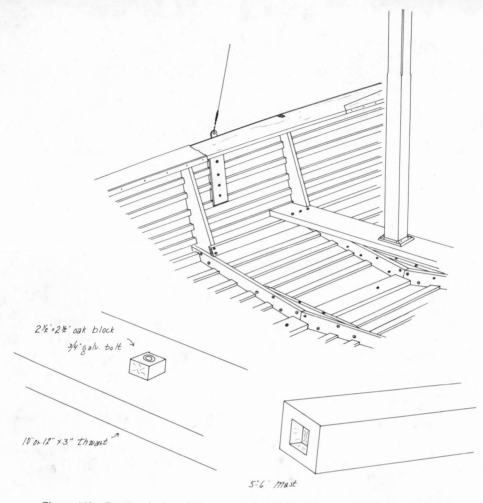

Figure 149 Details of a bench-type mast step as fitted to a small V-bottom launch

gested interior layout as a troller-gillnetter in Plate 135. The details of the mast step and its mounting are shown in Figure 149. This method of construction is required in powerboats where the mast is stepped aft of the engine and must have its heel raised to clear the propeller shaft. The mounting consists simply of a heavy thwart with its ends bolted to heavy stringers fastened to the side frames. The method of securing the mast step with a block and tenon is also shown. The chain plate fastenings for the shrouds should be secured by blocks set inside the outer planking at the sheer.

Optional Dimensions of Scantlings

The builder of these boats has an option as to the size of scantlings employed, dictated by either choice or the availability of materials. These can be varied within reasonable limits, as the loading factors of these hulls is not

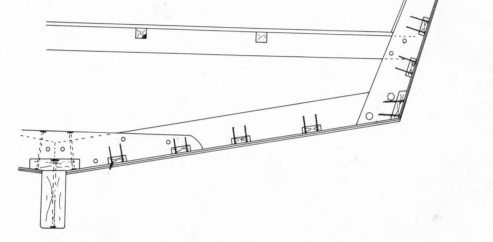

Typical Scantlings for 25'- 35' plywood Covered Hulls

Cabin sides ¾" plywood - Cabin Roof ½" plywood
Shelf at sheer - 1¾" stock
Side Frames 2"×6's - taper to 2½" at heads
Bottom frames 2"×6's - fasten at corners with ¾"galv bolts
Longitudinal Battens 1"×3" - fasten with 1¾, 3" screws or boat nails
Floors 2"×8" - ⅜" bolts - Chine 1¾"×5½"
Keel Bottom 2"×6" or 2"×8" net
Keel sides 4" or 6"
Deck Beams 2"×4"- ¼" bolts - 2"×8" longitudinal Stringers
Decking ½" or ¾" plywood. Ceiling ⅜" plywood
Planking - Two layers ½" plywood, or one layer ⅜", one layer ½"

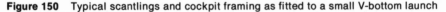

Figure 150 Typical scantlings and cockpit framing as fitted to a small V-bottom launch

critical and variation in immersion is not detrimental to the hull speed. Figure 150 shows a construction section of a typical hull with suggested scantling options in boats of 25 to 35 feet in length.

Offshore Longliner or Heavy-Duty Cruiser

A somewhat larger and more burdensome vessel built to this system is the 34 foot troller-longliner shown in Plate 136. This launch is very able and could serve a variety of heavy service applications including that of an offshore cruising boat if a cabin were built aft in the cargo hold area. Plate 137 shows the hull outline, a suggested interior arrangement, and offset tables. This boat should be built of heavy scantlings as outlined in Figure 150. Due to its generous displacement, about 1,000 lbs. of trimming ballast may be required to bring this boat down to its marks in light condition.

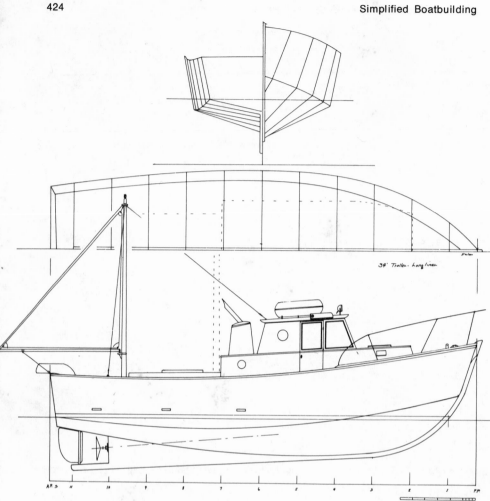

Plate 136   Profile and arrangement of a heavy-duty V-bottom offshore longliner

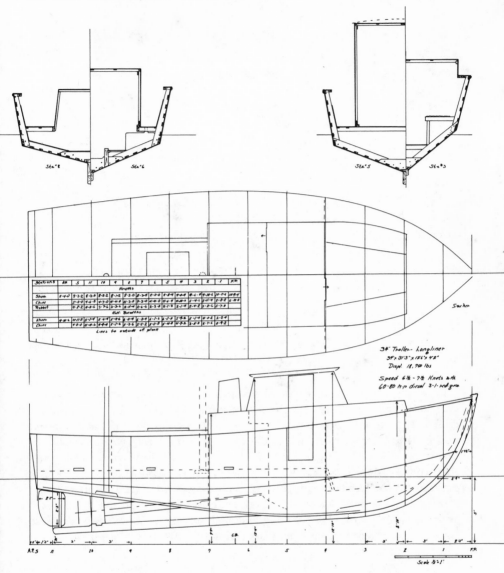

Plate 137   Construction details of a heavy-duty V-bottom offshore longliner

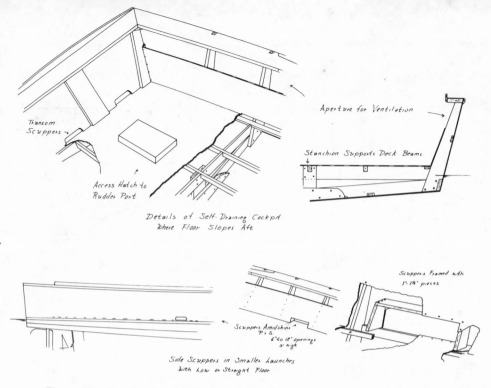

Figure 151 Construction details of cockpit and scupper arrangements for small V-bottom launches

A special feature of this type of design is the high bulwarks and sunken deck aft of the raised deck for the protection and safety of the crew. In these craft, adequate scuppers must be fitted to clear the decks of water coming aboard, and must be of sufficient size to empty solid water within seconds of boarding. Figure 151 shows both transom- and midship-type scuppers and their construction details. Aside from the necessity for substantial watertight decks and high hatch coamings on offshore power boats, the scuppers themselves should be well sealed throughout the orifice between the cockpit sole and the outer planking. The method of blocking is shown for adequate strength, together with the fiber glass lining that makes a contiguous surface through the opening.

3. THE "FRAMELESS" OR MONOCOQUE PLYWOOD HULL

The principal employment of this type of construction is an assembly line for series production of identical hulls. The boats are built upside-down over a jig or permanent framing, and a number of these may be used at the same time, according to the size of the operation.

As much of the strength of the hull and the maintenance of its shape depends mostly on the longitudinal stiffness of the plywood panels forming the sides and bottom, these must be applied as full length panels. They may

426

be made up of spliced pieces fabricated in the shop or purchased from the manufacturer on special order to the length required. The choice is optional with the builder, and the cost factor will influence the individual determination. If short panels are spliced, no joints should be placed in the way of the curve toward the bow, as there is danger of fracture or separation here if the forward part of the hull is subjected to a sharp blow. As most hulls produced today on this system are covered with fiber glass, this danger is minimized, but it is best to adhere to this rule.

While a fair number of hulls within the 25 to 35-foot class have been built by this method by both large and small boatyards in the past decade, they have not been generally successful from the standpoint of superior performance as sea boats. The stiff, plywood panels impose a rather wide bow angle which results in a somewhat wide waterline entrance angle. This, in turn, imposes a wide and shallow forefoot, as the developed shape of the bottom panels forward cannot be worked into a fine entrance angle. As most of these hulls are intended for pleasure cruisers, current fashion dictates a wide beam in order to contain spacious interior accommodations. This excessive beam-length ratio aggravates the condition still further. The result is a bluff-bowed hull with a very shallow forefoot that is hard driving, prone to pounding, and may be difficult to steer, especially in stern seas. In an attempt to remedy these defects, and in the constant search for more speed, these launches are usually fitted with excessive power, which enables them to plane effectively in smooth water. As most of these are built as pleasure boats and subject to use mostly in protected waters and in summer weather, their somewhat mediocre design features seem not to become too glaringly apparent. These boats are a compromise in several directions to answer the need for a mass-produced pleasure boat with interior styling to appeal to the customer who is not well versed in the fundamentals of small boat design (Plates 138, 139, and 140 may be cited as examples).

4. THE LIGHTLY FRAMED AND PLANKED BOAT WITH FIBER GLASS COVERING

Launches built on this system are of the lightest weight in proportion to their displacement when loaded than any of the commonly built types of plywood-covered boats. For this reason their various parts require very careful fitting and fastening to provide adequate structural strength. Their building should be undertaken only by those with some prior experience in small boat construction and possessing journeyman skills in carpentry and joinery.

The majority of the boats built to this method have been of the pleasure-boat type. In recent years, however, the growing popularity of high-speed workboats in certain types of fishing operations where better than average speeds are of economic benefit has fostered their adaptation to commercial uses.

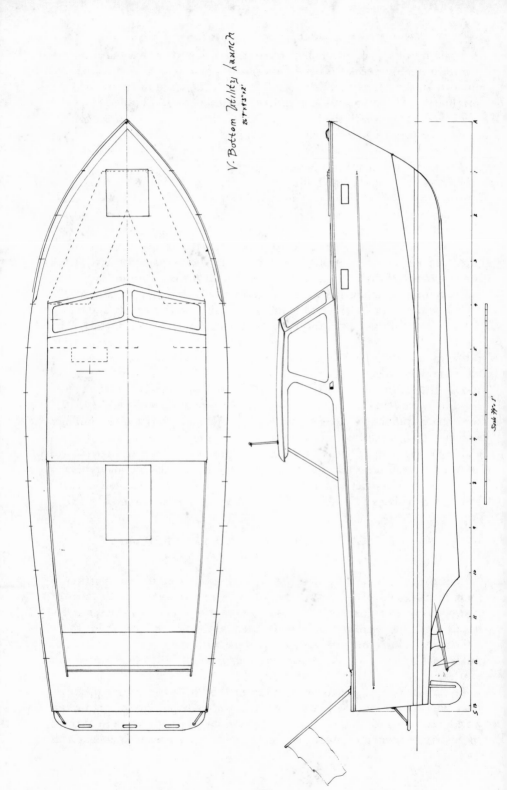

V-Bottom Utility launch
24'×8'3"×2'

Scale ⅜"=1'

428

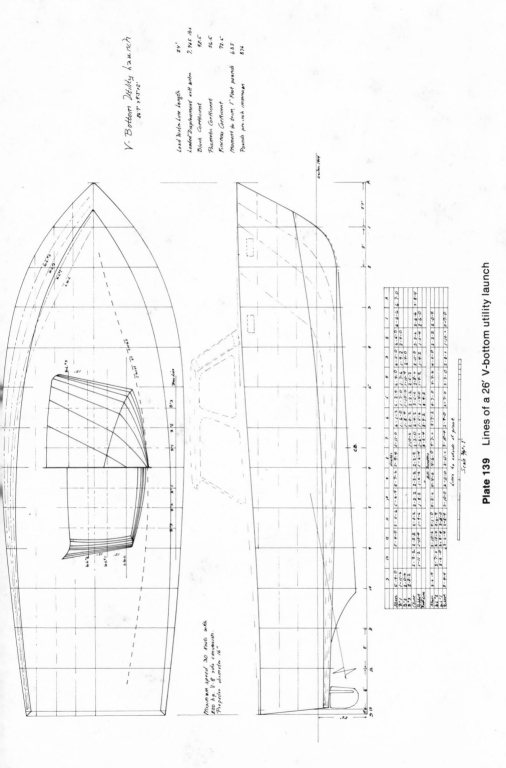

Plate 139 Lines of a 26′ V-bottom utility launch

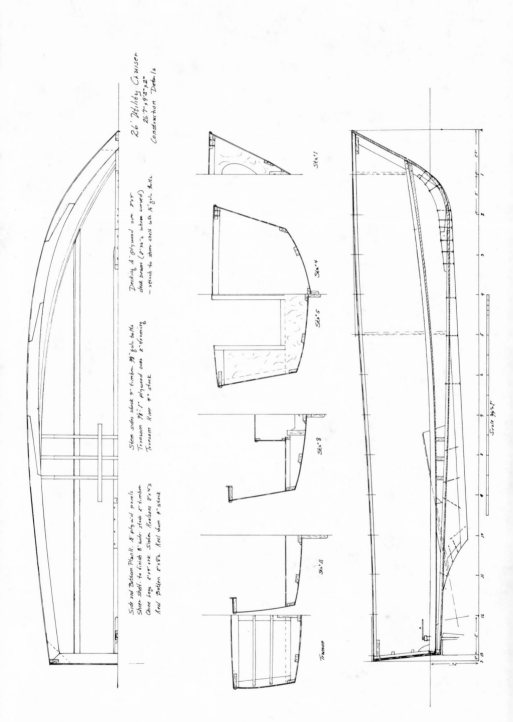

26' Whitby Cruiser
26'7" x 9'3" x 2"
Construction Details

Decking 3⁄8" plywood over 2" x 4"
deck beams (2" x 4"'s where curved)
– secured to sheer shelf with 3⁄8" galv. bolts

Stem sides stock 4" timber. 3⁄8" galv. bolts
Transom 1⁄2" plywood over 2" framing
Transom Knee 4" stock

Side and Bottom Plank 3⁄8" plywood panels
Sheer shelf to finish 8" wide. stock 2" timber
Chine logs 2" x 1" x 6". Stem Knees 2" x 4"'s
Keel Batten 2" x 8"'s. Keel shoe 4" stock

Sta' 1

Sta' 4

Sta' 5

Sta' 8

Sta' 11

Transom

Scale 3⁄4" = 1'

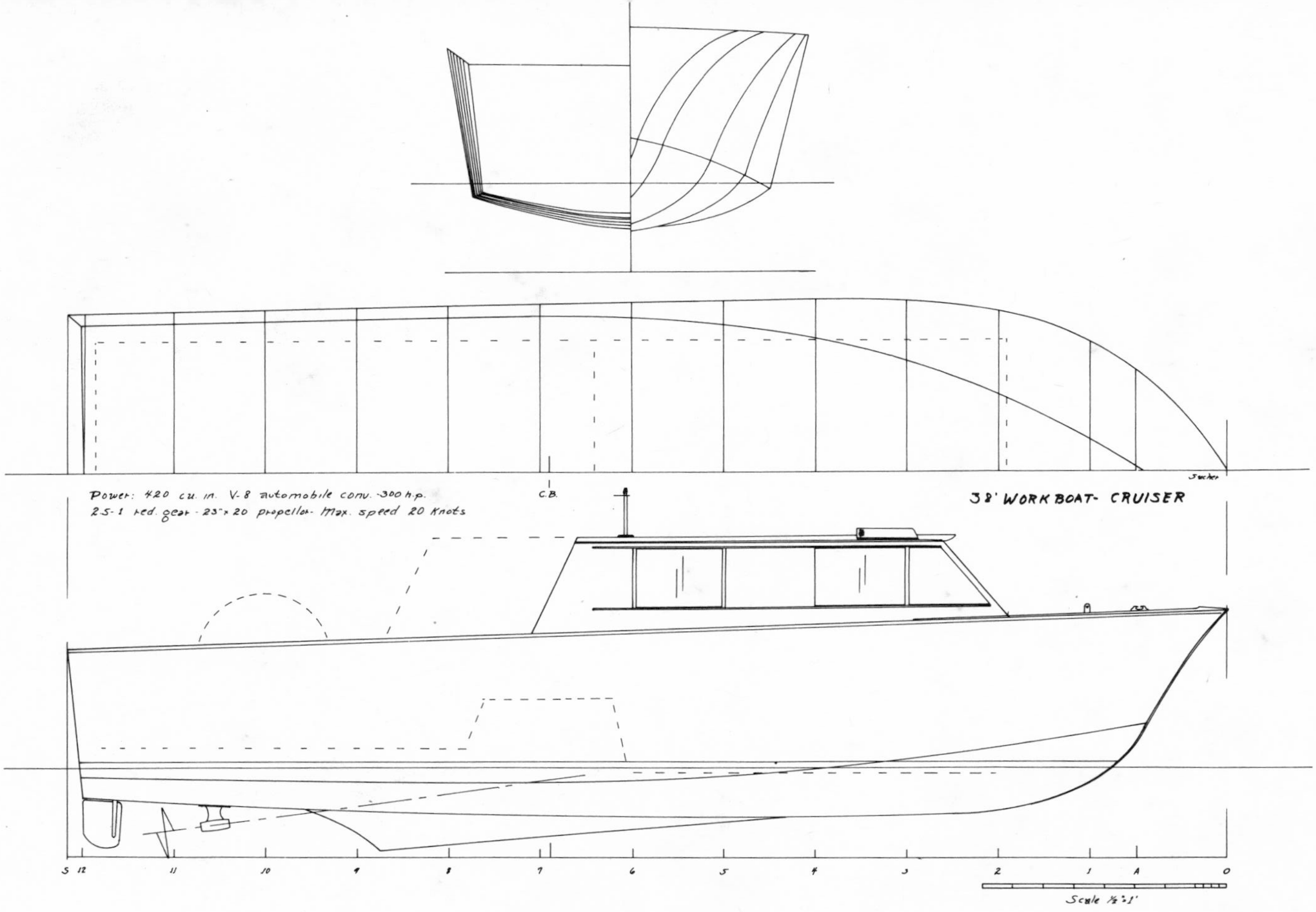

Power: 420 cu. in. V-8 automobile conv. 300 h.p.
2.5-1 red. gear - 23"x 20 propeller - Max. speed 20 Knots
C.B.
38' WORKBOAT- CRUISER
S 12 11 10 9 8 7 6 5 4 3 2 1 A 0
Scale ½"=1'

Plate 141 Profile and arrangement of a 38′ workboat-type cruiser

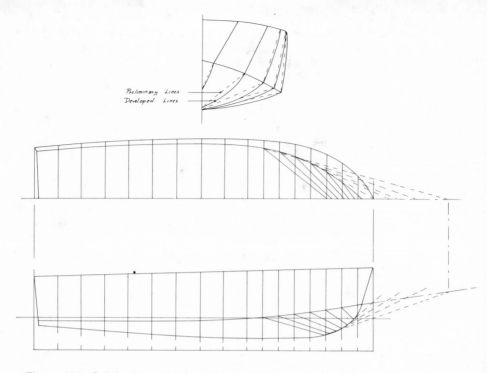

Preliminary Lines
Developed Lines

Figure 152 Schematic projection diagram of the conical projection of the bottom planking of a plywood-covered V-bottom launch

Pleasure-Workboat Type of Launch

A typical example of one of these dual purpose launches is represented by the 38-foot boat shown in Plate 141. With its generous freeboard and wide beam it offers substantial interior room, and its deep cockpit offers good weather protection and safety for the crew. Boats similar to this have been adapted by various designers during the past decade to trolling and gillnetting operations along the northwest Pacific coast of the United States.

Conically Developed Surfaces of Sheet Plywood Bent to Various Curves

The sectional drawing of the hull (Figure 152) shows curves which accommodate the conically developed form for the plywood panels used for planking, as described on page 430 for the frameless or monocoque type of building (Figure 153). The underwater form of these launches is such that they incorporate high-speed planing capabilities when fitted with large, powerful engines, yet they can perform acceptably as displacement boats when heavily loaded or when weather conditions make slow speed operation mandatory. Because of their easy lines and moderate resistance factors, their speed as displacement hulls is comparatively faster than conventional

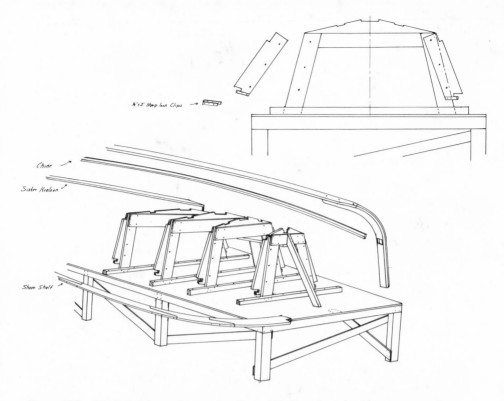

Chine

Sister Keelson

Sheer Shelf

$\frac{3}{4}"x3"$ Strap Iron Clips →

Figure 153 A building frame for constructing a V-bottom launch with monocoque-type planking

true displacement hulls. The somewhat bulbous forward section actually lowers resistance factors at displacement speeds, as proven by tank tests of models of large steamships having these contours under the bows. Sections of this form also inhibit diving when driven into steep, short seas.

Typical V-Bottom Cruiser-Workboat Launch

An outline of the hull with its offset tables and general characteristics is shown in Plate 142. The broad, flat after sections of the underbody, combined with the light construction, enable this boat to attain a speed of about 20 knots when powered with a 380 hp. automobile engine of 430 cu. in. displacement. As converted for marine use, this engine will develop about 300 shaft hp. turning a 23 x 20 inch three-bladed propeller. A critical factor in the hull design is the spray rail which follows the chine line from bow to stern. This aids in deflecting the water away from the chine line at planing speeds, and prevents the water from traveling up the sides of the hull when traveling at reduced or displacement boat speed. It must be emphasized that a boat such as this is designed for high performance and should be powered with an engine of the type specified. If a low-powered engine is installed, the overall performance will be disappointing.

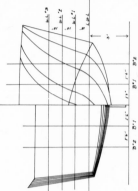

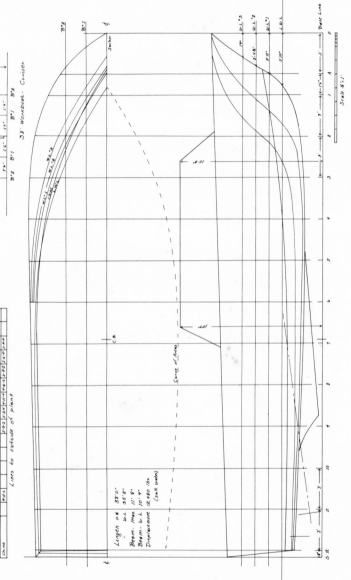

Plate 142   Lines and offset tables of a 38' workboat-type cruiser

Interior Arrangement of Cruiser-Workboat Launch

A drawing of the interior arrangement for pleasure boat use is shown in Plate 143. If built as a commercial fishing boat with a fish box in the cockpit, the engine should be moved forward about two feet to balance this load.

Framing Details for a Plywood-Covered Cruiser-Workboat

The main frames erected on the station lines are somewhat widely spaced and interconnected with closely set longitudinal battens fastened at identical intervals from the keel to the sheer. The upper part of the hull is secured by a sheer shelf made up of horizontally laid timbers that are notched at their outer edges to receive the heads of the side frames. This is good construction in a lightweight hull as it makes a very strong but light structure that effectively prevents the hull from wringing or changing shape. As there is adequate longitudinal strength in the sheer shelves, backbone structure, and chines, the battens are not let into the outer sides of the frames but merely nailed to them at the proper intervals. Their principal function is to support the plywood plank panels. Their after ends are notched into the transom frame, however, which makes a strong and rigid joint between the side plank and the transom face.

Details of Hull Construction

In building, the hulls are put together in the inverted position. The sheer shelves are made up of flat planks scarphed to the proper curves from the loft plan, and the notches are cut for the frame heads. As most of these designs show a straight or flat sheerline, the sheer shelves may be laid out on a large table which forms a building jig. Care must be taken to insure that the frames engage the sheer shelves at the proper angle before bolting the parts together—the frames, if laid out on a horizontally flat table, will be seen to cant forward. After the frames are set in place, the assembled stem and backbone pieces are bolted to the floors (Figure 154).

Battens at Forward Portion of Hull

A diagram of the forward portion of the hull with the battens that support the plywood plank panels is shown in Figure 155. It will be noted that the stem is not rabbeted, the battens running out to the edge of the stem bevel which is taken from that of the side plank. The latter extends even with the stem face, the hood ends of the plank panels then being covered with a steam-bent oak stem face or galvanized iron strap.

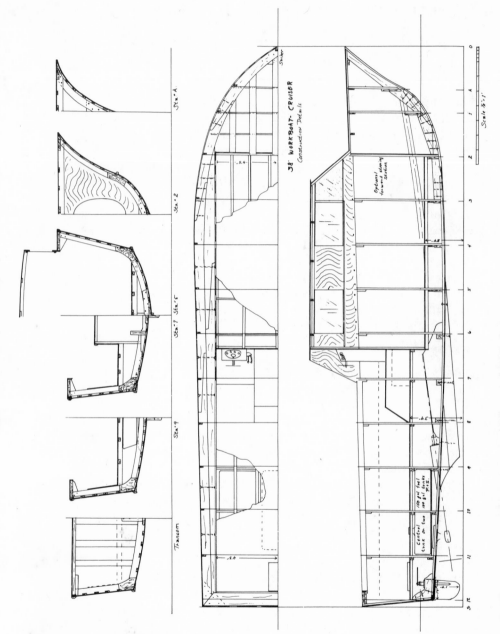

38' WORKBOAT- CRUISER
Construction Details

Plate 143. Construction details of a 38' V-bottom workboat-type cruiser.

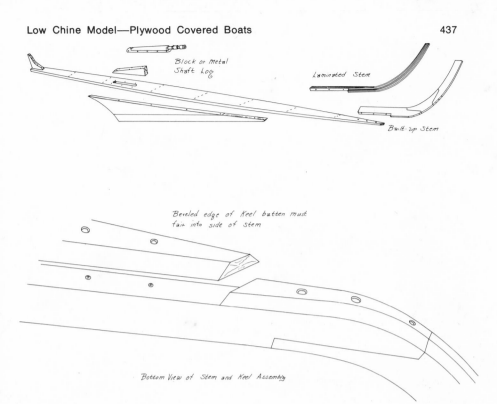

Block or Metal
Shaft Log

Laminated Stem

Built-up Stem

Beveled edge of Keel batten must
fair into side of stem

Bottom View of Stem and Keel Assembly

Figure 154 Construction details of the stem and backbone timbers for a small V-bottom plywood-covered launch

Figure 155 Details of seam batten construction for a small V-bottom plywood-covered launch

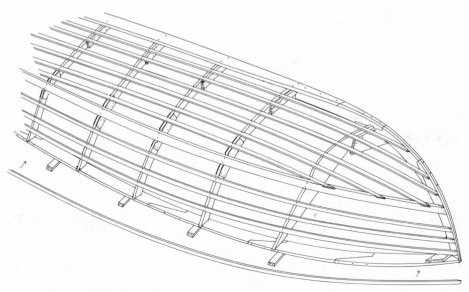

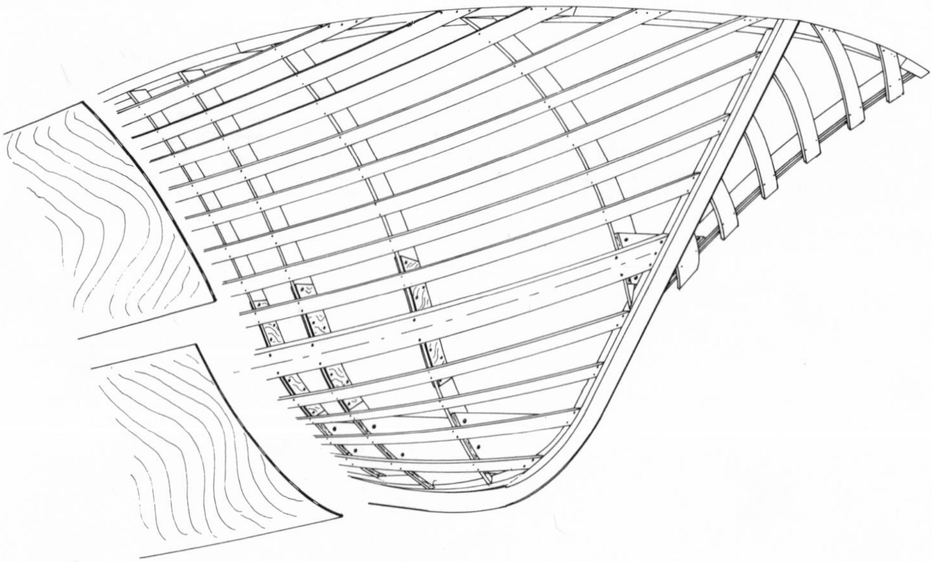

Figure 156 Details of seam batten construction at the bow sections of a small plywood-covered V-bottom launch

Conical Plank Development Allowing for Bow Flare and Flam

Some of these latterly designed hulls show a marked flare and flam in the bows. In most cases these are projected so that the developed shape of the planking will allow it to be sprung into place with very little forcing. The conical development of the flat surfaces will follow a convex curve as readily as a concave one (Figure 156).

Construction Details at Transom

The fitting of the battens at the stern is shown in Figure 157, with the notches cut into the transom frame only. The sheer batten is run out to a feathered end to make a smooth fitting for the after edges of the plank panels against the sides of the transom face. Also shown on this drawing is an optional method of bracing the ends of the side and bottom battens where they bear against the stem. The use of blocks here could save some building time as the ends should otherwise be rabbeted into the stem liner.

Construction Details of Sheer Shelves, Breast Hooks, and Quarter-Knees

Figure 158 shows construction details of the sheer shelves and their attachment to the heads of the side frames. The sides of the cabin may be

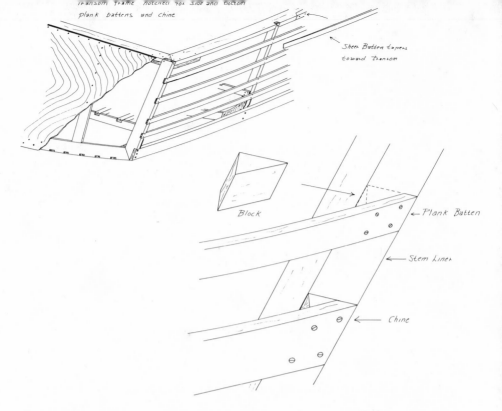

Transom frame notched for side and bottom plank battens and chine

Sheer Batten tapers toward transom

Block

Plank Batten

Stem Liner

Chine

Figure 157 Construction details at bow and stern for a small V-bottom plywood-covered launch

Figure 158 Construction details of clamps and shelves for a small V-bottom launch

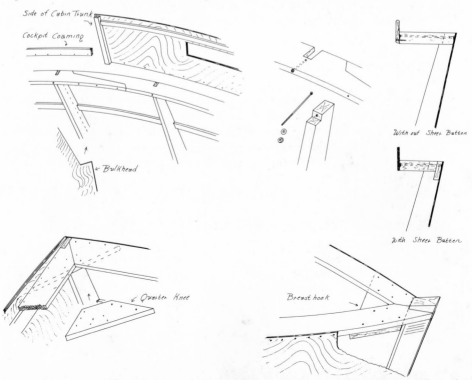

Side of Cabin Trunk

Cockpit Coaming

Bulkhead

With out Sheer Batten

With Sheer Batten

Quarter Knee

Breasthook

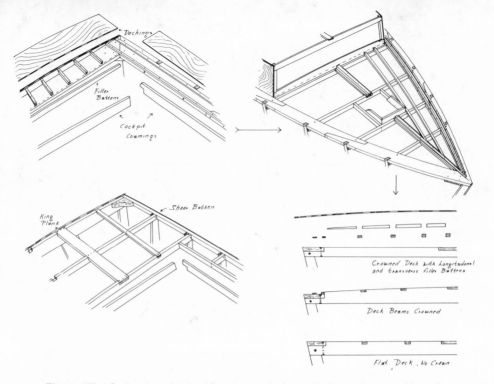

Figure 159 Optional methods of framing decks in small plywood-covered launches

fastened to the inside face of the sheer shelves, as the hulls are covered with fiber glass or polypropylene which will make a continuous watertight joint that can be extended to the midline of the roof top. Breast hooks and quarter-knees are made from short pieces, of similar dimensions to the sheer shelves, and fastened at the underside of the angles at bow and stern.

Optional Methods of Deck Construction

Optional methods of constructing the forward and after decks are shown in Figure 159. The most simple and quickest operation is to lay a flat un-crowned deck. If crowning is desired, the curve may be worked into the deck beams themselves. Another method is to lay a flat beam and build up the correct crown with fillets, which form backing pieces for the plywood deck panels.

Construction Details of Side Decks

Construction details of the side decks are shown in Figure 160. If the forward and after decks are uncrowned, the side deck plank is laid directly on top of the sheer shelves. If the former are crowned, the side decks must be built up with the use of longitudinal battens as indicated.

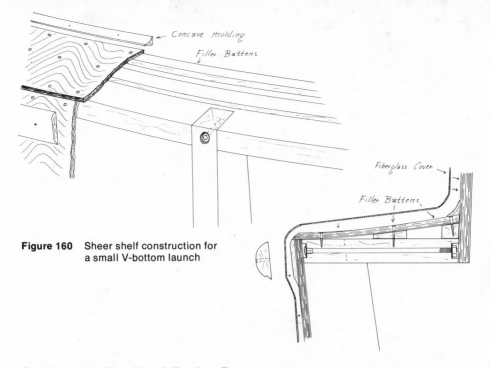

Concave molding

Filler Battens

Fiberglass Cover

Filler Battens

Figure 160 Sheer shelf construction for
a small V-bottom launch

Construction Details of Engine Bearers

In a lightly built hull carrying a powerful engine, some special attention should be given to constructing the engine bearers so that vibration can be minimized. The engine foundation should be made up of heavy timbers well braced and made long enough to extend over several bottom frames. As various makes of engine will vary as to the position of their mounting lugs, the builder will have to adapt the construction to suit a specific condition. Optional types of engine mountings are shown in Figure 161.

Figure 161 Optional methods of engine mounting construction employed in small
V-bottom launches

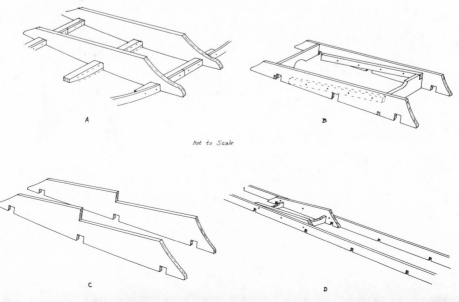

A

B

not to Scale

C

D

Use of Metal Frame Brackets in Bottom Planking

In cases where the propeller shaft passes through the point where the bottom frame futtocks intersect or through the top of a floor, much of the material may have to be cut away to accommodate its passage. The loss of the central support of one frame may not be critical in a low-powered displacement type hull, but it could be a source of weakness in lightly built high-speed planing launches fitted with large engines. In these cases it is therefore good practice to fit one of the available manufactured frame brackets. These are made from either naval bronze or galvanized iron and have a flat plate that bolts to the keel or keelson below and two arms on each side that are through bolted to the lower frame members (Figure 162).

Twin Engine Layout

High-speed planing or semiplaning hulls with substantial beam are sometimes fitted with twin engines, even if originally designed for single engine power. While the increase in speed in such cases is only nominal, maneuverability and handling qualities are enhanced, and it is possible to attain nearly 100 percent dependability of engine power if each engine is outfitted as an independent unit as to fuel supply and electrical components.

Figure 162   The use of metal floors in bottom frame futtocks of small V-bottom launches

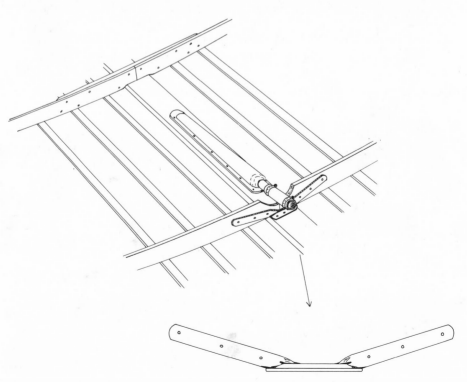

Use of Two Small Capacity Engines for Economy

In some cases increased economies of operation can be realized from a twin screw installation where two somewhat smaller engines are substituted for a single large one, so the boat can be operated at reduced speeds on only one engine. In any event the initial cost of such an installation will be substantially higher, due to the need for dual fuel systems, extra fuel tanks, shaft logs, rudders, and propellers, which are always expensive in any case.

Importance of Substantial Engine Mountings

As in any lightly built hull, vibration can be a problem and some thought must be given to provide substantial engine mountings. Such an installation is shown in Figure 163. The engine bearers should be made from heavy timbers, and the transverse supports should extend clear across the hull under both. This is especially critical, as the engines do not have the direct support of the keel and backbone timbers underneath as is the case with a single engine. A heavy batten or sister keelson should extend from beneath each engine mounting aft on either side to support the shaft logs, strut mounting, and rudder ports. It will effectively tie each system together as a unit.

Figure 163   Details of a typical twin-screw installation in a small V-bottom launch

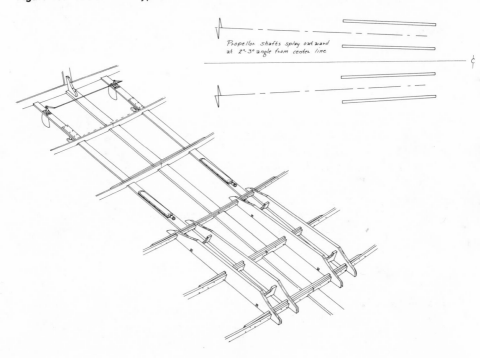

Weight and Balance Factors in Twin Engine Installations

As twin engine installations inevitably weigh more than a single unit, weight and balance factors that might affect performance factors must be carefully considered. Loading a hull with extra weights can be critical, and an excess here might nullify the supposed advantage of changing the design. The advice of a competent naval architect or experienced boatbuilder should be sought before proceeding.

To those who are well versed in small boat design and are able to perform the necessary weight and balance calculations, the procedure is routine. After the engine position is projected in relation to the dimensions of the hull, their lateral positions must be established. A rough guide is to locate the shaft couplings approximately at a point that is one third the distance from the centerline to the chine. Handling will be improved if the engines are mounted so that the shafts splay outward 2 or 3 degrees from the centerline of the hull.

A 28′ Workboat-Cruiser

A smaller 28-foot launch of similar form built to the same system is shown in Plate 144. It is arranged as a pleasure cruiser, but may be easily adapted to commercial or utility uses. The interior layout is shown in Plate 145, and is typical of the modern small yacht. The hull outline and offset tables are shown in Plate 146. If built to the suggested scantlings, the boat will attain a top speed of about 28 knots with a lightweight high-speed V-8 car-type engine of 175 to 200 hp. If twin engines are desired, a pair of light 100 hp. six-cylinder machines will result in slightly more speed and greater maneuverability.

Construction Details of a Stern Boarding Platform

The details of a boarding platform built on the transom slightly above the load waterline are shown in Figure 164. This is a very useful addition to any powerboat with high freeboard and combined with a ladder extending to the deck line, with suitable handrails, will accommodate a party of swimmers. It also offers a valuable safety factor in enabling a person overboard to be recovered easily. The platform also protects the transom when working around docks and other obstructions. Two optional methods of attachment are shown in the drawing. Handholds should be cut into the after edge of the platform.

Cross Section of V-Bottom Hull Showing Typical Scantling Dimensions

A drawing of a typical cross section of a hull built to this system is shown

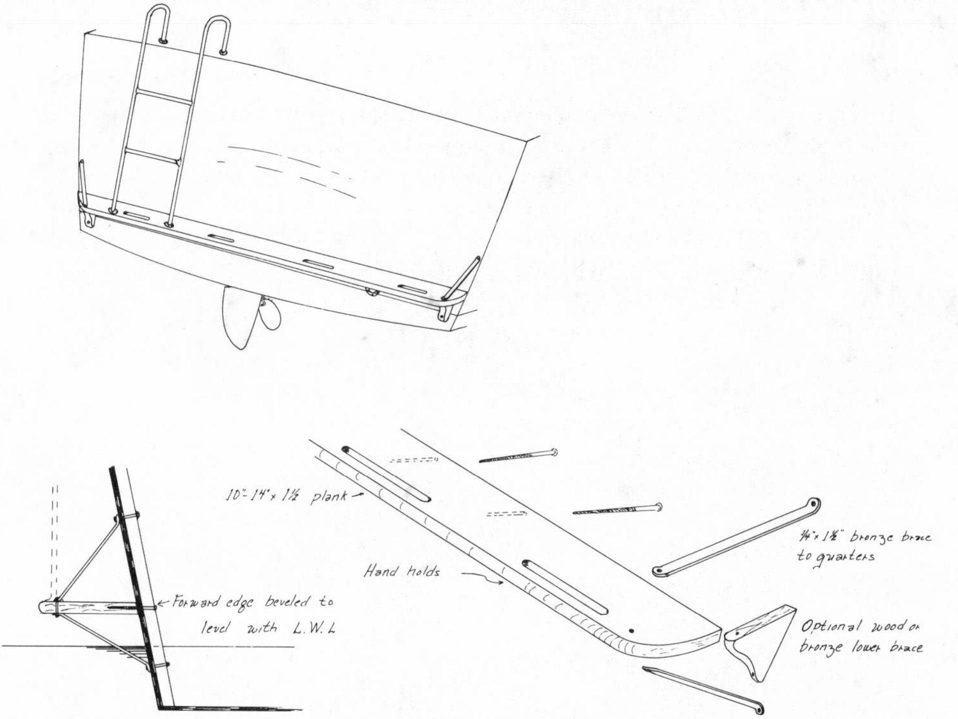

Figure 164 Construction details of a stern boarding platform used in small launches

Figure 165 Typical scantlings used in V-bottom plywood-covered hulls of 25′ to 40′

	25–30′ Hulls	35–40′ Hulls
Cabin Roof	⅜″ plywood	⅜″ plywood
Roof Beams	½″ × 3″ pine, fir, etc.	½″ × 3″ pine, fir, etc.
Cabin Sides	¾″ plywood	¾″ plywood
Sheer Shelves	1¼″ pine, fir, cedar	1¼″ pine, fir, cedar
Side and Bottom Frames	1″ × 3½″	1⅛″ × 4″
Frame Gussets, doubled	⅜″ plywood, ¼″ galv. bolts	⅜″ plywood, ¼″ galv. bolts
Plank Battens	¾″ × 2½″	¾″ × 2½″
Planking	⅜″ plywood sides and bottom	½″ plywood, or two layers ¼″ plywood
Chine Stringers	1¼″ × 5½″	1¼″ × 7½″
Floor Timbers	1⅛″ ¼″ galv. bolts	1¼″ ⅜″ galv. bolts
Keel Batten	1½″ × 10 ⅜″ floor bolts	1¾″ × 12 ½″ bolts
Keel and Stem Liner	3″ stock ⅜″ bolts to keel batten	4″ stock ½″ bolts to keel batten
Decking	⅜″ plywood	½″ plywood
Transom Face	½″ plywood	¾″ plywood

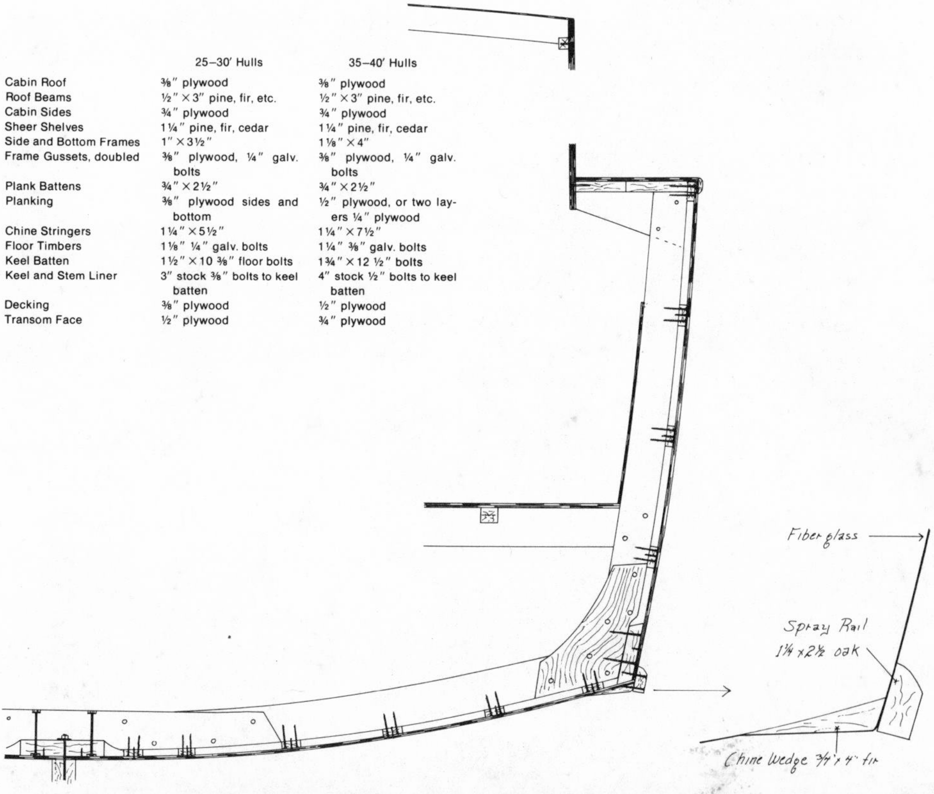

in Figure 165, with suggested scantling dimensions covering launches from 25 to 40 feet in length. While experienced builders may wish to vary these somewhat in the light of their own ideas or experience, it must be emphasized that the overall weight must be kept low to insure proper performance. The construction of the spray rail at the chine is shown in detail, and must be fitted as shown as it is critical to this type of hull form.

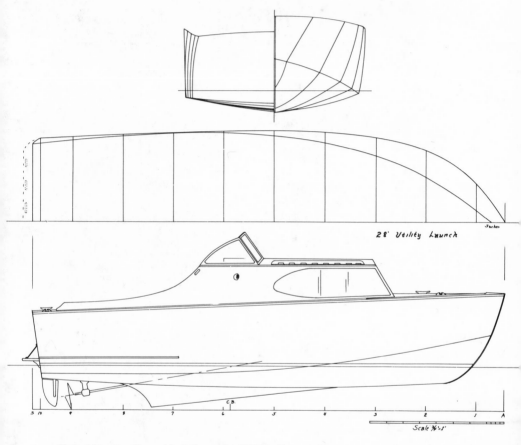

28' Utility Launch

Scale ¾":1'

Plate 144   Profile and hull lines of a 28' V-bottom cruiser

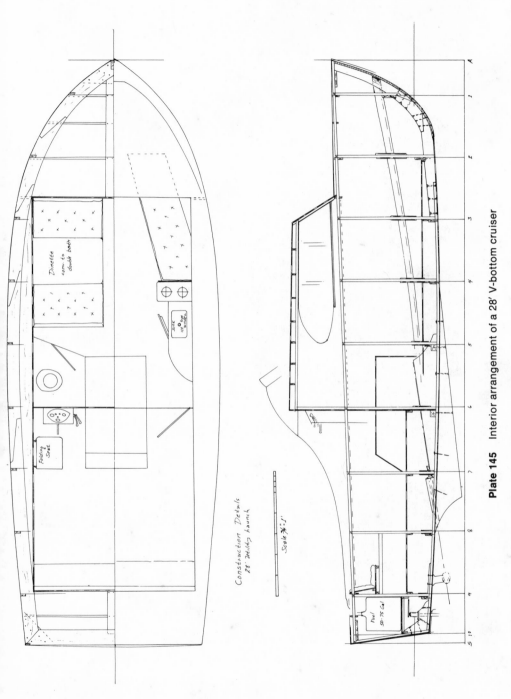

Construction Details
28' Utility Launch

Scale ¾ = 1'

Dinette
converts to
double berth

Sink
LG sliding
window

Folding
Seat

Fuel
50-75 Gal.

Plate 145 Interior arrangement of a 28' V-bottom cruiser

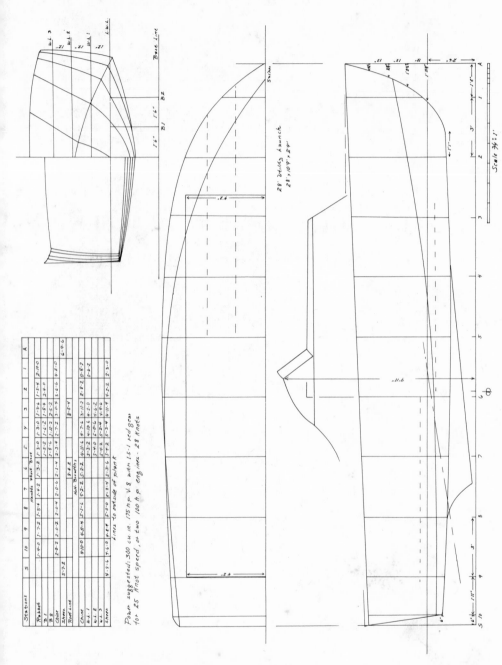

Stations	S	10	9	8	7	6	5	4	3	2	1	A
					Knots about Base							
Pocket		1-9-0	1-7-2	1-5-4	1-4-2	1-3-2	1-3-0	1-3-0	1-3-4	1-5-4	2-10-0	
B.1							1-5-2	1-6-2	1-8-4	2-9-0		
B.2							1-8-6	1-12	2-5-2			
Chine		2-0-2	2-0-2	2-0-4	2-0-6	2-1-4	2-3-4	2-7-2	3-0-8	3-6-6	4-2-0	
Sheer	S-7-2											6-9-6
Roof Line						P & Z				8-5-V		
						Half Breadths						
Chine		4-10-0	4-9-4	5-1-6	5-2-2	5-2-2	4-11-6	4-7-6	3-11-2	2-4-2	0-8-2	
W.L. 1							3-3-2	3-9-0	4-2-0		0-6-2	
W.L. 2							3-4-0	3-6-6	4-6-2			
W.L. 3							3-4-2	3-2-4	4-9-6			
Sheer		4-5-6	4-6-4	5-0-0	6-2-V	5-3-6	5-7-2	5-3-4	4-10-4	4-2-2	2-3-0	

Lines to outside of plank

Power suggested: 300 cu in. 175 h.p. V.8 with 15-1 red gear
for 25 knot speed, or two 100 h.p. engines - 28 Knots

28' Deddys launch
28' x 10' 3" x 29"

Scale ¾":1'

Plate 146 Construction details of a 28' V-bottom cruiser

448

Bibliography

Chapelle, Howard I. *Boatbuilding.* New York: W. W. Norton & Company, Inc., 1941.

Chapelle, Howard I. *Yacht Designing and Planning,* rev. and enlarged. New York: W. W. Norton & Company, Inc., 1971.

Bradley, Cliff. *Building the Small Boat.* New York: The Macmillan Company, 1946.

Crosby, William F. *Amateur Boat Building.* New York: The Rudder Publishing Co., 1938.

Editors of *Rudder* Magazine. *How to Build 20 Boats.* New York: Arco Publishing Co., 1958.

Kinney, Francis S. *Skene's Elements of Yacht Design,* rev. ed. New York: Dodd, Mead & Co., 1972.

Rabl, Samuel S. *Boatbuilding in Your Own Back Yard* (2nd ed.). Cambridge, Md.: Cornell Maritime Press, Inc., 1958.

Monk, Edwin. *Small Boat Building for the Amateur.* New York: C. Scribner's Sons, 1934.

Seward, Robert M. *Small Boat Construction.* New York: The Rudder Publishing Co., 1950.

British Publications

Ashcroft, Herbert J. *Boat Building Simplified.* London: Thomas Reed Publications, Ltd., 1936.

Griffiths, Maurice. *Dreamships.* London: Hutchinson & Co., Ltd., 1948.

Phillips-Birt, D. *Rigs and Rigging of Yachts.* London: George G. Harrap & Co., Ltd., 1962.

Sutton, John F. *Small Sailing Craft: Design and Construction.* London: Sir Isaac Pitman & Sons, Ltd., 1936.

Symonds, A. A. *Introduction to Yacht Design.* London: E. J. Arnold & Son, Ltd., 1938.

Verney, Michael. *Building Chine Boats.* London: Macmillan & Co. Ltd., 1961.

————. *Complete Amateur Boat Building,* 2nd ed. London: John Murray Ltd., 1967.

————. *Yacht Repairs and Conversions,* 3rd ed. London: John Murray Ltd., 1966.

Index